Masters of War

Other *New Political Science* Readers

Violence and Politics:
Globalization's Paradox
Edited by Kenton Worcester,
Sally Avery Bermanzohn,
and Mark Ungar

Liberation, Imagination,
and the Black Panther Party:
A New Look at the Panthers
and Their Legacy
Edited by Kathleen Cleaver
and George N. Katsiaficas

After the Fall: 1989 and
the Future of Freedom
Edited by George N. Katsiaficas

Explorations in African
Political Thought:
Identity, Community, Ethics
Edited by Teodros Kiros, with
a preface by K. Anthony Appiah

Latino Social Movements
Edited by Rodolfo D. Torres
and George N. Katsiaficas

The Promise of Multiculturalism:
Education and Autonomy in
the 21st Century
Edited by George N. Katsiaficas
and Teodros Kiros

The Politics of Cyberspace
Edited by Chris Toulouse
and Timothy W. Luke

Masters of War
Militarism and Blowback in the Era of American Empire

Edited by Carl Boggs
With a Foreword by Ted Rall

ROUTLEDGE
NEW YORK AND LONDON

Published in 2003 by
Routledge
29 West 35th Street
New York, NY 10001
www.routledge-ny.com

Published in Great Britain by
Routledge
11 New Fetter Lane
London EC4P 4EE
www.routledge.co.uk

Library of Congress Cataloging-in-Publication Data

Masters of war : militarism and blowback in the era of American empire /
edited by Carl Boggs ; with a foreword by Ted Rall.
    p. cm.
Includes bibliographical references and index.
   ISBN 0-415-94498-8 (hardcover : alk. paper) — ISBN 0-415-94499-6
(pbk. : alk. paper)
   1. United States—Foreign relations—1989–   2. United States—Foreign relations—
Philosophy.   3. United States—Military policy.   4. Intervention (International law)
5. Militarism—United States.   6. Imperialism.   7. Imperialism—Social aspects—
United States.   I. Boggs, Carl.
  E840.M375 2003
  355′.033573—dc21

                                 2003004050

Contents

Acknowledgments

This anthology is the outgrowth of an earlier project that I assembled and edited for *New Political Science* (March 2002), a special issue titled "U.S. Militarism in an Era of Globalization and Blowback," completed in the immediate aftermath of 9/11. Most of the articles that appeared there are included in this new project, in generally revised and expanded form, along with several additional contributions that cover a range of themes and issues beyond the focus of the special journal issue. The result is a more comprehensive treatment of the role of U.S. military power, both domestically and globally, and one that takes into account the epic events of 9/11 and their continuing fallout. From its inception, this work was strongly encouraged and supported by George Katsiaficas, then editor of *NPS*, and was later facilitated in many ways by Routledge editor Eric Nelson, both of whom are owed special gratitude. Every contributor to this volume has given generously to the editorial process, helping define and strengthen the work as it has evolved during the past two years. Thanks are also owed to several colleagues, including Mona Afridi, Takis Fotopoulos, Tim Luke, and Laurie Nalepa. I would like to further acknowledge the difficult and splendid work of Donna Capato, Angela Chnapko and Nikki Hirschman at Routledge, whose energies helped make this a far more readable and engaging volume than it would have been—qualities we hope will bring this urgent topic the power and vitality it deserves.

Carl Boggs
April 2003

Foreword

TED RALL

NO MAN IS AN ISLAND, BUT WE ARE.

IF YOU'RE A CITIZEN OF THE UNITED STATES OF AMERICA, YOU LIVE IN AN OASIS OF CIVILITY AND ORDER.

YOUR BUSINESS HERE?

CUSTOMS

COMING HOME.

SURE, THERE ARE PROBLEMS. IF YOU'RE BLACK, FOR EXAMPLE, YOU PROBABLY LIVE IN A SLUM.

FOR THE MOST PART, HOWEVER, LIFE IS RELATIVELY GOOD.

COMING UP ON "THE BACHELORETTE": WHO WILL WIN A CHANCE AT WEDDED BLISS TO SWEET, WEALTHY MELISSA—THE RAKISH DAMIAN OR PERRY THE GEEK?

THOUGH SOMEWHAT EMASCULATED, THE BILL OF RIGHTS PROTECTS AMERICANS FROM EXTREME GOVERNMENT ABUSE.

MOST OF THE BASIC NEEDS OF LIFE — FOOD AND SHELTER — ARE PLENTIFUL.

THE ODDS OF DYING IN WAR ARE LOW.

MOST OTHER COUNTRIES AREN'T LIKE THAT.

IN MANY NATIONS, MILITARY DICTATORS RULE WITH AN IRON FIST.

REVOLUTION IS IMPOSSIBLE AGAINST REGIMES ARMED AND FUNDED BY THE U.S.

OUR RELATIONS WITH DICTATORS INEVITABLY SOUR — SO WE END UP BOMBING THEIR CITIES.

DEMOCRATIC MOVE- MENTS — PEOPLE WHO WANT THEIR NATIONS TO LOOK MORE LIKE AMERICA — ARE TARGETED FOR DESTRUCTION SO NEW DICTATORS CAN BE INSTALLED.

"A reliable ally" - Prez

THE WORLD SEES ALL THIS AND CONCLUDES THAT WE'RE MILITARIST AND HYPOCRITICAL.

BUT WE DON'T SEE ANYTHING... AND WE IGNORE THE FEW THINGS THEY LET US SEE.

SOMETIMES FOREIGNERS TRY TO WAKE US UP.

IT NEVER WORKS, THOUGH. HOW COULD IT?

Introduction
Empire and Globalization

CARL BOGGS

To speak of a distinctive *American* militarism at the start of the twenty-first century may seem odd to many observers of the political scene, something in sharp
conflict with the peace-loving, democratic sensibilities generally understood to
be part of the long U.S. historical experience. After all, there have been no dramatic military coups or juntas since the founding of the Republic, nor has the
power of generals and admirals ever overwhelmed the integrity of civilian political rule. Indeed the military has always performed essentially instrumental
functions, in the service of institutions, laws, goals, and ideals presumably beyond the scope of Pentagon decision making. The U.S. military, in other words,
has been subordinate to the liberal-democratic principles of freedom, citizen
participation, national self-determination, and Constitutional governance,
both domestically and abroad. The well-worn preoccupation with national security, heightened in the aftermath of the terrorist attacks, has taken on meaning within this framework. Woodrow Wilson's view of a strong America
"making the world safe for democracy" seemed to capture the spirit and essence
of U.S. foreign and military policy throughout the twentieth century, as did
later apparently selfless and democratic motives during the World War II mobilization against fascism. Moreover, the U.S. has not typically been known for its
string of foreign conquests or extensive network of colonies around the globe,
as with earlier Spanish, French, and British empires. Few Americans today
would entertain the notion of a U.S. Empire or the idea that their nation stands
for anything but peaceful, democratic, humanitarian ends. As for the concept of
"militarism," that could only describe such demons as Napoleon or Hitler, Slobodan Milosevic or Saddam Hussein. At the same time, whatever role the military has played throughout American history would now appear to have
diminished at a time when globalization, with its overwhelming stress on economic interests and discourses (growth, trade, investment, balance of payments, etc.), would appear to supersede the old-fashioned, clumsy, destructive
tools of military violence—a major reason, perhaps, why the specter of U.S.
global military power has commanded surprisingly limited attention from
scholars, journalists, and other observers.

The uncomfortable reality, unfortunately, scarcely fits this kind of fanciful
mythology: U.S. militarism remains more alive than ever, more potent and

1

menacing than even at the height of the Cold War—a generalization likely to be even more valid in the wake of September 11, 2001, with the specter of an endless war on terrorism, mobilization for invasion of Iraq, and the promise of future "resource wars." A legacy of military power runs long and deep, lending added thrust to the contemporary expansion of American imperial rule through the mechanisms of economic, political, and cultural domination often concealed behind a façade of democratic structures and discourses. As Howard Zinn writes, "aggressive expansion was a constant of national ideology and policy . . . ," which, of course, uniformly depended upon lofty moral claims and justifications.[1] The actual history is one of conquest and dominion, of territorial aggrandizement and imposition of social order through outright coercion—genocidal war against Indian tribes, theft of land from Mexico and Spain, invasion of Russia after World War I, followed by a succession of military interventions in Korea, Indochina, Central America, Iraq, and more recently the Balkans. Today the ethos of militarism—of conquest, domination, violence, and Empire—permeates the American economy, political institutions, and culture. It could hardly be otherwise given the country's position as sole remaining superpower, as unchallenged world hegemon. At the moment the U.S. has unparalleled military domination over the world's landmasses, sea lanes, and air spaces, with great aspirations toward colonization of outer space, revealing (in Chalmers Johnson's words) "an imperial project that the Cold War obscured."[2] Consuming nearly 350 billion dollars annually (as of 2002), or roughly 22 times the *combined* total of the seven most purportedly menacing states, the sprawling Pentagon imperium deploys more than 350 major bases around the world, crucial to monitoring and protecting the New World Order. As in the past, American global power today requires ongoing military research and development, preparedness, and intervention, suggesting that it was Theodore Roosevelt and not Woodrow Wilson who may have best capsulized the thrust of U.S. foreign policy. Speaking in 1897, just seven years after the Wounded Knee massacre of Sioux men, women, and children and only a year before the U.S. would go to war with Spain as the first step toward Empire, TR commented: "In strict confidence . . . I should welcome almost any war, for I think this country needs one."[3] For Roosevelt, as for most subsequent American leaders, war never amounted to the opposite of peace but was rather viewed as a redemptive, purifying, ennobling form of human activity, just another extension of modernity and progress.

As the U.S. continues to celebrate the virtues of international order, human rights, and democracy—never missing an opportunity to lecture nations like China for their human-rights abuses—its ruling elites have become increasingly reckless and violent, brazenly violating every global norm they pretend to uphold. Internationally, the U.S. has become an outlaw country, the Rogue State of all rogue states intent on transforming the supposedly abstract process of globalization into the building blocks of Empire and military domination—so far with considerable success. In spring 1999, the U.S., working beneath the umbrella of NATO, bombed Yugoslavia for 79 consecutive days, destroying factories, apartment buildings, schools, hospitals, water-treatment plants, electrical and communications systems, and transportation networks, largely wiping out the Serb civilian infrastructure—a clear act of military aggression violating every canon of international law, the United Nations Charter, even the NATO Charter itself. Bombs were dropped on densely populated urban areas. Anti-personnel bombs were used on civilian targets, along with radium-tipped missiles. NATO Commander General Wesley Clark boasted that the aim of the air war was to "demolish, destroy, devastate, degrade, and ultimately eliminate the essential infrastructure" of Yugoslavia. As Takis Fotopoulos has persuasively argued, the NATO destruction of Serbia can best be understood as the first war systematically waged in defense of the global market system, a "war" involving few if any casualties for the perpetrators.[4] Along much the same lines, Michael Parenti writes: "The motive behind the intervention was not NATO's newfound humanitarianism but a desire to put Yugoslavia—along with every other country—under the suzerainty of free-market globalization."[5]

The great "efficiency" with which the U.S. and its allies rained death and destruction upon Yugoslavia was made possible in part by lessons drawn from the Persian Gulf War, which began in 1991 as part technowar massacre, part media spectacle and then became a protracted nightmare for 22 million Iraqis forced to endure suffering imposed by a decade of harsh economic sanctions and recurrent aerial assaults supposedly intended to make Saddam Hussein jettison his "weapons of mass destruction" and cease his human rights violations. Having bombed a small, oil-rich country into submission, the U.S. was able to enter the post-Cold War era as the only legitimate superpower—a nation prepared to oversee the entire New World Order, with an established armed presence in the Middle East and its own vast arsenal of deadly weapons of mass destruction (and, moreover, a proven willingness to use them). The Gulf War represented more than anything a celebration of pure militaristic ideology along with the worship of high-tech weaponry shown on CNN and other TV outlets, the representation of a "perfect war." A venture to protect Western oil interests, the intervention was cloaked (as usual) in a good deal of high-sounding phraseology about national self-determination, human rights, and the need to contain a Hitler-like demonic outlaw. The mass media, ever obedient to Pentagon priorities and discourses, fueled this mythology through a perpetual barrage of lies, distortions, caricatures, and sensationalism that would have made the old Hearst press rather proud.[6] This brutal "war" that never seems to end has cost the lives of tens of thousands of (mainly civilian) Iraqis over the past decade.

The immorality and hypocrisy of such U.S.-engineered catastrophes deserve far more attention than they have received in the media, the academic world,

and the political arena. No doubt the Iraqis retain some potential for manufacturing and deploying weapons of mass destruction, although surely quite limited by world standards. Other regimes in the Middle East (above all Israel)
possess far more deadly weaponry than Iraq. More to the point, the self-righteous hectoring of American elites and pundits obscures the fact that the U.S.
has been in the forefront of selling and distributing such weapons to countries
around the globe, including regimes with some of the worst human rights
abuses of the twentieth century. Indeed Iraq itself has been one of the many
beneficiaries of American weapons largesse. Moreover, the U.S. has built, stock-
piled, and *used* more weapons of mass destruction than all other nations combined. It has dropped atomic bombs on two occasions, threatened enemies with
nuclear response throughout the postwar years, and presently maintains more
than 10,000 nuclear warheads ready to be unleashed at a moment's notice. It
has conducted far more nuclear tests than any other country, disseminating
massive amounts of radiation beneath and above ground. It carried out extensive chemical and biological warfare in Vietnam (thanks to products manufactured by Monsanto, Dow, and Dupont), dumping millions of tons of Agent
Orange, napalm, white phosphorous, and other deadly toxins into a fragile
ecosystem, where they remain today. It used horrific fuel-air bombs over Iraq,
not to mention universally banned anti-personnel bombs in Iraq, Yugoslavia,
and Indochina. It conducted murderous terror bombings against densely populated cities throughout World War II, employing special incendiary devices to
produce firestorms, including a massive raid on Tokyo (with nearly 1100
bombers) just the day before the armistice was signed.[7] Throughout the postwar era American elites consistently made the first move in the arms race with
the USSR, managing to keep ahead while stimulating new phases in the balance
of terror at every turn. When it comes to weapons of mass destruction, the U.S.
can readily lay claim to the status of world champion.

   The military assaults on Iraq and Yugoslavia, along with the midnight invasion of Panama in late 1989, were part of an American foreign policy shift
intended to exorcise the demons of Indochina defeat—to purge the famous
"Vietnam syndrome" from the national psyche and thus free the country from
a mood of depression and impotence. A powerful resurgence of military
prowess—accompanied by strong resolve to use it—would presumably revitalize a sense of national pride and mission. The military planners would be
given much greater freedom of maneuver. A tough foreign policy approach
was now needed in the service of the New World Order. Of course there is no
public reflection today upon the horrific criminal venture that was the Indochina war, upon the long string of atrocities essentially ordered by three
American presidents—much less any call for official governmental reckoning
or apologies of the sort U.S. leaders regularly demand of Japan for its World
War II atrocities. (The relatively deafening public silence following revelations
of ex-Senator Bob Kerrey's grotesque war crimes in Vietnam, where he led a

Navy Seal unit in the massacre of at least 13 defenseless women and children, offers a strong clue to denial in the national psyche.) The U.S. generally behaved without moral restraint in Vietnam, dumping seven million tons of bombs on the country, destroying rural and urban regions with equal abandon, leaving an unparalleled legacy of death and destruction in an impoverished Third World country. What overcoming the "Vietnam Syndrome" means in this context is the obsession with getting beyond military failure and learning the crucial lesson of defeat: namely, break the reliance on ground warfare through vast implementation of high-tech (mostly aerial) weaponry. While politically "rational" in certain respects, this is nothing less than a recipe for rekindled militarism which, not surprisingly, has become a durable feature of the New World Order. At the same time it is a militarism that, dedicated as ever to the defense of Empire, acquires some important new dimensions.

What might be described as a "new militarism" is best understood through its convergence with the process of economic globalization—a process driven by corporate domination with its headquarters in the powerful host nations of North America, Europe, and Japan along with the international agencies they control. Today the concentration of economic and political power in the hands of a few elites is unprecedented, as are its terrible consequences. The rapid spread of informational technology is just one linchpin in this developmental mechanism. While the overriding goal of G-8 elites today is to maximize corporate freedom from external (i.e., public sector and local movement) constraints, the arena in which controls and regulations can be introduced (namely political governance) winds up narrowed and degraded to the point where it cannot function as a counterweight to huge business and financial interests. Except in the case of the U.S. and perhaps a few other industrialized nations, the gargantuan world economy driven by megacorporations is moving beyond the effective reach of local and national decision-making bodies. At the same time, the global system as a whole—and of course many of the countries that comprise it—is beset with increasing fragmentation, chaos, and instability, with civic violence (including terrorism) that often lacks clear ideological definition.[8] The signs are abundantly clear: a growing divide between rich and poor (both within and between countries), massive social dislocations, local warfare, threats of terrorism and nuclear war, spread of devastating new diseases, and proliferation of arms and munitions, including weapons of mass destruction. This Hobbesian disorder provides an ideal setting for military intervention, for the assertion of a highly authoritarian, coercive Leviathan in a context where "order" (read: New World Order) threatens to unravel. A U.S. Empire will have difficulty sustaining itself within a matrix of market relations, instrumental rationality, consumerism, and rampant local disorder that infuses the whole panorama of corporate colonization. The inevitable loss of community, social infrastructure, ecological balance, and democratic practices is sure to nourish conditions leading to social polarization, upheaval, and violent conflict—consequences fruitful to the growth of popular movements, but also to virulent superpower military response.

Globalization has undeniably eroded the autonomy and decision-making capabilities of most nation-states, yet the crucial fact remains that no international body has yet taken up specifically territorial, coercive, military functions historically assigned to particular governments. Most states today still possess a monopoly over deployment of "legitimate violence" and will continue to have it in the absence of any internationalized military force. This is notably the case with countries that have built strong military forces, above all the U.S. in its self-appointed, heightened role as world hegemon. The persistence, indeed growth, of U.S. military domination at the start of the twenty-first century requires greater attention—and more patient analysis—at a time when American military, political, and cultural influence around the world has deepened precisely in tandem with *economic* globalization. At the present juncture the U.S. presides over a reconstituted Empire, made possible by its controlling presence in world production and finance, its vast military power, its leading role in the spread of information technology, and its capacity to disseminate the neoliberal "American model" with its emphasis on privatization, deregulation, technology, and consumerism. Using that awesome leverage, the U.S. reasserts its dominion over weaker (i.e., virtually all) nations, over international structures, and of course over nature as it pursues its mania for growth and profits.

In the midst of dramatic transformations within global affairs, in the aftermath of Soviet collapse and end of the Cold War, and despite years of Pentagon moves toward downsizing and "modernization," U.S. militarism is more robust and expansionary than ever. The renewed threat of global terrorism can reinforce this tendency. American foreign and military policies are tied to the same agendas—buttressing the permanent war economy, pursuit of worldwide power, the perpetual search for new "enemies"—that held sway for most of the Cold War years. While forms of intervention remain local, they are nonetheless brutal, systemic, and globally oriented at a time when high-tech warfare renders military ventures more cruelly one-sided and less costly for the superpower. Here "globalization" takes on yet another meaning—integral to the struggle of American elites to remake the world according to their neoliberal, corporate-driven values. The familiar enemies of the past (fascists, Communists) have been replaced by a new set of demons: rogue states like Libya, Iraq, and North Korea, terrorists, local tyrants, drug traffickers, and the like. Imperial stratagems within the New World Order take many forms, including control over international bodies (United Nations, World Bank, International Monetary Fund, World Trade Organization), covert actions, global surveillance methods, direct military intervention, political machinations, and deadly economic sanctions of the sort used against Iraq. Political atrophy throughout the international arena helps to further clear away obstacles to U.S. pursuit of world domination.[9]

As Noam Chomsky argues, the 1990s witnessed development of a new era of international relations: shrouded in moralizing discourses of peace and human rights, American policymakers, setting themselves up as guardians of the world system, are more inclined than ever to simply disregard international laws and conventions if they get in the way of unrivaled military supremacy.[10] Every instance of U.S. armed intervention during the 1980s and 1990s represents a flagrant violation of regional treaties and laws, not to mention the UN Charter itself, which explicitly prohibits military attacks against sovereign nations (for example, Grenada, Nicaragua, Haiti, Panama, Serbia, and even Iraq after it signaled its strong preference for a negotiated settlement of the Kuwaiti crisis). In any event, the U.S. has consistently shown its contempt for international bodies, agreements, and procedures that might conflict with its hegemonic aspirations.

The "Clinton Doctrine" of the 1990s fits the pattern of an aggressive foreign policy in the service of neoliberal arrangements based in free trade, privatization, deregulation, and open foreign investment and backed by flexible, deadly military power. As the first president of the new global era, Clinton visited more than 70 countries, set up the WTO, boosted the international budget, maintained high levels of Pentagon spending, militarized the drug wars in South America, continued the military and economic assault on Iraq, laid the groundwork for "humanitarian" interventions, bombed the Sudan and Afghanistan, and carried out protracted aerial raids on Serbia. His "doctrine" actually broadened the parameters of U.S. military involvement around the world, despite all the talk of Pentagon cutbacks, arms reductions, base closings, and armed services demobilizations. Meanwhile, the U.S. failed to confront such growing international problems as poverty, disease, and human rights abuses within or outside regions of American influence, in fact lending its political, economic, and military support to nations (Israel, Turkey, Indonesia, Colombia) generally recognized as the worst abusers of democratic rights and human welfare. During the Clinton years, moreover, the U.S. balked at paying its UN dues, rejected a ban on land mines, dragged its feet on nuclear reductions, and kept alive the Reagan-Bush Star Wars fantasy. Enthused by prospects for total surveillance of the world, Clinton raised intelligence spending levels to more than 30 billion dollars, with increasing emphasis on the supersecret National Security Agency. The planned, systematic, and brutal destruction of the Serb infrastructure must be considered one of the great war crimes of the postwar years.

Clinton's brand of globalism was quickly ratified by the incoming George W. Bush administration, when Secretary of State Colin Powell, speaking in January 2001, insisted that it should be possible to use American military force anywhere in defense of a neoliberal system regarded as morally and politically superior to any conceivable rival. In Powell's view, the U.S. occupies a very special niche in its historic commitment to worldwide peace, security, prosperity, and democracy—all guaranteed, of course, by the great achievements of corporate capitalism and backed by unchallengeable military force—echoing almost word for word what Secretary of State Madeleine Albright had repeated throughout the Clinton presidency. Powell blithely commented that "other systems do not work. We are going to show a vision to the world of the value system of America." He added: "The U.S. has a special role in the world and should not adhere to every international agreement and convention that someone thinks to propose."[11] For the U.S. power structure, at least, economic globalization and military power go perfectly hand in hand.

Already during the second Bush's brief tenure in office, the U.S. has turned its back on the crucial Kyoto accords on global warming, endorsed Clinton's rejection of the land mine treaty, refused to go along with the universal ban on chemical and biological weapons (under pressure from the big chemical firms), and, most fearsome, has abrogated the 1972 ABM arms control agreements in order to resume nuclear testing. Equally menacing is the U.S. threat to overthrow the landmark 1967 Outer Space Treaty prohibiting the militarization of space. There are proposals afoot to terminate environmental restrictions on military operations within the country. Bush's doctrine of "preemptive warfare," allowing the U.S. to attack any country, any time it desires, is a flagrant violation of the UN Charter. Under guise of the war on terrorism the U.S. has empowered itself to drop bombs or send missiles against any target its surveillance manages to identify for destruction. This strident, reckless, lawless unilateralism is designed precisely to give the U.S. military a freer hand in policing the world. If the first Bush administration brought us the New World Order, the second Bush presidency can be expected to formulate what might come to be known as the new militarism in defense of that same order.

The new militarism is located at the intersection of globalization and entrenchment of American economic and political power. A confluence of developments—intensifying globalism, the information revolution, end of the Cold War, growth of high-tech weaponry—has brought the U.S. to the apex of a maturing world system. The U.S. stands as a lone superpower capable of using its many structural, material, and cultural advantages in a global arena otherwise riven with fragmentation, chaos, and conflict. Sophisticated arms production and deployment gives warfare a certain remoteness and efficiency, while high-tech communications allow for unprecedented surveillance and control, making Orwell's predictions seem ultimately rather tepid. The American military option is shaped by a combination of factors: local or regional chaos within the world order, challenge from rogue states, threat of terrorism, proliferation of weapons of mass destruction (conventional *and* nuclear), the imminent threat of China as rival superpower, and the all-important struggle for vital material resources (oil, water, timber, minerals, etc.) at a time when scarcity, population pressures, and ecological crisis will likely bring longstanding conflicts to a military plane. As Michael Klare writes, "whereas international conflict was until recently governed by political and ideological considerations, the wars of the future will largely be fought over the possession and control of vital economic goods—especially resources needed for the functioning of modern industrial societies."[12] As the largest consumer of material resources by far, the U.S. finds itself in the deepest predicament, one reason its elites are so anxious to sustain maximum military power and flexibility.

The result has been, and surely will continue to be, a heightened, more aggressive U.S. military increasingly reliant on worldwide mobility, sophisticated technological warfare and surveillance, and search for new villains which, given prevailing tendencies in the direction of Hobbesian disorder (including a possible new cycle of militarism and terrorism) should be readily available. The stepped-up militarization of the drug wars, most visible in Plan Colombia designed to justify a U.S. strategic presence in resource-laden South America, fits this pattern exactly.[13] The idea of Plan Colombia, already earmarked for several billion dollars, is to exterminate both widespread coca production and armed insurgency that could threaten corporate interests. In this region the drug lords and narco traffickers provide the ideal demons, but here again the time-honored distinction between "military" and "civilian" targets begins to collapse, allowing for a much greater percentage of casualties among innocent noncombatants. But this is no deterrent to aggressive warfare, any more than it was in the cases of Indochina, Panama, Iraq, and more recently the Balkans, where civilian death and suffering were enormous.

A vital ingredient of the new militarism, championed by Bush and his Defense Secretary Donald H. Rumsfeld, is the projected militarization of space—a frightening scheme going well beyond the familiar Star Wars missile defense shield originally proposed by Reagan. Politicians and the media have dwelled upon the purely *defensive* character of a missile-shield system that, despite its astronomical projected costs, could never protect against most forms of nuclear attack. Debates have correctly focused on the utter inadequacy of such a scheme, yet these debates have fallen short of taking up the broader *strategic* issues raised by a potential American *offensive* military presence achieved through new forms of space surveillance, orbiting battle stations, multipurpose satellites, and ballistic early-warning radar systems.[14] The Pentagon goal would make the U.S. the "master of space," using technological supremacy to solidify global military domination and make the world vulnerable to an American nuclear first strike. Such a weapons-in-space program, with its arrogant junking of the Outer Space Treaty, involves unprecedented costs and risks, yet is moving ahead without significant public debate or media attention—typical for important military departures. The program is urgently needed, according to Rumsfeld, since "more than any other country, the U.S. relies on space for its security and well-being."[15]

As U.S. military power veers out of control, beyond the reach of democratic mechanisms or countervailing forces, the *consequences* of such power flexed throughout the Empire will likewise be uncontrollable. American dominion breeds widespread dysfunction, resistance, and opposition even as its institutional power expands. The twenty-first century is bound to be a time of sustained, generally unanticipated "blowback," to use the apt title of Chalmers Johnson's landmark book mentioned above. The struggle to achieve and maintain global domination is destined to bring, in response, a perpetual spiral of authoritarianism, decay, violence, insurgency—and indeed terrorism. If the U.S. military can deliver massive blows anywhere with relatively few *immediate* risks and costs, blowback follows a more protracted, delayed, torturous, uncertain path: local attacks on U.S. military targets, various "incidents," popular movements, terrorist crusades, and mounting general revulsion against American power around the world. The problem is that military strength, whatever its geographical scope or technological capacities, cannot provide its own legitimacy or the foundations of global stability over the long run—as lengthy popular insurgencies against huge military machines in settings as diverse as Vietnam, South Africa, Algeria, and Israel have amply demonstrated. The very logic of military domination, of empire, guarantees blowback on a rather large scale. Hardt and Negri refer to the essential "novelty" of the imperial situation: "Empire creates a greater potential for revolution than did the modern regimes of power because it presents us, alongside the machine of command, with an alternative: the set of all the exploited and the subjugated, a multitude that is directly opposed to empire, with no mediation between them."[16]

The phenomenon of blowback has far-reaching domestic repercussions too, contributing to decay and lopsided development in the economic sphere, a narrowing of civic culture and political life in the "security state," and a culture of militarism that has come to permeate every corner of American life. Since the late 1940s the Pentagon has consumed a staggering twelve trillion dollars in resources—without doubt mostly wasteful or destructive consumption—and continues to spend roughly $300 billion yearly (a figure that will reach more than $500 billion within the next several years) to maintain empire. Nuclear weapons have consumed at least one trillion dollars of that total. Government officials and politicians like to speak of military reductions and troop demobilizations but these are simply code words for strategic "modernization": fewer bases, armed personnel, and weapons deployed but much greater reliance on high-tech weaponry (sophisticated planes, ships, bombs, missiles, communications networks, etc.), minimizing the need for large standing armies and navies. The new arms systems have far greater efficiency and firepower. In reality it is the Pentagon itself, often over strenuous objections from Congress, that generally begs to shut down obsolete facilities. Meanwhile, the American social infrastructure deteriorates as the Pentagon's sphere of control widens. Today we find an inverse relationship between growth of the U.S. empire and various measures of domestic well-being. What Petras and Morley wrote several years ago remains even more valid today: "The growth of international financial networks and the resurgence of U.S. global, political, and military power has been accompanied by rising economic and personal insecurity for the vast majority of America's urban dwellers: more real estate speculation, drug money laundering, deindustrialization, crime, prison spending, less social services, housing, well-paid manufacturing jobs. The ideology of 'national security' used to justify global empire is one side of the coin; deteriorating cities and worsening life circumstances inside the empire is the other."[17]

While the permanent war economy reproduces material decay, inequality, and disruption within home boundaries of the superpower, an expanded national-security state (expanded in the aftermath of the terrorist attacks) lends yet another definition to blowback: a drastic narrowing of the public sphere that has the distorted the very meaning of citizen participation and democratic decision making. The steady decline of American politics over the past few decades (lower voter turnout, weakening sense of efficacy, less civic involvement, meaninglessness of electoral campaigns, spread of anti-political attitudes) can be attributed to the impact of corporate colonization throughout public life, but the growing influence of military power as well as intelligence and law-enforcement resources *domestically* enters into this matrix.[18] In the U.S., as elsewhere, the security state thrives on secrecy, a huge intelligence network, techniques of surveillance and control, and centralized bureaucratic power that overrides popular inputs, especially in the realm of foreign and military policy. With vast resources committed to Empire and warmaking, elites naturally want to sidestep open debates that might undermine national "unity" and "security." Thus decisions to intervene militarily are rarely preceded or accompanied by genuine political discussion of the complex questions involved. The Gulf War, for example, was made popular by an immense propaganda barrage unleashed by the Pentagon, the media, and government, creating an ideological milieu in which 45 percent of the population said it would be prepared to use nuclear weapons against Iraq. Military actions were transformed into a grotesque national spectacle, a great celebration of warmaking that obliterated any rational critique of U.S. ambitions and stratagems in the Persian Gulf. As in the cases of Panama (Noriega) and Yugoslavia (Milosevic), the Iraqi demon (Hussein) had to be exorcised. One can readily point to other vital areas of military policy—Star Wars, nuclear testing, abrogation of various international treaties, refusal to pay UN dues, NATO expansion— where political debate has been nonexistent. When it comes to such issues the already narrow differences between Republicans and Democrats vanish altogether, as any close inspection of recent presidential "debates" will quickly reveal. (During Election 2000 it was actually the Democratic candidate, Al Gore, who adopted the harder military line, outflanking the Republican Bush in his zeal for boosts in Pentagon spending.)

Blowback also finds its way into the growing culture of militarism that seems to have established deep roots in the national psyche, nourishing a certain sacralization of violence, guns, and war.[19] It is hardly coincidental that the U.S. ranks as the most violent of all industrialized countries, averaging 22,000 murders yearly, with gang warfare in major cities, paramilitary militias enlisting hundreds of thousands of citizens, terrorist bombings on a regular basis, serial killings that have few parallels in other societies, and a burgeoning prison population now well past two million. The connections involving Empire, militarism, media culture, and civic violence (including regular glorification of that violence) have become more visible over time. As Richard Rhodes argues, militarism inevitably transforms the personalities of those who experience it: in making people into killers—and in sacralizing killing—the military generates callousness toward violence, traversing ethical restraints that otherwise might discourage people from violent aggression.[20] In fact the U.S. military itself regularly violates moral standards as part of its international conduct, to the extent that atrocities nowadays draw little interest from the media or political establishment. Such violations are made easier by the advent of high-tech warfare that depersonalizes aggressive attacks and shields perpetrators from their gruesome consequences. The popular media is saturated with images of violence, many of them grotesque and pointless, many of them linked to fetishism of the military. The emergence of local militias as a mass phenomenon is rather instructive: they represent a convergence of patriotic sentiments, conspiracy theories, racial antagonisms, and gun culture within a virulent reactionary populism. It was precisely this "harvest of rage," no doubt driven by a sense of military valor, that inspired Timothy McVeigh and his veteran cohorts to action in the Oklahoma City bombing.[21] William Gibson writes of the emergence of the "new warrior hero" on the social landscape beginning in the 1980s—a typically young, white, masculine hero fighting to conquer impotence while dedicating himself to personal and national redemption, to restoring a fallen nation in the wake of earlier military defeats (the Vietnam syndrome). The preferred modus operandi—though most often fortunately relegated to the sphere of romantic mythology—is that of direct, violent action with plenty of big weapons, following in the path of *Rambo*, *Lethal Weapon*, and *Patriot Games*.[22]

The role of the mass media in reproducing a culture of militarism cannot be stressed too much. We have seen how U.S. interventions in the Persian Gulf and the Balkans were presented to the American public as TV spectacles glorifying the achievements of high-tech weaponry and communications—spectacles crucial to mobilizing popular support behind military action and, by extension, the defense of empire (though this word is studiously avoided). The Hollywood war machine has been preoccupied with making films that depict something akin to a "good war," furnishing positive images of (U.S.) military operations that, not surprisingly, draw largely on the World War II experience where the supposedly unmediated struggle between good and evil can be mined for patriotic inspiration today. (Interestingly, no less than *eight* of Steven Spielberg's 17 films deal with World War II, including his celebrated *Saving Private Ryan* in 1998.) Motion pictures like *The Thin Red Line, U-571, Pearl Harbor, Schindler's List,* and *The Patriot,* like *Saving Private Ryan,* offer a powerfully redemptive, even purifying though often false vision of American military power and the masculine heroics that help shape it. At the hands of skillful directors like Spielberg war is turned into an epic struggle framed by remarkably graphic violence situated within the context of a "good war" aimed at saving civilization; the entire experience is aestheticized. Much like the earlier *Star Wars* episodes and comparable epics, a movie like *Saving Private Ryan* is transformed into a larger-than-life spectacle serving both to romanticize and valorize the military experience. Spielberg's work reflects once again the long and intimate partnership between the Hollywood film industry and the military establishment, with drastic consequences for American popular culture. As Zinn observes: "Our culture is in deep trouble when a film like *Saving Private Ryan* can pass by, like a military parade, with nothing but a shower of confetti and hurrahs for its color and grandeur."[23] This could happen because the culture of militarism, viewed as both cause and effect of American Empire, is so deeply embedded in the national fabric that it has now become nearly invisible.

Viewed in its larger historical and social context, therefore, the new militarism—sure to be fueled by what promises to be an interminable U.S. war on terrorism—can be seen as an extension of the frontier ethos of conquest and domination, where the outright destruction of enemies is undertaken as a sacred national right and duty. There will always be "good" wars to be fought and won by imperial elites. While embedded in a certain institutional rationality, this is nothing less than the culture of a dangerous outlaw nation which, at a time when the menace of mass-destruction weapons is surely greater than ever, appears as the most threatening force in the world today.

At the time of this writing (November 2002), in the immediate wake of the Republicans' smashing midterm election victory, a reinvigorated President Bush seems even more intent on military action in Iraq despite continued U.S. isolation (except for Britain) on the world scene. Planned invasion and occupation of Iraq, designed to secure oil and other natural resources in the region while further solidifying U.S. global domination, is guaranteed to sow additional blowback within an intensifying cycle of militarism and terrorism. The main generalizations recurring throughout this anthology—expansion of U.S.

imperial power across the globe, growth of the permanent war economy and security state, weaponization of space, further militarization of American society and culture, likelihood of future terrorist actions, etc.—are bound to ring *more* true with the passage of time. Given the severe narrowing of the public sphere exacerbated by the post 9/11 resurgence of militarism and patriotism, it will matter little whether Republicans or Democrats occupy the White House.

There is nothing fortuitous or innocent, much less "humanitarian," about such frightening trends. Indeed the Bush elites appear more openly and arrogantly dedicated to the aims of U.S. economic, political, and military domination of the world than any previous U.S. administration. A blueprint for renewed Pax Americana was outlined by such Bush acolytes as Rumsfeld, Cheney, Richard Perle, and Paul Wolfowitz already in September 2000, under the heading "American Grand Strategy," for the right-wing think-tank New American Century.[24] The plan involves a "core mission" to fight and win multiple wars around the world, through augmented Pentagon spending and modernization along with militarization of space. Describing U.S. military forces as "the cavalry on the new American frontier," the blueprint calls for the invasion of Iraq as one step toward securing full control over Middle East oil reserves. Equally disturbing, the authors identify several countries *beyond Iraq* as possible future targets of U.S. military intervention and "regime change." It should be emphasized that *all* the imperial plans were clearly laid out well *before* the events of 9/11.

Such plans, of course, reveal nothing less than the predatory ambitions of a rogue nation willing to use every means at its disposal—and those means are the most destructive in world history. Despite all the blather emanating from Washington about "weapons of mass destruction," a cornerstone of U.S. military policy has been and continues to be nuclear weaponry. It is this most horrifying technology of mass annihilation that the U.S. has used in the past and has considered unleashing on numerous other occasions. The U.S. is still opposed to the abolition of nuclear weaponry, refining and "modernizing" its huge arsenal even while it pretends to oppose "proliferation." Rather than rejecting nuclear weapons as totally barbaric and unthinkable, the Bush administration has fully dismissed antiballistic missile and other arms control treaties so that it can develop even more lethal nukes. The U.S. emphasis on Star Wars reflects yet another tendency in the direction of nuclear strategy. In 2001 the Pentagon authored a Nuclear Posture Review document calling for a more flexible, space-based approach to nuclear warfare, stressing the importance of renewed weapons testing and outlining "contingencies" that might require nuclear attacks on such countries as Russia, China, North Korea, Libya, Syria, Iraq, and Iran.

Given this barbaric imperial posture on the part of American elites—not to mention the new global milieu produced by 9/11 and the war on terrorism—it is easy to understand how the sole superpower has emerged as an out-of-control Empire. U.S. imperial domination is to be unfettered by any international treaties, laws, or conventions, uncompromised by messy UN deliberations or provisions. Of course this is a recipe for the most systemic, overt, reckless global domination by any nation in history.

As the war against terrorism continues, therefore, U.S. superpower arrogance is destined to aggravate the existing Hobbesian state of nature in which violence, chaos, fear, and lawlessness rule as daily features of life around the world, particularly in the great megacities tied to globalization—only now the phenomenon of blowback will negate any future American "exceptionalism" here. This increasingly fragile state of affairs means that ethical principles will be irrelevant, that political and legal methods of solving the spread of militarism, warfare, and terrorism will be checkmated in an atmosphere of mounting social polarization, disorder, and mutual blowback.

This unprecedented global crisis calls forth more urgently than ever the need for mass oppositional movements—not only against "globalization" but against the fearsome power of U.S. economic and military domination. It also calls for strong, militant voices of critical intellectuals willing to speak out against the worldwide death and destruction being carried out (and further planned) by the architects of Empire, in the name of American citizenry. We are fortunate in this volume to have an assemblage of such intellectuals, comprising an array of powerful, incisive voices ready to challenge the enormous barrage of myths and lies surrounding U.S. foreign and military policy in the early twenty-first century—myths and lies, it might be added, that can be said to span at least two centuries of U.S. history. The critical intellectuals represented in this anthology may come from somewhat diverse political experiences and outlooks but all share a passionate, reasoned hostility to U.S. militarism and the horrific impact it has exerted both domestically and globally. Owing to the frightening intensification of militarizing and warmaking trends in the aftermath of 9/11, the publication of this anthology could not be more timely.

Notes

1. Howard Zinn, *Howard Zinn on War* (New York: Seven Stories Press, 2001), 153.
2. Chalmers Johnson, *Blowback* (New York: Henry Holt, 2000), 5.
3. Cited in Howard Zinn, *A People's History of the United States* (New York: HarperCollins, 1995), 290.
4. Takis Fotopoulos, "The First War of the Internationalized Market Economy," *Democracy and Nature* (July 1999).
5. Michael Parenti, *To Kill a Nation* (London: Verso, 2000), 2.
6. See Douglas Kellner, *The Persian Gulf TV War* (Boulder, CO: Westview Press, 1992), chapter 1.
7. John W. Dower, *War Without Mercy* (New York: Pantheon, 1986), 300–301.
8. See Hans Magnus Enzensberger, *Civil Wars* (New York: The New Press, 1993), chapter 1.
9. See Carl Boggs, "Economic Globalization and Political Atrophy," *Democracy and Nature* (March 2001).
10. Noam Chomsky, *A New Generation Draws the Line* (London: Verso, 2001), 1–4.
11. *Los Angeles Times* (January 22, 2001).
12. Michael Klare, *Resource Wars* (New York: Henry Holt, 2001), 213.

13. James Petras, "The Geopolitics of Plan Colombia," *Monthly Review* (May 2001), 30–48.
14. Karl Grossman, *Weapons in Space* (New York: Seven Stories Press, 2000).
15. *Los Angeles Times* (August 3, 2001).
16. Michael Hardt and Antonio Negri, *Empire* (Cambridge, MA: Harvard University Press, 2000), 393.
17. James Petras and Morris Morley, *Empire or Republic?* (New York: Routledge, 1995), 88.
18. Carl Boggs, *The End of Politics: Corporate Power and the Decline of the Public Sphere* (New York: Guilford, 2000), chapter 1.
19. Barbara Ehrenreich, *Blood Rites* (New York: Henry Holt, 1997), chapter 10.
20. Richard Rhodes, *Why They Kill* (New York: Random House, 1999), chapter 21.
21. Joel Dyer, *Harvest of Rage* (Boulder, CO: Westview Press, 1997), chapter 11.
22. William Gibson, *Warrior Dreams* (New York: Hill and Wang, 1994), chapter 2.
23. *Howard Zinn on War,* 104.
24. See the report in *The Sunday Herald* (September 15, 2002).

PART I

The Expanding U.S. Imperial Domain

CHAPTER 1

The Logic of U.S. Intervention

MICHAEL PARENTI

Human motives are impossible to observe in any direct empirical way. We can view behavior and listen to utterances but we cannot observe the actual intent that is attributed to such things. People may profess all sorts of intentions, but they are also capable of outrageous deception, including self-deception. How then can we determine what their actual motives might be? The problem becomes crucial when attempting to divine the intent of political leaders, many of whom make a regular practice of lying about their actions. Some of us maintain that the overriding purpose of U.S. global interventionism is to promote the interests of transnational corporations and make the world safe for free-market capitalism and imperialism.[1] Washington policymakers claim that intervention is propelled by an intent to bring democracy to other peoples, maintain peace and stability in various regions, protect weaker nations from aggressors, defend U.S. national security, fight terrorism, protect human rights, oppose tyranny, prevent genocide, and the like. Are we to accept these claims uncritically? If not, how can we demonstrate that they are often false or incomplete, and that the intent *we* ascribe is the real agenda? How can we determine that U.S. interventionism is engendered by imperialist concerns rather than, say, humanitarian ones?

A Global Military Empire

If U.S. policy is respectful of other nations' sovereignty and other peoples' needs, then we might wonder why U.S. leaders engage in a relentless push for global military domination. The United States presides over an armed planetary force of a magnitude never before seen in human history. It includes about a half-million troops stationed at over 395 major bases and hundreds of minor installations in thirty-five foreign countries; more than 8,000 strategic nuclear weapons and 22,000 tactical ones; a naval strike force greater in total tonnage and firepower than all the other navies of the world combined, consisting of missile cruisers, nuclear submarines, nuclear aircraft carriers, and destroyers that sail every ocean and make port at every continent. With only five percent of the earth's population, the United States expends more military funds than all the other major powers combined.

U.S. bomber squadrons and long-range missiles can reach any target, delivering enough explosive force to destroy the infrastructures of entire countries—as demonstrated against Iraq in 1990–91 and Yugoslavia in 1999. U.S. rapid deployment forces have a firepower in conventional weaponry vastly superior to that of any other nation. U.S. satellites and spy planes conduct surveillance over the entire planet. And today the United States is developing a capacity to conduct war from outer space.

Worldwide U.S. arms sales to cooperative capitalist nations rose to $36.9 billion in 2000, up from $34 billion in 1999. In addition to sales, since World War II, the U.S. government has given some $240 billion in military aid to train, equip, and subsidize some 2.3 million troops and internal security forces in more than eighty countries, the purpose being not to defend these nations from outside invasion but to protect ruling oligarchs and multinational corporate investors from the dangers of domestic anti-capitalist insurgency.

How can we determine that? By observing that (a) with few exceptions there is no evidence suggesting that these various regimes have ever been threatened by attack from neighboring countries; (b) just about all these "friendly" regimes have supported economic systems that are subserviently integrated into a global system of transnational corporate domination, open to foreign penetration on terms that are singularly favorable to transnational investors; (c) there is a great deal of evidence showing that U.S.-supported military and security forces and death squads in these various countries have been repeatedly used to destroy popular reformist movements and insurgencies that advocate some kind of egalitarian redistributive politics within their own countries.[2]

For decades we were told that a huge U.S. military establishment was necessary to contain an expansionist world Communist movement with its headquarters in Moscow (or sometimes Beijing). But after the overthrow of the Soviet Union and other Eastern European Communist nations, Washington made no move to dismantle its costly and dangerous global military apparatus. All Cold War weapons programs continued in full force, with new ones being added all the time, including plans to militarize outer space. Immediately the White House and Pentagon began issuing jeremiads about a whole host of new enemies—for some unexplained reason previously overlooked—who menace the United States, including "dangerous rogue states" like Libya with its ragtag army of 50,000. The elder George Bush, as Richard Barnet noted, even "proclaimed the new American enemy to be 'instability,' a vague but ominous political science metaphor."[3] These claims were swiftly and uncritically embraced by defense establishment academics and media pundits who pretend to an expertise on foreign affairs.

Supporting the Right

The intent of U.S. national security state leaders[4] can be revealed in part by noting whom they assist and whom they attack. U.S. leaders have consistently supported rightist regimes and organizations and opposed leftist ones. The terms "Right" and "Left" are seldom specifically defined by policymakers or media commentators—and with good reason. To explicate the politico-economic content of leftist governments and movements is to reveal their egalitarian and usually democratic goals, making it much harder to demonize them. The "Left," as I would define it, encompasses those individuals, organizations, and governments that advocate egalitarian redistributive policies benefiting the common people and infringing upon the privileged interests of the wealthy propertied classes.

The Right also is involved in redistributive politics, but the distribution goes the other way, in an upward direction. Rightist governments and groups, including fascist ones, are dedicated to using the land, labor, markets, and natural resources of countries as so much fodder for the enrichment of the owning and investing classes. In almost every country, including the U.S., rightist groups, parties, or governments pursue tax and spending programs, wage and investment practices, methods of police and military control, and deregulation and privatization policies that primarily benefit those who receive the bulk of their income from investments and property, at the expense of those who live off wages, salaries, fees, and pensions. That is what defines and distinguishes the Right from the Left. In just about each instance, rightist forces abroad are deemed by U.S. opinion makers to be "friendly to the West," a coded term for "pro-free market" and "pro-capitalist." Conversely, leftist ones are labeled as hostile, "anti-democratic," "anti-American," and "anti-West."

While claiming to be motivated by a dedication to human rights and democracy, U.S. leaders have supported some of the most notorious right-wing autocracies in history, governments that have tortured, killed, or otherwise maltreated large numbers of their citizens because of their dissenting political views, as in Turkey, Zaire, Chad, Pakistan, Morocco, Indonesia, Honduras, Peru, Colombia, Argentina, El Salvador, Guatemala, Haiti, the Philippines, Cuba (under Batista), Nicaragua (under Somoza), Iran (under the Shah), and Portugal (under Salazar). Assistance is also given to counterrevolutionary groups in leftist revolutionary countries. These groups have perpetrated some of the most brutal bloodletting against civilian populations, as have Unita in Angola, Renamo in Mozambique, the Contras in Nicaragua, the Khmer Rouge (during the 1980s) in Cambodia, the counterinsurgency ethnic slaughter in Rwanda, the *mujahideen* and then the Taliban in Afghanistan, and the right-wing Albanian separatist KLA in Kosovo.

U.S. support of right-wing conservatism has extended to the furthest reaches of the political spectrum. After World War II, U.S. leaders and their Western capitalist allies did little to eradicate fascism from Europe, except for putting some of the top Nazi leaders on trial at Nuremberg. In a short time, former Nazis and their collaborators were back in the saddle in Germany.[5] Hundreds of Nazi war criminals found a haven in the United States, either living in comfortable anonymity or employed by U.S. intelligence agencies during the Cold War.[6]

In France, too, very few Vichy collaborators were purged. As Herbert Lottman writes, "No one of any rank was seriously punished for his or her role in the roundup and deportation of Jews to Nazi camps."[7] U.S. military authorities also restored fascist collaborators to power in various Far East nations. In South Korea, for instance, police trained by the fascist Japanese occupation forces were used immediately after the war to suppress left democratic forces. The South Korean Army was commanded by officers who had served in the Imperial Japanese Army, some of whom had been guilty of horrid war crimes in the Philippines and China.[8]

In Italy, within a year after the war, almost all Italian fascists were released from prison while hundreds of Communists and other leftist partisans who had been valiantly fighting the Nazi occupation were jailed. Allied authorities initiated most of these measures.[9] From 1945 to 1975, U.S. government agencies gave an estimated $75 million to right-wing organizations in Italy, including some with close ties to the neofascist *Movimento Sociale Italiano* (MSI). From 1969 to 1974, high-ranking elements in Italian military and civilian intelligence agencies, along with various secret and highly placed neofascist groups, embarked upon a campaign of terror and sabotage known as the "strategy of tension," involving a series of kidnappings, assassinations, and bombing massacres (*i stragi*), including an explosion that killed eighty-five people and injured some two hundred in the Bologna train station in August 1980. Fueled by international security agencies including the CIA, terrorism was directed against the growing popularity of the democratic parliamentary Left. The objective was to "combat by any means necessary the electoral gains of the Italian Communist Party" and create enough terror to destabilize the multiparty social democracy and replace it with an authoritarian "presidential republic," or in any case "a stronger and more stable executive." Implicated in this terrorist campaign, the CIA refused to cooperate with an Italian parliamentary commission investigating *i stragi* in 1995.[10]

In the 1980s scores of people were murdered in Germany, Belgium, and elsewhere in Western Europe by extreme rightists in the service of state security agencies. As with the earlier strategy of tension in Italy, these attacks attempted to create enough popular fear and uncertainty to undermine the existing social democracies. The U.S. corporate-owned media largely ignored these acts of right-wing terrorism in Western Europe while giving prominent play to tiny and far less effective left terrorist grouplets found in Italy and West Germany.

In Italy, as long as the Communist party had imposing strength in parliament and the labor unions, U.S. policymakers worked with centrist alternatives such as the Christian Democrats and the anticommunist Italian Socialist Party. With Communism in decline by the 1990s, U.S. leaders began to lend more open encouragement to extreme rightist forces. In 1994 and again in 2001, national elections were won by the National Alliance, a coalition of neofascists, ultraconservatives, and northern separatists headed by media tycoon

Silvio Berlusconi. The Alliance played on resentments over unemployment, taxes, and immigration. It attempted to convince people that government was the enemy—especially its social service sector. At the same time it worked to strengthen the repressive capacities of the state and divide the working class against itself by instigating antagonisms between the resident population and immigrants, all the while preaching the virtues of the free market and pursuing tax and spending measures that redistributed income upward. U.S. leaders have had not a harsh word to say about the Italian neofascists.

Opposing the Left

We can also infer intent by looking at who is targeted for attack by the U.S. national security state, specifically just about all leftist governments, movements, and popular insurgencies, either in direct military attacks by U.S. forces and surrogate mercenary forces such as the Contras in Nicaragua, or by subversion and destabilization from within. The U.S. has subverted reformist and leftist governments by financing and controlling their internal security units and intelligence agencies, providing them with counterinsurgency technology, including instruments of torture; imposing crippling economic sanctions through IMF austerity programs; bribing political leaders, military leaders, and other key players; inciting retrograde ethnic separatists and supremacists within the country; subverting their democratic and popular organizations; rigging their elections; and financing collaborationist political parties, labor unions, academic researchers, journalists, religious groups, nongovernmental organizations (NGOs), and various media.[11]

U.S. leaders profess a dedication to democracy. Yet over the past five decades, democratically elected reformist governments—guilty of introducing redistributive economic programs—in Guatemala, Guyana, the Dominican Republic, Brazil, Chile, Uruguay, Syria, Indonesia (under Sukarno), Greece, Cyprus, Argentina, Bolivia, Haiti, the Congo, and numerous other nations—were overthrown by their respective military forces funded and advised by the U.S. The newly installed military rulers then rolled back any reforms and opened their countries all the wider to foreign corporate investors. The U.S. national security state has participated in covert actions or proxy mercenary wars against reformist or revolutionary governments in Cuba, Angola, Mozambique, Ethiopia, Portugal, Nicaragua, Cambodia, East Timor, Western Sahara, Egypt, Cambodia, Lebanon, Peru, Iran, Syria, Jamaica, South Yemen, the Fiji Islands, Afghanistan, and elsewhere.[12] In many cases the attacks were directed at "soft targets" such as schools, farm cooperatives, health clinics, and whole villages. These wars of attrition extracted a horrific toll in human life and frequently forced the reformist or revolutionary government to discard its programs.

Since World War II, U.S. forces have invaded or launched aerial assaults against Vietnam, Laos, the Dominican Republic, North Korea, Cambodia,

Lebanon, Grenada, Panama, Libya, Iraq, Somalia, Yugoslavia, and most recently Afghanistan—a record of military aggression unmatched by any Communist government in history. U.S./NATO forces delivered round-the-clock terrorist bombings upon Yugoslavia for two and a half months in 1999, targeting housing projects, private homes, hospitals, schools, state-owned factories, radio and television stations, government-owned hotels, municipal power stations, water supply systems, and bridges, along with hundreds of other non-military targets at great loss to civilian life. In some instances, neoimperialism has been replaced with an old-fashioned direct colonialist occupation, as in Bosnia, Kosovo, and Macedonia.

The September 2001 terrorist attacks against the World Trade Center and the Pentagon, causing a great loss of innocent lives, provided U.S. leaders with a perfect excuse to intensify their policies of armed intervention, surveillance, and repression, and reactionary rollback of domestic public services—all in the name of national security. "Terrorism," defined only as something that others do to the U.S., became something of a national obsession, an all-encompassing imperative that elevated U.S. leaders beyond the reach of critical protest and allowed them to pose yet again as defenders of national security, peace, and justice. Easily overlooked in all this is the fact that for over the last half century or more, U.S. leaders have been the greatest purveyors of violence and terrorism throughout the world.

Even before World War II, there existed a notable frequency of violent intervention. U.S. military forces waged a bloody and protracted war of conquest in the Philippines in 1899–1903. U.S. expeditionary forces fought in China along with other Western armies to suppress the Boxer Rebellion and keep the Chinese under the heel of European and North American colonialists. Along with fourteen other capitalist nations, the U.S. invaded socialist revolutionary Russia in 1918–21. U.S. Marines invaded and occupied Nicaragua in 1912 and again in 1926 to 1933; Cuba, 1898 to 1902; Mexico, 1914 and 1916; Panama, 1903 to 1914, Haiti, 1915 to 1934; Honduras six times between 1911 and 1925.

Governments that strive for any kind of economic independence, or apply some significant portion of their budgets to the public sector, to not-for-profit services that benefit the vast majority of the people, are those most likely to feel the wrath of U.S. intervention or invasion. The designated "enemy" can be (a) a *populist military government*, as in Panama under Omar Torrijos (and even under Manuel Noriega), Egypt under Gamal Abdul Nasser, Peru under Juan Velasco, Portugal under the MFA, and—before long—Venezuela under Hugo Chavez; (b) a *Christian socialist government*, as in Nicaragua under the Sandinistas; (c) a *social democracy*, as in Chile under Salvador Allende, Jamaica under Michael Manley, Greece under Andreas Papandreou, Cyprus under Mihail Makarios, and the Dominican Republic under Juan Bosch; (d) an *anti-colonialist radical reform government*, as in the Congo under Patrice Lumumba; (e) a *Marxist-Leninist government*, as in Cuba, Vietnam, and North Korea;

(f) an *Islamic revolutionary order,* as in Libya under Omar Qaddafi; or even (g) a *conservative militarist regime,* as in Iraq under Saddam Hussein if it should attempt an independent course on oil quotas and national development.

Exceptions that Prove the Rule

U.S. leaders have striven with much success to repress (1) the emergence of *competing forms of production* (socialist, collectivist, communitarian); and (2) *competing capital formations* (prosperous autonomous capitalist economies, or mixed ones, in emerging nations, and with FTAA and GATS, all public sector services except police and military in *all* capitalist countries). The goal is the Third Worldization of the entire world, including Europe and North America, a world in which capital rules supreme with no public sector services; no labor unions to speak of; no prosperous, literate, effectively organized working class with rising expectations; no pension funds or environmental, consumer, and occupational protections, or medical plans, or any of the other insufferable things that cut into profit rates.

While described as "anti-West" and "anti-American," just about all leftist governments—from Cuba to Vietnam to the late Soviet Union—have made friendly overtures and shown a willingness to establish normal diplomatic and economic relations with the United States. Only in a few rare cases have U.S. leaders treated leftist governments or forces in a friendly fashion: Yugoslavia during the Cold War, the Khmer Rouge (if it could be considered leftist) against a socialist government in Cambodia during the 1980s, China today as it allows business investments and labor exploitation within its "enterprise zones." In such instances U.S. support has been dictated by temporary expediencies or the promise, as in the case of China, that the country is moving toward incorporation into the global capitalist system.

In the post-World War II era, U.S. policymakers sent assistance to Third World nations and put forth a Marshall plan, grudgingly accepting reforms that produced marginal benefits to the working classes of Western Europe and elsewhere. They did this because of Cold War competition with the Soviet Union and the strong showing of Communist parties in Western Europe.[13] With no competing lure today, Third World peoples (and working populations everywhere) are given little consideration in the ongoing campaigns to roll back benefits and wages.

After the Counter-Revolution

One can judge the intentions of policymakers by the policies they pursue in countries that have been successfully drawn into the Western orbit. For decades we were told by U.S. leaders, media commentators, and academic policy experts that the Cold War was a contest between freedom and an expansionist Communism, with nothing said about the expansionist interests of global capitalism. But immediately after Communism was overthrown in the USSR and Eastern Europe, U.S. leaders began intimating that there was something more on their agenda than just free elections in the former "captive nations"—namely free markets. (By "free markets," of course, we are referring to the investment processes related to global neoliberal corporate domination, which are neither free nor a market.) Getting rid of Communism clearly meant getting rid of public ownership of the means of production. Of what use was political democracy, they seemed to be saying, if it allowed retention of an economy that was socialistic or even social democratic? So the kind of polity seemed to weigh less than the kind of economy.

The newly installed private market governments in Eastern Europe, under strong direction of Western policymakers, eliminated price controls and subsidies for food, housing, transportation, clothing, and utilities. They reduced medical benefits and support for public education. They abolished job guarantees, public employment programs, and workplace benefits. They forbade workplace political activities by labor unions. They have been selling off publicly owned lands, factories, and news media at bargain prices to rich corporate investors. Numerous other industries have been simply shut down. The fundamental laws were changed from a public to private ownership system. There was a massive transfer of public capital into the coffers of private owners. Throughout the former Soviet Union and Eastern Europe, "reforms" brought severe economic recession and high unemployment; a sharp increase in crime, homelessness, beggary, suicide, drug addiction, and prostitution; a dramatic drop in educational and literacy standards; serious deterioration in health care and all other public services; and skyrocketing infant mortality with plummeting life expectancy rates.[14]

Another of many examples is Grenada. In 1983, U.S. forces invaded the tiny and relatively defenseless sovereign nation of Grenada (population 110,000) in blatant violation of international law. The invasion could not be denied, but what of the intent? The Reagan administration justified the assault by claiming (a) it was a rescue operation on behalf of American students whose safety was being threatened at the St. George medical school; (b) the island harbored a large contingent of Cuban troops and "deadly armaments"; (c) the New Jewel revolutionary government had allowed the island to become a Soviet-Cuban training camp "to export terror and undermine democracy," and was planning to build a Soviet submarine base and a Soviet military air base; (d) Cuba and the USSR could use Grenada to control crucial "choke points" along oil tanker lanes that came to the U.S.[15] When it was determined that these various charges were without foundation, some critics concluded that White House policy toward Grenada had been unduly alarmist and misguided. But the fact that officials offer confusing and misleading rationales is no reason to conclude ipso facto that they are themselves confused or misled. It may be that they have other motives which they prefer not to enunciate.

In actuality U.S. global free-market policy was quite rational and successful with regard to Grenada. Under the New Jewel revolutionary government, free milk and other foodstuffs were being distributed to the needy, as were materials for home improvement. Grade school and secondary education were free for everyone for the first time. Free health clinics were opened in the countryside, thanks mostly to assistance rendered by Cuban doctors. Measures were taken in support of equal pay and legal status for women. The government leased unused land to establish farm cooperatives and turn agriculture away from cash-crop exports and toward self-sufficient food production.[16] We can conclude something about the motivation underlying the U.S. invasion by noting how *the U.S. counterrevolutionary occupation put an immediate end to almost all these government-sponsored programs.* In the years that followed, unemployment in Grenada reached new heights and poverty new depths. Domestic cooperatives were suppressed or starved out. Farm families were displaced to make way for golf courses as the corporate-controlled tourist industry boomed. Grenada was once more firmly bound to the privatized free-market world, once again safely Third Worldized.

The same process occurred after the U.S. invaded Panama in December 1989, supposedly to bring Manuel Noriega, described as a drug-dealing dictator, to justice. With Noriega and his leftist military deposed and the U.S. military firmly in control, conditions in that country deteriorated sharply. Unemployment, already high because of the U.S. embargo, climbed to 35 percent as drastic layoffs were imposed on the public sector. Pension rights and other work benefits were abolished. Public sector subsidies were eliminated and services were privatized. Publicly owned media were shut down by U.S. occupation authorities, while a number of Panamanian editors and reporters critical of the invasion were jailed. The U.S. military arrested labor union leaders and removed some 150 local labor leaders from their elected positions within their unions. Crime, poverty, drug trafficking, and homelessness increased dramatically.[17] Free-market Third Worldization was firmly reinstated in Panama.

Consistent Inconsistencies

U.S. foreign policy is often criticized for being "self-contradictory." Thus critics have pointed out that Communist Cuba has been subjected to every hostile stratagem short of war, including travel and trade embargoes, while Communist China—guilty of numerous human rights violations—has been granted "most favored nation" trading status. U.S. policymakers have repeatedly tried to assure fundamentalist hawks in Congress that a political litmus test should not be applied to China while one is regularly imposed on Cuba—so the argument goes. Washington's China policy is no doubt markedly different from its Cuba policy, but behind the apparent double standard rests the same underlying dedication to capital accumulation. China has opened itself to private capital and free market "reforms," including "enterprise zones" where Western investors can superexploit the country's huge and cheap labor supply with no worry about wage and occupation standards or other restrictive regulations. Cuba has so far refused to go down that road.

Lacking any class perspective, all sorts of experts come to conclusions based on surface appearances. While attending a World Affairs Council meeting in San Francisco, I heard some participants smilingly refer to the irony of Cuba's having come "full circle" since the days before the revolution. In prerevolutionary Cuba the best hotels and shops were reserved for the foreigners and the relatively few Cubans who had Yankee dollars; today it is the same. But this judgment overlooks some important differences. Strapped for hard currency, the revolutionary Cuban government decided to use its sunny climate and beautiful beaches to develop a tourist industry, so that by 2000 tourism had become one of the island's most important sources of income. To be sure, tourists are given accommodations that few Cubans can afford. But in prerevolutionary Cuba, the immense profits from tourism were pocketed by big corporations, generals, gamblers, and mobsters. Whereas today profits are split between the foreign investors who build the hotels and the Cuban government, which uses its portion for health clinics, education, the importation of fuel and machinery, and the like. In other words, some portion of the surplus value is still socialized; the people reap much of the benefits of the tourist trade—as is true also of the export earnings from Cuba's publicly owned sugar, coffee, tobacco, rum, seafood, honey, and marble industries.

When the Cuban government no longer utilizes the public sector to redistribute a major portion of the surplus value to the common populace, when it privatizes the factories and lands and allows the productive wealth to be pocketed by rich private owners, removing all labor protections for workers, then it will have come full circle, being once more reduced to capitalist client-state servitude. Then Havana will be warmly embraced by Washington, as have other ex-Communist newly established free-market nations.

U.S. immigration policy is another area criticized as "inconsistent." Cuban refugees regularly have been granted entry into this country while refugees from Haiti during the 1980s were turned away in great numbers. From this, some people concluded that the difference in treatment can only be ascribed to racism, since the Haitians were more noticeably of African descent. More often, however, the decisive consideration seems to be not the complexion of the immigrants but the political complexion of the governments in question. Generally, refugees from anticapitalist countries like Cuba are readily categorized as victims of political oppression and allowed entry, while those fleeing from brutal procapitalist military dictatorships like Haiti during the 1980s are sent back (often to face incarceration or extermination). During the 1980s refugees from right-wing, client states like El Salvador and Guatemala had a difficult time getting into the U.S., while refugees from Nicaragua—of the same Latino stock as the Salvadorans and Guatemalans—had relatively no trouble since they were considered to be fleeing a communistic Sandinista government. Likewise, refugees from Eastern Europe were embraced with open arms when that region was socialist, but after Communist governments were replaced by conservative free-market ones, Eastern Europeans met with an unreceptive entry policy from the State Department. Far from being inconsistent, U.S. policy in this area has been chillingly predictable.

When Words Speak Louder than Actions

It should not go unnoticed that leaders occasionally do verbalize their commitment to making the world safe for the transnational corporate system. At such times words seem to speak louder than actions, for the words are an admission of intent. For example, as President Woodrow Wilson contemplated sending U.S. troops as part of the expeditionary force of Western nations to overthrow the newly installed government in Russia in 1917, his Secretary of State, Robert Lansing, recorded in a confidential memorandum the administration's class concerns. Lansing ignored all the blather that U.S. leaders were publicly mouthing about Lenin and the Bolsheviks being German agents. Instead he perceived them to be revolutionary socialists who sought "to make the ignorant and incapable mass of humanity dominate the earth." The Bolsheviks wanted "to overthrow all existing governments and establish on the ruins a despotism of the proletariat in every country." Their appeal was to "a class which does not have property but hopes to obtain a share by process of government rather than by individual enterprise. This is of course a direct threat at existing social order [i.e., capitalism] in all countries." The danger was that it "may well appeal to the average man, who will not perceive the fundamental errors."[18] Almost four decades later, in 1953, President Dwight Eisenhower uttered a forbidden truth in his State of the Union message: "A serious and explicit purpose of our foreign policy [is] the encouragement of a hospitable climate for [private] investment in foreign nations."[19] In 1990, General Gray, commandant of the U.S. Marines, observed that the United States must have "unimpeded access" to "established and developing economic markets throughout the world."[20]

U.S. opinion makers treat capitalism as inseparable from democracy. The preferred terms are "free market," "market economy," "economic reforms," and "free market democracies," labels that sound less capitalistic by appearing to include more people than just the Fortune 500. So President Clinton announced before the United Nations on September 27, 1993: "Our overriding purpose is to expand and strengthen the world's community of market-based democracies."[21] In a similar vein, the *New York Times*, supportive of the repressive and murderous measures perpetrated against parliamentary democracy by Russian president Boris Yeltsin in 1993, opined that "Yeltsin remains the best hope for democracy and a market economy in Russia."[22] Electoral democracy is useful when it helps to destabilize one-party socialism and serve as a legitimating cloak for capitalist restoration. But when it becomes an obstacle to untrammeled capitalism, democracy runs into trouble. Far from being wedded to each other, capitalism and democracy are often on a fatal collision course, as U.S. leaders demonstrated in Guatemala in 1954, Chile in 1973, Greece in 1967, Indonesia in 1965, and in a score of other countries.

Another example of how the supporters of capitalism are coming out of the closet came to my attention in 1994 when I wrote a letter to Representative Lee Hamilton, then Chair of the House Foreign Affairs Committee, urging normalization of relations with Cuba. He wrote back that U.S. policy toward Cuba should be "updated" in order to "put Cuba in contact with the ideas and practice of democracy . . . and the economic benefits of a free market system." The embargo was intended to "promote democratic change in Cuba and retaliate for the large-scale seizure of American assets by the Castro regime." Needless to say, Hamilton did not explain why his own government, having supported a brutal pro-capitalist Batista dictatorship in Cuba for decades, was now so insistent on installing Western-style democracy on the island. But he did let us know that a fundamental U.S. commitment was to make Cuba safe for "a free market system."

Over the past decade U.S. policymakers have explicitly demanded free market "reforms" in one country after another in the former Communist nations of Eastern Europe. We no longer have to impute such intent to them. The most recent example is Yugoslavia. As Michel Chossudovsky notes, "multi-ethnic, socialist Yugoslavia was once a regional industrial power and economic success," with a 6.1 percent annual growth rate, free medical care, a literacy rate over 90 percent, and a life expectancy of 72 years. But after a decade of IMF restructuring, years of war, boycott, and embargo, "the economies of the former Yugoslavia are prostrate, their industrial sectors dismantled." None of this was a matter of simple happenstance. As early as 1984 the Reagan administration issued U.S. National Security Decision Directive 133: "United States Policy towards Yugoslavia," labeled "secret sensitive." It followed closely the objectives laid out in an earlier directive aimed at Eastern Europe, one that called for a "quiet revolution" to overthrow Communist governments while "reintegrating the countries of Eastern Europe into the orbit of the World [capitalist] market."[23] The economic "reforms" pressed upon Yugoslavia by the IMF and other foreign creditors mandated that all socially owned firms and worker-managed production units be transformed into private capitalist enterprises.[24]

In February 1999, U.S. officials at Rambouillet made their determined goal of capitalist privatization perfectly clear. Chapter 4a, Article 1, of the Rambouillet "agreement," actually an ultimatum imposed upon what remained of Yugoslavia (Serbia and Montenegro), stated in no uncertain terms: "The economy of Kosovo shall function in accordance with free market principles." There was to be no restriction on the movement of "goods, services, and capital to Kosovo," and all matters of trade, investment, and corporate ownership were to be left to the private market.[25] In 2000, the "Stability Pact for Southeastern Europe," calling for "creating vibrant market economies" in the Balkans, was hailed by the White House for offering advice on investment to all the countries of southeast Europe. That same year the Overseas Private Investment Corporation (OPIC) inaugurated a fund to be managed by Soros Private Funds Management. Its purpose, as stated by the U.S. embassy in Macedonia, is "to provide capital for new business development, expansion and privatization."[26] Meanwhile the Agency for International Development (USAID) announced its intention to undertake "assistance programs to support economic reform and restructuring the economy . . . to advance Montenegro toward a free market economy."[27]

In April 2001, according to the London *Financial Times*, the newly installed rulers of Yugoslavia, beneficiaries of millions of dollars in U.S. electoral funds, launched "a comprehensive privatization program as part of economic reforms introduced following the overthrow of former president Slobodan Milosevic." This included the sale of more than 4,500 publicly owned or worker controlled companies to private investors.[28]

"Conspiracy," "Incompetence," and "Inertia"

In law, people are assumed to intend the reasonably foreseeable consequences of their actions. If they pursue acts that produce predictable outcomes, and avoid ones that would produce other outcomes, it is assumed that there is some link between their actions and their intent. But when one applies this principle to the U.S. national security state, orthodox social scientists and media pundits dismiss it as "conspiracy theory." Policies that produce undeniably unfortunate effects on others are explained away as "unintended consequences." Of course, unintended consequences do arise, and upheavals do sometimes catch U.S. leaders off guard, but that is no reason to reduce so much of policy outcome to stochasticism, to argue again and again that things occur by chance; stuff just happens, as innocently befuddled leaders grope about unburdened by any hidden agenda. To say, as I do, that U.S. national security leaders know more, intend more, and do more than they let on is not to claim they are omnipotent or omnicompetent. It is to argue that U.S. policy is not habitually misguided and bungling, although mistakes are made and indeterminacies certainly arise. U.S. foreign policy is generally quite consistent and cohesive, a deadly success, given the interests it represents. Those who see it as repeatedly befuddled are revealing their own befuddlement.

Sometimes policymakers themselves seize upon incompetence as a cover. In 1986 it was discovered that the Reagan administration was running a covert operation to bypass Congress (and the law), using funds from secret arms sales to

Iran to finance counterrevolutionary mercenaries (the "Contras") in Nicaragua and probably GOP electoral campaigns at home. President Reagan admitted full knowledge of the arms sales, but claimed he had no idea what happened to the money. He was asking people to believe these operations were conducted by subordinates, including his very own National Security Advisor, without being cleared by him. Reagan publicly criticized himself for his slipshod managerial style and lack of administrative control over his staff. His admission of incompetence was eagerly embraced by various analysts and pundits who prefer to see their leaders as suffering from innocent ignorance rather than deliberate deception. Subsequent testimony by his subordinates, however, revealed that Reagan was not as dumb as he was pretending to be, and that he had played an active and deciding role in the entire Iran-Contra affair.[29]

Throughout its history the CIA and other agencies of the national security state have resorted to every conceivable crime and machination, using false propaganda, sabotage, bribery, rigged elections, theft, collusion with organized crime, narcotics trafficking, death squads, terror bombings, torture, massacres, and wars of attrition. At the same time, U.S. leaders have pretended to have had nothing to do with such things. Their denials are to be expected, as are their claims that they were caught completely off guard by one or another event. No less a political actor than Henry Kissinger repeatedly pretended to innocent ignorance and incompetence when confronted with the dirty role he and his cohorts played in East Timor, Indochina, Chile, Bangladesh, and elsewhere. Kissinger's writings and speeches are heavily larded with exhortations about the importance of maintaining the efficacy of U.S. policy and the need to impress the world with the mettle of U.S. resolve. As Christopher Hitchens observes, ". . . in response to any inquiry that might implicate him in crime and fiasco, he rushes to humiliate his own country and its professional servants, suggesting that they know little, care less, are poorly informed and easily rattled by the pace of events."[30]

Secrecy is another phenomenon that would suggest the existence of hidden agendas. If policymakers have nothing to hide, why do they hide so much? An estimated 21,500 U.S. government documents are classified *every workday* of the year.[31] Some of these materials eventually come to light thirty or forty years later—and can still be quite revealing. Thus, a recently uncovered October 1970 cable to CIA operatives in Chile from Kissinger's "Track Two" group states, "It is firm and continuing policy that [the democratically elected government of] Allende be overthrown by a coup. . . . We are to continue to generate maximum pressure toward this end utilizing every appropriate resource. *It is imperative that these actions be implemented clandestinely and securely so that the USG* [United States Government] *and American hands be well hidden.*"[32] If public utterances of policymakers represent their real intentions, if they have no hidden agendas, then why do they find it necessary to hide their actions not only from the U.S. public but from their own staff?[33]

Sometimes outcomes are explained away as the result of a disembodied organizational inertia. With this mode of analysis there is no intentional human application to speak of. Interventions are said to occur because a national security agency wants to prove its usefulness or is simply carried along on its own organizational momentum, as supposedly happened with the CIA and Pentagon intervention in the Bay of Pigs. To be sure, organizational interests do come into play, but to see them as the predominant force behind policies is like claiming that the horses are the cause of the horse race.

The "Other Variables" Argument

Some people might complain that the analysis presented here is simplistic and insufficiently nuanced because it ascribes all events to purely economic and class motives while ignoring such other variables as geopolitics, culture, ethnicity, nationalism, ideology, morality, and leadership psychology. It is a passion among certain academics to claim authorship to *nuanced* views. These views often turn out to be so much polished evasion whose primary function is to deny the existence of a material and economic base to any social conflict. Furthermore, what is more simplistic and mechanistic than to assume, without benefit of empirical investigation, that a proliferation of variables ipso facto brings us closer to the truth? Such a question should be settled by empirical investigation rather than fiat.

In any case, I do not argue that the struggle to maintain capitalist global hegemony explains everything about world politics nor even everything about U.S. foreign policy. However, it does explain quite a lot; so is it not time we become more aware of it and more willing to speak its name? If politically safe academics and other orthodox opinion makers really want to portray political life in all its manifold complexities, then we might expect that they be less studiously reticent about the immense realities of imperialism. They might consider how the process of global capitalist domination assumes many dimensions, including the economic realm as well as the political, military, and cultural domains.

The presence of other variables such as nationalism, militarism, the search for national security, and pursuit of power and hegemonic dominance neither compels us to dismiss economic realities nor to treat these other variables as insulated from class interests. Thus, to argue that U.S. leaders intervene in one or another region not because of economic considerations but for strategic reasons may sound to some like a more nuanced view, but in most cases, empirical examination shows that the desire to secure or extend U.S. strategic power is impelled at least in part by a desire to stabilize the area along lines that are favorable to politico-economic elite interests—which is usually why the region becomes a focus of concern in the first place. Various considerations are not mutually exclusive but work upon each other. The growth in overseas investments invites a need for military protection, just as military interventions open opportunities for overseas investment. All this, in turn, creates a need to secure bases and establish alliances with other nations, helping to expand the defense perimeter that must be maintained. So a particular country becomes not only an "essential" asset in the support of U.S. defenses but must itself be defended, like any other asset.

To repeat, I am not denying that U.S. leaders may have other concerns, such as advancing their nation's prestige, maintaining national security against potentially competing capitalist nations, developing strategic military superiority, distracting the American public from domestic problems and scandals, advancing the heroic macho image of the president, and the like. But these purposes almost always dovetail with dominant capitalist interests, or certainly do not challenge those interests in any serious way. No U.S. president, for instance, would ever think of promoting his macho image by heroically supporting the cause of socialist revolution in this or any other country. That officeholders seek to achieve many other purposes, Ralph Miliband once noted, "should not obscure the fact that *in the service of these purposes*, they become the dedicated servants of their business and investing classes."[34] The point is not that nations act imperialistically for purely material motives but that the ideological and psychic motives, embraced with varying degrees of sincerity by individual policymakers, unfailingly serve the overall system-sustaining material interests of a particular class.

In sum, U.S. politico-corporate elites have long struggled to make the world safe for the system of transnational corporate capital accumulation; to attain control of the markets, lands, natural resources, and cheap labor of all countries; and to prevent the emergence of revolutionary socialist, populist, or even military nationalist regimes that challenge this arrangement by seeking to build alternative or competing economic systems. To achieve this, a global military machine is essential. The goal is to create a world populated by client states and compliant populations completely open to transnational corporate penetration, on terms that are completely favorable to the penetrators. It is not too much to conclude that such an activist and violent global policy is produced not by dumb coincidence but by conscious design.

Notes

1. "Imperialism" is a term not normally applied by orthodox political scientists to anything that U.S. leaders do. So perhaps it needs a definition: Imperialism, as used in this article, is the process whereby the rulers of one country use economic and military power to expropriate the land, labor, markets, and natural resources of another country in order to attain ever greater capital accumulations on behalf of wealthy interests at home and abroad.

2. For evidence in support of this see Michael Parenti, *Against Empire* (San Francisco: City Lights, 1995); Michael Parenti, *Inventing Reality*, 2nd edition (New York: St. Martin's, 1993); William Blum, *Killing Hope: U.S. Military and CIA Interventions since World War II* (New York: Black Rose Books, 1998); and the writings of James Petras, Morris Morely, and Edward Herman. For Petras's latest treatment of imperialism and capitalism, see his "Neo Mercantilist Empire in Latin America: Bush, ALCA and Plan Colombia" (unpublished monograph, 2001).

3. Richard Barnet, "The Uses of Force," *New Yorker*, April 29, 1991, 84.
4. By the "U.S. national security state" I mean the Executive Office of the White House, the National Security Council, National Security Administration, Central Intelligence Agency, Federal Bureau of Investigation, and other such units that are engaged in surveillance, suppression, covert action, and forceful interventions abroad and at home. Also included are the various monitoring committees set up by the NSC, such as the "54/12 Group," later known in the Nixon era as the "40 Committee," composed of top players from State, Defense, the CIA, the Joint Chiefs of Staff, the White House, and the NSC itself.
5. See Ingo Muller, *Hitler's Justice* (Cambridge, MA: Harvard University Press, 1991), part 3, "The Aftermath."
6. Jon Wiener, "Bringing Nazi Sympathizers to the US," *Nation*, March 6, 1989, 306–309. Nazi war criminals have been aided by Western intelligence agencies, business interests, the military, and even the Vatican. In October 1944, German paratroop commander Major Walter Reder slaughtered 1,836 defenseless civilians in a village near Bologna, Italy, as a reprisal against Italian partisan activities. He was released from prison in 1985, after Pope John Paul II, among others, made an appeal on his behalf—over the strenuous protests of families of the victims.
7. Herbert Lottman, *The Purge* (New York: William Morrow, 1986), 290.
8. Hugh Deane, "Korea, China and the United States: A Look Back," *Monthly Review*, Feb. 1995, 20 and 23.
9. Roy Palmer Domenico, *Italian Fascists on Trial, 1943–1948* (Chapel Hill: University of North Carolina Press, 1991), passim.
10. *La Repubblica,* April 9, 1995; *Corriere della Sera*, March 27 and 28, 1995, April 12, 1995, and May 29, 1995.
11. On the widescale use of terrorism by the U.S. national security state, see Edward Herman, *The Real Terror Network* (Boston: South End Press, 1982). The most insidious form of intervention should not go unnoticed, namely the circumvention of an already inadequate democratic sovereignty by international agreements such as NAFTA, GATT, GATS and the like, which in effect give transnational corporations the power to overrule the laws and public protections of nation-states, in what amounts to a global coup d'état by the plutocratic class; see Lori Wallach and Michelle Sforza, *World Trade Organization? Corporate Globalization and the Erosion of Democracy* (Washington, D.C.: Public Citizen, 1999); and *FTAA for Beginners* (Boston: United for a Fair Economy, January 2001).
12. See John Quigley, *The Ruses for War: American Intervention since World War II* (Buffalo, NY: Prometheus Books, 1992).
13. Peter Gowan, "The NATO Powers and the Balkan Tragedy," *New Left Review*, March-April 1999, 103–104.
14. Michael Parenti, *Blackshirts and Reds: Rational Fascism and the Overthrow of Communism* (San Francisco: City Lights, 1997), chapters 6 and 7.
15. Network news reports, October 27 to November 4, 1983; *New York Times*, November 6 to 20, 1983; John Judis, "Grenadian Documents Do Not Show What Reagan Claims," and Daniel Lazare, "Reagan's Seven Big Lies about Grenada," both in *In These Times*, November 6, 1983.
16. "A Tottering Structure of Lies," *Sojourner*, December 1983, 4–5; and Michael Massing, "Grenada Before and After," *Atlantic Monthly*, February 1984, 79–80.
17. See "Special Report," *Labor Action* (publication of the Labor Coalition on Central America, Washington, D.C.), July/August 1990; Clarence Lusane, "Aftermath of the US Invasion," *CovertAction Information Bulletin*, Spring 1991, 61–63; *San Francisco Examiner*, April 9, 1991.
18. Quoted in William Appleman Williams, "American Intervention in Russia: 1917–1920," in David Horowitz (ed.), *Containment and Revolution* (Boston: Beacon Press, 1967), 36, 38.
19. *New York Times*, February 3, 1953.
20. Quoted in Barnet, "The Uses of Force," 90.
21. When the text of Clinton's speech was printed the next day in the *New York Times,* the sentence quoted above was omitted.
22. *New York Times*, October 5, 1993. For a full account of Yeltsin's repression, see my "Yeltsin's Coup and the Media's Alchemy," in Michael Parenti, *Dirty Truths* (San Francisco: City Lights, 1996), 133–140.
23. Sean Gervasi, "Germany, U.S., and the Yugoslav Crisis," *CovertAction Quarterly*, winter 1992–93, 41–42.

24. Michel Chossudovsky, "Dismantling Former Yugoslavia, Recolonizing Bosnia," *CovertAction Quarterly*, Spring 1996; and Chossudovsky's "Banking on the Balkans," THIS, July-August 1999.

25. *Interim Agreement for Peace and Self-government in Kosovo* (the "Rambouillet Agreement"), February 23, 1999, reproduced in full in *The Kosovo Dossier*, 2nd ed. (London: Lord Byron Foundation for Balkan Studies, 1999).

26. Gregory Elich, "The CIA's Covert War," *CovertAction Quarterly*, April-June 2001, 35–36.

27. Elich, "The CIA's Covert War," 38–39.

28. *Financial Times*, April 11, 2001. By July 2001, the number of companies slated for privatization had grown to over 7,000, according to a communication to me from Barry Lituchy, editor of *Eastern European Review*.

29. Jonathan Marshall, Peter Dale Scott, and Jane Hunter, *The Iran-Contra Connection* (Boston: South End, 1988); *Report of the Congressional Committee Investigating the Iran-Contra Affair* (Washington, D.C.: Government Printing Office, 1987).

30. Christopher Hitchens, *The Trial of Henry Kissinger* (London & New York: Verso, 2001), 98–99.

31. See Information Security Oversight Office, *Report to the President* (Washington, D.C.: National Archives and Records Administration, 1995 and 1996); Office of Management and Budget, "Information Security Oversight Office; Classified National Security Information," 32 CFR Paret 2001, *Federal Register*, vol. 60, no. 198, October 13, 1995.

32. Cable of October 16, 1970, quoted in Hitchens, *The Trial of Henry Kissinger*, 60.

33. See Daniel Ellsberg, "Lying About Vietnam," *New York Times*, June 29, 2001.

34. Ralph Miliband, *The State in Capitalist Society* (New York: Basic Books, 1969), 84 (italics in the original).

CHAPTER 2

Oil Politics and U.S. Militarism in the Middle East

IRENE GENDZIER

One year after September 11, 2001, with the "war on terror" a permanent feature of the U.S. political landscape, the dominant question in Washington and much of the world was Iraq. When would the U.S. act on its threat of "preemptive action" against Iraq, the first stage in the Bush administration's reordering of the Middle East? Locked into the hallucinating vision of a recolonized Middle East designed to suit Washington's taste and that of the Israeli right wing was the related question of Middle East oil. And assigned to guarantee U.S. victory, as the public was repeatedly informed, were American forces in the Gulf. Their deployment was estimated to include some 35,000 U.S. military personnel by the end of October 2002.[1] Is this, then, what the "war on terror" was all about? Was oil politics and its connection to the military a response to the events of 9/11? Or was it those key features of U.S. Middle East policy that had always assumed a global reach, whose significance was dramatized in the light of American power and its open claims to global hegemony, a product of the post-Cold War?

In the long year that elapsed since the events of September 11, the Middle East came to occupy center stage in media and official talk. From a long taboo subject judged to be inordinately sensitive and complex, the Middle East and more generally, the Islamic world, acquired an unwelcome notoriety as the media and public grappled with what appeared to be entirely unknown and terrifying political developments with an Eastern address. Making sense of the Taliban's rise to power, or that of its Saudi militant collaborator, Osama bin Laden, or their collective antagonism towards the U.S., was a formidable task. In the ensuing tumultuous coverage of the Middle East, Pakistan, and Afghanistan, the veritable condition of these states and their societies remained distorted if not invisible. As the fearful images of the Taliban gave way before an illusory declaration of a U.S. victory in Afghanistan, the infamous figure of Saddam Hussein came to dominate public attention—in deference to Washington's initiatives.

As the U.S. "war on terror" centered on Iraq, the question of oil politics compelled increasing attention. For those familiar with U.S. Middle East policy,

however, the question was hardly new, and the events of 9/11 offered no fundamental change in this regard. But the impact of 9/11 was hardly negligible, leading to reinforcement of U.S. military support in the Gulf and throughout the
Caucasus and Central Asia. Of these areas, the former was the historic center of
U.S. oil interests and epicenter of U.S. military preparations in 2002. U.S. oil
company advances into the former Soviet republics of the Caucasus and Central Asia were a more recent phenomenon, one whose turning point was not
9/11 but 1989 and the collapse of the USSR. Nonetheless, as the pages that follow indicate, the allied role of the U.S. military was part of this expansion.

In the aftermath of 9/11, that role was justified in this region as in the Middle
East partly as an expression of the "war on terror." U.S. oil policy was explained
in this context, as motivated by the exigencies of dependency and the needs of
diversification. Its past history, and the relevance of that history to the crises
confronting the U.S. after 9/11, was not readily discussed. Yet on this and on the
heady affairs of contemporary oil politics and the expanded role of the military,
far more evidence was available than presented in public debate. For those who
demanded to know, the records were available, whatever their limitations.

From Oil Dependency to Diversification

Barely a month after the September 11 attacks, *Business Week* reminded readers that the U.S. economy was ailing and that the country was more vulnerable
to an "oil shock," a reference to the feared hike in oil prices, than it had been at
the time of the first Gulf War. The reason was to be found in diminished global
reserves, the combined product of U.S. sanctions on Libya and Iran, and "tight
national budgets in oil-producing nations."[2] The same journal warned its
readers that oil accounted for "40% of the nation's energy." In that light, it recommended diversification of U.S. sources given that the country was import-
ing "51.6% of its oil needs and relies on OPEC for about half of that—roughly
26% of total consumption." The eleven oil-producing states represented in
OPEC, in turn, accounted for roughly two thirds of the world's crude oil exports, with Saudi Arabia responsible for 7.8 millions of barrels per day, or 18.9
percent of the "world share" according to a November 2001 estimate.[3] Considered in other terms, Saudi Arabia exported 7.8 millions of barrels per day, followed by Venezuela at 2.7 million barrels per day, Iran at 2.6 million barrels
per day, United Arab Emirates at 2.2 million barrels per day, and Iraq at 2.1
millions barrels per day.[4] Among non-OPEC states, Russian production stood
at 4.3 million barrels per day, with an estimated 10.4 percent of the world's
output, according to the same source. While Russian oil producers appeared
open to exploiting their advantageous position, they alternately emerged as
competitors in the global oil rush and on other occasions as partners of the
U.S. committed to challenging OPEC's influence.

Given the reality of U.S. oil dependency, there was a predictable response in
the media and among interested constituencies. There were those who favored

greater reliance and expansion of the U.S. Strategic Petroleum Reserve, drilling in the Arctic National Wildlife Refuge of Alaska, and/or diversifying energy sources outside of the Middle East. Not only did these positions reflect the range and lack of consensus, they were indicative of the different constituencies represented by environmentalists and advocates of alternative energy, U.S. oil independents, and the giant U.S. and international companies.[5] Virtually all adopted a critical view of existing U.S. policy, without however being in agreement with one another. Some called for more conservation, for more environmentally friendly policies, for greater concentration on domestic production, and an opening to countries blocked by sanction policies.

The Bush administration put forth its views on the matter of oil dependency prior to the events of 9/11. U.S. National Energy policy was defined in the Report of the National Energy Policy Development Group, issued in May 2001. Entitled "Reliable, Affordable, and Environmentally Sound Energy for America's Future," it predicted increasing oil dependence and recommended increasing diversification. "Our projected growing dependence on oil imports is a serious long-term challenge. U.S. economic security and that of our trading partners will remain closely tied to global oil market developments. Without a change in current policy, the share of U.S. oil demand met by net imports is projected to increase from 52 percent in 2000 to 64 percent in 2020."[6] Noting that more of U.S. imports came from the Western hemisphere, the authors underlined the proposition that two decades' worth of diversification had not rendered "the U.S. and global economies" immune from the risks of "major disruption of oil supplies," emphasizing the double role of the U.S. as the "second largest natural gas producer and its third largest oil producer," as well as its role as consumer of "over 25 percent of the oil produced worldwide, slightly more than half of which it imports."[7] As a result, the authors of the Report recommended that "the President make energy security a priority of our trade and foreign policy."[8]

In the same section of its review of foreign energy sources, the Report underlined the Saudi role as "linchpin of supply reliability to world oil markets," with the Gulf "projected to supply between 54 and 67 percent of the world's oil." But the NEPD paper did not stop there. It pointed to the growing importance of sources in the Western hemisphere, from Canada to Latin America, where Venezuela and Colombia, along with Brazil, figured prominently. Going further afield, the same report pointed to the increasing importance of Africa's producers, in a period when U.S. interests in Nigerian, Angolan, and French West African oil sources were on record.[9] The National Energy Policy Development group also pointed to the actual and potential roles of Russia and the former Soviet republics in the Caucasus and Central Asia.

The NEPD report appeared before September 2001. Its policy recommendations were operative before that date, as the expansion of U.S. and foreign oil companies into Russia, the Caspian-Caucasus, and Central Asia, attests.

The events of 9/11 however, served to highlight U.S. anxiety over what was loosely described as political instability in the Middle East. Insofar as U.S.-Saudi relations were concerned, they entered a difficult phase in the aftermath of 9/11. The Saudi identity of the majority of the hijackers involved in the attacks, along with that of their alleged leader Osama bin Laden, increased Washington's pressure on Riyadh. Washington demanded the arrest of supporters of Al Qaeda and the backers of bin Laden. The Saudi kingdom was subjected to an unprecedented level of public criticism, its protected status increasingly open to question.

In the months that followed, Riyadh responded with a sense of evident frustration, mounting publicity campaigns on the one hand and taking more pointed actions, such as the withdrawal by Saudi private investors of an alleged $200 billion from U.S. markets, on the other. Within a year of the September attacks, the Saudi regime moved to close its natural gas fields to U.S. and Western companies, as reported in *The Wall Street Journal* early in September 2002. That move attracted the notice of U.S. and foreign companies as it "appeared to all but end a yearlong plan by the companies to invest $25 billion in Saudi Arabia, in what was billed as a historic reopening of the kingdom's petroleum sector. Saudi Arabia has produced all of its own oil and gas since the 1970s, when it bought out four U.S. oil companies' interests in Aramco. Western oil companies haven't been allowed to produce oil or gas within Saudi borders, though there is some Western ownership of Saudi petrochemical plants."[10]

The response was predictably negative. But it was not Saudi politics so much as frustration with limited opportunities in the oil and natural gas sectors reported on by *The Petroleum Intelligence Weekly* (May 15, 2002 online). "No majors are bailing out yet, but the frustration is palpable as upstream openings in Iran and Kuwait, and Saudi Arabia's more recent natural gas initiative, have all become bogged down in tortuous negotiations. As enthusiasm fizzles, attention is turning back to Russia and the Caspian, where the IOCs (International Oil Companies) last flocked in early 1990s." But the oil giants did not move out of the Gulf, as the continuing lucrative activity of ExxonMobil, Royal Dutch/Shell, BP, Total Fina Elf, and ChevronTexaco in Abu Dhabi, indicated.

But there were other aspects of the impact of 9/11 on oil politics that revealed some of the internal tensions and directions of oil markets. The attacks on the U.S. were followed by a fall in oil prices, a drama into which Russia immediately moved. Russian companies, among those outside of OPEC, first moved to challenge the organization of petroleum exporters before withdrawing to cooperate with it. The Russian response did not go unnoticed. It was read in Washington as a reminder of the role that Russian oil was now playing in the international market. Less than a month later, ExxonMobil was reported to have invested some $4 billion in offshore oil and gas development in far eastern Russia—the "largest single foreign investment so far" in Russia.[11] The origins of that project, however, did not lie in the events of September 11. Work had begun in fields off the Sakhalin island in the sea north of Japan in 1996. ExxonMobil owned 30 percent of what was a joint venture, with Japanese, Indian, and Russian partners. The stakes were reputed to be some 2.3 billion barrels of oil, equal to a third of Canada's reserves.

Other movements in the oil business were well underway in this period, such as those of U.S. and international oil interests into the Caucasus and Central Asia. U.S. activity in the region included the steady aggrandizement of U.S. political and military support. In November 2001, President Bush congratulated Russia, Oman, and Kazakhstan, along with U.S. oil giants ExxonMobil and Chevron Texaco, for their work on the Caspian Pipeline Consortium (CPS) and its pipeline plans in the region. More congratulations were in order in the following year.

In summer 2002, officials from Turkmenistan, Afghanistan, and Pakistan were reported to be planning to meet to plan a gas pipeline for the transport of gas from Turkmenistan across Afghanistan to Pakistan. Their respective presidents had reportedly signed an agreement in May for a project that would involve a 1500-kilometer pipeline, opening Turkmenistan's reserves of natural gas to outside powers for the first time. The U.S. ambassador to Turkmenistan was reported as "saying the pipeline could play a key role in ensuring stability in Afghanistan, helping to diversify gas export routes for the ex-Soviet republic."[12] And indeed Moscow announced plans in summer 2002 to forge a vast alternative transport project across the Caspian Sea that would carry liquefied gas and oil from Turkmenistan and Kazakhstan in a different direction, to the Black Sea. The U.S. secretary of energy, Spencer Abraham, was reported shortly thereafter as studying "energy deposits off Russia's Arctic coast."[13]

Along with oil and pipelines, the Bush administration advanced economic aid and military assistance to its new friends in the Caucasus and Central Asia, provoking Russian concern about U.S. intentions. It became increasingly clear that U.S. ambitions in the region were hardly limited in time or place. In spring 2002, the U.S. secretary of defense gave a joint press conference with his opposite number in Kazakhstan, Mukhtar Altynbayev, in which the latter reported on meetings with President Nazarbayev and U.S. Defense Secretary Rumsfeld. Kazakhstan, Rumsfeld had informed his audience, was "involved with NATO through Partnership for Peace arrangements, and we discussed improving and strengthening our military-to-military relationship."[14] That relationship involved Kazakh military officers, who would be trained at the "CENTCOM headquarters in Florida with coalition forces, and they will be responsible for operational planning."

In summer 2002, Kansas was host to an official government conference and roundtable. The government was that of Kazakhstan, the roundtable was on investment and trade, and the guests were Kazakh and U.S. representatives. Within a matter of weeks, the U.S. agreed to provide the Kazakh Defense Ministry with assistance, arms, and training. At the same time, 2002, General

Tommy Franks, commander of U.S. forces in Afghanistan, Central Asia, and the Persian Gulf, visited Kazakhstan, Kyrgyzstan, and Uzbekistan, confirming long-term U.S. interests in the region, a matter of evident concern to Russia, China, and Iran.[15] These were not the only areas of interest: U.S. military support for Azerbaijan and Georgia further deepened Moscow's suspicions. Considered in conjunction with the U.S. military presence throughout the Gulf and Saudi Arabia, the Center for Defense Information analyst on Central Asia, Hoonan Peimani, observed that the U.S. military role was "not proportional to the declared objective of neutralizing the remnants of the Taliban and al-Qaeda."[16]

That conclusion assumed knowledge of U.S. policy in the region that neither the media nor Administration officials publicized. The preceding history of U.S. involvement in the Caucasus and Central Asia was as little known outside of specialized circles as were the dealings of U.S. officials with the Taliban, or the U.S. role in supporting the anti-Soviet *mujahideen* under Saudi and Pakistani auspices. In the absence of such information, the terrifying events of 9/11 and the ensuing "U.S. war on terror" provided justification for policies that went largely unquestioned by the U.S. media or public.

There was no effort to consider the impact of such policies on local regimes, the manner in which they strengthened the repressive apparatus of authoritarian states, or their impact on Russia. Loose talk about reform and democratization hid the harsh realities in Central Asia, as well as in the zones marked off by Russia for its own interests, such as Chechnya and Georgia. After 9/11 the former USSR was simultaneously extolled as a major U.S. ally in the "war on terror" and as an oil-producing state whose exports would soon rival those of OPEC majors. What such political images failed to convey was the price extorted by Moscow for supporting the "war on terror" as well as its apprehensions concerning a U.S. military strike on Iraq.

Where did it all begin? Some ingredients of U.S. oil politics and the larger framework of American foreign policy should have been clear within the public record, but much in fact remained off limits. Still, a consideration of what we knew or should have known is a sobering introduction to the subject of oil, politics, and the military in U.S. policy.

The Way it Was

Several weeks after 9/11, Assistant Secretary of State William J. Burns addressed the Middle East Institute in Washington. His remarks were designed to assure his audience that the Middle East remained a major concern of the Bush administration. "Since the end of the Second World War," Burns insisted, "the United States has understood that a secure, prosperous and stable Middle East is an essential ingredient not only in defending vital American interests, but also the interests of the world economy." Thus Burns reiterated the administration's claims that it was committed to a resolution of the major political conflicts in the region, and that it was fully appreciative of the fact that a region "mired in internal conflict serves neither the interests of the people of the region nor the people of the United States."[17]

In practice, U.S. endorsement of political change in the Middle East—as in Latin America and Southeast Asia—penalized reformers who resisted U.S. policies and promoted ruling elites of similar outlook; no princes, clerics, or secular reformers with serious political intent were in demand. The fate of Gulf elites who aspired to more representative political systems was equally dismal. The logic of Washington's Middle East policy was centered around maintaining the status quo in the oil sector—that is, the continuity of U.S. oil company operations without risk of interruption by nationalist, populist, or reformist leaders who had independent views on domestic, much less foreign policy, matters.

The short history of U.S. policy in the Middle East confirms the centrality of oil and its role in justifying U.S. intervention. The succession of presidential "doctrines" from Eisenhower to Carter to Bush II leaves no doubt as to U.S. commitment to use force in securing its interests, including "regime change." That is precisely what was done in Iran in 1953, when as a result of Iranian Prime Minister Mohammed Mossadegh's nationalization of the Anglo–Iranian oil company, the U.S. and U.K. collaborated in a covert coup to bring down that regime. It was replaced by the Shah, who remained in power until 1979. In 1956 the British and French, along with Israel, invaded Egypt in response to Nasser's nationalization of the Suez Canal Company. Two years later, President Eisenhower resisted the British prime minister's call to intervene in Iraq, where revolution brought down the Hashemite monarchy and the entire political edifice on which it rested, which was a product of the British mandate and continuing British power. Within hours of that event, Eisenhower called for U.S. troops to intervene in Lebanon, then in the midst of its first civil war, while also backing British intervention in Jordan. U.S. action in Lebanon, preceding the events in Baghdad, was designed to assure the emergence of a politically reliable leadership that excluded the socialist Kamal Jumblatt. His leadership, U.S. oil companies feared, would put the U.S. pipeline (TAPLINE) that carried Aramco's oil to the Mediterranean at some risk.

Further East, the U.S. was supporting counterrevolutionary policies in the Arabian peninsula in a covert campaign that attracted little attention in the U.S. The U.S. not only armed its allies in Saudi Arabia, but by the early 1970s, Kuwait, North Yemen, Oman, Bahrain, Qatar, and the United Arab Emirates had also become eligible to receive U.S. military assistance. "Everyone has heard of the Bay of Pigs invasion of Cuba in 1961," wrote Fred Halliday in a major work on the Arabian peninsula, "but not its Arabian counterpart—the September 1972 attack on South Yemen, when thousands of right-wing exiles and their tribal allies hurled themselves against the boundaries of the beleaguered anti-imperialist republic."[18] The U.S. relied on Iran during the 1973 oil crisis to send some 10,000 troops into Dhofar province in Oman in order to crush its guerrilla movement. Iran was active in support of U.S. policy outside of the Middle East as well in this period, as the Shah's support for U.S. military action in Vietnam made clear.

With the fall of the Shah in 1979 and the emergence of the Khomeini regime in Teheran, Washington's calculations concerning the Middle East underwent a major shock but its objectives did not change. In supporting the repressive regime of Saddam Hussein, the U.S. used Iraq to contain Iran's influence in the Arabian peninsula and the Middle East, a policy the Saudis actively promoted. To that end Washington, along with its allies and other states with compatible interests, supported Baghdad in the long and bloody war that ensued between 1980 and 1988.

These were the very years singled out in the U.S. State Department's information sheet on Iraq's "Crimes Against Humanity."[19] As the statement indicated, the Iraqi dictator "ordered the use of chemical weapons against Iranian forces in the 1980–1988 Iran-Iraq war, and against Iraq's Kurdish population in 1988. The 1980–1988 Iran-Iraq war left 150,000 to 340,000 Iraqis and 450,000 to 730,000 Iranians dead." It was in this very period, between 1981 and 1988, that both Iran and Iraq received arms from foreign sources, including the U.S., the Soviet Union, and France, with North Korea and Israel providing arms to Iran. Assessments of this arms traffic demonstrate, however, that "between 1981 and 1988 Iraq received 77 percent of the arms delivered to the two belligerents (in dollar terms) while Iran received only 23 percent."[20]

It was in the period 1985–1992, according to Henry Gonzalez, former chairman of the House Banking Committee, that the U.S. Commerce Department "approved at least 220 export licenses for the Iraqi armed forces, major weapons complexes, and enterprises identified by the CIA as diverting technology to weapons programs."[21] Former deputy Defense Undersecretary Stephen Bryen reported on the same occasion that the U.S. encouraged its "companies to go to Iraq and do business there, and a lot of that that was sold was going right into the military programs." As Bryen said: "the [Bush] administration's policy was to support Saddam Hussein, and not to look backwards, not to look sideways, look straight ahead and give him what he wanted. We coddled him, we supported him, he was 'our guy.' And just because he was building missiles, or just because he had a nuclear potential—the CIA warned about that, we know that now for sure—didn't matter. They simply didn't care."

Details of the "U.S. Chemical and Biological Warfare-Related Dual Use Exports to Iraq and their Possible Impact on the Health Consequences of the Gulf War," known as the Riegle Report, were issued by Donald W. Riegle, Jr., chairman, and Alfonse D'Amato, ranking member of the Senate Committee on Banking, Housing and Urban Affairs with Respect to Export Administration, on May 25, 1994.[22] According to the Riegle Report, "records available from the supplier for the period from 1985 until the present show that during this time, pathogenic (meaning 'disease producing'), toxigenic (meaning 'poisonous'), and other biological research materials were exported to Iraq pursuant to application and licensing by the U.S. Department of Commerce."

More recently, *The New York Times* reported on previously undisclosed aspects of the covert U.S. program carried out under the Reagan administration, indicating that it "provided Iraq with critical battle planning assistance at a time when American intelligence agencies knew that Iraqi commanders would employ chemical weapons in waging the decisive battles of the Iran-Iraq war, according to senior military officers with direct knowledge of the program."[23] These sources revealed the following: "Though senior officials of the Reagan administration publicly condemned Iraq's employment of mustard gas, sarin, VX and other poisonous agents, the American military officers said President Reagan, Vice President George Bush and senior national security aides never withdrew their support for the highly classified program in which more than 60 officers of the Defense Intelligence Agency were secretly providing detailed information on Iranian deployments, tactical planning for battles, plans for airstrikes and bomb-damage assessments for Iraq." Further, it was apparent that Defense intelligence officers recognized Iraq had used chemical weapons in the Fao Peninsula, which was attacked with U.S. "planning assistance" in 1988. The Pentagon's response was a tolerant one: " 'It was just another way of killing people—whether with a bullet or phosgene, it didn't make any difference,' as a representative of the military said."

As the April 14, 2002, issue of *Newsweek* in 2002 indicated, "It is hard to believe that, during most of the 1980s, America knowingly permitted the Iraq Atomic Energy Commission to import bacterial cultures that might be used to build biological weapons. But it happened."[24] With Iraq's invasion of Kuwait on August 1, 1990, U.S. policy towards Saddam Hussein underwent a dramatic shift—the record of which has yet to be made public. "Air Force sources said the allies dropped about 1,200 tons of explosives in 518 sorties against 28 oil targets. The intent, they said, was "the complete cessation of refining [in Iraq] without damaging most crude oil production." Targets included "major storage tanks; the gas/oil separators through which crude oil must pass on its way to refineries; the distilling towers and catalytic crackers at the heart of modern refineries; and the critical K2 pipeline junction near Beiji that connects northern oil fields, an export pipeline to Turkey and a reversible north-south pipeline inside Iraq."[25] Iraq's three major refineries in Daura, Basra, and Beiji were bombed.

Remembering the Taliban and Other Deals

Other developments in this period cast comparable light on U.S. policy toward the Taliban in Afghanistan, including the extent of U.S. and Western oil interests in the region of the Caucasus-Caspian and Central Asia in the period following collapse of the Soviet Union. The expansion of U.S. oil companies within this area was matched by offers of military training and support that assumed increasing importance after 9/11. It was during 1986 that the CIA authorized direct U.S. military support and training for Pakistan and Saudi backed anti-Soviet *mujahideen* in Afghanistan. These efforts resulted in mobilization of large numbers of international recruits under the direction of the Saudi, Osama bin Laden. Some ten years later, bin Laden's influence on the Taliban, which had succeeded in consolidating its power in Kabul, gave him a strong role in their leadership. The network of so-called "Arab Afghans" included many non-Arab and non-Afghan militants who eventually came to constitute the core of Al Qaeda.

In 1998, the year in which Al Qaeda attacked U.S. forces in Kenya and Tanzania, President Clinton responded by bombing Taliban bases of Osama bin Laden and his forces in Afghanistan. One outcome of this was the derailing of attempts by a U.S. oil company (Unocal) adviser, Zalmay Khalilzad, to bring about U.S. recognition of the Taliban regime. In 2001, Khalilzad became the U.S. Ambassador to Afghanistan, and Unocal was fully back in business.

Unocal, the twelfth largest U.S. oil company, was involved in Afghanistan and the Caspian after the mid-1990s until 1998, during which it competed and clashed with the Argentinian oil company Bridas, among the largest independent Latin American oil and gas companies in the region. Unocal eventually displaced Bridas in 1995, signing an accord along with Delta Oil, a Saudi affiliate, with Turkmenistan. At the time Henry Kissinger was advising Unocal and Alexander Haig was advising Turkmenistan. Several years later, Khalilzad, an official in the State and Defense Departments under Presidents Reagan and George Bush, emerged as adviser to Unocal. In that capacity he met with Taliban officials in 1997, after their consolidation of power, to forge an agreement on pipeline construction. Negotiations were broken off by Unocal in 1998 after attacks on the U.S. in Kenya and Tanzania attributed to Osama bin Laden. Three years later Khalilzad expressed regrets over apparent U.S. lack of interest in Afghanistan.

Prior to this, in 1996, U.S. Senate hearings were held to consider Afghan development. The State Department had plans to send officials to Kabul in 1996, in advance of establishing diplomatic relations with the Taliban. In the winter of 1998, Unocal Vice President for International Relations John J. Maresca testified before the House International Relations Subcommittee on Asia and the Pacific, emphasizing the "tremendous uncapped hydrocarbon reserves, much of them located in the Caspian Sea basin," along with "natural gas reserves throughout Azerbaijan, Uzbekistan, Turkmenistan and Kazakhstan."[26] Maresca talked about pipelines, underlining the critical issue of "export routes" without which the liquid gold could never reach potential markets. As Maresca put it, "one of the main problems is that Central Asia is isolated," and as he also conceded, its resources are both geographically and politically "land-locked." Assuming that the markets with the greatest potential would be those of the Asia/Pacific region, Maresca reviewed possible pipeline routes.

Aside from prohibitive costs associated with projects involving such great distances, including routes through China, there were political obstacles, as in the case of pipelines crossing Iran. That option, as he explained, was unavailable to U.S. companies because of U.S. sanctions against Iran. It was in this context that the significant role of Afghanistan emerged, along with a projected pipeline system that would coordinate an entire network of pipelines transporting oil through Turkmenistan, Uzbekistan, Kazakhstan, and Russia. Unocal's planned Central Asian Oil Pipeline Consortium was to be part of this pipeline system, assuring connections linking Turkmenistan through Afghanistan to Pakistan to the Arabian Sea. But, as Maresca explained, Unocal's pipeline projects, whether for oil or gas, were dependent on an internationally recognized government in Kabul; hence, his support for such recognition. All such plans were dismissed in 1998, however, when the attacks on U.S. property in Kenya and Tanzania were attributed to Al Qaeda and its leader, who was now closely involved with the Taliban.

In the intervening years, as Maresca's testimony revealed, the attention of U.S. and international oil companies and their respective governments was devoted to oil and gas fields in the Central Asian republics as well as in the regions surrounding the Caspian Sea. By the early 1990s the former Soviet republics were open fields for Western investors.

In 1993 Chevron and the Kazakh regime signed a contract to develop Tengizoil fields, a project that had Washington's full backing. The Tengizchevroil and Lukoil-Russia companies joined to establish the Caspian Pipeline Consortium, specifically to transport Tengizoil to the Black Sea port of Novorossiysk. That was followed in 1994 by establishment of the Azerbaijan International Operating Company including companies such as Amoco, British Petroleum (BP), Russian Lukoil, and U.S. Unocal, Pennzoil, and Statoil, among others.

The Azerbaijani deal was indeed a major coup, setting off numerous other political coups and military actions revealing the stakes and states involved. It was preceded by a political coup in June 1993, when President Elchibei was ousted in favor of Heydar Aliyev. In 1994 the new regime entered into the so-called "contract of the century," only to find it condemned by Moscow and undermined by yet another attempted coup that failed. The next phase focused on pipeline routes—those proposed by Moscow on the one hand and by Turkey on the other. The former passed through Grozny to transport oil from Baku to Novorossiysk, the latter involving a proposed route from Baku through Chechnya terminating in Ceyhan on the Mediterranean (favored by Washington).

The prospect of huge U.S. oil companies active in a region stretching from the Caspian to the states of Central Asia, involving also the interests of the U.S. military, was indeed appealing to Washington, especially among the circles of

Newt Gingrich, who "received support from a number of the multinationals most deeply involved in the titanic struggle already underway for control of Transcaucasian oil, including Amoco, Chevron, and Mobil."[27] Following the 1994 election, President Clinton underlined the importance of U.S. relations with Turkey and "personally telephoned the president of Azerbaijan to win support for a pipeline leading down through Georgia and eventually through Turkey, instead of one running only through Russian-controlled territory."[28]

That was not the preferred route from the Russian vantage point. Moscow's map led through Chechnya, which by 1995 resulted in deployment of Russian troops there. Two years later, however, the Baku to Novorossiysk pipeline faced yet another challenge, this one from OPEC. Under Saudi direction, OPEC's increased oil production served to lower its price, thereby undercutting hoped-for high profit levels associated with the new pipeline. In February 1998 another attempt, this time by the Azerbaijani International Operating Consortium, led to a proposal for a pipeline route extending from Baku through Tbilisi to Supsa, on the Black Sea. Here too Georgian ambitions crossed those of separatist movements in the region of Abkhazia. Attempts on the life of the Georgian president, followed by an attempted coup in Georgia, put an end to that pipeline project. The Baku-Tbilisi-Ceyhan pipeline, allowing for movement of Azerbaijani oil through Georgia and Turkey, won Washington's approval. In 1999 the leaders of Turkey, Georgia, and Azerbaijan were invited to the Clinton White House, with the U.S.-based Bechtel corporation ready to work on pipeline construction. Clinton's support, along with that of the Republicans, reflected a consensus on the significance of aggressive political-military support for U.S. corporate dominance in the Caspian region—a policy based upon the enhancement of Turkey and containment of both Iranian and Russian interests in the very region.

The U.S.-Uzbekistan military connection was developed as early as 1995. In 1997 military exercises were held in Kazakhstan involving U.S. troops as well as military forces from Uzbekistan, Kyrgyzstan, and Russia. In 1998 Azerbaijan, Georgia, and Armenia, along with the Ukraine and Belarus, were integrated into the U.S. military command in Europe, while in 1999 military exercises were held by joint U.S. and Uzbek forces. In the same year, "Turkmenistan, Kazakhstan, Uzbekistan, and the lesser relevant non-Caspian basin nations of Tajikistan and Kyrgyzstan were added to the U.S. Central Command's (CENTCOM) area of responsibility."[29]

The State Department estimated that U.S. aid in 1998–2000 to states in the Caspian region, including Armenia, Azerbaijan, Georgia, Kazakhstan, Kyrgyzstan, Tajikistan, Turkmenistan, and Uzbekistan, was "an astonishing $1.06 billion, of which $175 million was intended for regional security, arms transfers, nonproliferation activities, and military training."[30] Of course this was not the only source of support: an analysis published in the 1999 *Strategic Review* confirmed that indeed "the United States' greatest tool is financial leverage. The dollar counts. The U.S. wields this powerful tool through its Overseas

Private Investment Corporation (OPIC), the Export-Import Bank (EX-IM Bank), and the Trade Development Authority (TDA)."[31] Their collective support had been reportedly offered for the Baku-Tbilisi-Ceyhan pipeline. Developments through 2001 and 2002 confirmed the increasing significance of Russia as a major oil producer, as well as continuing U.S. ties with the Caucasus and Central Asian republics. Implicit in the pronouncements of U.S. officials was the concern with "unstable" oil states, notably those in the Middle East. Saudi Arabia was being warned.

On June 20, 2002, U.S. Secretary of Energy Spencer Abraham testified before the House International Relations Committee to the effect that the administration was "committed to ensuring that U.S. energy needs are not held hostage by politically unstable foreign suppliers." Reiterating the well-known concern for increasing U.S. oil dependence, Abraham reminded House members that Saudi Arabia figured as the second principal foreign oil supplier to the U.S., and that its role in OPEC's pricing practices was of particular importance. The implication was clear: oil diversification was critical, and the U.S. had its options outside the OPEC circle, including Russia, reportedly the "second largest world crude oil producer and exporter." But Abraham also referred to the riches of the Caspian basin and Central Asia, making note of his role at the inauguration of the Caspian Pipeline Consortium linking Kazakhstan to the Black Sea. Several months after Abraham's testimony to the House, news of an imminent high level Russo-American meeting on energy planned for September 2002 in Houston, Texas, was publicized. According to Grigori A. Yavlinsky, head of the liberal Yabloko Party, the idea of Russo-American collaboration meant "tearing down the OPEC monopoly," thus removing "the stick that they [OPEC] are using to terrorize everyone."[32]

In fall 2002, Kazakh newspapers reported on an international oil and gas conference held in Almaty, citing U.S. oil company officials as affirming that Kazakhstan might well become a player in the international oil economy so long as it resolved the key matter of pipeline routes. "The investment potential of Kazakhstan's oil and gas branch will be about 20 billion dollars in the next five years," General Manager of ExxonMobil Kazakhstan Inc. James Taylor said.[33] Taylor pointed to the need of a "more favourable investment climate," citing figures of the U.S. Department of Energy indicating that the "total volume of investments in Kazakhstan since 1991 was 13 billion dollars." Added to this was the prediction by the ChevronTexaco CEO that his company was planning to invest five percent of the some 80 billion dollars it projected for worldwide investments in Kazakhstan. In the same period, there was news of a major Caspian oil and gas deal involving a BP (British Petroleum) led consortium, including Azerbaijan, Turkey, and Georgia.[34]

Israel and Iraq

Far from the oil and natural gas fields of Central Asia was yet another area whose oil wealth was of major concern: Iraq. The Iraqi oil fields were not the subject of public discussion among U.S. officials. "The only interest the United States has in the region is furthering the cause of peace and stability, not his [Hussein's] country's ability to generate oil," claimed President Bush's spokesperson.[35] The question of Iraq was not so apologetically broached in White House circles, however. Pursuit of the region was advocated by some, in and outside of government, who also had ideas about how to achieve peace and stability in the Middle East—the same kind of ideas involved in the pacification of Palestinians.[36]

Within a week of the September attacks, *The New York Times* reported differences within the administration as to what the scope of the U.S. response should be. Deputy Secretary of Defense Paul Wolfowitz and Chief of Staff to the Vice President I. Lewis Libby urged a military campaign against Osama bin Laden as well as "other suspected terrorist bases in Iraq and in Lebanon's Bekaa region."[37] At the time, neither Vice President Dick Cheney nor Defense Secretary Donald Rumsfeld were viewed as supporting a campaign against Iraq, nor was Secretary of State Colin Powell sympathetic to such a move. At the same time, Wolfowitz and Libby were hardly alone: their allies included colleagues with whom they had served in unofficial circles of neoconservative think tanks in Washington.

In a critical letter addressed to the Speaker of the House and the Senate in 1998, then Majority Leader Newt Gingrich and Trent Lott, and former members of the State and Defense Departments, as well as a former CIA director, combined their efforts to call for the removal of Saddam Hussein's regime. The group included Richard Perle, Donald Rumsfeld, James Woolsey, Elliot Abrams, and others.[38] Among the reasons offered was that Hussein risked adversely influencing the "Middle East peace process." What the same letter never disclosed was that some of its signatories were actually *opposed* to the "peace process," at least as the term was routinely understood. Their views on both Iraq and Israel emerged more clearly in other contexts, as in the private institutions and think tanks that functioned as informal lobbying groups in Washington. One of them, to which most of the above letter writers belonged, was PNAC, or Project for the New American Century.

PNAC was described as a "non-profit educational organization whose goal is to promote American global leadership." Its chair was William Kristol, editor of the neoconservative *Weekly Standard,* joined by Gary Schmitt, executive director of the organization.[39] Along with a host of other compatible institutions, such as the Institute for National Security Affairs, the American Enterprise Institute, the Hudson Institute, the Washington Institute, the Middle East Forum, and the Center for Security Policy, these institutions and think tanks acted as lobbying groups giving voice to past political insiders, some of whom were in Washington during the years between Reagan and Clinton. Of these a number assumed official positions in the Bush administration, while others remained on the margins of officialdom—though scarcely without influence derived from their connections.[40]

Although describing itself as a Jerusalem-based think tank with an office in Washington, the Institute for Advanced Strategic and Political Studies should be included in this group. Richard Perle and Douglas Feith were among its advisers at a time when the Institute produced an important study on the Middle East for Israeli Prime Minister Benjamin Netanyahu. The Institute's "Study Group on a New Israeli Strategy Toward 2000" was chaired by Perle,[41] at the time a member of the American Enterprise Institute. He was joined by Feith, Jonathan Torop, and James Colbert, among others: the last two were, respectively, members of the Washington Institute for Near East Policy and the Jewish Institute for National Security Affairs. Perle became Chairman of the Defense Policy Board in the Bush Administration, while Feith was appointed Under Secretary of Defense for Policy in July 2001.

Akiva Eldar, Israeli columnist for the daily *Ha'aretz*, recalled that Perle and Feith had been asked to advise Likud leader Netanyahu when he first became Prime Minister. The result of their efforts was a working paper produced by the Institute in 1998. "They could not have known," Eldar wrote, "that four years later the working paper they prepared, including plans for Israel to help restore the Hashemite throne in Iraq, would shed light on the current policies of the only superpower in the world."[42] That superpower would then unabashedly endorse the policies of the Israeli Right, justifying such support in the name of "peace," the nature of which was clearly articulated in the Institute's paper.

The main thrust of the group's proposals was a critique of Israeli politics directed at the Labor party and its "statist excesses." The problem, it proclaimed, was "Labor Zionism, which for 70 years has dominated the Zionist movement, [and] has generated a stalled and shackled economy."[43] In its place, privatization and economic reforms were recommended, along with "stressing self-reliance, maturity, strategic cooperation on areas of mutual concern, and furthering values inherent to the West. This can only be done if Israel takes serious steps to terminate aid, which prevents economic reform." In terms of Middle East policy, the advice of the group was to work closely with Turkey and Jordan to contain, destabilize, and roll back the most dangerous threats in the region. This implies a clean break from the slogan "comprehensive peace," embracing instead a more traditional concept of strategy based on balance of power. In its place, "a new approach to peace" was called for that the authors believed would be enthusiastically welcomed in Washington, involving slogans like "peace for peace," "peace through strength" and self-reliance: *the balance of power*."[44]

The foundations of such an approach were described as resting on the specific proposition Netanyahu was advised to emphasize in the U.S., namely: "Our claim to the land—to which we have clung for 2000 years—is legitimate and noble. . . . Only the unconditional acceptance by Arabs of our rights, *especially* in their territorial dimension, '*peace for peace*,' is a solid basis for the future."[45] Under such conditions, Israel could "embrace negotiations, but as *means, not ends*, to pursue those ideals and demonstrate national steadfast-ness." The group also had something to offer on the subject of "securing the Northern border" with Syria. They urged sympathetic support in the U.S. "if Israel seized the strategic initiative along its northern borders by engag-ing Hesballah, Syria, and Iran, as the principal agents of aggression in Leba-non. . . ."[46]

At the same time, Iraq was not to be forgotten. Here the authors of the working paper recommended that Israel should not merely cooperate with Jordan and Turkey in "rolling back Syria," but also "focus on removing Saddam Hussein from power in Iraq—an important Israeli strategic objective in its own right—hoping thereby to foil Syria's regional ambitions."[47] The instru-ment for such a policy was ultimately to be the Hashemite restoration of power in Iraq, that is, completely undoing the revolution of 1958. Attributing the idea of such a restoration to King Hussein of Jordan, the working-group authors viewed such an outcome as breaking the control exercised by Hesbal-lah over the Lebanese south. To this end they recommended that the Ne-tanyahu government offer the Jordanian monarch protection while arranging for U.S. investments to undermine Jordan's ties with Iraq.

As for Palestine, Israel's security might necessitate "hot pursuit into Pales-tinian-controlled areas, a justifiable practice with which Americans can sym-pathize," according to the authors.[48] The Oslo arrangements were to be considered in this spirit, including the prospect of undermining PLO leader Yasir Arafat in the event of noncompliance with existing agreements. But the Palestinian question was to be transcended, according to the authors, and the Israeli relationship with Washington was to be secured by cultivating mutual interests based less on achieving peace with Palestinians than on supporting "anti-missile defense in order to remove the threat of blackmail which even a weak and distant army can pose to either state." They believed the U.S. Con-gress would respond positively.

The PNAC had a somewhat different approach to the Middle East, focusing on the U.S. position in the Persian Gulf and its impact on American oil inter-ests in the context of overall U.S. military power. They wanted to undermine the Saudi position and advocated a U.S. invasion of Iraq, although neither was justified in terms of Israeli interests. The overall thrust of PNAC's most influ-ential paper on American defense strategy emphasized the need for military expansion along lines announced by President Bush in his $379 billion Penta-gon budget for Fiscal Year 2003.[49] Their 2000 report, entitled "Rebuilding America's Defenses: Strategy, Forces and Resources for a New Century," was written by a team that included Wolfowitz, Dov Zakheim, Undersecretary of Defense under Bush junior, and Libby. It provided a review of U.S. forces in the Gulf since the end of Desert Storm, making clear they were in the region to stay and emphasizing reliance on such states as Kuwait, Qatar, and Bahrain to help protect U.S. interests. It identified U.S. adversaries as Iran and Iraq while recommending a downgraded status of the Saudi position in the larger constellation of U.S. policy. That position was further emphasized in testimony offered by the PNAC chair before the House in the spring of 2002. The earlier report underlined the extent to which there had been "a geometric increase in the presence of U.S. armed forces, peaking above 500,000 troops during Operation Desert Storm, but rarely falling below 20,000 in the intervening years."[50] According to their estimate, about 5,000 U.S. airmen were stationed along with a fleet of aircraft patrols, "often complemented by Navy aircraft from carriers in the Gulf" based in Saudi Arabia, Kuwait, and "neighboring states."

In spring 2002, William Kristol appeared before the House International Relations Subcommittee on Middle East and South Asia to urge the U.S.-Saudi connection be revamped and its OPEC leverage undermined. In addition, he supported a U.S. invasion and control of Iraq, where the U.S. could proceed with "regime change" to construct a decent Iraqi society and economy that would be a "tremendous step toward reducing Saudi leverage."[51] Writing in *The New American Century* on May 2002, the PNAC executive director Gary Schmitt reinforced this position. "From a military and strategic perspective, Iraq is more important than Saudi Arabia," he maintained, advocating a U.S. invasion of Iraq as a way of "building a representative government in Baghdad [that] would demonstrate that democracy can work in the Arab world."[52] He strongly endorsed the Bush Doctrine, extolled as an instance of "American 'exceptionalism'" that recalled the heady days of post-World War II policy under President Truman. To turn from this vision of America to the Islamic Middle East and Central Asia was, in Schmitt's view, to embrace historically retrograde regions which "for some sound and some not-so-sound reasons" the U.S. had been led to "exempt from the requirements of liberal rule." Schmitt's views on the Arab and Islamic worlds echoed talk of civilization clashes and the superiority of the West.

Support for an attack on Iraq came from other sources, including those involved in deliberations on U.S. oil politics and plans for military action. Less ideological in their approach, less overtly sympathetic to an expansive Israeli politics along lines of Netanyahu or Sharon, those talking oil politics here were bent on thinking through other kinds of problems. Questions would have to be posed. In the event of a U.S. attack on Iraq, what would be the reactions of U.S. allies with stakes in Iraqi oil? Who would be the beneficiaries of such a move among U.S. and international oil companies? The answers of course assumed an eventual U.S. military victory that war preparations and "bombing runs" on Iraq were precisely designed to achieve.

Deploying Troops and Practicing War

According to foreign sources, the Bush cabinet agreed as early as April 2001 that "Iraq remains a destabilizing influence to the flow of oil to international markets from the Middle East" which justified military intervention.[53] Neil

Mackay, the journalist who published this account in *The Sunday Herald*, disclosed that Vice President Cheney had requested a study from the Baker Institute for Public Policy which endorsed such a policy. James Baker, Secretary of State under George Bush senior, sought counsel from Kenneth Lay, the ex-Enron chief indicted for fraud, along with a director of Shell, the regional head of British Petroleum, the head of ChevronTexaco, and an ex-oil minister from Kuwait. Cheney himself, as *The Sunday Herald* reminded its readers, had been at the head of the oil services company Halliburton, although it omitted to mention that "Halliburton subsidiaries submitted $23.8 million worth of contracts with Iraq to the United Nations in 1998 and 1999 for approval by the sanctions committee."[54]

Baker's advisers at BP and ChevronTexaco represented the interests of big oil, as opposed to the Independents. The distinction is worth noting as some analysts had described Bush's foreign policy initiatives in the oil sector, in fall 2001, as inadequately responsive to the interests of the oil giants that were disposed to favor a more internationalist policy, concluding there was a disjuncture between the Bush administration and "the true long-term interests of Big Oil in the U.S."[55] In their estimate "the Bush team is asking the U.S. oil industry to wait until it is ready to accommodate U.S. IOGC [International Oil and Gas Companies] interests." The benefits to big oil were broached in *The Washington Post* on September 15, 2002. Citing industry officials and leaders of the Iraqi opposition, David Ottaway and Dan Morgan suggested that "a U.S.-led ouster of Iraqi President Saddam Hussein "could open a bonanza for American oil companies long banished from Iraq, scuttling oil deals between Baghdad and Russia, France and other countries, and reshuffling world petroleum markets, according to industry officials and leaders of the Iraqi opposition."[56] Former CIA director James Woolsey, a signer of the 1998 letter to Trent Lott and Newt Gingrich calling for Saddam Hussein's ouster, was cited in the same article. Woolsey addressed the sensitive question of the fate of foreign investors in Iraq whose governments did not support the U.S. position, a matter of direct concern to Russian and French investors who were heavily engaged in Iraq and/or seeking contracts with the Hussein regime. The price of resisting U.S. policy was economic blackmail, as Woolsey's position suggested. If a new government was set up in Baghdad, it might well choose to ignore existing contracts and favor U.S. firms such as ExxonMobil and ChevronTexaco.

Would there be international recourse against such actions? The question was posed by oil specialists who acknowledged that "European and Russian oil companies face losing their grip on Iraqi oilfield projects to U.S. energy firms if the country's opposition party is brought to power in a U.S.-forced coup."[57] Moreover, there was widespread speculation and anxiety concerning the impact of U.S. military action against Iraq on oil prices, a position shared by oil producers around the world not to mention consumers who can recall past experiences. The subject, however, was not openly aired by the Bush White House, although analysts in the U.S. warned of significant risks posed by U.S. preemptive action for "treasuries and foreign ministries around the world."[58]

At the public level Washington spoke of Iraq in altogether different terms: the anticipated U.S. invasion of Iraq was justified by the President's Special Assistant for Near East, Southwest Asian, and North African affairs, Zalmay Khalilzad, in terms of democracy. The former Unocal adviser who favored recognition of the Taliban was now advocating U.S. intervention "to achieve the disarmament mission and to get Iraq ready for a democratic transition and then through democracy over time."[59] Through the fall of 2002, on the other hand, it was not a "democracy" but rather invasion that was being planned as the U.S. escalated its deployment of military forces in the Gulf. The planned transfer of General Tommy Franks and some 600 senior level officers from their base in Florida to al Udeid in Doha, Qatar, was viewed by many observers "as a precursor to the initiation of combat, as the officers involved are responsible for the management of all U.S. forces in the region."[60]

By October 2002, U.S. forces were deployed throughout the Middle East and the Gulf, as follows.[61] In Turkey some 4,000 U.S. forces were stationed at the Incirlik air base, with its array of fighters and electronic aircraft used to conduct flights over northern Iraq. Jordan had an estimated 1,400 U.S. Special Operations troops, with continuous exercises involving British forces, along with personnel from Jordan, Oman, and Kuwait. In Saudi Arabia there were reported an estimated 6,000 U.S. troops, with the main command center at al Kharj, located south of the Saudi capital. In Kuwait, 10,000 troops were reported stationed or expected to arrive in the coming month, including 3,000 Air Force personnel active in U.S.-U.K. Operation Southern Watch over Iraq. Bahrain was reported to be the locale of some 4,200 U.S. troops, in addition to the Fifth Fleet, with a new air base under construction in Musnana'h along with British bases at Masirah and Seeb. The United Arab Emirates was reported as housing the 380th Air Expeditionary Wing at al Dhafra, along with reconnaissance squadrons. In Qatar, the much publicized site of the expanded U.S. command center at al Udeid, there were some 3,300 U.S. military personnel, including a fleet of Air Force and refueling tankers used by the U.S. in Afghanistan. Yemen, Djibouti, and Diego Garcia were also sites of U.S. military activity.[62]

Mention should also be made of the significant role played by private military contractors, including a subsidiary of Halliburton, Kellogg, Brown and Root, that was "contracted to provide comprehensive logistical support for U.S. bases in Afghanistan, Uzbekistan and elsewhere in the region."[63] Such private supports were available in other states as well, including Saudi Arabia, where they helped reinforce the defense and national guard, along with safety of the ruling family that had helped to subsidize the first Gulf War.

What did it all mean? What was it for? Where would it lead? Had the first stage of the undeclared U.S. war for oil and global hegemony been justified in the name of the U.S. "war on terror," just what many feared would inspire yet further acts of the same kind?

U.S. troop deployments in the Gulf and continued "bombing runs" over Iraqi "no flight zones" represented the ongoing reality of an undeclared war, the proximate origins of which stemmed from the first Gulf War and involved the long-term struggle for control of oil resources.[64] That the U.S. has been able to mount such operations from its Gulf bases without challenge is indicative of another undeclared condition, namely, the transformation of the Gulf into a U.S. protectorate—a policy the U.S. has been pursuing in Central Asia. There, as Andrew Bacevich pointed out in *The National Interest,* the U.S. "war on terror" in what was former Soviet-controlled territory promoted the conversion of "Central Asia into a quasi-protectorate—much as it did the Persian Gulf after Great Britain departed," with the purpose of assuring U.S. exploitation of the region's resources.[65]

Notes

1. "U.S. Forces in the Middle East," Terrorism Project, *Weekly Defense Monitor,* vol. 6, no. 36, Oct. 24, 2002 (online edition: http://www.cdi.org/terrorism/forces-centcom.cfm)
2. "What to do About Oil," *Business Week Online,* Oct. 19, 2001, 2.
3. David Barboza, "OPEC's Pain is U.S. Gain," *The New York Times,* Nov. 16, 2001, C1.
4. According to the Energy Information Administration, cited in David Barboza, ibid.
5. See Michael Tanzer's remarks on the subject at the end of his essay, "Oil and the Gulf Crisis," in Phyllis Bennis and Michel Moushabeck, eds. *Beyond the Storm* (New York: Interlink Publishing Company, 1991), 267.
6. Report of the National Energy Policy Development Group, "National Energy Policy: Reliable, Affordable, and Environmentally Sound Energy for America's Future," U.S. Government Printing Office, Washington, D.C., 2001, 1–13.
7. Ibid., Section 8, 3.
8. Ibid., Section 8, 4.
9. Juan Forero, "New Role for U.S. in Colombia: Protecting a Vital Oil Pipeline," *The New York Times,* Oct. 4, 2002, 1. On Africa, see: Douglas A Yates, "The Scramble for African Oil," *West Africa* April 29–May 5, 2002, 29; and Ken Silverstein, "U.S. Oil Politics in the 'Kuwait of Africa,' " *The Nation,* April 22, 2002, 11–20.
10. Bushan Bhtree and Thaddeus Herrick, "Saudis Put a Stopper in Big Plans for Investment by Western Firms," *The Wall Street Journal,* Sept. 9, 2002, A1.
11. Sabrina Tavernise, "Exxon Says Way is Cleared for Development in Russia," *The New York Times,* Oct. 30, 2001.
12. AFX European Focus, July 8, 2002, online.
13. Sabrina Tavernise, "For Big Oil, Open Door in Far East of Russia," *The New York Times,* Aug. 6, 2002, W1.
14. April 28, 2002, "Secretary Rumsfeld Joint Press Conference in Kazakhstan," in U.S. Dept of Defense News Transcript (online): http://www.defenselink.mil/new/Apr2002/t0428 2002_t0428kzk.html
15. Hoonan Peimani, "American Military Presence in Central Asia Antagonizes Russia," Center for Defense Information Weekly, #28, 1 (online access: http://www.cdi.org/russia/228–11.dfm)
16. Ibid.
17. Assistant Secretary of State William J. Burns, "Towards a Positive Agenda for the Middle East," Oct. 19, 2001. Asst. Secretary of State Burns' speech can be read at: http://usinfo.stategov/regional/nea/iraq/offtxts/1020brns.htm
18. Fred Halliday, *Arabia Without Sultans* (New York: Vintage Books, 1975), 23. For Halliday's more recent assessment of this work, see by the same author, "Arabia Without Sultans Revisited," *MERIP,* July–September 1997, 27–29.

19. Iraq: Crimes Against Humanity-U.S. Department of State/IIP, May 7, 2002. http://usinfo. state.gov/regional/nea/iraq/crimes/

20. Michael T. Klare, "Prelude to Desert Storm: Arms Transfers to Iran and Iraq During the Iran-Iraq War of 1980–1988 and the Origins of the Gulf War," unpublished paper prepared for the Conference "Reassessing the Gulf War," Boston University, Feb. 21, 2001, 7.

21. As reported in the transcript record of ABC News Show, *Nightline*, Oct. 28, 1992, at which Gary Milhollin, Director of the The Wisconsin Project, who testified before the Committee on Banking, Housing and Urban Affairs, U.S. Senate, 102nd Congress, on Oct. 27, 1992, appeared.

22. The Riegle Report can be found on the web site of the Gulf War Veterans (http://www. gulfweb.org/bigdoc/report/riegle1.html)

23. Patrick E. Tyler, "Officers Say U.S. Aided Iraq in War Despite Use of Gas," *The New York Times*, August 18, 2002, 1.

24. Christopher Dickey and Evan Thomas, "How Saddam Happened," *Newsweek*, Sept. 23, 2002, 36.

25. Barton Gellman, "Allied Air War Struck Broadly in Iraq; Officials Acknowledge Strategy Went Beyond Purely Military Targets," *The Washington Post*, June 23, 1991, A1.

26. Feb 12, 1998, Hearings on "U.S. Interests in the Central Asian Republics," before the House Subcommittee on Asia and the Pacific, Doug Bereuter, Chairman, House International Relations. The preceding document was accessed through the online Nexis database.

27. Thomas Ferguson, "Blowing Smoke: Impeachment, the Clinton Presidency, and the Political Economy," in William J. Crotty, ed., *The State of Democracy in America* (Washington, D.C.: Georgetown University Press, 2001), 212.

28. Ibid., 212–213.

29. Maj. Adrian W Burke, USMC, "U.S. Strategy for the Caspian Sea Basin," *Strategic Review*, Fall 1999, 27.

30. Klare, op. cit., 95.

31. "U.S. Strategy for the Caspian Sea Basin," op. cit., 26.

32. Sabrina Tavernise, "Russia and U.S. to Discuss Collaborative Oil Ventures," *The New York Times*, Sept. 28, 2002, B2. See also the earlier analysis by Ariel Cohen, "Why Russia's Accession to the WTO is in America's Economic and Strategic Interests," The Heritage Foundation Reports, May 22, 2002.

33. "USA Could be 'Promising' Importer of Kazakh oil," *Novosti Nedeli*, Almaty, Kazakhstan, Oct. 9, 2002, as reported in BBC worldwide monitoring.

34. Aug. 20, 2002, Michael Lelyveld, "Western Companies Prepared to Invest in Caspian Gas Fields," EurasiaNet, Business and Economics. (http://www.eurasianet.org/departments/ business/articles/pp.081702.shtml) See also, Sept. 19, 2002, Richard Allen Greene, "Work Begins on Oil Pipeline Bypassing Russia and Iran," *The New York Times*, W1.

35. Serge Schmemann, "Controlling Iraq's Oil Wouldn't be Simple," section 4, Week in Review, *The New York Times*, Nov. 3, 2002, 1.

36. The present analysis does not include discussion of the role of the organized Christian backers of Israel in the U.S., an important subject for an examination of the domestic constituencies supporting Bush's policies toward Israel.

37. Patrick E. Tyler and E. Sciolino, "Bush Advisers Split on Scope of Retaliation," *The New York Times*, Sept. 20, 2001, 1.

38. May 29, 1998, Letter addressed to The Honorable Newt Gingrich and The Honorable Trent Lott and signed by the following: Elliot Abrams, William J. Bennett, Jeffrey Bergner, John R. Bolton, Paula Dobriansky, Francis Fukuyama, Robert Kagan, Zalmay Khalilzad, William Kristol, Richard Perle, Peter Rodman, Donald Rumsfeld, William Schneider, Jr., Vin Weber, Paul Wolfowitz, R. James Woolsey, Robert B. Zoellich. The text appears in: http://www. newamericancentury.org/iraqletter1998.htm

39. See also the American Enterprise Institute, the Hudson Institute, the Washington Institute, the Institute for National Security Affairs (also known as the Jewish Institute for National Security Affairs), the Center for Security Policy (CSP), and the Middle East Forum. For example, the "Project for the New American Century," described as "a non-profit educational organization whose goal is to promote American global leadership."

40. For an uncritical description of the Institute for National Security Affairs, see Mark H. Milstein's "Strategic Ties or Tentacles? Institute for National Security Affairs," *Washington Report*, (http://www.washington-report.org/backissues/1091/9110027. htm) For a critical

account, see Jason Vest, "The Men From JINSA and CSP," *The Nation*, Aug. 15, 2002 (online at: http://www.TheNation.com/doc.mhtm/?i=20020902)

41. "A Clean Break: A New Strategy for Securing the Realm," The Institute for Advanced Strategic and Political Studies, Jerusalem, Washington. (online: http://www.israel.economy.org/strat 1.htm)

42. Akiva Eldar, "Perles of Wisdom for the Feithful," *Ha'aretz,* Oct. 1, 2002 (online: http://www.haaretzdaily.com/hasen/pages/ShArt.jhim1? itemNo=214635)

43. "A Clean Break," Ibid. 1.

44. Ibid., 2.

45. Ibid., 2.

46. Ibid.

47. Ibid., 3.

48. Ibid., 4.

49. For a discussion of the Bush military budget, see Michael Klare, "The Pursuit of Perpetual Supremacy—Decoding the Administration's Military Budget," *The Nation*, July 15, 2002.

50. "Rebuilding America's Defenses: Strategy, Forces and Resources for a New Century," a report of the Project for a New American Century, issued September 2000. Available online at: http://www.newamericancentury.org/RebuildingAmericanDefense.pcf, 17.

51. William Kristol, Testimony before the House Committee on International Relations Subcommittee on Middle East and South Asia, published in Project for the New American Century, May 23, 2002. Memorandum to Opinion Leaders on Saudi Arabia. (online: http://www.newamericancentury.org/saudi-052302

52. May 23, 2002, Gary Schmitt, Memorandum: Opinion Leaders, 3. http: www.newamericancentury. org/saudi-052302.htm

53. Neil Mackay, "Official: U.S. Oil at the heart of Iraq Crisis," *The Sunday Herald* (Scotland), Oct. 6, 2002 (online: http://sundayherald.com/)

54. Cited in Nicholas D. Kristof, "Revolving-Door Monsters," *The New York Times*, Oct. 11, 2002, A 31.

55. Ibid., 19.

56. Sept.15, 2002, Dan Morgan and David B Ottaway, "In Iraqi War Scenario, Oil is Key Issue; U.S. Drillers Eye Huge Petroleum Pool," *The Washington Post*, A01.

57. Martyn Wingrove, "Non-U.S. Oil Interests at Risk Says Iraq Opposition," *Lloyd's List*, Oct. 18, 2002; and "Iraqi Opposition Prepared to Revise Oil Contracts with Foreign Companies," *Kommersant*, Moscow, Oct. 21, 2002.

58. Thomas Ferguson and Robert A Johnson, "Oil Economics Lubricates Push for War," *Los Angeles Times*, Oct. 13, 2002.

59. David E. Sanger and Eric Schmitt, "U.S. Has a Plan to Occupy Iraq, Officials Report," *The New York Times*, Oct. 11, 2002, 14.

60. Michael T. Klare, "War Plans and Pitfalls," *The Nation*, Oct. 21, 2002, 16.

61. The following sources—which may include differing estimates—have been used in compiling this data: Eric Schmitt and Thom Shanker, "American Arsenal in the Mideast is Being Built Up to Confront Saddam Hussein," *The New York Times*, Aug. 19, 2002, A8; the *Weekly Defense Monitor*, vol. 6, #36, Oct. 24, 2002, Terrorism Project, Center for Defense Information (online: http://www.cdi.org/terrorism/forces-centcom.cfm); Arms, Arms Trade Resource Center, The World Policy Institute, Oct. 4, 2002; "Growing US Military Presence Since 9/11/01," *The Nation*, Oct. 21, 2002.

62. The following sources of U.S. funding should also be noted since they were designed to facilitate compatible activities. They include Congressional allocations for Economic Support Funds, Foreign Military Financing, International Military Education and Training, Non-proliferation Anti-terrorism Demining and Related Programs, Assistance for Independent States of the Former USSR, and others. Beneficiaries include Israel, Turkey, Egypt, Jordan, Oman, Yemen, Afghanistan, Pakistan, India, Azerbaijan, Uzbekistan, Kyrgyzstan, Kazakhstan, Tajikistan, and Georgia.

63. "War, Inc.," *The Nation*, Oct. 21, 2002, 23.

64. Michael R. Gordon, "U.S. Pilots in Gulf Use Southern Iraq for Practice Runs," *The New York Times*, Nov. 3, 2002, 1; and Serge Schmemann, "Controlling Iraq's Oil Wouldn't Be Simple," Week in Review, *The New York Times*, Section 4, 1.

65. Andrew Bacevich, "Bases of Debate; America in Central Asia: Steppes to Empire," *The National Interest*, summer 2002 (issue 68), 48–49.

CHAPTER 3

Star Wars
Imperialism in Space

LORING WIRBEL

Opponents of the Bush administration who expected an exponential increase in rhetoric on the use of space for global military supremacy have found it difficult to follow the tortuous path of space doctrine under Secretary of Defense Donald Rumsfeld. On the one hand, rapid deployment of multitiered missile defense has been promoted from the White House to a level not seen since Ronald Reagan's seminal 1983 Star Wars speech. The Rumsfeld Commission report on military space, released in early 2001 just as Bush took office, seemed to go beyond the United States Space Command's aggressive *Long-Range Plan* of 1998 in advocating global space dominance in order to prevent a new "space Pearl Harbor."[1]

But Rumsfeld's decision in the spring of 2002 to merge the U.S. Space Command into Strategic Command left military leaders puzzled. True, a new domestic military command was formed in the process, Northern Command, which could make use of space-based technologies for the ill-defined mission of "homeland defense." But what would be gained by melding the unified Space Command and former Strategic Command into an expanded Strategic Command at Offut Air Force Base in Nebraska, particularly if all service-specific Space Commands remained in Colorado Springs? Was Rumsfeld punishing the Air Force for its lead role in U.S. Space Command, or was he losing interest in exploiting space for planned preemptive regional battles in the war on terror?

Two fundamental errors are made in the way such questions are posed: too often, tactical critics of missile defense accept the excuse that such weapons systems truly are intended for defense against rogue short-range missiles, rather than as elements in an offensive preemptive military strategy. Similarly, critics of the general militarization of space assume that space represents a unique dimension in the overall military strategy of an unchallenged superpower.

Rumsfeld is carrying out the conclusions of two panels he served on just before assuming office in early 2001: one on the future of the National Reconnaissance Office, another on the militarization of space.[2] Both panels echoed many general conclusions of the earlier and more famous Rumsfeld Commission on "missile defense." The domination of near-earth space is considered necessary to protect U.S. interests as the largest economic and military power. Total control of 24-hour global reconnaissance, targeting, and navigation from space is seen as necessary to realize that goal. Missile defense is a necessary arrow in the quiver of precision conventional weapons, as well as nuclear weapons utilized to enforce that dominance.

It follows that analysts should not have their attention diverted by minor wrinkles in what otherwise is a seamless blanket of space superiority. Supporters of a "revolution in military affairs" based on conventional weapons, for example, have criticized the tactical marriage between Space Command and the "nuclear dinosaur" of Strategic Command. The belief that Strategic Command is arcane stems from an observation that Bush was willing to limit strategic nuclear weapons in conjunction with Vladimir Putin, and that nuclear weapons are "obsolete" in an era of "precision warfare." But the harsh language contained in the recent Nuclear Posture Review,[3] as well as Rumsfeld's suggestion that the Missile Defense Agency consider nuclear warheads on interceptor missiles for missile-defense, indicates that the administration considers nuclear weapons a vital element in its quest for space domination. What appeared as a tactical gaffe has become one more step in the goal of ensuring absolute U.S. global supremacy in all theaters of war.

The familiar "documents of domination" of the U.S. Space Command—*Vision for 2020, Long-Range Plan, 2001 Almanac*—remain reliable high-level explications of U.S. military strategy in space, despite the demise of the sponsoring agency. Peace activists can thank the Space Command for being so frank in suggesting that the purpose of U.S. space dominance is to ensure preservation of the current international gulf between haves and have-nots. This indicates not only a major role for space forces in supporting preemptive unilateralism, but provides an enlightening view of the role of the military in supporting U.S. corporate interests.

Interestingly enough, most Space Command planning documents were prepared in the era preceding Bush's assumption to power. Long before Bush's underlings elected to flaunt their unilateralism with pride, Clinton officials like Secretary of State Madeleine Albright and NRO Director Keith Hall were touting the advantages of unilateralism and world domination. As military analyst Michael Klare pointed out, in several mid-1990s studies on "permanent preeminence," Clinton officials took the path of least resistance at the end of the Cold War, keeping the old military networks in place and looking for new targets against which to apply intelligence and targeting technologies. There never was a thought to scaling back intelligence networks, as Russia did, in order to gain peace dividends. Democrats and Republicans were united in the Clinton era in supporting the unspoken notion that the U.S. must establish global supremacy, both militarily and economically, and that the slightest move to scale back military networks would indicate a lack of U.S. resolve. The path to the June 1, 2002 "Bush Doctrine" speech on the omniscient U.S. right of preemptive war was in fact prepared on the basis of a decade's worth of incremental steps.

This path has the full support of all branches of government, and both major parties, with only minor exceptions like Representative Dennis Kucinich (D-OH) giving partial critiques of U.S. space supremacy. The General Accounting Office, for example, normally is regarded as an aggressive watchdog of government malfeasance. Yet its two analyses of Space Commission conclusions in 2002 accepted as given that unilateral control of space was a worthwhile and achievable objective.[4] The bipartisan support of space supremacy is as misguided as the broad congressional support for Bush preemptive warfare strategy, yet critics must go back to first principles in order to delineate all that is wrong with such a strategy.

A full comprehension of the building blocks of space supremacy requires a brief overview of the past 50 years in the history of military space. Elements of the military C3ISR network—command, control, communications, intelligence, surveillance, and reconnaissance—are as important in this overview as development of space weapons. This implies an important baseline assumption to apply when analyzing the question of U.S. space supremacy. Supporters of space weapons bans, as proposed in legislation sponsored by Kucinich and others, insist that a more important and realizable goal is to ban the *weaponization* of space, as opposed to the *militarization* of space.[5] Because space has been militarized for more than 40 years, the argument goes, peace activists should concentrate on the achievable goal of stopping space weapons before they are deployed. But weapon systems can use space for the bulk of their infrastructure, while the weapons themselves can be based on land or sea. National technical means of verification fielded by the NRO and National Security Agency, originally used for the stabilizing goal of verifying arms control treaties, have been reoriented toward tactical warfighting and improved with faster and higher-resolution sensors. When used in tactical situations in theatres such as Afghanistan and Iraq, the precision targeting of programs like Talon Knight become weapons based largely upon space assets, which are both more dangerous and more immediate threats than futuristic Star Wars platforms like the space-based laser.

Consequently, the real litmus test for those concerned with arms control should be: Does this particular satellite system or launch vehicle or ground station serve the interests of stabilization and multilateral control, or does it serve the interests of unilateral (U.S.) dominance? In the current portfolio of U.S.-government-owned space-based platforms, at least two thirds of these systems would fail this test. And these systems so overwhelmingly dominate privately-financed space systems or those launched by other nations, the latter can almost be ignored as falling into the background noise. In this model, analyzing the history of missile-defense and space-based weapons is necessary but scarcely sufficient. Understanding space dominance requires an understanding of the evolution of the NSA, NRO, and C3ISR networks.

From Verification to Warfare

The National Security Agency has tried to emphasize the passive nature of its electronic intelligence tasks since the creation of the agency in 1952 from the remnants of the Armed Forces Security Agency. For those few in the know about the agency's structure 50 years ago, NSA officials tried to stress the idea that direction-finding and triangulation antennas were systems intended to pick up hints of the possible aggressive military intent on the part of Communist nations, primarily the Soviet Union and China. The forward projection of the NSA always was clear, however, given the basing strategy the U.S. employed for nuclear weapons stockpiling and conventional-force projection. As soon as the U.S. began setting up strategic nuclear bases on a global basis in the mid-1950s, the NSA followed, signing secret pacts with host nations to allow for establishment of specialized antenna fields, either "broomstick" deployments of vertical dipole antennas or the later massive "elephant cage" systems based on the FLR-9 circularly-disposed antenna arrays. NSA bases were virtually the only sites treated with higher security than nuclear weapons bases in the early history of the Cold War.

To the extent that NSA used such bases to assemble order-of-battle analyses of Soviet forces, the understanding that the bases would serve "defensive" purposes could be taken at face value. From the beginning, however, the NSA adopted the Pentagon view that all sea lanes and overhead air lanes belonged inherently to Western powers, and that any use of open sea and air space by the Soviets constituted prima facie evidence of aggressive intent. Thus the early ancestors of the Echelon global snooping network, formed under auspices of the UK/USA Treaty, constituted a network of control based on the similar default assumption that the U.S. managed the planet.

But NSA aggression extended beyond the establishment of global passive antenna networks. Revisionist historians covering the Cold War's secret history, including James Bamford and Jeffrey Richelson,[6] have unearthed several instances of U.S. aggressive overflights of Chinese and Soviet territory, performed on behalf of the NSA, which predated the well-known U-2 flights for joint CIA and NSA use. The cases of downed RB-47 planes along the China coast and interior are fairly well known, if only because many pilots and crew were treated as prisoners of war (while remaining unacknowledged by their government). Defenders of such actions could claim that, if the characteristics of defense radar were to be learned, aggressive intrusions into national air spaces were required in order that Soviet and Chinese forces activate these radar long enough for the NSA to obtain "signatures" of their electromagnetic characteristics. Of course, one only need know all details of defense radar if one plans on aggressive attack of an adversary's home territory, but the argument had at least partial validity.

Bamford, however, disclosed details in 2001 of Operation Homerun, a massive intrusion of Soviet airspace by RB-47s and B-52s flying across the North Pole in March 1956. This mission, approved directly by President Eisenhower, was justified on the basis of forming an entire map of electronic military installations in the Russian interior, although there was little to distinguish one such run on March 21, 1956, from a preemptive military attack against the USSR.[7] The later, more provocative U-2 program was intended as a direct response to the Soviet Union's refusal to discuss the Open Skies program promoted in the United Nations. The audacity of White House efforts to preserve plausible deniability was exposed for all to see after Francis Gary Powers was shot down in May 1960. But Eisenhower had promoted a concurrent spy satellite program since before the launch of Sputnik in late 1957. Simultaneous programs were designed to explore imaging and signals-interception from space. Before the first satellite launches, Eisenhower secretly created the National Reconnaissance Office in August 1960 to take control of all spy-satellite launches; the very existence of NRO remained classified for 32 years, until the waning days of the first Bush administration. Today NRO is proud to reveal details of the only spy satellite declassified to date, the KH-4 Corona. This imaging satellite used the legitimacy of the Discoverer program, the "scientific" series of launches observed by Americans as a belated (and chaotic) response to Sputnik. Far less has been said about GRAB, the Galactic Radiation and Background electronic intelligence satellite launched by the Naval Research Labs in June 1960, or a follow-on developed in conjunction with NSA and NRO, Poppy.

Imaging satellites were developed as informal "competitive" efforts pitting the Air Force/NRO against the CIA, due to the latter agency's expertise in handling image interpretation through its National Photographic Interpretation Center. The Corona family was based on analog image capture on film, and on delayed drops of film rolls to planes that picked up film canisters in large nets. The familiar KH-9 satellite nicknamed Big Bird represented the last of these non-real-time film-based satellites, but served the U.S. reasonably well with image resolution of a few feet. The goal for the succeeding KH-11 imaging satellite was not just higher resolution but a turn to "real-time" imaging by cutting the delay associated with film processing and retrieval. KH-11 turned to charge-coupled devices rather than film as an imaging medium, relaying data from the CCDs to one key ground station, the notorious Pine Gap base, opened in the Australian outback in the early 1970s. Because Pine Gap ground equipment accepted unencrypted traffic from satellites, this drove the need for NRO to develop a highly-secure and highly-classified relay system in space called the Satellite Data System or SDS.

Desmond Ball, an Australian arms researcher who wrote one of the earliest studies of Pine Gap, realized something critical had changed with the shift from Big Bird to KH-11, or Kennan. While the purpose of the upgrade may have been an innocent case of "technological creep," the result was to make the spy satellite a highly-accurate, time-sensitive system that was of more use in warfighting than in treaty verification. Ball had been paying close attention to the arguments made by former Lockheed engineer Robert Aldridge, who insisted in an Institute for Policy Studies report that the turn to highly accurate multiple independently targeted re-entry vehicles, or MIRVs, made the U.S. nuclear arsenal a first-strike system by default, if not by definition. The claims Aldridge made in his *Counterforce Syndrome* pamphlet were later validated when President Jimmy Carter revealed policy directives 57 and 59, committing the U.S. to a first-strike nuclear doctrine. Similarly, Ball said, intelligence platforms should not have been developed to the point where subtle distinctions of a few meters could be made and relayed in real time to an intelligence agency headquarters. The mere existence of such technology, he argued, would turn intelligence technology from a stabilizing function to warfighting. (Christopher Boyce and Dalton Lee made some of the same arguments when they were charged with selling secrets of Rhyolite signals intelligence satellites to Soviet agents.)[8]

The KH-12, or Advanced Crystal, was the first generation of geosynchronous satellite to experiment with light shielding and limited maneuverability. It has represented the mainstay of imaging architectures since the 1980s. NRO has had a program on its books since 1995 called 8X Future Imagery Architecture, which will upgrade imaging satellites by 2004 with advanced image filtering and processing capabilities on board, as well as maneuvering capabilities beyond KH-12. Boeing is the prime contractor for this multi-billion-dollar project, said to be the most expensive intelligence satellite program in history. An adjunct program to imaging in visible light is the radar imaging program, which possesses an ability to see through clouds and add "multispectral" analysis. Lacrosse satellites with Synthetic Aperture Radar have been in orbit since 1988 and have aided mapping capabilities in Iraq (Desert Storm), Somalia, Yugoslavia, and Afghanistan. NRO has fought for years to fund an ambitious next-generation radar platform, the Space-Based Radar, which the agency described as having direct target-acquisition capability.[9]

The highest classification in satellites has come in NRO's joint work with the NSA on adding space-based signals intelligence capability. Following the early GRAB and Poppy experiments, the NRO achieved regular interception capabilities from its first geosynchronous satellites of the 1970s, known in different versions as Canyon, Rhyolite, and Aquacade. These were improved in the 1980s with larger, unfurlable antennas and improved signal-processing, in a series of giant satellites dubbed Chalet, Vortex, Magnum, and Orion. During the Reagan era, geosynchronous satellites were augmented with high-earth-orbit "close-listen" satellites called Jumpseat. The latter had short lifetimes and usually were launched to provide region-specific analysis of hot spots. In the 1990s, the Mercury and Mentor series of geosynchronous satellites had become so large they could only be launched by Titan-4 rockets. At the same time that NRO promoted its 8X program, it consolidated electronic and communications intelligence programs into a unified Integrated Overhead SIGINT Architecture program, or IOSA. Boeing won the primary IOSA contract, just as it had in the case of 8X, and plans to launch a mid-decade monster called Intruder, as well as a spinoff satellite, Prowler, to be used in the Precision SIGINT Targeting System for spotting relocatable targets (moving vehicles and radars, etc.) from space.[10]

Congress had asked the NRO to examine micro-satellite architectures in a special IOSA-2 program, and even worked with NRO to create an office for small satellites within the agency—only to have the effort scotched through lobbying from Boeing. This mirrored an earlier lobbying program in the 1990s, in which Martin Marietta's chairman at the time, Norm Augustine, worked with Newt Gingrich to kill small satellite programs with the excuse that large geosynchronous satellites, and the companies that made them, must be protected in the name of national security.[11] This was scarcely the first time the NRO had fallen victim to corrupt practices and undue lobbying by contractors; the path to a space-based radar had proven difficult for the agency and its supporters. The Navy had been able to field an ocean surveillance system, White Cloud/Classic Wizard, in the 1980s, but failed to expand the program to tactical monitoring of ships. NRO proved no luckier in promoting a Wide-Area Surveillance System in the early 1990s, and Congress took the unusual step in 1994 of publicly denouncing the agency for continuing to spend money on a project Congress had canceled. By mid-decade attacks were coming from every direction. The agency was raked over the coals in Congress for opening a posh new $350-million headquarters in Chantilly, Virginia, even though Congress itself had approved the expenditure. Later, NRO Director Jeffrey Harris was forced to resign after being unable to account for more than $3 billion of the agency's budget. Later probes showed inadequate accounting for at least $4.5 billion in funds.

NRO sought solace by moving closer to two post-Cold War friends: it consolidated more work with NSA by moving a larger percentage of signals intelligence missions to space, and it openly collaborated with the U.S. Space Command in advertising the use of its resources to "serve the warfighter." As NSA closed many ground-based antenna farms and turned others into remotely managed facilities, the bulk of its communications intelligence collection moved to space. NSA and NRO jointly opened several Regional SIGINT Operation Centers, or RSOCs, to more effectively manage space-based intelligence. The expansion required at bases such as Menwith Hill, England, and Bad Aibling, Germany, helped spur later paranoia about the Echelon program, though this global system of keyword-search computers had in reality been around since the 1980s and was a natural follow-on of systems in place since the 1960s.[12]

The NSA/NRO collaboration was not nearly as visible as NRO's work with Space Command: NRO touted the idea that national satellites could be used in tactical programs such as TENCAP (Tactical Exploitation of National Capabilities) and TIARA (Tactical Intelligence and Related Activities). And it encouraged collaboration with commercial imaging companies—the initial threats of exercising "shutter control" to prevent companies like Space Imaging Inc. from taking pictures of certain regions. During the 2001 war in Afghanistan, the Pentagon bought up all imaging products from commercial space-imaging companies worldwide, achieving a censorship through free enterprise that would have raised hackles if it was enforced through U.S. military power.

What does the NSA and NRO shift to tactical warfighting support mean in practice? When strategic satellites can be used in a single region to provide all possible information about an adversary, it gives the Pentagon "total situational awareness" that enables it to achieve lopsided victories. In the fall of 2002, for example, Advanced Crystal and Lacrosse satellites were used in coordination with Mentor SIGINT satellites and UAVs to provide a 24-hour multispectral view of Iraq.[13] If all imaging information were used optimally by the National Imagery and Mapping Agency, the information available to cruise missiles, UAVs, fighter pilots, and bombers would allow total control of a battlefield. Similarly, if information collected by signals intelligence satellites were actually analyzed, the fears expressed by critics of Echelon would hold merit. The latest class of SIGINT satellite does have, in theory, the ability to scoop up any call, fax, or e-mail of merit. But NSA has fought a running battle to keep from depleting storage space before human analysts have a chance to study what is collected. Despite using the latest storage technology of disk arrays and optical jukeboxes, NSA analysts end up analyzing only a tiny percentage of the daily results. But with the transfer from intelligence collection platforms to autonomous battle vehicles in the field becoming more and more automated, we end up with a more frightening prospect: real-time transfer of intelligence from "sensor to shooter," in a common Space Command term, without human analysis of the information. The hazards associated with future autonomous warfare here are obvious.[14]

Communications, Navigation, Distribution, and Missile Warning

When a state is committed to preemptive warfare, even the supposedly benign and defensive realms of navigation and information distribution can take on an offensive character. In reality, systems such as Navstar (the navigation network enabling the Global Positioning System) and Milstar (the survivable communications network) were developed with first-strike warfare in mind. These capabilities appear more ominous when shifted from the Cold War target of the Soviet Union to any chosen adversary du jour, particularly when those adversaries are far smaller than the U.S. The fearsome prospects of such abuse of space resources are underscored by the aggressive posture of the new U.S. national security doctrine of preemptive war announced in September 2002.[15]

Navigation, for example, has been promoted to the public as a benign spinoff of technologies pursued for basic military capabilities. Ask most people who own a Global Positioning System receiver, and they will agree that the Navstar system primarily benefits civilian applications. But the Pentagon has always designated certain frequencies in the GPS satellite system for military use only, and has sought ways to deny even the civilian signals to adversaries. As the Navstar network has been upgraded several times, new capabilities added under the GPS III-Navwar and GETS (GPS for Enhanced Theatre Support) programs have turned military frequencies of the network to a first-strike tool for preemptive attack. Because the Pentagon wants these capabilities to be available to the U.S. alone, it has worked to encourage degradation of the old Soviet Glonass system, even as it also demands that the European Space Agency stop financing the Europe-based Galileo navigational satellite system. A similar transition has taken place in the Defense Support Program family of satellites, which use infrared sensors to watch for missile launches. DSP was considered a passive and stabilizing means of watching for possible Soviet and Chinese rocket plumes during the Cold War. The satellites also played an important role, along with Vela nuclear-blast detectors, in watching for possible nuclear tests in South Africa, Israel, India, and Pakistan. Further, the aging DSP satellites provided information leading to bombing effectiveness in the Tora Bora region during the war in Afghanistan.[16]

A distinct shift in purpose for DSP took place in the early 1990s, however. While the original "Follow-On Early-Warning System," or FEWS, fell victim to cost overruns and charges of corporate favoritism, Space Command initiated a special tactical program called Project Alert in the mid-1990s. DSP was used as a fused element in information distribution experiments conducted by the Space Warfare Center at Schriever AFB. Slowly but surely infrared sensing of missile launches became a direct element of missile defense systems.

The two-tiered successor to DSP, Space-Based Infrared System High and Low, was promoted as a direct component of missile defense systems. From its first promotion in the late 1990s SBIRS became a particular target of Russia and China because it could be used in tactical warfare as well as in a traditional missile-defense mode. Russia saw SBIRS-Low as the system most likely to violate the then-active ABM Treaty of 1972, while China feared the use of the SBIRS system in conjunction with sea-based theatre missile defense on board Aegis cruisers, particularly when these integrated systems were used in the Taiwan Straits. Both SBIRS systems will fall far short of their mid-decade launch plans. SBIRS-High, under a prime contract awarded to Lockheed-Martin, spurred a mandated congressional review after overruns drove costs from $1.8 billion to $4.5 billion. SBIRS-Low has faced criticism from Congress and the GAO for similar reasons.

An oft overlooked element in space supremacy is that of real-time intelligence distribution. In the 1970s the NRO realized the importance of in-space intelligence distribution when it designed a highly classified satellite network, Satellite Data System, which used advanced inter-satellite links to move imaging information from the Keyhole/Kennan series of satellites to the ground station at Pine Gap, Australia. Information distribution gained more broadband capabilities and became less secret in the 1990s, when the NRO and the Navy helped design the Global Broadcast Service. This multiple-band, multiple-agency service is carried on dedicated transponders on board the Navy's UHF Follow-On satellite. GBS played a crucial role in the development of the Talon intelligence-distribution experiments conducted at Schriever in the mid-1990s. During the war in Afghanistan, GBS played an important role in relaying intelligence information to ships, fighter jets, and individual special operations soldiers. Using a relay station on the island of Diego Garcia, GBS fed video data from Predator UAV flights directly to special operations soldiers on horseback in the Afghan countryside.[17]

The Real Goal of Multi-Tiered Missile Defense

Since the dawn of the intercontinental missile age, military researchers have dreamed of a magic bullet capable of halting missiles in mid-trajectory. Missile defense in its most primitive form began in the Eisenhower era, with ineffective short-range systems developed for air defense, such as Jupiter, Thor, and Nike, serving as precursors to the anti-ballistic missile networks of the LBJ years. Advocates of missile defense steeped in international strategy have had fundamental disagreements with its opponents, stemming from the bomber-gap years of the 1950s, carrying on through the ABM Treaty debates of the 1960s, and lasting well into the twenty-first century. In short, the public is led to believe that a revolutionary technology will provide an impenetrable shield for the continental United States, or some other region of interest to U.S. leaders. In reality, "missile-defense" proponents realize that a true defense works best only to absorb a second strike, when used as part of a program of offensive strategic attack by the nation fielding the strategic defense system.[18] Declassified documents of 1950s war plans belatedly made this goal abundantly clear throughout the years that Curtis LeMay headed the Strategic Air Command, but it remains true in the current Bush administration at a time when there is little to challenge the U.S. outside small "rogue" states fielding ineffective intermediate-range missiles.

While public association of missile defense with space-based "Star Wars" concepts began with President Ronald Reagan's famous March 1983 speech, the earliest attempts to design laser and particle-beam weapons began in the Carter years, as an adjunct to strategic force modernization. But only when Edward Teller and Lowell Wood sold Reagan a bill of goods on the potential of concepts like the H-bomb-fueled X-ray laser did the notion of a "protective umbrella" sheltering the public from enemy missiles become engrained in the American consciousness. With each succeeding president, missile defense has been scaled back in ambition and scaled up in test regimes, as its proponents failed to demonstrate a system capable of working, even in theory. It is a waste of time, however, to argue the case for more rigorous tests of airborne lasers or exoatmospheric kill vehicles. The main point is that missile defense theory at its heart does not aid the cause of disarmament, but instead encourages a dangerous new arms race.

The primary anti-missile weapon for the past 50 years has been a missile attacking a warhead in re-entry phase, favored due to the difficulty of attacking a missile in its initial launch or boost phase without use of space-based weapons. In the early years this goal was met through nuclear-tipped rockets such as Nike-Zeus, which evolved to Nike-X. (It is interesting and frightening to note that the original air-defense missile, Nike-Hercules, was deployed to the suburbs of dozens of U.S. cities, using tactical nuclear weapons under the control of National Guard troops in many instances.) The original model called for explosion of a 400-kiloton warhead at an exoatmospheric (beyond the atmosphere, at 60 miles in altitude) height. Because tracking radar of the 1950s and 1960s was so primitive, the system relied on massive overkill of a nuclear weapon, with the release of radiation and electromagnetic pulse over the defending nation which such use implied.

Nike-X turned to use of a phased-array radar, along with an improved nuclear warhead called Sprint. As missile technology was upgraded to the Sentinel and Safeguard systems during the mid-1960s, the Johnson administration shifted to a strategy of "thin" defense of key cities and weapons manufacturing sites—owing to recognition of radiation deaths possible in a missile-defense scenario, and because U.S. weapons were taking an unannounced turn to first-strike use due to their growing accuracy.[19]

By the time a supposedly viable system for defending major missile fields and Strategic Air Command bases had been developed at the start of the Nixon administration, missile defense had fallen into disfavor because it was seen, correctly, as possibly encouraging a first strike. The limitation of missile defense to no more than two missile fields was seen as critical to the success of limiting nuclear weapons in general. In this context the Anti-Ballistic Missile Treaty of 1972 was the centerpiece of the first Strategic Arms Limitation Treaty, or SALT-I.

Nixon's National Security Advisor, Henry Kissinger, was well aware during negotiations that many stabilizing aspects of SALT-I would be negated by the use of Multiple Independently-Targeted Re-Entry Vehicles, or MIRVs, on nuclear missiles, but the Air Force was still committed to MIRVs. Similarly, when the Soviet Union elected to use MIRVs on many of its own intercontinental missiles, the Safeguard system was perceived as next to useless. The only viable ABM system in Grand Forks, North Dakota, became operational on October

1, 1975, but moved into caretaker status in February 1976. (It is interesting to note that SALT-I negotiators insisted there was no way to "legislate technology development," and thus ban MIRVs before deployment, but Strategic Arms Reduction Treaty negotiators were able to ban MIRVs in the 1990s—albeit not before 18 years of the most wanton nuclear proliferation of the Cold War.) Even though nuclear-armed ABM weapons became obsolete virtually as soon as they were fielded, the combined cost of the Nike and Safeguard systems totaled close to $34 billion, according to the Brookings Institution.

During his earlier stint in the Ford administration, Donald Rumsfeld planted the seeds of a newfound interest in conventional re-entry anti-missile weapons, and in laser-based weapons that would attack missiles in the boost phase. Rumsfeld and many of the officials who would later go on to positions in the present Bush administration worked with conservative activists like Retired General Daniel Graham to spread fears of a Soviet particle-beam research facility in Saryshagan. While Saryshagan later was exposed as a paper tiger, the furor spurred the Carter administration to raise funding for advanced chemical laser, excimer laser, and particle-beam development to be applied in new space-based weapons. Carter's National Security Advisor, Zbigniew Brzezinski, became an enthusiastic supporter of these research efforts following the Soviet invasion of Afghanistan.

By the time Reagan was persuaded, two years into his administration, to focus attention on missile defense once again, there was little new to show the president that had not been under advanced development during the Carter years. Reagan was swayed by Edward Teller's claims for an H-bomb powered X-ray laser that could wipe out missiles in boost phase through advance deployment in space, though such a weapon later was proved to be all but impossible to develop in practice. Other than the magical X-ray laser, the suite of weapons proposed to Reagan was based on conventional ABMs and lasers touted during the Carter years, with the addition of some advanced technologies such as adaptive mirrors that could send laser beams even through atmospheric turbulence.

What Reagan added was a populist vision suggesting that a large-scale network might be possible to deploy, one that could defend more than 3,500 targets against a full-scale Soviet attack. The U.S. government created the Strategic Defense Initiative Organization, spending more than $4 billion on it annually through the end of 1988, though it was clear by 1986 that Mikhail Gorbachev would place arms reduction ahead of a Star Wars arms race. Gorbachev's changed strategy eventually won Reagan over to placing Strategic Arms Reduction Treaty talks ahead of Strategic Defense Initiative dreams.

By the time of the first Bush administration, there was no "evil empire" left to utilize ABM weapons against, though that did little to stop the star warriors. SDIO representatives turned attention to small-satellite and microsatellite kill vehicles, dubbed Brilliant Pebbles, that could disable warheads in mid-trajectory, as well as similar microsatellite imaging systems, called Brilliant Eyes (both conceived and promoted, like the X-ray laser, by Edward Teller and Lowell Wood). It's important to emphasize that funding throughout the Bush Sr. and Clinton administrations remained in the $3 to $4 billion annual range, despite significantly scaled-back goals for the program. Bush was the first to suggest shifting the focus of SDI from the then-collapsing Soviet Union to the rather tenuous threat of "rogue" states, when the Global Protection Against Limited Strikes (GPALS) program was unveiled in early 1991.

It is likely that strategic defense would never have survived during the Clinton years were it not for two trends that kept ABM dreams alive: first, Clinton had little interest in continuing the START-1 and START-2 treaties to achieve greater arms cuts and hence depended more on nuclear weapons as a hedge against the smaller non-Communist Russia, as well as against China and smaller adversary states. Second, the flap about Scud missiles fired by Iraq and the defensive role of Patriot missiles over Israel (never as effective as Israel or the Patriot manufacturers would have us believe), led to a revitalization of interest in conventionally armed anti-missile missiles following the Gulf War. As Frances FitzGerald pointed out in her book on the Reagan Star Wars program, however, the Army Patriot missile program and the proposed Star Wars ground-based interceptors had so little to do with each other that to try and imply such a connection "was the equivalent of saying that anyone who could build a barn could build a skyscraper."[20]

The first exposures of failures in both the Reagan-era Homing Overlay Experiment and the Bush-era ERIS missile began to leak out at the end of the first Bush administration, dashing pro-SDI hopes of a system fielded within the 1990s and leading to hopes in the anti-SDI camp that the concept could be killed while Clinton was president. Despite early skepticism expressed by Clinton's Defense Secretary, Les Aspin, the only real shift was a slight cut in annual budget from $4.1 to $3.8 billion. The Clinton administration changed the name of SDIO to the Ballistic Missile Defense Organization and reoriented the program to two "low-tier" battlefield-missile interceptors, the Army's PAC-3 and the Navy's Aegis; and a unified "high-tier" program based on the Army's Theater High Altitude Air Defense missile, or THAAD. The prospect of re-entry phase conventional missiles and boost-phase lasers kept interests high among defense contractors and Republicans.

In the 1996 presidential race the Republicans came up with the Defend America Act, which called for a multi-tiered defense program slated to include ground-based and sea-based missiles, ground-based chemical lasers, airborne chemical and excimer lasers, and space-based lasers. The full system, which Republicans wanted to see by 2003, was estimated to cost more than $60 billion. Clinton responded with a "three plus three" proposal, calling for three years of testing, followed by the fielding of a system based on THAAD by 2003. Unfortunately for its proponents, tests of THAAD and ERIS throughout the late

1990s were utter failures. Meanwhile, the Republican-led Congress established a commission under Donald Rumsfeld to study missile defense, and a report by that commission in July 1998 warned of an imminent threat of intermediate-range missile attacks from North Korea, Iraq, and Iran. The Clinton administration responded by pledging $6.6 billion for missile defense in early 1999.

So where do we stand at a time when the Bush administration plans to expand National Missile Defense for global duties? The U.S. has spent close to $70 billion since Reagan's speech, with little to show for it. Clinton's official NMD program had six components: initial launch and detect, consisting of existing Defense Support Program (DSP) satellites and the new Space-Based Infrared System-High (SBIRS-High); new ground-based early-warning UHF radars to coordinate the tracking of missiles carried out by DSP and SBIRS-High; four to nine X-band radars to distinguish between warheads and decoys; the interceptor booster, a three-stage rocket with exoatmospheric kill vehicle; the kill vehicle itself, with a multi-bandwidth optical and infrared sensor; and a Battle Management Command/Control/Communications network for controlling the kill vehicle. A proposed seventh element of NMD, the 24 satellites of the low-orbit SBIRS-Low, is a network that could provide better discrimination against decoys, but is also one of the factors that Russia originally saw as violating the ABM Treaty, though its decision to demur in the face of U.S. treaty abrogation meant its suspicions of SBIRS-Low were muted in practice. SBIRS (High and Low) has also experienced significant software and sensor problems, and so will be fielded in phases beginning in 2006 as an experimental network.

Various Army and Navy programs have been proposed to allies as Theater Missile Defense weapons systems, designed to respond to intermediate-missile threats in particular regions. These programs often resemble tactical missile programs from the 1970s, with additional tracking and surveillance pieces added on. This can raise the ire of adversaries beyond simply their connection with the NMD program. China, for example, is outraged over Pentagon plans to sell Taiwan the full Aegis radar sea-defense system, not only because of the Aegis connection to missile defense but because of the broader surveillance capabilities of such a system.[21]

The exotic directed-energy weapons systems admired by Reagan live on, in the Airborne Laser and Space-Based Laser programs. The former is a continuation of a test program dating from the 1980s, called the Airborne Laser Lab. Enhanced in 1992 with the establishment of an Airborne Laser Program Office at Kirtland AFB in New Mexico, the program initially was kept on minimal-funding stage until a new laser, the Chemical Oxygen Iodine Laser (COIL), combined with the use of deformable mirrors, could demonstrate an ability to propagate a beam through the atmosphere. Since 1995, the airborne program has escalated to a full-scale weapons development program. Boeing, TRW, and Lockheed-Martin are corporate partners in the $1 billion program, which is scheduled to demonstrate its ability to shoot down a ballistic missile from a modified 747 plane by the end of fiscal 2003. In March 2001, subcontractor Raytheon Electronic Systems achieved "first light" of the solid-state tracking laser that will track the target for the COIL laser.[22]

While the Reagan/Teller dreams of an H-bomb-fueled X-ray laser are thankfully dead, the dream of conquering space lives on in the Space-Based Laser Program, an 18-month, $127 million test program awarded to "Team SBL," consisting of Lockheed-Martin, TRW, and Boeing. The contractors, along with Air Force personnel, will use the new Stennis Space Center in Mississippi as headquarters for a program aimed at an Integrated Flight Experiment in 2012. The program will use a space-based version of the Alpha hydrogen fluoride laser developed during the Reagan SDIO years. The current program will use ground facilities to test the feasibility of the space-based program, estimated to cost more than $3 billion by launch date in 2012, and more than $30 billion for a fielded system. A full system capable of conducting boost-phase missile defense would require at least 20 armed satellites in orbit, necessitating abrogation of both the Outer Space and ABM Treaties.[23]

President Reagan reportedly became intrigued with Star Wars before his presidency, after a visit to the NORAD Cheyenne Mountain headquarters in the summer of 1979, when he was surprised to discover that the U.S. had no missile defense. Similarly, most Americans refuse to believe that missile-defense does not already exist. At first blush, it would seem natural to support the "magic bullets" that an effective missile defense would seem to represent. But there is more to find fault with than gross expenditure of money with little to show for it. To understand why missile defense has been so problematic, it is necessary to examine how nuclear weapons policies have changed in the past 40 years, particularly since the end of the Cold War.

Assumptions Driving the Nuclear Weapons State

The very notion of the nuclear "triad" of air-, sea-, and space-based nuclear forces was developed in part as a response to the hopelessness of achieving effective missile defense. The U.S. did not become fully committed to a policy of forward-basing its B-52 bombers until initial studies by Alfred Wohlstetter of the RAND Corporation showed that achieving a 95 percent kill rate against incoming missiles would require an expenditure of one third of the Gross National Product of the nation. The maturation of ballistic missiles led to the demise of virtually all forms of continental air defense, including first generation Nike missiles. Because thermonuclear weapons were replacing fission weapons in the first generation of intercontinental ballistic missiles, the think-tank experts at RAND and other facilities recognized that fighting and winning a nuclear war in the manner of LeMay was not feasible. Before the official jargon of "Mutually Assured Destruction" was developed, insiders already were talking about the three elements of a weapons-delivery triad providing "deterrence." While Eisenhower and Kennedy went through a series of debates regarding the wisdom of holding cities hostage, the creation of a massive nuclear infrastructure virtually required that missile defense not be attempted to any great extent.

Less appreciated at the time, in the late 1950s, when the Strategic Air Command went on a global base-creation frenzy, was the fact that space-defense and intelligence communities came right behind the SAC—and the connections between them were direct ones. MAD (Mutually Assured Destruction) required not just constantly patrolling submarines, dispersed ICBM missile fields, and bomber bases surrounding the Soviet Union, but also a global intelligence network that could provide "total situational awareness." That meant Ballistic Missile Early Warning Systems to augment the North American DEW and Pinetree radar lines. Large BMEWS radars were erected at Thule, Greenland, and Fylingdales, U.K., in 1961.

It also meant that the NSA had become an international basing specialist precisely to serve the interests of nuclear doctrine. The NSA could not only pick up electronic communications, it also could pick up telemetry information from missile tests, dubbed "Telint" or "ELINT," and measurement tests of electromagnetic properties of atmospheric disturbances, dubbed "Masint." Few Americans were aware of the number of NSA agents who had been captured in the Soviet Union and China when overflights were shot down in the 1950s. Fewer still were aware of the NSA's efforts to establish bases in the U.K., Germany, Turkey, Diego Garcia, Australia, Pakistan, and many other nations around the world, in order to create a global intelligence web necessary for missile defense. In some nations, like Turkey, NSA took control of both radar and interception-antenna duties in order to obfuscate the role of certain types of technical equipment. The role of intelligence in supporting space warfare would not become obvious until nearly 40 years later.

In the McNamara era of Kennedy and Johnson, the U.S. had achieved a certain stability through its acknowledged policy of MAD and flexible response. Why then, did ABM find new supporters late in LBJ's administration? For one, conservatives in the Pentagon were worried about a new ABM field surrounding Moscow and insisted on a tit-for-tat response. For another, the "technological creep" of improved Sprint warheads and Nike-X radars made it likely that ABM systems would be deployed without proper debate. Recognition that ABM was an open-ended excuse for a new arms race was the catalyst driving the SALT-I talks. A 1974 addendum to the original 1972 treaty limited both superpowers to a single ABM site, which in the case of the U.S. was only operational for a matter of months. But SALT-I carried the unfortunate combination of limiting missile launchers and ABM missiles, without however limiting strategic warheads themselves. This was a virtual invitation to increase the use of MIRV warheads, ushering in the era of greatest warhead expansion in the Cold War.

Because newer weapons planned for the Triad—MX missile, Trident D5 missile, air-launched cruise missile—offered much greater accuracy than predecessors, activists charged during the Carter administration that the U.S. had turned quite explicitly toward a first-strike policy. Robert Aldridge, in his seminal pamphlet *The Counterforce Syndrome*, argued that any continued effort to achieve ABM capabilities in the absence of future arms reduction, in particular without cutting down on MIRVs or limiting warhead accuracy, would only to serve to enhance first-strike capabilities. While Carter officials initially denied that counterforce strategies amounted to a first-strike policy, later presidential directives such as PD-59 all but admitted that this was the announced policy of the United States. President Clinton reaffirmed this in his December 1997 Presidential Directive 60, which not only reserved the right to first use of nuclear weapons but added the response to chemical or biological weapons as an instance justifying first use.[24]

With first-strike policies an explicit intention since 1979, the Reagan era became a time when schizophrenia reigned supreme. Reagan initiated the greatest arms buildup of the Cold War, relying on the conservatives of the Committee on the Present Danger who held the most paranoid views on Soviet intentions. Many supporters of Daniel Graham and Edward Teller within this group wanted to push for space-based ABM capabilities right away. But Pentagon advisors cautioned Caspar Weinberger that too much faith in a nuclear "umbrella" could undermine support for arms buildups. As a result, Reagan's SDI speech was delayed for two years, and even then was accepted with a certain amount of bemusement by the military establishment. It took another two years before SDIO became a viable agency, and it immediately took on the accouterments of a pork-barrel project intended to placate the Gipper, rather than as a crash development effort where short-term results could be expected.

By the time Gorbachev came to power in the Soviet Union, Reagan had moved into a true arms-reduction mode, shocking conservatives with the deep cuts he proposed in Reykjavik. Because START concepts had strong bipartisan support as Soviet society opened up, the warhorses within the White House and Pentagon could do little but redirect SDIO toward alternative threats.

In retrospect, the first Bush era represented a high watermark in true arms reduction. It was only because of START negotiations that the U.S. pulled back to its current level of approximately 7,200 strategic warheads. START II and III would bring this down to 3,000 and 1,500 warheads, respectively, but the Clinton administration did little to accelerate warhead reductions. Ever since the collapse of the Soviet bloc in the late 1980s, the peace community has been searching for a "peace dividend" that never materialized, at least insofar as strategic forces are concerned. As would be expected from any mammoth bureaucracy, the Pentagon has been concerned with retaining all its former base of power. While military base reduction acts have scaled back some of the forward basing in foreign nations, the strategic arms and intelligence infrastructure of the Cold War has changed very little since the Soviet Union finally self-destructed in 1991.

A de facto ban on MIRVs was implemented during the Clinton years, and real arms reduction has indeed taken place over the last decade, but the U.S. uses its "stockpile stewardship" rationale as an ongoing cover for developing new weapons, spending more than $4.5 billion annually on nuclear weapons research and development. The covert development of the B-61-11 gravity bomb for the B2 Stealth bomber in the mid-1990s is a case in point. The second Bush administration has revived interest in a low-yield, earth-penetrating nuclear warhead designed for hardened targets.[25] Western States Legal Foundation has pointed out that even the National Ignition Facility at Lawrence Livermore, a laser used in nuclear weapons simulation, has a direct role to play in support of missile defense.

On the intelligence-infrastructure front, virtually the entire network inherited from the Cold War remains in place worldwide. Ever since the establishment of Space Command as a unified military structure in the early 1980s, the U.S. has emphasized space-based communications and intelligence, not for verification of treaties but as a "force multiplier" for fighting wars. Leaders of the Space Command, from Charles Horner in the early 1990s to the present, have continuously insisted that the U.S. reserve for itself the right to maintain the only global 24-hour reconnaissance of the planet. Should another nation attempt to duplicate the U.S. space presence, they will be stopped, Space Command warns.

During the Clinton years a Space Warfare Center was established at Schriever (then Falcon) Air Force Base in Colorado to test concepts for using space-based intelligence in tactical battle environments. The Air Force later established a larger Joint National Test Center around the Space Warfare Center to expand SWC's mission. As the new Bush administration was sworn in, JNTC (later renamed Joint National Integration Center, or JNIC) made an unusual high-profile attempt to bring in the press to discuss its simulated battles in a special wargame exercise. But the uses of JNIC and SWC are far more commonplace than that, as intelligence fusion programs like the Talon series reveal.

The end result of the "serving the warfighter" movement for space resources is that strategic nuclear interests and tactical counterinsurgency interests of the U.S. have become inextricably connected. This means that no nuclear drawdown can be expected unless START II and III are ratified and further arms negotiations are undertaken, not a likely scenario with the current Congress or president. It also means that nuclear weapons *use* is more likely in the current environment because the so-called tripwire that treats nuclear war as something special and different is eroded as all elements of the U.S. arsenal become part of a unified whole. What does this mean for ABM? We expect Russia, China, and smaller nations to acquiesce in our existing arsenal advantages, and to ignore our warfighting rhetoric, because we are simply too benevolent a nation to contemplate a first strike. Yet policies allowing for a first strike remain on the books and the U.S. actions clearly demonstrate that no military advantages would be ignored.

An informative view of nuclear policies can be seen in analysts' response to the leaked "talking points" for ABM Treaty revisions, which U.S. Ambassador John Holum prepared for his Russian counterparts in early 2000. Holum was trying to convince the Russians that some ABM capabilities would work to their advantage, and that X-band radar deployment would serve everyone by increasing the availability of information regarding missile flights. Bruce Blair, president of the Center for Defense Information, pointed out that "In reality, a surprise offensive U.S. strike could destroy all but a few tens of Russian warheads." And Jack Mendelsohn of the Lawyers Alliance for World Security pointed out that Russia is even more nervous about new X-band radars and SBIRS-Low satellites than it is about kinetic kill vehicles, because the new radar and infrared intelligence could "substitute for land-based ABM engagement radars."[26] U.S. political leaders of both parties reject such a view, insisting that it is inconceivable the U.S. would exploit its superpower role by engaging in offensive actions. But as a nation, we are judged by our actions and announced policies. It is here that the biggest problem in missile defense and space warfare lies.

A fair analysis of U.S. missile-defense schemes cannot be made without addressing the surreal environment in which a unilateral superpower with overwhelming military capabilities sees itself as threatened by Lilliputian "rogues." As Michael Klare pointed out in a recent survey, the unspoken military policy of the United States in the 12 years since the Cold War ended can best be described as "permanent preeminence."[27] Until Bush's West Point speech of June 1, 2002, this policy was never discussed in any explicit sense, by either Democrats or Republicans, because the U.S. does not like to present itself as a visibly imperial power. It is only since the attacks of September 11 that the U.S. felt comfortable in stating for the record that it was building an empire, as implicitly laid out earlier in the Space Command's *Vision for 2020* and *Long-Range Plan*.[28]

The preeminence strategy accepts as given that the U.S. will retain overwhelming control over the planet, retaining in the process the sole right to maintain 24-hour space-based reconnaissance networks to monitor the globe. It will define which nations are good and bad on its own terms and will expect allies to comply with those definitions. During the Clinton administration, the Albright Doctrine took the subtler yet still arrogant path of a nation that will act "multilaterally when we can, but unilaterally when we must." Under Bush, the pressure for acting unilaterally has increased under Reagan-era defense officials like Paul Wolfowitz and Richard Armitage, to such an extent that multilateralism has all but disappeared. At the same time, infrastructural networks of nuclear weapons support and always-on C3I (Command, Control, Communications, and Intelligence) have been maintained at Cold War levels despite the fact that Russia's capabilities are but a shadow of the former Soviet

Union's, and Chinese military capabilities are only a fraction of the American. This is why it was so important for the 1998 Rumsfeld Commission on missile defense to significantly inflate the missile capabilities of North Korea, and why the 2001 Rumsfeld Commission had to invoke totally inappropriate images of a "Space Pearl Harbor."

Rumsfeld's "Space Pearl Harbor" analogy, of course, is patently absurd. In 1941, the U.S. was very much aware that its embargo of oil would elicit a Japanese response. It knew of the Japanese navy's imperial reach and was anticipating a move at some Pacific location, and only the inability to process intelligence pointing specifically to Hawaii made Pearl Harbor a surprise. Today, the U.S. has no adversaries that are within a tenth of its force-projection capabilities. The two would-be superpowers, Russia and China, are subject to U.S. attempts to limit their freedom of military action. Smaller powers have such limited missile capabilities that the idea of even a limited surprise missile attack is simply laughable. While some Americans became more supportive of missile defense following September 11, it is obvious that money spent on defenses against missiles is money that is not used to challenge far cruder but more effective weapons wielded by non-state adversaries. Indeed, a reverse notion of a "Space Pearl Harbor" remains the most plausible—Russia, China, and developing nations can fear a surprise space-based attack from the U.S., using space coordination platforms for terrestrial weapons today and direct space-based weapons in the future.

The fact that the U.S. declares its intentions to be benevolent is entirely irrelevant. When American capabilities allow unilateral control of planetary resources, when the elite boasts of its power to act unilaterally, when U.S. military exercises highlight the ability to use strategic resources at any tactical point on the globe, we must anticipate that the rest of the world perceives the U.S. as an arrogant, brutal empire that severely abuses its superpower status to play endless games parading as King of the Mountain.

From Space Down to Earth

In the 1970s, those interested in true arms reduction correctly criticized members of the arms control community for stressing "throw-weights" and "circular error probable," arguing that the institutionalization of SALT-II would do nothing to stop the arms race. Where can we find a constituency to explore the issue of "permanent preeminence," when it is precisely this area of policy that neither Republicans nor Democrats want to discuss? We can begin by recognizing the ties between the military's use of space, the corporate globalization campaigns, and U.S. counterinsurgency campaigns in foreign nations. Addressing the problem of missile defense means confronting the way the U.S. behaves as an unchallenged superpower throughout the world and in space. We can start by demanding a virtual halt to all missile-defense funding: no systems have been shown to add to national security, and all are guaranteed to create a new arms race. As Ted Postol, Kosta Tsipis, and others have pointed out, any defense can be overwhelmed by offense-based countermeasures—and little has changed in 50 years of missile research.

Given the Russians' interest at examining early boost-phase technologies, and recognizing that analysts such as Richard Garwin and Ted Postol may develop plausible uses for boost-phase defense, it is reasonable to conduct basic studies on how a multilateral, international regime might be developed for future defenses. But such studies should take as a given the Outer Space Treaty's strict ban on weapons in space. It should also take into account warnings from researchers that boost-phase attacks on missiles could send nuclear warheads plummeting down on an unsuspecting third state. It should finally ensure that new weapons related to boost-phase defense are not developed merely in the name of "technology creep," or because they represent a boon to some arms manufacturer.

Replacing unilateral interests and strategies with multilateral treaty agendas implies establishment of new monitoring systems such as the Missile Technology Control Regime. While some arms control groups have been only too happy to provide MTCR and similar organizations with the fig leaf of respectability, it is important to keep in mind the degree to which developing nations see MTCR and the Non-Proliferation Treaty as inherently unfair owing to the behavior of the U.S. Indeed, the NPT almost collapsed three years ago, due to the failure of the major nuclear weapons states to show progress in further arms reduction, with the U.S. cited as the worst offender. If we are to provide legitimacy to MTCR, it must show how it can self-police the current "keepers of the keys," so that existing nuclear states are not given special exemptions from the rules. If new global organizations are created to monitor space weapons or space intelligence, they must not be structured to give the U.S. special rights other nations do not have.

As for the special case of intelligence, it is useful to heed the warnings of Australian military analyst Desmond Ball, who argued almost 25 years ago that too much intelligence automatically serves a first-strike policy. When imaging intelligence alone is used in a delayed-processing fashion, the data can be useful for treaty verification; this is roughly the state of commercial space imaging today. But when imaging intelligence is combined with electronic intelligence, and processed and disseminated to tactical battlefields with great rapidity, it inevitably serves the offensive warfighter, as the Space Command actually boasted in its documents. It may not be possible or desirable to halt development of certain technologies for intelligence-gathering. But nations can agree on self-limiting their application of technology, *provided* the world's most powerful nation sets an example for others to follow. This in turn requires that space warfare intelligence centers be open for limited scrutiny in a manner similar to weapons manufacturing plants. Does this mean that every radome at direct intelligence downlink bases like Menwith Hill and Buckley be open for scrutiny, and every frequency band for interception antennas be published in the open literature? Not necessarily. But it does mean that centers like Joint National Integration Center and Space Warfare Center be open for general inspection by other nations, and that applications such as real-time delivery of tactical intelligence to localized battlefields be subject to international rules.

Eliminating the need for NMD means getting rid of more strategic nuclear weapons that remain in the arsenals of the major nuclear states, above all the U.S. There will be debates on whether a true zero option is viable, or whether a Tsipis or Butler vision for 100 or 1000 nukes within any state proves more realizable—at least for the short term. But the world must move beyond the total inactivity in arms reduction that characterized the Clinton years and demand that "stockpile stewardship" programs leading to new weapons be halted immediately. Is this too massive a shift in outlook to imagine when taking opposition against missile defense and unilateral space militarization? There is yet a larger cultural block that needs to be confronted. Just as the Pentagon can claim to be accurately representing civilian leaders when it uses the language of space dominance and control, heads of the State and Defense Departments can claim, with some justification, to be responding to an American public sold on the idea that being Number One means everything, and the pursuit of absolute domination in a material sense takes precedence over global sharing and governance.

The Space Command accurately concluded in 1998 that its task was to preserve the current global separation between haves and have-nots, and there are many citizens of the U.S. who would advocate an overwhelming display of military power in order to maintain that privilege. Just as one cannot protest Bush's rejection of the Kyoto Treaty without looking at the larger issue of U.S. resource utilization, one cannot reject the Space Command's stated mission of preserving inequity without looking at the fact that the U.S. represents 4 percent of the world's population while consuming up to 70 percent of the planet's resources.

Opponents of space militarization can find common purpose with those opposed to U.S. military intervention abroad, those opposed to globalized free-market capitalism, and those advocating a more ecologically balanced lifestyle. The U.S. defines the terms of when an insurgent group is legitimate and how the U.S. will intervene, simply because it has the power to do so. The U.S. demands first rights to natural resources and manufactured goods at the prices it desires, because it has the power. The U.S. promulgates a global culture that runs rampant over indigenous localized cultures, because it has the power. If it is time to place opposition to missile defense in a larger context, it also is time to look for an alternative vision for space exploration and near-earth space use. Is space a legitimate venue for military-related communications and intelligence and, if so, must that venue be multilateral by design? What leverage can be brought to bear against a future "rogue state" that chooses to abrogate the Outer Space Treaty by weaponizing near-earth space? What responsibility does the commercial space industry have for handling space junk in earth orbit? What scope and goals should be set for deep space exploration, particularly when launches play a significant role in ozone destruction? In the meantime, however, the main goal is to end the type of space unilateralism that places the economic, political, and military interests of the U.S. above those of other nations and the world in general—a vast undertaking, to be sure.

Notes

1. Report of the Commission to Assess United States National Security Space Management and Organization, January 2001; US Space Command, *Long-Range Plan*, Peterson AFB, March 1998. For an analysis of the implications of Space Command goals, see Karl Grossman and Michio Kaku, *Weapons in Space (Open Media Pamphlet Series)* (London: Seven Stories Press, December 2000).
2. Ibid.; Report of the National Commission for the Review of the NRO, Nov. 2000.
3. See William Arkin, "March Madness," *Bulletin of the Atomic Scientists*, May/June 2002, 76.
4. General Accounting Office, *Defense Space Activities: Status of Reorganization*, GAO-02–772R, June 2002; GAO, *Military Space Operations: Planning, Funding and Acquisition Challenges Facing Efforts to Strengthen Space Control*, GAO-02–738, September 2002.
5. Cf., Phillip E. Coyle and John B. Rhinelander, "Drawing the Line: The Path to Controlling Weapons in Space," *Disarmament Diplomacy*, Issue No. 66, Sept. 2002.
6. Cf., Bamford, *The Puzzle Palace* (Boston: Houghton-Mifflin, 1982); Bamford, *Body of Secrets* (New York: Doubleday, 2001); Richelson, *American Espionage and the Soviet Target* (New York: William Morrow, 1987).
7. Bamford, *Body of Secrets*, ibid., 35–37.
8. Robert Aldridge, *The Counterforce Syndrome*, Washington, D.C.: IPS Press, 1978; Desmond Ball, *A Suitable Piece of Real Estate* (Sydney: Allen & Unwyn, 1980); Robert Lindsey, *The Falcon and the Snowman* (New York: Simon & Schuster, 1979).
9. Bill Sweetman, "Spies in the Sky," *Popular Science*, April 1997, 43; U.S. Space Foundation, *National Space Symposium 2002 Proceedings.*
10. See the Federation of American Scientists' Space Policy Project Web site, http://www.fas.org/spp, for a concise analysis of several systems. Its associated web site, the Intelligence Reform Project, http://www.fas.org/irp, covers the agencies involved.
11. Robert Dreyfuss, "Orbit of Influence: Spy Finance and the Black Budget," *The American Prospect*, March–April 1996; Loring Wirbel, "Confronting the New Intelligence Establishment: Lessons from the Colorado Experience," *The Workbook*, Fall 1996.
12. Nicky Hager, *Secret Power* (Nelson, New Zealand: Craig Potton Publishing, 1996).
13. Craig Covault, "Secret NRO Recon Eyes Iraqi Threats," *Aviation Week & Space Technology*, Sept. 16, 2002, 23.
14. Office of the Secretary of Defense, Director of Defense Research and Engineering, *DoD Space Technology Guide, FY2000–2001.*
15. Office of the White House, *The National Security Strategy of the United States*, Sept. 20, 2002.
16. The most comprehensive analysis of DSP is Jeffrey Richelson's seminal work, *America's Space Sentinels: DSP Satellites and National Security* (Lawrence, KS: University of Kansas Press, 1999). See also Leonard David, "Update: The War On Terror On Earth, In Orbit, and In the Future," www.space.com/businesstechnology/technology/911_space_war, Sept. 11, 2002.
17. Teets speech, US Space Symposium, Colorado Springs, April 2002; Loring Wirbel, "Space Command Plans," *Electronic Engineering Times*, April 10, 1998, 1; "Global Broadcast Service," www.fas.org/spp/military/program/com/gbs.htm
18. Col. Daniel Smith, *A Brief History of Missiles and Missile Defense (Missile Defense Issue Brief)* (Washington, D.C.: Center for Defense Information, 2001), http://www.cdi.org/hotspots/issuebrief/ch3/index.html
19. Frances FitzGerald, *Way Out There in the Blue: Reagan, Star Wars, and the End of the Cold War* (New York: Touchstone/Simon & Schuster, 2000), 482–483.
20. FitzGerald, op. cit., 486.

21. Gordon, Michael R., "Secret U.S. Study Concludes Taiwan Needs New Arms," *New York Times*, March 31, 2001, 1.

22. Federation of American Scientists, Airborne Laser Program, http://www.fas.org/spp/starwars/program/abl.htm; Airborne Laser Program Office, http://www.airbornelaser.com; "Airborne Laser on Track to Illuminate Missile," http://www.spacedaily.com/news/laser-01c.html

23. Federation of American Scientists, Space-Based Laser, http://www.fas.org/spp/starwars/program/sbl.htm; SBL IFX Project Office, http://www.sbl.losangeles.af.mil/Divisions/FrontOffice/body.htm

24. For an analysis of the ties between first-strike policies and missile defense, see Andrew Lichterman et al., "U.S. Nuclear Weapons Policies, Ballistic Missile Defense, and the Quest for Weapons in Space: Military Research and Development and the New Arms Race," *Western States Legal Foundation Information Bulletin*, Summer 2000.

25. *Washington Post*, "U.S. Considers Low-Yield Nuclear Weapon," April 16, 2001, 1.

26. See *Bulletin of the Atomic Scientists*, special online May–June 2000 series on the ABM Treaty talking points, http://www.bas.org/issues/2000/mj00/treaty_blair.html

27. Michael T. Klare, "Permanent Preeminence: U.S. Strategic Policy for the 21st Century," *NACLA Report on the Americas*, Nov.–Dec. 2000, 8–15.

28. Op. cit.

CHAPTER 4

The Geopolitics of Plan Colombia

JAMES PETRAS
MORRIS MORLEY

Plan Colombia, to be understood properly, should be located in a historical perspective both with relation to Colombia and to the recent conflicts in Central America. Plan Colombia is both "new" policy and a continuation of past U.S. involvement in Colombia. Beginning in the early 1960s, under President Kennedy, Washington launched its regional counterinsurgency program, forming special operations forces to enable client regimes to fend off attacks by "popular movements."[1] The principal target in Colombia was the autonomous peasant self-defense communities, particularly those based in Marquetalia. Plan Colombia was President Clinton's extension and deepening of President Kennedy's counterinsurgency doctrine for Latin America.

But the earlier version of the internal war doctrine and its current reincarnation are not identical. The first major difference is the ideological justification for U.S. intervention: under Kennedy, the rationale for counterinsurgency programs was the threat of international communism; Clinton's Plan Colombia was justified on the basis of the threat posed by the narco-drug trafficking industry. The second major difference is the scale and scope of U.S. involvement. Plan Colombia is a long-term billion-dollar program involving large-scale modern arms shipments, whereas the earlier counterinsurgency agenda was a much smaller operation. The explanation for this difference is to be found in the changed Colombian and global political contexts. In the 1960s the guerrillas were a small isolated group; today they are a formidable army operating on a national scale. During Kennedy's presidency, U.S. military policy became increasingly concentrated on Indochina, whereas today Washington has a relatively free hand. Plan Colombia is thus both a continuation and an escalation of U.S. politico-military policy—based on imperialist strategic goals adapted to new local and global realities.

The third major difference is the changed regional context for U.S. intervention. Plan Colombia has been heavily influenced by Washington's successful reassertion of hegemony in Central America in the 1980s, culminating in the signing of "peace accords" that triggered a series of political changes, bringing to governmental power forces supportive of U.S. political and economic objectives. These gains were achieved through the use of state terror, the mass displacement of populations, large-scale military spending, Pentagon advisors and expertise, and the "carrot" of political settlements involving the reincorporation of the guerrilla commanders into electoral politics. In the post-Cold War era, Clinton and Bush policymakers maintained the belief that Washington's successful 1980s "terror for peace" formula in Central America could be replicated in the Andean region in the first decade of the new century by means of Plan Colombia.

What follows is an analysis of the geopolitical interests and ideological concerns that guide Plan Colombia, the consequences of U.S. military escalation, and a critique of Washington's misdiagnosis of the "Colombian question." The essay will conclude with a discussion of some of the adverse unanticipated consequences that Washington may incur in pursuing its military policy in Colombia.

Plan Colombia and the "Radical Triangle"

While its critics described Plan Colombia as a U.S.-authored and -promoted policy directed toward militarily eliminating the guerrilla forces in Colombia and repressing the rural peasant communities that support them, American policymakers initially characterized it as an attempt to eradicate drug production and trade by attacking the sources of production located in areas of guerrilla influence or control. Since the latter were concentrated in the main coca producing regions, they argued, the primary objective of U.S. military assistance and Pentagon advisory teams in Colombia was to destroy the "narco guerrillas." In response to political and military successes of the two major guerrilla movements—the Revolutionary Armed Forces of Colombia (FARC) and the National Liberation Army (ELN)—statements by Clinton officials increasingly focused on the "guerrilla insurgency" as the key target of Washington's interventionist policy. Although the economic stakes for both the U.S. and Bogota's ruling oligarchy remained substantial, the larger and more important explanation for growing U.S. military involvement in Colombia was geopolitical. From the perspective of the White House, there are several key political issues that could adversely affect U.S. imperial power in the hemisphere.

The Colombian insurgency is part of a geopolitical matrix that poses a major challenge to U.S. hegemony in northern South America and the Panama Canal Zone. This matrix includes the oil factor (production, supply, and prices); the core conflicts in Colombia, where the guerrilla movements pose a formidable challenge to the state and regime, in Venezuela, where the "Bolivarean appeals" of President Chavez mobilize the lower classes, and in the Ecuadorean highlands, where peasant-Indian movements reject the political-economic status quo (the "radical triangle"); growing leftist and nationalist discontent in key adjoining countries (Brazil and Peru), and in countries further south (Paraguay and Bolivia); and massive anti-imperialist consciousness in Argentina.

Plan Colombia cannot be extrapolated from the geo-economic matrix of the oil rich triangle of northern South America, a strategic resource to fuel the empire as well as an economic lever allowing nationalists to challenge any boycott and to finance potential allies. Oil diplomacy remains a trump card of the "radical triangle" countries: Venezuela is the third biggest petroleum supplier to the U.S., providing 1.5 million barrels daily or just under 15 percent of total net oil imports, and has the largest reserves outside the Middle East;[2] and Colombia is a producer state with substantial untapped reserves, as is Ecuador on a lesser scale. This has resulted in the oil issue becoming a two-edged sword. While it acts as a stimulus to heightening U.S. interventionist actions to make and unmake political regimes (as the U.S.-backed coup against Chavez on April 10–11, 2002, demonstrates), it also provides a powerful lever, as Venezuela's Chavez has demonstrated, to challenge U.S. regional domination. Venezuela's resource power, augmented by the new president's more independent positions can strengthen the resolve of Caribbean and Central American governments to resist U.S. efforts to reassert its total dominance over the subregion.

The major beneficiary of Venezuela's favorable oil deals with its neighbors has been Cuba. Subsidized petroleum exports to Havana have not only facilitated the island's further integration into the regional economy but challenged and further undermined Washington's failed and tattered, but continuing, efforts to maintain the regional isolation of the Cuban Revolution. If guerrilla and popular movements represent a serious political and social challenge to U.S. supremacy on a continent-wide basis, Chavez's Venezuela, through its leadership role in OPEC and its nonaligned foreign policy, offers a potential diplomatic and political-economic challenge to the imperial state in the Caribbean basin and beyond. Together, the movements and governments that define the "radical triangle" have the potential to undermine the mystique surrounding the invincibility of U.S. regional hegemony and Washington policymakers' efforts to entrench the notion of the free market development model.

In more specific terms the conflict between the "radical triangle" and U.S. imperial power focuses attention on the fact that much of what is described as "globalism" rests on the foundations of the social relations of production and the balance of class forces in the nation-state. Recognition of this fact has particular relevance to the conflict in Colombia. Our argument is based on the assumption that without solid political, social, and military foundations within the nation-state, the imperial enterprise and its accompanying global networks are imperiled. Thus there is a need to examine closely the nature of the Clinton-Bush proxy war in Colombia where Washington, through its client regimes, has been attempting to destroy the guerrilla movements, and decimate and demoralize their supporters in order to restore the local foundations of imperial power.

Geography of the Anti-U.S. Challenge

In the 1960s and 1970s the challenge to U.S. imperial power was located in Latin America's southern cone—Chile, Argentina, Uruguay, and Bolivia. Washington responded by backing military coups and state-authored violence as a means of terrorizing and atomizing highly politicized mass-based opposition movements into submission. During the 1980s, Central America became the new locus of revolutionary challenge in the hemisphere. The toppling of the Somoza regime in Nicaragua by radical nationalist guerrillas and the rise of popular guerrilla movements with substantial rural support in El Salvador and Guatemala posed a serious challenge to U.S. client regimes and geo-political-economic interests. The Reagan White House attempted to counter this challenge by militarizing the region, allocating billions of dollars to finance and arm an anti-Sandinista mercenary force in Nicaragua and to fund state terrorism in El Salvador and Guatemala. This war of attrition cost hundreds of thousands of lives and wrecked economies but ultimately produced a set of peace accords, based on a return to electoral politics, that Washington exploited to restore U.S. client regimes to power, bolstering the imperial state's hegemonic position.[3]

Since the late 1990s and into the new millennium, the geography of resistance to the U.S. empire has shifted to northern South America—principally Colombia, Ecuador, and Venezuela. In Colombia, the Pastrana regime (1998–2002) confronted a nationwide challenge: guerrilla forces that controlled or exercised influence over a wide swath of territory south of Bogota toward the Ecuadorean border, northwest toward Panama, and in several pockets to the east and west of the capital; large-scale peasant mobilizations; and trade union-led general strikes. In Venezuela, the Chavez leadership partially reformed key state institutions (Congress, the constitution, the judiciary) and adopted an independent foreign policy that ranged from supporting higher OPEC oil prices, to developing ties with Iraq, to extending diplomatic and commercial links with Cuba, to signing military agreements with China and Russia, to opposing Plan Colombia, to criticizing the U.S. global anti-terrorist campaign. But Chavez's failure to reform the military or the Supreme Court led to a U.S.-supported coup in April 2002 that had the backing of several top generals. The Supreme Court subsequently voted (10 to 8) to exonerate the self-declared *golpistas*—in effect legalizing the coup. In Ecuador a powerful Indian-peasant movement (CONAIE) linked with lower military officials and trade unionists toppled the Jamil Muhuad government in early 2000. Although the new president, Gustavo Noboa, later pledged support for Plan Colombia, began cooperating with Washington's regional counter-narcotics program, and gave the Pentagon and CIA access to the Manta air force base, CONAIE and its allies retained its formidable popular base, enabling it to sweep legislative elections in the Ecuadorean sierra. As a result, the Pentagon's military strategy of encircling the Colombian guerrillas by building a "forward operating" military presence at Manta came under serious attack.

Plan Colombia originated, in part, as a strategy to contain and undermine the appeal of the revolutionary alternative in other Latin American countries. It recognized that the "radical triangle" countries were adjacent territories that, in turn, served to reinforce their mutual support of one another. While Venezuela's nationalist-populist project has its roots in popular revulsion against the corruption and decay of national political institutions and the destitution of the majority of its people, the fact of a powerful social-revolutionary movement at its doorstep in Colombia strengthens Venezuela's borders from any U.S. inspired destabilization policy. Likewise, the Chavez regime's refusal to allow U.S. reconnaissance overflights in Venezuelan airspace to search and target Colombia's guerrillas lessens military pressures on the FARC/ELN forces. The existence of a large-scale, peasant-Indian movement in Ecuador opposing U.S. militarization of its border with Colombia also weakens the imperial war effort. Indirectly, so too does the Quito government's embrace of dollarization of the economy and agreement to allow Washington to establish a military and covert presence at the Manta air force base. Both decisions have simply fuelled the existing legitimacy crisis of the regime amid growing impoverishment of the populace, further heightening socio-political tensions.

The "radical triangle" and its conflict with the U.S. empire can spill over in neighboring countries. In Peru, a staunch U.S. client "autogolpista," Alberto Fujimori, and CIA secret police chief "asset" Vladimiro Montesinos were toppled from power in late 2000. But new head-of-state Alejandro Toledo's refusal to pursue policies independent of Washington's demands has resulted in ongoing confrontation with mass movements that reject this neoliberal agenda. In Brazil, the left Workers Party candidate for the 2002 presidential elections, Luiz Inacio de Silva ("Lula"), is poised to succeed Fernando Henrique Cardoso as the country's new leader. Mid-year polls show "Lula" with almost 45 pecent of the popular vote compared with around 16 percent for Cardoso's protégé and chosen heir, Jose Serra.[4] As the economic crisis deepens, the Cardoso government continues its downward spiral. The Landless Workers Movement (MST) continues to organize and occupy large estates (30,000 families were settled in 2001) and to resist state repression in a tense, conflictual countryside where dozens of peasant activists have been killed over the past two years. Further south, major peasant and urban mobilizations have, with increasing frequency, paralyzed the economies of Bolivia and Paraguay. In Argentina, four presidents were ousted in 2001 by urban uprisings throughout the country that blocked highways, attacked municipal political institutions, and engaged in other forms of popular resistance. Plan Colombia must be understood within this context of growing continental mobilization, as an attempt to behead the most advanced, radicalized, and well-organized opposition to U.S. efforts to break down the remaining barriers to its political and economic domination of the hemisphere.

The upsurge of multifaceted opposition inside the "radical triangle" has to date checkmated or reversed U.S. policies at the edge of imperial concerns. Washington's four-decades-long effort to isolate the Cuban Revolution from Latin America and the Caribbean has for all practical purposes collapsed—accelerated by developments within the "radical triangle." Political and/or economic relations have been reestablished with virtually every country in the region; governments as diverse as Venezuela's and Brazil's sign oil agreements with Havana or open up their markets to Cuban biotechnology exports; Rio and Ibero-American conferences regularly denounce the extraterritorial Helms-Burton law, totally isolating U.S. diplomats attending these meetings. Meanwhile, Washington's efforts to overthrow the Chavez regime have been contested and repulsed: Venezuela's Ali Rodriguez was elected OPEC Secretary-General; while a number of Caribbean nations eagerly sought out and signed beneficial oil agreements with Caracas, and Chavez's public attacks on Plan Colombia have elicited favorable diplomatic responses from key Latin countries, including Brazil and Mexico.

Washington's hemispheric strategy is based on a variation of the "domino approach": The first objective of Plan Colombia is to defeat the FARC/ELN guerrillas, the second is to surround and pressure Venezuela and Ecuador, and the third is to more actively escalate internal destabilization within the "radical triangle" countries. The strategic goal is to reconsolidate power in northern South America, secure unrestricted access to a vital raw material (oil), and enforce the "no alternatives to globalization" ideology for the rest of Latin America.

Maintaining the Mystique

Plan Colombia is about maintaining the mystique of the invincibility of empire and the irreversibility of neoliberal policies. The power elite in Washington knows that beliefs held by oppressed peoples and their leaders are as effective in retaining U.S. power as the actual exercise of force. As long as Latin American regimes and their internal opponents continue to believe there is no alternative to U.S. hegemony they will conform to the major demands and diktats laid down by the White House and its representatives in the international financial institutions. The belief that U.S. power is untouchable, that its authority and pronouncements are beyond the reach of the nation-state (reinforced by globalization rhetoric) has been a prime factor in sustaining U.S. economic exploitation and the Pentagon's physical presence on the continent. Once U.S. dominance is tested and successfully resisted by popular struggles in one region, the mystique is eroded and people and even regimes elsewhere begin to question the U.S.-defined parameters of political action. Once the mystique is challenged and skepticism spreads across the continent, opposition forces receive a new impetus in challenging neoliberal rules and regulations that facilitate the pillage of their economies. Once the rules are questioned, capital, ever fearful of a revival of nationalist and socialist reforms, and redistributive structural changes, will flow outward. The reversion to more restricted markets and the constraints of risk and declining profit margins will weaken the dollar. The flight from the dollar will, in turn, make it difficult for the U.S. economy to finance its huge current account imbalances.

Fear of this chain reaction is at the root of Washington's hostility to any regional challenge that could set in motion large-scale and extended political opposition. By itself, the U.S. economic and political stake in Colombia is not overly substantial. Yet the possibility of a successful emancipatory struggle led by guerrilla and popular movements could undermine the mystique of imperial dominance and unleash movements in other countries, and perhaps put some backbone in the spine of key Latin leaders. Plan Colombia is about preventing Colombia from becoming an example which demonstrates that alternatives are possible and that Washington is vulnerable. What particularly looms large in Washington's strategy is the specter of an alliance between Bogota, Havana, and Caracas that would constitute a powerful political and economic bloc. Cuban social welfare and security expertise harnessed to Venezuela's energy clout and Colombian oil, labor power, and agricultural resources could make these complementary political-economies an alternative pole to the U.S.-centered empire. Plan Colombia is organized to destroy the potential centerpiece of that political alliance: the Colombian insurgency.

Plan Colombia has the virtue of being a straightforwardly military operation directed by the U.S. to destroy its class adversary in order to consolidate its empire in Latin America. The anti-drug rhetoric is more for domestic consumption than any operational guide to action. Guerrilla leaders and their movements understand this and act accordingly, mobilizing their social basis of support, securing their military supplies, and fashioning an anti-imperial strategy. Faced with this stark political-military polarity, clearly defined by each adversary, many "progressive" academics and other intellectuals retreat to apolitical abstractions—obscurantist and reified concepts divorced from real power configurations and class-struggle politics. They speak of "the world capitalist system," "accumulation on a world scale," "the age of extremes," and "historic defeats"—vacuous phrases that explain nothing and obscure the specific class and political basis of growing anti-imperialist movements and popular struggle.

The strategic importance that first Clinton and now Bush attach to the outcome of the Colombian conflict, and the potential that struggles of this kind have as a cutting edge for the breakup of U.S. hegemony in Latin America, serves to underline the degree to which U.S. capital accumulation depends critically on the results of political struggle within nation-states. Moreover, because oil is *the* primary source of energy for the American economy, an imperial politico-military victory in Colombia would isolate, and facilitate efforts to overthrow, the Chavez government in Venezuela that is attempting to combine liberal domestic reforms with a nationalist foreign policy. Chavez has followed a relatively orthodox fiscal policy, privatized the electricity sector, adopted a favorable approach toward foreign investors (e.g., new oil concessions), deregulated the financial sector, and scrupulously met the country's foreign debt obligations. Even if FARC and the ELN are perceived as the radical "greater evil," U.S. policy planners shifted from cautious pressure on Chavez prior to September 11, to virulent opposition culminating in the April 2002 coup attempt. Since September 11, Washington has followed a singular military approach toward its adversaries in the "radical triangle," sharply escalating its support for war against the guerrilla movements and their allies in Colombia, while militarizing Ecuadorean politics.

Colombia: Washington's Multitrack Policy

Washington is pursuing a multitrack policy in relation to different kinds of opposition it faces in the Andean region. In relation to Colombia, where a U.S. client controls the state apparatus and guerrilla formations represent a systemic challenge, the Clinton and Bush administrations have declared all-out war, centralized and expanded their military machine, and advocated marginalization of autonomous popular organizations in civil society. The demilitarized zone where peace negotiations took place during 1998–2002, for instance, turned into a war zone as U.S. military involvement expanded, tightening control along the borders (particularly the Ecuadorean-Colombian frontier). This strategy received an enormous boost in 2002 when the White House-supported candidate and paramilitary sponsor Alvaro Uribe was elected president, whereupon he swiftly launched an all-out military assault on the guerrilla forces.

During the mid-1990s, the Clinton administration terminated most U.S. aid to Colombia on human rights grounds. In 1998, rising levels of narcotics production and trafficking notwithstanding, the White House decided to recertify the Samper government as "fully cooperating" in the war against drugs, which paved the way for $289 million in counter-narcotics aid in fiscal year 1999—catapulting Colombia to the third biggest recipient of U.S. foreign aid worldwide behind Israel and Egypt.[5] FARC military successes were partly responsible for this policy shift. The impetus for "cautiously reengaging" the Colombian armed forces was to support a renewed offensive against those coca growing areas of southern Colombia controlled by guerrillas who derived a large part of their funds from taxing drug traffickers and coca and opium plant growers. But if the primary focus at this time was on the counter-drug strategy, a senior U.S. official warned that "we may go in the [counterinsurgency] direction in the future."[6] This was no idle threat. In March 1999, Washington began sharing intelligence information on drug trafficking and guerrilla movements with the Colombian military; within months, over 300 Pentagon, Drug Enforcement Agency, and CIA personnel were operating in Colombia.

Some months earlier, in November 1998, the new government of Andres Pastrana had embarked on a peace strategy with the guerrillas by withdrawing army troops from a 42,139-square-kilometer "demilitarized zone" in south central Colombia where FARC's authority predominated. Negotiations between the two sides continued until July 1999, when they were temporarily suspended; soon after, the FARC initiated a nationwide offensive against the regime, which merely reinforced U.S. policymakers' belief that FARC would only capitulate if defeated militarily. "Pastrana seems to have bent all the way over in a Gumby-like way," a Pentagon official dismissively commented. "He's about used up what he's got to offer, and it is not working."[7] The perceived failure of Pastrana's strategy combined with the growing strength of the guerrilla forces transformed Colombia into a major foreign policy "problem" for the Clinton administration. National Security Council Adviser Samuel Berger and Undersecretary of State Thomas Pickering were assigned responsibility for coordinating an overall approach. At an interagency meeting to discuss the matter, Berger warned that this was "a third-order issue" en route to becoming "a first-order issue."[8] Pickering and White House Office of National Drug Control director Barry McCaffery visited Colombia in late August (1999) and bluntly told Pastrana that any new concessions to the FARC to revive peace negotiations could threaten continuing U.S. support for his regime. Although senior Pentagon officials expressed limited enthusiasm for any significant counterinsurgency intervention in Colombia, the internal policy debate could not disguise a consensus (supported by Congress) that Pastrana had conceded too much to the FARC in pursuit of a negotiated solution, in particular his decision to allow the guerrillas control over a demilitarized zone.[9] The undersecretary promised a big increase in aid if "he [Pastrana] develops a comprehensive plan to strengthen the military, halt the nation's economic free fall and fight drug trafficking."[10] In subsequent testimony before the Senate Foreign Relations Committee, Pickering described Washington's longer-term policy objective: "the end goal is not [sic] taking over the country by the guerrillas."[11]

This was the genesis of "Plan Colombia" which was developed in close consultation with the Clinton administration. The Pastrana government hoped to obtain $3.5 billion of the proposed $7.5 billion cost from foreign governments and global financial institutions. In February 2000, the White House proposed a major aid package for Colombia that President Clinton and Secretary of State Madeleine Albright insisted was for exclusive use in the war against the drug traffickers even though the funds were destined mainly for the army and security forces. For his part, the architect of the proposal, drug czar Barry McCaffery, made no effort to hide the broader, overriding purpose of the aid. It was, he said, to enable the military to "recover the southern part of the country currently under guerrilla control."[12] In July 2000, Congress approved a $1.32 billion aid package as part of emergency funding ostensibly for Andean region anti-drug operations. Vigorous lobbying by American oil, helicopter, and other companies likely to benefit most from the administration's aid package immensely facilitated passage of the supplemental.[13] Over $862 million of the total was programmed for Colombia, more than 70 percent of which was to be used to train and equip the nation's military and police forces and (indirectly) the paramilitary forces. However, responding to documented evidence of widespread human rights abuses by the armed forces and its rightist paramilitary allies, the legislators attached seven "human rights" conditions to the release of any security assistance to the coercive institutions of the Colombian state. In late August, the White House revealed the depth of its commitment to human rights in Colombia by waiving six of these conditions on "national security" grounds. The official justification was the need to combat a "drug emergency," even as the State Department reported that the security forces were colluding with the paramilitaries. U.S. Embassy officials told Human Rights Watch investigators that they could not imagine any abuse perpetrated by the armed forces that would induce them to recommend a halt to military aid. They were in no doubt that similar sentiments predominated in the State Department and the White House. As one Embassy official put it: "I think we will waive human rights conditions indefinitely."[14]

U.S. military strategy increasingly focused on the expansion and operational efficacy of the estimated 10,000-strong paramilitary forces that assumed a key role in Plan Colombia: aggressively "social cleansing" entire regions of peasant activists suspected of guerrilla sympathies. For over a decade the CIA aided in the formation of these groups, allegedly to combat the drug cartels. Yet Carlos Castano, head of the "United Self-Defense Forces (AUC)," publicly boasted of his narco-trafficking activities and acknowledged that drugs were an important source of income for his organization. During the latter half of the 1990s, the Clinton White House escalated clandestine support to the paramilitaries via its funding of the Colombian armed forces, all the while tolerating their drug activities. Based in the northern part of the state and financed by coca barons, other large landowners, and drug traffickers, these armed rightist groups were Washington's "card" for scuttling peace negotiations and turning the Colombian conflict into a total war. The tactic was to push for the presence of paramilitary forces in the peace negotiations and then allow Pastrana to mediate as a centrist between the two extremes, imposing a settlement that sustained the socio-economic status quo.

The demilitarized zone continued in place from late 1999 to February 2002, when the Pastrana regime abruptly ended peace negotiations and launched a military assault on the region, hoping to defeat the guerrillas and capture the FARC leadership. The "surprise attack" failed and, with strong White House backing, the war resumed on a more extensive and violent scale. In April 2002, the Bush administration's "candidate," ultra-rightist Alvaro Uribe, won the presidential election (with only 46 percent of eligible voters participating), ensuring there would be no letup in the Colombian state's effort to destroy the guerrilla movements. Upon his inauguration Uribe declared a state of siege ("*conmocion*") and announced a special tax to fund 3,500 special forces, 50,000 additional police, 100,000 part-time militia, and one million civilian informers. Plan Colombia has been taken to its logical extreme—a total war directed by a scorched earth policy.

Clinton's policy followed an almost exclusively military track (accompanied by minor financial incentives to co-opt NGOs to work on alternative crops), combining "paper criticism" of the paramilitary forces in annual State Department reports with indirect, large-scale material support. This contrasts with the posture adopted toward Venezuela that was shaped principally by the need to avoid triggering a premature confrontation with the Chavez regime. Until early 2001, American diplomats were savvy enough to realize that the balance of forces within Venezuela was unfavorable to any direct military political action. Chavez had won presidential and congressional elections by overwhelming majorities, appointed some constitutionalist officers to a few senior command positions, and secured solid majority support among the populace in his partial efforts to reform the constitution and judicial system.[15] Anti-regime and pro-U.S. allies among the business elite, the traditional parties, and in the state apparatus were not strong enough to provide effective channels for a Washington-funded and -orchestrated destabilization effort; the preferred strategy centered on a propaganda war directed toward creating favorable conditions for a future civilian-military coup. This approach involved highlighting the authoritarian dangers of Chavez's centralization of power, attempts to promote greater autonomy for its elite supporters in civil society, and efforts to fragment power and provide a platform on which to reorganize the discredited traditional political parties.

Following September 11 and Chavez's refusal to join Washington's anti-terrorist campaign, the Bush administration began systematic efforts to overthrow his government. In early October 2001, Chavez had the audacity to criticize Bush's war on terrorism and attacks on Afghanistan, stating that "you cannot fight terrorism with terrorism." After the U.S. recalled its ambassador, the State Department's Marc Grossman headed a delegation to Caracas to meet with Chavez. According to Venezuelan foreign affairs officials at the meeting, Grossman openly threatened Chavez, telling him "you will pay for this policy [opposition to Bush] and so will future generations."[16] Between November 2001 and April 2002, Assistant Secretary of State for Inter-American Affairs Otto Reich and other senior U.S. officials conferred on a regular basis with anti-Chavez military, business, and labor leaders—the future coup-makers.[17] As the coup unfolded, U.S. Ambassador Charles Shapiro welcomed it—and then stood by impotently as the popular multitude rose up in defense of the constitutional regime. In the months that followed, undeterred by its April "setback," Washington continued preparations for a second *golpe*, establishing an office for a "transitional government" in Caracas.

Under both Clinton and Bush the White House articulated and implemented a highly complex pattern of intervention in the "radical triangle": support for IMF-World Bank-Pastrana austerity programs and military confrontation via the state apparatus and paramilitary forces in Colombia; diplomatic and political pressure followed by a military coup via elite media, business, and military groups in Venezuela, and targeting of disaffected upper and middle class groups and the trade union bureaucracy; and political-economic cooptation of the Ecuadorean government together with support for repression of the social movements, and the marginalization of elected political opposition.

While Plan Colombia led to a more aggressive use of paramilitary forces and greater civilian casualties, it produced no effective "rollback" of the guerrillas and presided over a further deterioration of the Colombian economy, which increased urban disaffection and weakened Pastrana's political position, setting the stage for total war under Uribe. However in September 2002, shortly after Uribe announced an austerity budget, the trade union confederation (the CUT) and peasant unions called a successful general strike, with 150,000 marching in Bogota. In Venezuela, the Chavez regime retained shaky control over institutional power, organizing popular support in Bolivarean circles while still pursuing liberal economic policies. In Ecuador, the social movements and peasant-Indian coalition retained power to engage in political mobilization even as the U.S. client regime at least temporarily succeeded in pushing through bilateral military agreements and, as a result of dollarization, relinquished key decisions affecting the national economy to U.S. Treasury officials.

Washington's commitment to funding Plan Colombia and waging counterinsurgency war against the FARC showed no signs of abating following the election of Republican George W. Bush in November 2000. The new President not only endorsed his predecessor's policy but also drew on the experience of his father's 1989 "Andean Initiative," a five-year plan to finance a more effective prosecution of the war against popular insurgent movements under

pretext of a war against drugs in the heartland of the South American continent—Colombia, Bolivia, and Peru. The program provided "expanded assistance" to police, military, and intelligence officials in all three countries,[18]
bolstering the firepower of those state institutions specializing in repression
of popular unrest. In April 2001, the White House requested almost $900 mil-
lion in economic and "counter-narcotics" and counterinsurgency aid as part
of a new "Andean Regional Initiative" (ARI). In a slight departure from the
Clinton strategy, the proposed funding allocations reflected even greater emphasis on limiting the regional impact of the popular struggle in Colombia;
while Bogota was allocated $399 million of the total, the other $500 million
was distributed between Peru, Bolivia, Ecuador, Brazil, Panama, and
Venezuela.[19] When Congress passed the ARI legislation in December it had
pared back the original request to $625 million and attached conditions re-
stricting the aid to use in the anti-narcotics trafficking struggle—a dead letter
in practice.[20]

Throughout its first twelve months in office, defeating the guerrillas was the
first priority of the Bush White House. Like Clinton, Bush has not allowed
human rights abuses or the Colombian military's collusion with rightist paramilitary death squads to obstruct efforts to prosecute a counterinsurgency war
against the guerrilla movements, peasant communities, human rights leaders,
and trade unionists. In early February 2002, the administration requested an
additional $98 million to train an elite Colombian army battalion to protect
U.S. Occidental Petroleum's 490-mile Cano Limon oil pipeline against FARC
attacks. This submission coincided with a joint report issued by Amnesty International, Human Rights Watch, and the Washington Office on Latin America documenting the continued failure, or refusal, of the Pastrana government
to break close operational ties between the armed forces and paramilitaries resulting in almost 30,000 deaths over the previous decade. The report also
noted that Congress had placed clear and unequivocal restrictions on counter-
narcotics funding to Colombia as long as these ties remained in place and
military officers accused of human rights abuses were not prosecuted:
"Colombia's government has not, to date, satisfied the conditions, and that the
military's human rights record, if anything, has gotten worse."[21]

On February 20, the Pastrana government broke off peace talks with the
FARC leadership and ordered the armed forces to reoccupy the demilitarized
zone. Within weeks, the Colombian military had extended its operations from
the former guerrilla safe-haven into surrounding departments. Church organizations based in these areas reported that the major casualties of this renewed military offensive were civilians who were bombed, massacred, forcibly
displaced, and unable to get access to sufficient water and basic foodstuffs.[22]
Washington's response to the collapse of negotiations—which they opposed
from the start—was immediate and predictable: increased military aid to the

armed forces with the goal of pursuing a simultaneous war against drugs and guerrillas. Seeking to extend the global "anti-terrorist" war to Colombia, Bush officials began describing the FARC as "narco-terrorists" and lobbied Congress to remove all restrictions on U.S. military funding of the Pastrana regime and its coercive institutions.[23]

With the presidential election victory of U.S.-backed death squad organizer Alvaro Uribe in late May 2002, greater direct U.S. intervention in Colombia's counterinsurgency war became inevitable. The former governor of Antioquia, and strong supporter of Plan Colombia, campaigned on a platform of waging a more aggressive military struggle against the guerrillas. He promised to double defense spending (with significant U.S. support), to give military commanders a free hand in waging all-out war against the FARC, to double the size of the armed forces and the national police, and to create a one-million strong civilian intelligence network along the lines of a similar program he supported during his governorship in the mid-1990s when armed civilian groups (Cooperatives for Surveillance and Private Security, or Convivirs) were established to act as informers and "death squads" allied to the military. They were eventually banned in 1999 because of their involvement in widespread human rights abuses against civilians.[24] Retired General Rito Alejo del Rio, a senior election campaign adviser to Uribe, had been a strong ally of the then governor when he commanded the Seventeenth Brigade in Antioquia between 1995 and 1997, only to be subsequently relieved of his post by Pastrana "for his alleged support of paramilitary groups [during that period]."[25]

The Bush administration welcomed Uribe's election victory and, according to White House Director of the Office of National Drug Control Policy John P. Walters, was "eager to begin work with him."[26] However, Walters and other American officials also linked any new major U.S. financial commitment to substantial increases in Colombian government military and security spending. Some weeks later, U.S. Ambassador Anne Patterson conveyed the same message to 800 Colombian business leaders. The United States, she said, "is ready to invest more if the Colombians invest more in their own security."[27] Nonetheless, Congress approved a $28.9 billion counter-terrorism bill in late July that included $35 million for Colombia, primarily to bolster Uribe's ability to wage war against the FARC, which U.S. policymakers now characterized as "the most dangerous international terrorist group based in this hemisphere."[28] When Bush signed the aid package into law at the beginning of August, it promised to immensely facilitate the conterinsurgency war in Colombia because it also rescinded the provision limiting the application of U.S. anti-drug aid to counternarcotics programs. In effect, it gave Uribe the "green light" to use the approximately three quarters of Plan Colombia and ARI funds (a requested $731 million for 2003, see Table 2, page 108) that come in the form of military aid to prosecute the war against the guerrillas.

Emboldened by strong White House support, Uribe set about implementing his "total war" agenda. Within days of his inauguration, the new president suspended all constitutional freedoms and declared a "state of *conmocion interior*" to raise a war tax, increased military and paramilitary forces over a hundred thousand strong, and began organizing his network of one million civilian informers. The FARC and ELN, in turn, organized urban guerrilla units that bombarded Uribe's inauguration, firing cylinders in the direction of the Presidential Palace and Congress. Since the election, the urban centers, now populated by almost two million peasants displaced from their land and homes in the countryside, have become a recruiting ground for both the popular insurgency and Uribe's paramilitary allies.

On September 10, 2002, constitutional guarantees took a further battering when the Uribe regime expanded its emergency powers by allowing military commanders to declare curfews, control movements, and detain without warrants any citizen in specially designated "zones of rehabilitation and consolidation." Twenty-four hours earlier, the Bush administration released $42 million in new military aid, certifying that the Colombian armed forces had satisfied the limited human rights improvements mandated by Congress. This justification brought a withering retort from Jose Miguel Vivanco, executive director of the Americas Division of Human Rights Watch: "But the fundamental problems remain the same: no serious progress toward suspending officers implicated in abuses, toward effective judicial investigations of abuses, or toward breaking the persistent links between the military and the paramilitary groups."[29]

Consequences of U.S. Military Escalation

Clinton's Plan Colombia unfolded as a typical low-intensity war (combining large-scale U.S. financing and arms and relatively limited military and covert personnel) which had a high intensity impact on peasants and workers that, in turn, began to internationalize the conflict.[30] Despite predictable denials, U.S. military and intelligence agencies actively promoted Colombian paramilitary forces to decimate anyone vaguely associated with guerrilla movements or sympathetic to any part of their program. Dozens of suspected peasants, community activists, schoolteachers, and others were tortured and assassinated in order to terrorize the rest of the population.

Between 1988 and 1997, over 23,000 civilians were killed by nongovernmental armed organizations, of whom all but 3,500 were casualties of rightist paramilitary groups, drug cartels, and "private justice" groups.[31] In a blunt assessment of the Samper government's (1994–1998) approach toward dealing with the paramilitaries, a June 1997 CIA intelligence report not only acknowledged that civilian noncombatants suspected of ties to the guerrillas were primary targets of these death squads but also the regime's failure to translate its anti-paramilitary rhetoric into practice: "We see scant indications that the military is making an effort to directly confront the paramilitary groups. . . ."[32] Little changed after Pastrana came to power in 1998. His reluctance to publicly acknowledge the collusive relationship between Colombia's military and security forces and the paramilitary groups, which continued to account for the overwhelming majority of human rights abuses during his presidency, was only exceeded by a failure to take effective measures to sever this alliance.[33]

As Plan Colombia escalated the violence, thousands of peasants fled toward and crossed the borders into Venezuela, Ecuador, Panama, and Brazil. Even then, these refugees fleeing for their lives were not safe from the depredations of cross-border attacks. The frontiers and borders were transformed into war zones in which squatter refugees living in squalor became targets of the Colombian military and its paramilitary allies. Rather than containing the civil conflict, Plan Colombia extended and internationalized it, exacerbating instability in the adjoining regions of neighboring countries.

By the end of 2000, over one million peasants had been displaced due to the activities of the armed forces and frequent sweeps by the paramilitary groups through regions under control of the Colombian military. In 2001, another 319,000 were forcibly displaced from their villages. Human Rights Watch described one particularly graphic, and not untypical, instance of this rightist violence against civilian noncombatants and the acquiescence of the Colombian state:

> Over a period of a week in early July [2001], in the town of Peque, Antioquia, over five hundred armed and uniformed paramilitaries blockaded roads, occupied municipal buildings, looted, cut all communications, and prevented food and medicines being shipped in, according to the Public Advocate's office. Over 5,000 Colombians were forced to flee. When the paramilitaries left, church workers counted at least nine dead and another ten people "disappeared," several of them children. As a local official said: "*The state abandoned us. This was a massacre foretold. We alerted the regional government the paramilitaries were coming and they didn't send help.*"[34]

Paramilitary terror is an integral part of the repertoire of U.S. counterinsurgency tactics designed to empty the countryside and deny the guerrillas logistical support, food, and new recruits.

Plan Colombia also escalated the degree and visibility of U.S. involvement in Colombia. With hundreds of Pentagon advisors, and additional subcontracted mercenaries flying helicopters, this participation moved down the chain from planning, design, and direction of the war to the operational-tactical level. At the same time, Clinton policymakers used their financial levers to reward pliant and cooperative military officials and to punish or humiliate those who did not sufficiently respond to U.S. commands or advice. The perception began to take hold within a large sector of the country's populace that

Plan Colombia had essentially transformed a decades-long civil war into a national liberation struggle. The Colombian elites and sectors of the upper middle class emerged as the strongest advocates of increased direct U.S. military intervention. To the peasant population, however, this was a recipe for greater use of chemical defoliants, increasingly aggressive and destructive military chemical forays to eradicate coca and food plants, and a more violent regime-paramilitary response to those that stood in the way.

Plan Colombia's response to popular insurgency accelerated the militarization of Colombian society, triggering increased emigration of urban professionals fleeing the intimidation unleashed by the armed forces and their rightist paramilitary allies in the cities and countryside. By putting the nation on a war footing, Plan Colombia not only menaced the average citizen, it also intimidated the lower-middle class, who were subjected to arbitrary searches and interrogation. The loss of limited urban space to engage in civil discourse led some to shift to underground and clandestine anti-regime actions and others to further withdraw from public life. The Pastrana and Uribe governments characterized demands by trade unions and civic groups as "subversive to the war effort" and denounced urban opponents as "fifth columnists acting on behalf of the guerrillas." The result was an increase in the already record high number of state and parastate-authored assassinations of trade unionists, human rights advocates, journalists, indigenous and campesino leaders, and other perceived opponents of the anti-guerrilla conflict. Labor leaders have been an especially favored target of the paramilitaries, especially of the largest right-wing organization, the AUC. They have murdered close to 4,000 of their number over the past decade and a half.[35] Less than one month after Uribe's election, the *Washington Post* reported that the AUC "is still killing more Colombians than ever before."[36]

Not least, Plan Colombia imposes a multibillion-dollar drain on the Colombian treasury at a time when the Pastrana and Uribe governments were implementing austerity measures and social spending cuts that adversely affected wage and salaried groups. Responding to the consequences of skyrocketing military expenditures, that took the form of rising popular opposition to the Colombian state and regime, the armed forces leadership and Clinton policymakers began to call for an expanded military apparatus. Neoliberal austerity policies and the militarization of the conflict required a bigger centralized state and a shrinking, more constricted civil society—at least among the popular classes. The reinforcement of the state and its commitment to fight a two front war—in the countryside with arms and in the cities with harsh economic measures—not only deepened polarization between the regime and the civilian populace but increasingly isolated Pastrana and Uribe and made them more dependent on Washington along with the Andean nation's burgeoning military and paramilitary organizations. Instead of containing the conflict and bolstering support for the regime, the unintended consequences of Plan

Colombia have been to extend and deepen the struggle, isolating both the Pastrana government and its successor Uribe, elected by an estimated 24 percent of eligible voters. In large part, Washington and its Colombian clients are responsible for this outcome, blinded by single-minded pursuit of imperial power which led them to misread the revolutionary challenge.

Washington's Diagnosis: Foibles and Facts

Essentially Plan Colombia operates from three mistaken assumptions: a spurious analogy extrapolated from Reagan-Bush victories in Central America; a series of false equations about the Colombian guerrillas and their sources of strength; and a misplaced emphasis or exaggerated focus on the drug basis of guerrilla political power.

The FARC/ELN challenge to the Colombian state and regime cannot be compared to the Central American guerrilla struggles of the 1980s. *First*, it ignores the time factor; the Colombian movements have a longer trajectory, allowing them to accumulate an infinitely greater storehouse of practical experiences and making them far more sensitive to the pitfalls of peace accords that fail to transform the state and place structural change at the center of a settlement. The 1980s formal cease-fire between the FARC and the government, in particular, was a salutary learning experience: over 3,000 guerrilla supporters and sympathizers of the newly formed Patriotic Union political party were assassinated by paramilitary death squads and no progress was made in reforming the socio-economic system. *Second*, the FARC guerrilla leadership is made up largely of peasants or individuals with deep ties to the countryside, whereas their counterparts in El Salvador and Nicaragua were primarily middle class professionals eager to return to city life and careers in electoral politics.[37] *Third*, the geography of the Colombian conflict could not be more different: it encompasses a far larger territory and a topography much more favorable to guerrilla warfare. The FARC guerrillas' social origins and experiences have made them more familiar with this terrain than was the case with the Central American movements. *Fourth*, the FARC leadership has put socio-economic reforms at the center of their political negotiations, unlike the Central Americans who prioritized the reinsertion of ex-commanders into the electoral process. *Fifth*, the Colombian guerrillas are totally self-financing and are not subject to the pressures and deals of outside supporters—as was the case in Central America. *Sixth*, and finally, the guerrillas were not impressed by the results of the Central American accords: the ascendancy of neoliberalism; the immunity from prosecution of armed forces' leaders for major human rights abuses; and the enrichment of many of the ex-guerrilla commanders, some of whom have joined the chorus supporting U.S. intervention in Colombia.

Such differences profoundly undermined Clinton's two-track policy of talking peace and financing alternative crops while escalating the war and promoting crop eradication. The attraction of a peace settlement for the commanders and the war of attrition at the base failed to achieve its objective. FARC rejected a peace accord based on electoral politics, the continuity of the military with its power and prerogatives intact, and no brakes on rampaging neoliberal-free market economic policies.

U.S. policymakers' analysis of the sources of FARC power is based on an equally flawed assumption. It equates the FARC with the drug trade, accusing the movement of deriving its strength from accumulation of millions of drug-tax dollars to recruit fighters, and from the "terror tactics" they practice to intimidate the populace and gain control of large swaths of the countryside. Washington's strategic thinking about the FARC can be summarized in a set of simple equations: FARC=drugs, drugs=dollars, dollars=recruits, recruits=terror, terror=growth of control over territory.

This superficial approach lacks any historical, social, or geographical dimension, and thus completely bypasses the social dynamics of FARC's spreading influence during the 1990s. Above all, it overlooks or ignores two critical factors: the historical process of FARC formation and growth in particular regions and classes, and the role family ties, and living and working experiences in regions abandoned or harassed by the state have played in recruitment and movement support, along with the movement's insertion into the class structure via interlocking linkages with villagers and its defense of peasant interests. The depredations committed against the peasant population by the armed forces and the paramilitaries have swelled the number of recruits to the guerrilla armies over the past decade and a half. So too has the Colombian state's crop eradication programs, which have destroyed peasant livelihoods, thus creating more propitious conditions for listening to the FARC/ELN call to arms.

Over the past four decades, the FARC has become a formidable guerrilla formation, accumulating a vast store of practical understanding of the psychological and material bases of guerrilla warfare and mass recruitment—not in a linear fashion but through trial and error, setbacks and advances. Throughout its history of championing land reform and peasant rights the FARC has been able to create peasant cadres who link villagers and leaders and communicate in both directions. These historical ties and experiences have been far more instrumental in movement growth than any drug trade tax. Indeed, the tax has been one outcome of FARC's historical-political evolution and not vice versa. The decision to tax drug-traffickers and reinvest the funds back into the movement—notwithstanding isolated cases of personal enrichment—reveals its basic political character. In areas of FARC control, drugs are not sold or consumed and the guerrillas ensure that peasant producers are protected from the violence of the state and its paramilitary allies.[38]

The strength of Colombia's guerrilla movements is not only a function of arbitrary state-authored violence in the countryside at the service of the Bogota political elite and resident landlords but also derives from the pattern of state spending and consumption that is concentrated in Bogota and, to a lesser extent, in the other major cities. This process of urban-rural polarization has increased the distance between the political class and the peasant population, making the latter more sympathetic to the appeals of the guerrillas. Another consequence of this polarization has been the formation of rural armies under the control of powerful regional politicians. In the absence of the security provided by linkages to the guerrilla movements, local villages would be much more vulnerable to attack.

Finally, although the FARC drug tax remains an important and necessary source of revenue to finance arms and food purchases, U.S. policymakers have consistently overemphasized the centrality of drug income in the guerrilla war. What the ideologists of Plan Colombia ignore or underestimate is the importance of FARC's struggles on behalf of basic peasant interests (land, credit, roads, etc.), the social services and law and order they provide, and their political education and ideological appeals. In most of their dealings with the rural population, the FARC represents order, rectitude, and social justice. While drug taxes fund arms purchases, this cannot buy class loyalties or village allegiances. The strength of the FARC is based on the interplay of ideological appeals and the resonance of its analysis and socio-political practices with the everyday reality of peasant life. To undermine the FARC, Washington would have to change the Andean nation's socio-economic reality that Plan Colombia is designed to defend.

Conclusion: "Misdiagnoses" and "Blowback"

Plan Colombia originated as a typical example of an imperial power pouring arms and money to prop up loyal client regimes that rely on coercion (military and paramilitary forces) and political-economic allies who appropriate land and dispossess peasant families. The armed forces depend on conscripts with no stake in the outcome of the struggle and on trained, loyal, promotion-oriented military professionals unfamiliar with the terrain of struggle and lacking any rapport with the peasantry. The large-scale destruction of crops and villages has little attraction for normal recruits, which is why the military has increasingly relied on hired paramilitary assassins to carry out the "dirty war." The paramilitary formations recruit a limited number of uprooted peasant youth but Plan Colombia provokes fear and flight among the overwhelming majority of peasant communities. For reasons of history, biography, and social-economic background, it is unlikely that the paramilitary forces in the future will be able to match the FARC/ELN in securing new recruits.

The continuing and deepening war under Uribe means greater U.S. military engagement. Pentagon advisors are teaching and directing high-tech warfare, providing operational leadership in close proximity to the battlefield. State Deparment and White House officials extend operational bases to new regions, creating new garrison bases destined to become new targets of the guerrilla forces. If the Colombian forces are not up to the task of defending the forward bases from which U.S. advisors operate, that will be used as a pretext to send more U.S. troops to protect the bases—the beginning link in a chain leading to greater U.S. ground troop engagement.

While serious questions may be raised about the degree and depth of future U.S. military involvement, there is no question that Plan Colombia under the Uribe government means total war and that it will result in large-scale civilian casualties and further undermining of the Colombian economy. The nation's treasury is drained to finance the war, notwithstanding Uribe's new war tax. The increased air and land war provokes a massive increase in refugees and destabilizes regional (and ultimately national) economies. Refugee camps have frequently become hotbeds for radical politics—the politics of the uprooted. Drug, contraband, and other criminal activity will flourish, straining the capacity of border policing by neighboring countries. History teaches us that the U.S. will not be able to localize the effects of its war.

Contrary to assertions by White House policymakers and Plan Colombia's ideological defenders, the so-called narco-guerrillas and peasant coca growers are not the Andean nation's most prominent drug traffickers. These two groups receive less than 10 percent of total drug earnings because they only produce and tax the raw materials. The major financial beneficiaries are those engaged in processing the coca leaves, in commercializing the product for the export market, and in the laundering of drug profits. The real powers and beneficiaries of the narcotics traffic—the bankers and business elite—are all strategic U.S. allies in the counterrevolutionary war. The drug routes across the Caribbean and Central America to the U.S. mainland pass through important client regimes with official backing.

What confronts the U.S. in Colombia is a potential problem that even a hegemonic imperial state cannot control: the long-term, unanticipated, and often adverse, effects of its involvement in overseas (especially covert) operations. Throughout the Cold War era, strategic Third World allies and anti-Communist clients were longtime recipients of extensive military/covert assistance and training. Many ultimately turned against their imperial patron. Colombia presents a similar "blowback" potential in the post-Cold War era.[39] The narco drug-traffickers who buy the coca leaves, process the paste, and turn out the final product (powder) are typically either working with or members of paramilitary groups, high military officials, landowners, bankers, and other respectable capitalists who launder drug money as investments in real estate, construction, and other profitable "legitimate" businesses, or through multinational private banks in the United States and Europe. Key U.S. political allies in Colombia and influential economic elites located in the centers of American finance capital are the major players in the narcotics trade that undermines the fundamental ideology of Washington's Plan Colombia and reveals its true, imperial underpinning.

As the breach between U.S. anti-drug ideology and its links to the narco-military/paramilitary forces becomes clearer, the emergence of a large-scale domestic opposition movement in the United States remains a future prospect. Meanwhile, today in Bolivia, Venezuela, Ecuador, and the rest of Latin America—exposed to the full brunt of the war to save the empire—the advance of the revolutionary struggle in Colombia has revealed contradictions that cut right through their societies and extend beyond, into the world economic order, with profound implications both for their future and for the trajectory of U.S. imperial rule.

Notes

1. See Stephen G. Rabe, *The Most Dangerous Area in the World: John F. Kennedy Confronts Communist Revolution in Latin America.* (Chapel Hill: University of North Carolina Press, 1999).
2. Mark P. Sullivan, *Venezuela under Chavez: Political Conditions and U.S. Relations.* Congressional Research Service, Report for Congress, July 27, 2001, 4.
3. See William M. LeoGrande, *Our Own Backyard: The United States in Central America, 1977–1992.* (Chapel Hill: University of North Carolina Press, 1998).
4. See "Brazilian Elections: 'Lula' Surges Ahead," *Washington Report on the Hemisphere*, June 1, 2002, 10.
5. Quoted in Bruce Bagley, "Drug Trafficking, Political Violence and U.S. Policy in Colombia in the 1990s," *Working Paper*, University of Miami, Coral Gables, FL, February 7, 2001, 14. On U.S. policy toward the Samper government, see Russell Crandell, "Explicit Narcotization: U.S. Policy Toward Colombia During the Samper Administration," *Latin American Politics and Society*, Vol. 43, No. 3, Fall 2001, 95–120.
6. Quoted in Douglas Farah, "U.S. to Aid Colombian Military," *Washington Post*, December 27, 1998 [online edition, hereafter OE].
7. Quoted in Tim Golden and Steven Lee Myers, "U.S. Plans Big Aid Package to Rally a Reeling Colombia," *New York Times*, September 15, 1999 [OE].
8. Ibid.
9. Douglas Farah, "U.S. Ready to Boost Aid to Troubled Colombia," *Washington Post*, August 23, 1999 [OE]; Tim Golden, "U.S. Antidrug Plan to Aid Colombia is Facing Hurdles," *Washington Post*, February 6, 2000 [OE].
10. Quoted in Ingrid Vaicius and Adam Isacson, *Plan Colombia: The Debate in Congress, 2000.* (Washington, D.C.: Center for International Policy, December 2000) 2.
11. U.S. Congress, Senate, Committee on Foreign Relations, *Crisis in Colombia: U.S. Support for Peace Process and Anti-Drug Efforts*, 106th Cong., 1st sess., October 6, 1999, 51.
12. Quoted in Ana Carrigan, "Is It Aid—or a $1.6b Bomb?," *Boston Globe*, February 6, 2000 [OE].
13. See Vaicius and Isacson, *Plan Colombia: The Debate in Congress, 2000*, 9.
14. Quoted in Human Rights Watch, *The "Sixth Division": Military-Paramilitary Ties and U.S. Policy in Colombia, October 2000* [HRW web site]. Also see the statement of Jose Miguel Vivanco, Executive Director, Americas Division, Human Rights Watch, in U.S. Congress, House Committee on International Relations, Subcommittee on the Western Hemisphere, *Implementing Plan Colombia: The U.S. Role*, 106th Cong., 2nd sess., September 21, 2000, 44–50.
15. See Sullivan, *Venezuela under President Chavez: Political Conditions and U.S. Relations*, 1–2; Mark P. Sullivan and Tracy Bius, *Venezuela under President Chavez: Political Conditions and U.S. Policy.* Congressional Research Service, Report for Congress, August 8, 2000, 1–3.
16. Personal Interviews, Paris, October, 2001.
17. See Christopher Marquis, "Bush Officials Met With Venezuelans Who Ousted Leader," *New York Times*, April 16, 2002 [OE]; Karen DeYoung, "U.S. Details Talks With Opposition," *Washington Post*, April 17, 2002 [OE]; Hector Tobar et al., "Rapid-Fire Coup Caught Chavez Foes Off Guard," *Los Angeles Times*, April 22, 2002 [OE]; Maurice Lemoine, "Venezuela: A Coup Countered," *Le Monde Diplomatique*, May 2002, 11.

18. National Security Archive, "War on Colombia," Electronic Briefing Book No. 69, *National Security Directive 18*, from George Bush, White House, Washington, D.C., August 21, 1981.

19. K. Larry Storrs and Nina M. Serafino, *Andean Regional Initiative (ARI): FY2002 Assistance to Colombia and Neighbors*. Congressional Research Service, Report for Congress, September 7, 2001, 1–4. Also see Nina M. Serafino, *Colombia: Plan Colombia Legislation and Assistance (FY2000–FY2001)*. Congressional Research Service, Report for Congress, July 5, 2001.

20. See Karen DeYoung, "U.S. Eyes Shift in Colombia Policy," *Washington Post*, January 15, 2002 [OE].

21. Quoted in Karen DeYoung, "Wider U.S. Role in Colombia Sought," *Washington Post*, February 6, 2002 [OE].

22. Kim Alphandary, "Report from the Theater of Operations," *Colombia Report*, April 1, 2002 [www.colombiareport.org].

23. See Ana Carrigan, "Looking for Allies in Colombia," *New York Times*, March 10, 2002 [OE]; Karen DeYoung, "U.S. May End Curbs on Aid to Colombia," *Washington Post*, March 15, 2002 [OE]; Christopher Marquis, "U.S. Expects a Wider War on Two Fronts in Colombia," *New York Times*, April 28, 2002 [OE].

24. See Garry M. Leech, "A Vote for Madness," *Colombia Report*, May 28, 2002 [www.colombiareport.org].

25. Human Rights Watch, *Colombia: President-elect Uribe Visits Washington*, June 18, 2002 [HRW web site].

26. Quoted in Carol Rosenberg, "U.S. Prods Uribe on Drug War," *Miami Herald*, May 30, 2002 [OE].

27. Quoted in Scott Wilson, "Colombia Poised to Install Leader as Rebels Attack," *Washington Post*, August 7, 2002 [OE].

28. Garry M. Leech, "Washington Targets Colombia's Rebels," *Colombia Report*, July 29, 2002 [www.colombiareport.org].

29. Quoted in "Colombia Fails Rights Test," *Human Rights Watch*, September 10, 2002 [HRW web site].

30. For an interesting discussion, see William O. Walker III, "A Reprise for 'Nation Building': Low Intensity Conflict Spreads in the Andes," *NACLA Report on the Americas*, July/August 2001, 23–28.

31. Angel Rabasa and Peter Chalk, *Colombian Labyrinth*. (Santa Monica: Rand Corporation, 2001) 56.

32. National Security Archive, "War on Colombia," Volume III, *CIA, Intelligence Report, "Colombia: Paramilitaries Gaining Strength,"* June 13, 1997 [NSA web site].

33. See, for example, Testimony of Jose Miguel Vivanco, Executive Director, Americas Division, Human Rights Watch, before Foreign Operations Subcommittee, Senate Operations Committee, July 11, 2001 [HRW web site]. On the paramilitaries also see Fernando Cubides C., "From Private to Public Violence: The Paramilitaries," in Charles Berquist et al. eds., *Violence in Colombia 1990–2000: Waging War and Negotiating Peace*. (Wilmington, DE: Scholarly Resources, 2001) 127–148.

34. Human Rights Watch, *Human Rights Watch Report 2000: Americas* (our emphasis) [HRW web site]. Also see Testimony of Jose Miguel Vivanco.

35. Garry M. Leech, "Washington Targets Colombia's Rebels," *Colombia Report*, July 29, 2002 [www.colombiareport.org.]. Also see Human Rights Watch, *Colombia: Current Human Rights Conditions*, September 10, 2001 [HRW web site].

36. Quoted in "Colombia's Inaugural Strife," *Washington Report on the Hemisphere*, September 10, 2002, 5.

37. In contrast to the peasant origins of the FARC leadership, the ELN commanders were largely composed of students and graduates of the University of Santander. Nor were the primary external political relations identical: the FARC were more closely aligned with the Soviet Union whereas the ELN had its strongest ties with Cuba.

38. Estimates of FARC remuneration from drug taxes vary from $100 million to $500 million annually. See William M. LeoGrande and Kenneth E. Sharpe, "Two Wars or One? Drugs, Guerrillas, and Colombia's New *Violencia*," *World Policy Journal*, Vol. XVII, No. 3, Fall 2000, 6.

39. For a detailed exposition of this notion, see Chalmers Johnson, *Blowback: The Costs and Consequences of American Empire*. (New York: Henry Holt, 2000).

Appendix: United States Aid to Colombia

Table 1

Economic and Social Programs

	ESF [Economic Support Fund]	DA [Development Assistance]	CSD [Child Survival and Disease Programs]	P.L. 480 food assistance	INC [International Narcotics Control]	Econ/Social Total
1997	0	0	0	0	0	0
1998	0	0.02	0	0	0.5	0.52
1999	3	0	0	0	5.75	8.75
2000	4	0	0	0	208	212
2001	0	0	0	0	5.65	5.65
2002, est.	0	0	0	0	127.5	127.5
2003, req.	0	0	0	0	154.8	154.8

Military and Police Aid Programs

	INC [International Narcotics Control]	FMF [Foreign Military Financing]	IMET [International Military Education and Training]	Emergency Drawdowns of counter-drug assistance	"Section 1004" [Defense Dept. counter-drug aid]	"Section 1033" [Defense Dept. riverine counter-drug aid]	ONDCP discretionary funds	EDA [Excess Defense Articles]	ATA [Anti-Terrorism Assistance]	Mil/Pol Total
1997	33.45	30	0	14.2	10.32	0	0.5	0.09	0	88.56
1998	56.5	0	0.89	41.1	11.78	2.17	0	0	0	112.44
1999	200.11	0.44	0.92	58	35.89	13.45	0	0	0	308.81
2000	686.43	0.4	0.9	0	90.60	7.23	0	0	0	785.56
2001	46.35	0.42	1.04	0	150.04	22.3	0	0	?	220.15
2002, est. plus supp. req.	253	6	1.18	0	84.99	4	0	0	25	374.17
2003, req.	284.2	98	1.18	0	117.52	7.59	0	0	?	508.49

Source: Center for International Policy's Colombia Project, *The Current Outlook*, July 29, 2002.
Note: All figures in millions of dollars. 2002 figures are official U.S. government estimates; 2003 figures are amounts being requested of Congress. Numbers in *italics* are estimate amounts from averaging the previous two years.

Table 2
Andean Regional Initiative 2003 Aid Request ($m)

Country	Military/Police	Economic/Social	Total
Colombia	$275,000,000	$164,000,000	$439,000,000
Peru	$66,000,000	$69,000,000	$135,000,000
Bolivia	$49,000,000	$42,000,000	$91,000,000
Ecuador	$21,000,000	$16,000,000	$37,000,000
Brazil	$12,000,000	—	$12,000,000
Venezuela	$8,000,000	—	$8,000,000
Panama	$9,000,000	—	$9,000,000
Total	$440,000,000	$291,000,000	$731,000,000

Source: Center for International Policy's Colombia Project, *The 2003 Aid Request,* July 29, 2002.

PART II

Empire, Militarism, and Terrorism

CHAPTER 5

American Militarism and Blowback
CHALMERS JOHNSON

The suicidal assassins of September 11, 2001, did not "attack America," as United States' political leaders and news media want to maintain; they attacked American foreign policy. Employing the strategy of the weak, they killed innocent bystanders who then became enemies only because they had already become victims. It was probably the most successful instance in the history of international relations of the use of political terrorism to influence events.

The Nature of Political Terrorism

Political terrorism is defined by its specific strategic objectives. The first goal is to attempt to turn domestic or international conditions that the terrorists perceive to be unjust into a revolutionary situation. They intend to demonstrate to a wavering population that the incumbent authorities' monopoly of force has been broken. The idea is to disorient the mass of the population "by demonstrating through apparently indiscriminate violence that the existing regime cannot protect the people nominally under its authority. The effect on the individual is supposedly not only anxiety, but withdrawal from the relationships making up the established order of society."[1] Such a strategy rarely works as intended: indeed, it usually has the opposite effect of calling people's attention to the seriousness of the situation and encouraging them to support any strong reassertion of authority. That was precisely what happened within the United States following the attacks on the World Trade Center and the Pentagon on September 11, 2001, but not necessarily what followed throughout the Muslim world, where the objective of displaying the vulnerabilities of the United States was largely successful.

A second strategic objective of revolutionary terrorism is to provoke ruling elites into a disastrous overreaction, thereby creating widespread resentment against them. This is a classic strategy, and when it works its impact on a potentially revolutionary situation can be devastating. Carlos Marighella, the Brazilian guerrilla leader whose writings influenced many political terrorists of the 1960s and 1970s, explains its rationale as follows: "It is necessary to turn political crisis into armed conflict by performing violent actions that will force

111

those in power to transform the political situation of the country into a military situation. That will alienate the masses, who, from then on, will revolt against the army and the police and blame them for this state of things."[2] The Israeli-Palestinian struggle during the so-called Second Intifada of 2000 and 2001 illustrates this goal: terrorist attacks elicited powerful and disproportionate Israeli military reactions that led to an escalating cycle of more attacks and more retaliation, most of it to the political advantage of the Palestinians.

The overreaction does not have to alienate only domestic "masses." The bombing of Afghanistan that the U.S. launched on September 30, 2001, is likely to inflict great misery on innocent people, which has been the pattern in recent American bombing campaigns (Iraq, Serbia), and will almost certainly produce unintended negative consequences throughout the Islamic and underdeveloped worlds. Vacillating supporters of the terrorists will be drawn into joining militant organizations. Moderate Muslim governments, especially in Saudi Arabia and Pakistan, will almost certainly face growing internal dissent and may even be overthrown.

Perhaps the prime example of terrorism succeeding in its goal is the Philippeville massacre of August 20, 1955, in which Algerian revolutionaries killed a hundred and twenty-three French colonials. A conscious act of terrorism carried out by revolutionaries who until then had enjoyed only slight popular backing, the Philippeville massacre resulted in a massive and bloody retaliation by the French, as well as in the important French reformer Jacques Soustelle, then governor-general of Algeria, becoming an advocate of suppression. The French crackdown eliminated most of the moderates on the Muslim side and caused influential French citizens back home to turn against their country's policies. This chain of events ultimately provoked a French army mutiny, brought General Charles de Gaulle back to power as the savior of the nation, and caused a French withdrawal from Algeria. Franco-Algerian relations are still strained today.[3]

Terrorism by definition strikes at the innocent in order to draw attention to the sins of the invulnerable.[4] The United States deploys such overwhelming military force globally that for its militarized opponents only an "asymmetric strategy," to use the jargon of the Pentagon—that is, a David-and-Goliath-type contest—has any chance of success. Like judo, it depends on unbalancing the enemy and using his strengths against him. When it does succeed, as it did spectacularly on September 11, it renders the massive American military machine virtually worthless: the terrorists offer no comparable targets.

On the day of the disaster, President George W. Bush told the American people that the country was attacked because it is "a beacon of freedom" and because the attackers were "evil-doers." In his address to the U.S. Congress on September 20, he said, "This is civilization's fight." The president's attempt to define difficult to grasp events as only a conflict over abstract values—as a "clash of civilizations" in current post-Cold War American jargon—is not only disingenuous, but also a way of evading responsibility for the "blowback" that America's imperial projects have generated.

Blowback

"Blowback" is a CIA term first used in March 1954 in a report on the 1953 operation to overthrow the government of Mohammed Mossadegh in Iran.[5] It is a metaphor for the unintended consequences of covert operations against foreign nations and governments. The CIA's fears that there might ultimately be some blowback from its egregious interference in the affairs of Iran were well founded. Bringing the Shah to power brought twenty-five years of tyranny and repression to the Iranian people and ultimately elicited the Ayatollah Khomeini's revolution. In 1979, the entire staff of the American embassy in Teheran was held hostage for over a year. This misguided "covert operation" of the U.S. government helped convince many capable people throughout the Islamic world that the United States was an implacable enemy.

Blowback became inevitable in the wake of decisions by the Carter and Reagan administrations to plunge the CIA deep into the civil war in Afghanistan. The agency secretly undertook to arm every *mujahideen* volunteer in sight, without ever considering who they were or what their politics might be—all in the name of ensuring that the Soviet Union had its own Vietnam-like experience. The American public was led to believe that the destabilization of the Soviet Union was worth the 1.8 million Afghan casualties, 2.6 million refugees, and ten million land mines left in the ground there—but it did not fully grasp all the other "blowback" its Afghan adventure unleashed.

Not so many years later, these Afghan "freedom fighters" began to turn up in unexpected places. In 1993, some of them bombed the World Trade Center in New York City. They then murdered several CIA employees on their way to work in Virginia and some American businessmen in Pakistan who just happened to become symbolic targets. On August 7, 1998, they attacked American embassies in East Africa. In 2001, they flew hijacked airliners into the World Trade Center and the Pentagon, killing as many as 4000 people. "Blowback" has come to mean the unintended consequences of American policies kept secret from the American and other peoples—except, of course, for those on the receiving end.

The pattern has become all too familiar. Osama bin Laden, the leading suspect as mastermind behind the carnage of September 11, is no more (or less) "evil" than his fellow creations of the United States' Central Intelligence Agency, Manuel A. Noriega, former commander of the Panama Defense Forces until George Bush *père* in late 1989 invaded his country and kidnapped him, or Saddam Hussein, the president of Iraq, whom Washington armed and backed so long as he was at war with Khomeini's Iran and whose people the U.S. has bombed and starved for a decade in an incompetent effort to get rid of him. All of these men were once listed as "assets" of the CIA.

Osama bin Laden joined the U.S. call for resistance to the Soviet Union's 1979 invasion of Afghanistan and accepted its military training and equipment along with countless other *mujahideen* "freedom fighters." As with the misguided "covert" operation in Iran that was unraveling during the same year, strong evidence suggests that the U.S. was deeply involved in actually provoking the Soviet invasion of Afghanistan and that what followed in Afghanistan and in the United States was "blowback" in the most direct sense. In his 1996 memoirs, former CIA director Robert Gates writes that the American intelligence services began to aid the *mujahideen* in Afghanistan *six months before the Soviet invasion.*[6] Two years later, in an interview with the French weekly magazine *Le Nouvel Observateur*, President Carter's National Security Adviser, former professor Zbigniew Brzezinski, unambiguously confirmed Gates's assertion.[7]

In its interview, the *Nouvel Observateur* asked Brzezinski, "Is Gates's account correct?" He replied, "Yes. According to the official version of history, CIA aid to the *mujahideen* began during 1980, that is to say, after the Soviet army invaded Afghanistan on December 24, 1979. But the reality, closely guarded until now, is completely otherwise: Indeed, it was July 3, 1979, that President Carter signed the first directive for secret aid to the opponents of the pro-Soviet regime in Kabul. And that very day, I wrote a note to the president in which I explained to him that in my opinion this aid was going to induce a Soviet military intervention." What Carter signed in July 1979 was a secret "finding," the orders that a president must approve in order to set a clandestine operation in motion.

The *Nouvel Observateur*'s interview continues. "You don't regret any of this today?" Brzezinski: "Regret what? That secret operation was an excellent idea. It had the effect of drawing the Russians into the Afghan trap and you want me to regret it? The day that the Soviets officially crossed the border, I wrote to President Carter, essentially: 'We now have the opportunity of giving to the USSR its Vietnam War.'" "And neither do you regret having supported Islamic fundamentalism, which has given arms and advice to future terrorists?" Brzezinski: "What is more important in world history? The Taliban or the collapse of the Soviet empire? Some agitated Moslems or the liberation of Central Europe and the end of the Cold War?" It seems likely that the American people will remember the "agitated Moslems" Brzezinski helped bring into being much longer than they will the end of the Soviet empire in Eastern Europe he sought to engineer. Moreover, Brzezinski's native Poland was well on its way toward freeing itself of Soviet influence due to the activities of the trade union leader Lech Walesa—without any help from Washington.

It was only after the Russians bombed Afghanistan back into the stone age and suffered a Vietnam-like defeat, and the U.S. turned its backs on the death and destruction that the CIA had helped cause, that Osama bin Laden turned against his American supporters. The last straw as far as bin Laden was concerned was that, after the Gulf War, the U.S. based "infidel" American troops in Saudi Arabia to prop up that decadent, fiercely authoritarian regime. Ever since, bin Laden has been attempting to bring the things the CIA taught him home to the teachers. On September 11, 2001, he succeeded with a vengeance.

American Foreign Policy

Why has there been blowback against the role of the United States in international affairs? There are today, ten years after the demise of the Soviet Union, some 800 Department of Defense installations located in other people's countries.[8] The people of the United States make up perhaps four percent of the world's population but consume forty percent of its resources. They exercise hegemony over the world directly through overwhelming military might and indirectly through secretive organizations such as the World Bank, the International Monetary Fund, and the World Trade Organization. Although largely dominated by the American government, these are formally international organizations and so beyond Congressional oversight.

As the American-inspired process of "globalization" inexorably enlarges the gap between the rich and the poor, a popular movement against it has gained strength, advancing from its first demonstrations in Seattle in 1999 through protests in Washington, D.C., Melbourne, Prague, Seoul, Nice, Barcelona, Quebec City, and Göteborg and on to the violent confrontations in Genoa during early 2001. Ironically, although American leaders are deaf to the desires of the protesters, the U.S. Department of Defense has actually adopted the movement's main premise—that current global economic arrangements mean more wealth for the "West" and more misery for the "rest"—as a reason why the United States should place weapons in space. The U.S. Space Command's pamphlet "Vision for 2020," argues that "the globalization of the world economy will continue, with a widening between 'haves' and 'have-nots'" and that we have a mission to "dominate the space dimension of military operations to protect U.S. interests and investments" in an increasingly dangerous and implicitly anti-American world. Immediately prior to the September 11 attacks on New York and Washington, the U.S. president named Air Force Gen. Richard B. Myers, former head of the U.S. Space Command, chairman of the American Joint Chiefs of Staff, the first chairman to come from such a background. Unfortunately, while the eyes of military planners were firmly focused on the "control and domination" of space and "denying other countries access to space," a very different kind of space was suddenly occupied.

On the day after the September 11 attack, U.S. Senator Zell Miller, D-GA, declared, "I say, bomb the hell out of them. If there's collateral damage, so be it." "Collateral damage" is another of those hateful euphemisms invented by the Pentagon to disguise its killing of the defenseless. It is the term American defense spokesmen use to refer to the Serb and Iraqi civilians who were killed or maimed by bombs from high-flying American warplanes in the U.S. campaigns against Saddam Hussein and Slobodan Milosevic. Massive military retaliation with its inevitable "collateral damage" will, of course, create more desperate and embittered childless parents and parentless children, and so recruit more maddened people to the terrorists' cause. Moreover, a major crisis in the Middle East will inescapably cause a rise in global oil prices with, from the terrorists' point of view, desirable destabilizing effects on all the economies of the advanced industrial nations.

How America's Postwar Empire Began

In February 1998, the then U.S. Secretary of State, Madeleine Albright, defending the use of cruise missiles against Iraq, declared that "If we have to use force, it is because we are America. We are the indispensable nation. We stand tall. We see farther into the future."[9] The evidence suggests precisely the opposite. I believe that America's role is not disinterested but instead grew out of the structural characteristics of the Cold War and the strategies the U.S. pursued, particularly in East Asia, to achieve what it thought were its interests. The United States created satellites in East Asia for the identical reasons that the Soviet Union created satellites in East Europe. During the course of the Cold War, the USSR intervened militarily to try to hold its empire together in Hungary and Czechoslovakia. The United States intervened militarily to try to hold its empire together in Korea and Vietnam. The United States, incidentally, killed a great many more people in its two losing interventions than the USSR did in its two winning interventions.

The richest prize in the Soviet empire was the former East Germany; the richest satellite in the American empire remains Japan. Japan today, much like East Germany before the wall came down, is a rigged economy brought into being and maintained for America's benefit. During the Cold War and for the decade after its end, the U.S. offered unrestricted access to the American market and tolerated Japan's protectionism. In return Japan accepted and helped to pay for American troops based there and gave at least verbal support for America's foreign policies. For the first half of the Cold War, down to about 1970, the U.S. also encouraged Japan to take positive advantage of these terms in order to prosper economically. Economic growth was the American way of inoculating the Japanese against Communism, neutralism, socialism, and other potentially anti-American political orientations.

Over time, this pattern produced gross overinvestment and excess capacity in Japanese industries. It also produced the world's largest trade deficits in the United States (over $300 billion per year at the beginning of the new millennium), huge trade surpluses in Japan, and in general a lack of even an approximation of equilibrium in supply and demand across the Pacific. Moreover, contrary to the Communist accusations of neocolonialism, it was costly to the United States in terms of lost American jobs, destroyed American manufacturing industries, and smashed hopes of American minorities and women trying to escape from poverty.

The American government continued to accept these costs as the price of keeping its empire together. From about the Nixon administration on, the U.S. did start to negotiate more or less seriously with the Japanese to open their markets to American goods and to "level the playing field." But attempts to lessen trade friction and open reciprocal markets always collided with the security relationship. In order to level the economic playing field, the United States would also have had to level the security playing field, and this it was never willing to do.

Perhaps these American policies made strategic sense during the period from approximately 1950 to 1970, when they also had the desirable consequence of bringing real competition to such complacent industries as American automobile manufacturing. But today these old policies are utterly destructive to the security and economic well-being of both the U.S. and Japan. They continue to alter the American economic system away from manufacturing and toward finance capitalism, and they prevent Japan from producing an economy that can stand alone and trade with other economies on a mutually beneficial basis. The day of reckoning for American pride and Japanese myopia cannot be very far away.

The U.S.-Japan Security Treaty today is an anachronism left over from the Cold War. When during the Cold War Japan was used as a launching pad for American troops, ships, and aircraft, Japan had no voice in the matter. During the Korean War, Japan was still under American occupation, and during the Vietnam War, Okinawa was still under American occupation. Today, the Japanese Diet would have to approve any U.S. military action emanating from its soil. And it is not likely, despite the Security Treaty's nebulous assurances or the new so-called Security Guidelines, that Japan would countenance the U.S.'s launching air strikes against either North Korea or China from its Okinawan or mainland bases. Only Washington's so-called strategists, totally ignorant of East Asian history in the twentieth century, can seriously believe today that Japanese facilities could be used for American wars against Japan's former colony, Korea, or against China, where Japan still faces accusations of war crimes and crimes against humanity. The onset of detente on the Korean peninsula, begun by the Pyongyang summit meeting of June 2000, has made all these policies obsolete, but the Americans and Japanese still cling to them because of hegemonism on the one hand and dependency in the second instance.

In 1995 an incident occurred that revealed more clearly the relationship between the United States and Japan as one of an imperial power and its dependent satellite. On September 4, 1995, two U.S. Marines and a sailor from Camp Hansen, located in Kin village in central Okinawa, kidnapped and gang-raped a twelve-year-old schoolgirl they had picked out at random. This incident was bad enough, but it was what followed over the succeeding years that forces one to reexamine the American role in Japan and, by extension, to consider the American role in the world throughout the so-called Cold War era.

The Okinawan rape produced the most serious crisis in Japanese-American relations since the Security Treaty riots of 1960. It illuminated the costs to the 1.3 million Okinawans of the thirty-eight American military bases located in an overcrowded space smaller than the island of Kauai in the Hawaiian Islands. It revealed that Washington and Tokyo were quite prepared to force the Okinawans to bear burdens during peacetime that the citizens of the Japanese mainland or of the United States would not even contemplate assuming for themselves. The United States treated the Okinawan rape incident not as a symptom of a need for a change in policy but as a public relations problem. It endlessly spun the case as a singular tragedy, not typical of the American military or of its sixty-five major military installations located in other people's countries (even though Okinawa actually has a higher rate of rapes of local women than any other place on earth where the American military is located).

The Cold War in East Asia did not end when the Soviet Union disappeared. Instead, the United States worked strenuously to shore up its old Cold War structures in East Asia, including keeping its satellites, Japan and South Korea, in subordinate and obedient positions. This suggests that the deployments of American forces in East Asia over the years reflected not just Cold War requirements but constituted a new form of imperialism—an American determination to maintain hegemony over the nations of East Asia in much the same way that the former USSR maintained hegemony over the nations of Eastern Europe.

During the early Cold War years, the problem for the United States in East Asia was that national Communist parties had filled the vacuum of leadership of movements for liberation from European, Japanese, and American colonialism. Since the U.S. was supporting the Europeans in their attempts to keep their colonies, it inevitably ended up on the wrong side of history. In order not to see all of East Asia, possibly even including Japan, come under the influence of nationalistic Communist parties, the United States from time to time used the same brutal methods the USSR resorted to in Eastern Europe to hang on to its sphere of influence. The best example of this was the role played by the United States in South Korea from 1945 to the present, a history that until recently has been almost totally obscured in the United States. In the spring of 1980, for example, keeping the U.S.'s South Korean satellite securely under the control of an American puppet involved killing hundreds of South Korean civilians who were demonstrating for democracy and against the country's American-backed military dictator, General Chun Doo Hwan, at Kwangju. This incident, almost totally ignored by the American news media, is quite comparable to the Chinese government's suppression of democratic demonstrators at Tiananmen in 1989.[10]

One of the prime consequences of the long and persistent period of Cold War, as well as a major source of future blowback against the United States, is the development of militarism in America. By militarism, I mean the phenomenon in which a nation's armed services come to put their institutional preservation ahead of effectiveness in achieving national security or a commitment to the integrity of the governmental structure of which they are a part. Related to this internal transformation of the military is an enlargement and progressive displacement by the military of all other institutions within a government for the conduct of relations with other nations. A sign of the advent of militarism is a nation's relying on its armed forces for numerous tasks for which it is unqualified, indeed its particular capabilities almost guaranteeing to make a problematic situation worse. Classical tools of international relations, such as diplomacy, foreign aid, international education, and the making of one's country a model of international behavior, atrophy as the carrier task force and cruise missiles become the first choices as instruments to solve global problems. Militarism portends that the armed services have or are about to pass beyond effective political control and become the de facto or explicit governing class of a society. It is an increasingly common phenomenon around the world—examples include much of Latin America during the 1970s, Suharto's Indonesia from 1965 to 1998, South Korea from 1961 to 1993, Pakistan today. American political leaders, from Washington's farewell address to Eisenhower's identification of the "military-industrial complex," have warned against its dangers to a democratic society.

The Appearance of a Military Class

The onset of militarism is commonly marked by three broad indicators that suggest its presence. First is the emergence of a professional military class and the subsequent glorification of its ideals. This began to occur in the United States after the Vietnam War. When it became apparent that the military draft was being administered in an inequitable manner—university students were exempted while the weight of forced military service fell disproportionately on minorities and those with insufficient means to avoid it—the U.S. government chose to abolish the draft rather than apply it equitably. Henceforth, serving in the military in defense of the country was no longer a normal obligation of U.S. citizenship. Service in the armed forces is entirely voluntary and has become a route of social mobility for those for whom other channels of advancement are often blocked—much as was the case in the former Imperial Japanese Army during the 1930s, where conscription was in effect but city dwellers were commonly deferred for health reasons.

Vietnam also contributed to the advance of militarism because the United States lost the war. This defeat was disillusioning to American elites and set off a never concluded debate about what "lessons" were to be learned from it.[11] For the newly ascendant far right in American politics, Vietnam became a just war that the left wing did not have the will or courage to win. Whether they truly believed this or not, rightist political leaders came to some quite specific conclusions. As Christian Appy observes, "For Reagan and Bush, the central lesson of Vietnam was not that foreign policy had to be more democratic, but the opposite: it had to become ever more the province of national security managers who operated without the close scrutiny of the media, the oversight of Congress, or accountability to an involved public."[12] The result has been the emergence of a "general staff" of professional militarists that classifies as secret everything they do and has thoroughly infiltrated other branches of government.

Not all of these militarists wear uniforms. One consequence of the way the United States waged war in Vietnam was to undercut the professionalism of the Joint Chiefs of Staff (JCS), since they often opposed the decisions of President Lyndon Johnson. As the historian of the JCS, H. R. McMaster, explains: "The president and [Secretary of Defense Robert] McNamara shifted responsibility for real planning away from the JCS to ad hoc committees composed principally of civilian analysts and attorneys, whose main goal was to obtain a consensus consistent with the president's pursuit of the middle ground between disengagement and war. . . . As American involvement in the war escalated, Johnson's vulnerability to disaffected senior military officers increased because he was purposely deceiving the Congress and the public about the nature of the American military effort in Vietnam."[13]

The old and well institutionalized American division of labor between elected officials and military professionals who advise the elected officials and execute their policies was destroyed and never recreated. In the Reagan administration, a vast array of amateur strategists and Star Wars enthusiasts occupied the White House and sought to place their allies in positions of authority in the Pentagon. The result was the development of a kind of military opportunism, with the military paying court to the pet schemes of politicians while also preparing for lucrative post-retirement positions in the arms industry or military think tanks. Top military leaders began to say what they thought their political superiors wanted to hear, and they also undertook covertly to maintain and enlarge the interests of their individual services.[14]

These tendencies accelerated and became entrenched during the 1990s and the opening years of the twenty-first century. Lobbyists and representatives of groups wanting to maintain Cold War-type relationships took charge of making virtually all politico-military policy, particularly in East Asia, where the possibilities for a new Cold War seemed most promising to them.[15] They often sought to eliminate or counter expertise that stood in their way; the influence of the State Department within the U.S. government notably withered. For example, Kurt M. Campbell, former Deputy Assistant Secretary of Defense for East Asian and Pacific Affairs in the Clinton administration, notes approvingly that U.S. policy toward China has increasingly been taken over by a new "'strategic class'—that collection of academics, commentators and policy-makers whose ideas help define the national interest." He says that this new crop of military experts, of which he is a charter member, is likely not to know much about China but instead to have "a background in strategic studies or international relations" and to be particularly watchful "for signs of China's capacity for menace."[16] These are the attitudes of militarism.

The second political hallmark of militarism is the preponderance of military officers or representatives of the arms industry as officials of state policy. During 2001, the administration of George W. Bush filled many of the chief American diplomatic posts with militarists, including the secretary of state, General Colin Powell, a former chairman of the Joint Chiefs of Staff, and the deputy secretary of state, Richard Armitage, undersecretary of defense in the Reagan administration. The secretary of defense, Donald Rumsfeld, served previously as secretary of defense some twenty-six years earlier, in entirely different political times and circumstances. The vice president, Richard Cheney, was also a former secretary of defense. At the Pentagon itself, President Bush nominated Albert Smith, a Lockheed-Martin vice president, for the post of undersecretary of the Air Force; Gordon England, a vice-president of General Dynamics, for secretary of the navy; and James Roche, an executive with Northrup-Grumman and a retired brigadier general, for the post of secretary of the Air Force.[17] It should be noted that Lockheed-Martin is the world's largest arms manufacturer, selling $17.93 billion worth of military hardware in 1999. On October 26, 2001, the Pentagon awarded Lockheed-Martin a $200 billion contract, the largest military contract in American history, to build the F-35 "joint-strike fighter," an aircraft that might have been needed during the Cold War but that is irrelevant to the anticipated military problems of the twenty-first century.

Richard Gardner, a former U.S. ambassador to Spain and Italy, estimates that the United States spends more on preparing for war than on trying to prevent war by a ratio of at least 16 to 1.[18] Policies that attempt to prevent war by eliminating the underlying conditions that breed social discontent or that make resorting to violence relatively easy or that try to mitigate misunderstandings among nations include: programs for combatting AIDS, promoting health, seeking to achieve food security, providing humanitarian assistance to refugees, safeguarding nuclear materials and stopping their proliferation, economic aid generally in areas of potential conflict such as Afghanistan, in the Israeli-Palestinian confrontation, and in the Balkans, and activities such as the international exchange of students and scholars in the Fulbright program. The United States is notoriously delinquent in paying its dues to the United Nations and is at least $490 million in arrears to the various multilateral development banks. By comparison the United States will spend at least $340 billion on defense in 2002 and is well on its way, following the terrorist attacks, toward $400 billion defense budgets.

Military Preparedness as Highest Goal of the State

The third hallmark of militarism is devotion to policies in which military preparedness becomes the highest priority for the state. In his inaugural address, President George W. Bush said, "We will build our defenses beyond challenge, lest weakness invite challenge. We will confront weapons of mass destruction, so that a new century is spared new horrors." But there is no nation that has the capability to challenge the United States militarily. Even as the new president spoke, the Stockholm International Peace Research Institute was compiling the 2001 edition of its authoritative SIPRI Yearbook. It shows that global military spending rose to $798 billion in 2000, an increase of 3.1 percent from the previous year. The United States accounted for 37 percent of that amount, by far the largest proportion. It was also the world's largest arms salesman, being responsible for 47 percent of all munitions transfers between 1996 and 2000. The United States was thus already well prepared for war when Bush came into office. Since his administration is nonetheless devoted to enlarging America's military capability—a sign of militarism rather than of military preparedness—they had to invent new threats in order to convince the people who voted for them that more was necessary. China has long been one of the Republican Party's special targets of vilification, despite the fact that since 1978 China has turned decisively toward a strategy of commercial integration with the rest of the world.

On April 1, 2001, a U.S. Navy EP-3E "Aries II" electronic espionage aircraft collided with a Chinese fighter plane off Hainan Island. The American aircraft was on a mission to provoke Chinese defenses and then record the transmissions and procedures the Chinese use in sending up its interceptors. One Chinese pilot lost his life, while all twenty-four American spies landed safely on Hainan and were taken well care of by the Chinese authorities. It soon became clear that China, which is the third largest recipient of foreign direct investment on earth today, after the United States and Britain, was not interested in a confrontation with the U.S., where many of its most important investors have their headquarters. But it could not instantly return the crew of the spy plane without provoking powerful domestic criticism of its obsequiousness in the face of American provocation and belligerence. It therefore delayed for eleven days, until it received from the U.S. a pro forma apology for causing the death of a Chinese pilot on the edge of Chinese territorial air space and for making an unauthorized landing at a Chinese military airfield. Meanwhile, the American media labeled the crew as "hostages," encouraged their relatives to tie yellow ribbons around trees near their homes, claimed that Bush was doing "a first-rate job," and endlessly criticized China for its "state-controlled media." The incident allowed Washington's militarists to promote their view that hostility between a commercially oriented China and a jealously hegemonic United States is inevitable and that a war between them is likely to break out sometime in the first quarter of the twenty-first century.

The other main arena of war-scare propaganda has been the Bush administration's attempt to convince the American public and the other nations of the world that the United States needs to build a "ballistic missile defense" to protect itself from "rogue states," a euphemism for four very small and economically insignificant nations: Iran, Iraq, Libya, and North Korea. China opposes the so-called ballistic missile defense (BMD) because it suspects that it is actually aimed at neutralizing China's minuscule nuclear deterrent, and all of America's main allies are reluctant to go along with it, fearing that the BMD would unleash an arms race in missiles in order to overwhelm such defenses with numbers. Russia rejects it because it is incompatible with the Anti-Ballistic Missile Treaty of 1972, which is designed to prevent the signatories from achieving what they might think is a first-strike capability because they have constructed missile defenses. Nonetheless, the Bush administration is determined to go ahead with this unproven and highly destabilizing system, and the patriotic euphoria following the attacks of September 11, 2001, caused the Congress to vote all the money the Pentagon requested to get started. The U.S. military is also prepared to buy Russia's acquiescence by maintaining the shell of the 1972 treaty and by turning a blind eye to its war in Chechnya. This, then, leaves only China in opposition, which is likely to reinforce militarist and conservative elements within the Chinese leadership.

The Bush administration's BMD campaign included doing everything in its power to hide official information on how it is likely to malfunction and the hazards that entails. For example, the Pentagon has continued to suppress the report written in August 2000 by Philip E. Coyle, then director of operational testing and evaluation at the Department of Defense, despite six different Congressional requests for it. Among other things, Coyle documents how the command and control system of the BMD is easily confused and has in the past caused a simulated launch of multiple interceptors against missiles that did not exist. Representative John Tierney (D-MA) commented that "One immediate danger in these types of situations is that adversaries may interpret these launches as a hostile first strike and respond accordingly."[19] Defense Secretary Rumsfeld says he wants a national missile defense even if it has not been thoroughly tested and is admittedly not able to perform to specifications.

Suppression of information has become routine at the Pentagon. The most recent case is the doctoring of information about design flaws in the V-22 "Osprey" tilt-wing aircraft that the Marine Corps wants Congress to buy even though several crashes have killed more than twenty-five Marines.[20] The ease with which the Marine Corps has been able to defy the civilian leadership of the Pentagon and push for production may well be a precedent for the ballistic missile defense.

The U. S. nuclear arsenal today is comprised of 5,400 multiple megaton warheads atop intercontinental ballistic missiles based on land and sea; an additional 1,750 nuclear bombs and cruise missiles ready to be launched from B-2 and B-52 bombers; and a further 1,670 nuclear weapons classified as "tactical." Not fully deployed but available are an additional 10,000 or so nuclear warheads held in bunkers around the United States.[21] One would think this is more than enough preparedness to deter the four puny nations the United States identifies as potential adversaries—two of which, Iran and North Korea, have been trying to achieve somewhat friendlier relations with the U.S. despite the decades of hostility and clandestine interference in their societies. The overkill in the enormous American nuclear arsenal and its lack of any rational connection between means and ends is clear evidence of militarism in the United States.

An Out-of-Control Military

In addition to these three prime indicators of militarism—a military class, the predominance of the military in the administration of the state, and an obsession with military preparedness—there are other manifestations of militarism that may be less significant but are no less revealing. They all suggest that the military is in the process of passing beyond civilian control and is acting as a separate corporate body in order to preserve and enlarge its diverse spheres of influence. Let me discuss some of these, in no particular order of importance.

1. *Military Recruitment.* During the year 2000, President Clinton signed a new law promoted by the Pentagon that would give military recruiters the same access to American high schools that is granted to college and business recruiters. This law contained no penalties and exempted schools where an official district-wide policy had been adopted restricting military access. In order to overcome these obstacles, the Pentagon in 2001 engineered an amendment to a new law intended to help disadvantaged students. This law, which the House of Representatives passed, is called (without apparent irony) the "No Child Left Behind Act of 2001." The amendment, which the House adopted by a vote of 366–57, says that "Any secondary school that receives Federal funds under this Act shall permit regular United States Armed Services recruitment activities on school grounds, in a manner reasonably accessible to all students of such school." As Representative John Shimkus (R-IL) put it, "No recruiters, no money." As of this writing, the bill is stalled in a House/Senate conference committee, but the trend toward trying to attract high school students into military service is well advanced beyond the old Junior ROTC (Reserve Officer Training Corps) programs.[22]

Another aspect of the Pentagon's creative efforts to attract more recruits is its support for pro-war Hollywood films. The latest example of this strategem is the Pentagon's backing of Disney Studios' *Pearl Harbor*. The movie premiered on May 21, 2001, at a special showing on the flight deck of the nuclear-powered aircraft carrier *U.S.S. John C. Stennis* that had bleachers and a huge screen installed and that was moved without its aircraft from its home port in San Diego to Pearl Harbor specifically for this purpose. As the credits reveal, numerous U.S. military commands helped make the film and in turn extracted changes to the scenario in order to portray the American military in a favorable light and to promote the idea that service in the armed forces is romantic, patriotic, and fun. According to the *Chicago Tribune*, military recruiters set up tables in the lobbies of theaters where *Pearl Harbor* was being shown in hopes of catching a few youths on their way out after viewing the three-hour recruiting pitch.[23]

Disney and the Pentagon also worked closely with the American media to promote the idea that *Pearl Harbor* was an example of what the NBC broadcaster Tom Brokaw has called *The Greatest Generation* in his book of that title (New York: Random House, 1998)—as distinct from the Vietnam generation, which the Pentagon hopes the American public will forget. On May 26, the day after the film opened in theaters, the Disney-owned ABC-TV network ran a one-hour special on Pearl Harbor narrated by David Brinkley; and the next day, rival NBC broadcast a two-hour National Geographic special featuring Tom Brokaw himself. The NBC cable affiliate, MSNBC, put on a two-hour program about the survivors of the Pearl Harbor attack narrated by General Norman Schwarzkopf, commander in the Gulf War.[24] Until September 11, 2001, this propaganda blitz was the latest effort in an ongoing campaign to prettify war and make the armed forces a routine aspect of American daily life. After the September 11th attacks, television news broadcasts began their programs with a thematic logo, "America at War," and the *New York Times* began running a special news section it called "A Nation Challenged."

2. *Military Lobbying*. The Navy and Disney invited more than 2,500 guests to the film premier of *Pearl Harbor* on Battleship Row aboard the *John C. Stennis*. This suggests that the Navy did not learn any lessons from the case of the *U.S.S. Greeneville*, a 6,500-ton nuclear-powered attack submarine, that on February 9, 2001, only a few months before the party on the *Stennis*, performed an emergency surfacing off Honolulu and collided with and sank the 190-foot Japanese high-school training ship *Ehime Maru* with a loss of nine Japanese lives. It is also possible that the Navy high command was so confident of its coverup of what actually happened that it went ahead with the *Pearl Harbor* promotion undisturbed.

The *Greeneville* put to sea on February 9 solely in order to give sixteen rich civilian backers of the Navy a joyride. Even though the *Greeneville* was missing about a third of its crew and was operating close to land with several pieces of equipment out of commission, its captain, Cmdr. Scott D. Waddle, testified before a court of inquiry that he had not been distracted by the civilians and a Navy captain-escort crowded into the control room. Nonetheless, such a collision between a surfacing submarine and another ship could only be caused by negligence on the part of the submarine's crew. On April 16, 2001, the *Honolulu Advertiser* reported that Waddle had reversed himself and said that if he were court martialed for negligence, his main defense would be that he had been ordered to take the civilians on a cruise; and he said to *Time* magazine that "having them in the control room at least interfered with our concentration."[25] A Texas oil company executive was actually at the controls when the submarine shot to the surface.

In order to prevent any of this from becoming public, the Navy's court of inquiry did not call on any of the civilian guests to testify; and Adm. Thomas B. Fargo, commander of the Pacific Fleet, decided against court martialing Waddle because it would, he argued, be detrimental to morale.[26] Waddle was allowed to retire with full pension benefits. The *Greeneville* case revealed for the first time the extent to which the Navy was using public property to generate support for its operations. During the year 2000, the Pacific Fleet alone welcomed 7,836 civilian visitors aboard its vessels. It made twenty-one voyages using *Los Angeles*-class nuclear attack submarines like the *Greeneville* for 307 civilian guests and seventy-four voyages of aircraft carriers for 1,478 visitors. No member of Congress was recorded as questioning or even taking an interest in this lobbying by the Navy on its own behalf.

Another instance of Navy propaganda was the cover story in the March 11, 2001, issue of *Parade* magazine. *Parade* is the largest weekly in terms of circulation of any publication in the United States—more than 37 million copies are included as a supplement in Sunday newspapers across the country. The article was titled "Should We Leave Okinawa?" and was written by the former secretary of the Navy in the Reagan administration, James Webb. From its cover photo of a U.S. Marine helping an Okinawan woman and her baby during the Battle of Okinawa of 1945 (with no mention that a third of the Okinawan civilian population lost their lives in the battle) to its citing erroneous statistics on crimes committed by U.S. service personnel against Okinawans and its Mc-Carthyite insinuation that former Governor Masahide Ota, a retired professor and a former Fulbright scholar, is a communist, the article is a tissue of lies about this unlucky island and its thirty-eight American military bases. The only American commentary on this whitewash of the American military's record in Okinawa appeared in the *Rafu Shimpo*, a Japanese-American newspaper published in Los Angeles.[27]

3. *Military Tyranny over the Defenseless.* The American military enjoys its comforts on places like Okinawa and wants to preserve them. It is so confident of its independence from any form of effective oversight that it sometimes mistreats not only foreigners but also American civilians. For the past sixty years, the U.S. Navy has used the beautiful beaches of Vieques, a small, inhabited island off Puerto Rico, for bombing practice using live ammunition by ships and aircraft. Protests against this activity have had no effect on Washington's militarists, although in January 2000, President Clinton offered the then

governor, Pedro Rossello, $40 million in "development" funds if Puerto Ricans would continue to put up with the bombing. Needless to say, Vieques has not attracted much in the way of private development funds given that life there is constantly interrupted by the sounds of supersonic aircraft and explosions. It was never clear exactly what Clinton proposed to develop. Some 500 Puerto Rican protesters have been arrested at the bomb site over the past five years.[28]

In April 2001, the Navy took into custody another group of demonstrators, this time including Velda González, the 68-year-old vice president of the Puerto Rican Senate, and U.S. Congressman Luis Gutierrez of Illinois. It subjected them to "harsh, dangerous and at times sadistic treatment at the hands of Navy personnel" and conducted a public and humiliating strip-search of Ms. González. A Navy spokesman said that the Navy did not intend to investigate this incident because "We have not deemed that, in fact, we have had any cases of abuse or excessive force."[29]

A similar case of military arrogance and mistreatment of civilians exists in the atolls of the Marshall Islands, including Kwajalien, Bikini, Enniburr, Ebeye, and Boken. Kwajalien is one of the main test sites for the proposed ballistic missile defense and no Marshall Islanders are allowed to live there. Bikini and Boken are uninhabitable due to earlier atomic and hydrogen weapons tests. A third of the population of the Marshall Islands has thus been concentrated on Ebeye, which has been described by Howard W. French as "a scorching place with poor sanitation, inadequate water supplies and few trees—one of the most densely inhabited islands on earth."[30] America's military colonialism in the Marshall Islands is comparable to its long imperial reign over Okinawa and Vieques. The fact that in all three places it is virtually immune from any form of supervision by elected American officials is a further sign of militarism.

4. *The Terrorism Threat.* The United States Constitution of 1787 establishes a clear separation between the activities of the armed forces in the defense of the country and domestic policing under the penal codes of the various states. The Posse Comitatus Act of 1878 was enacted to prevent the military from engaging in police activities in the United States without the consent of Congress or the president. However, with the rise of militarism and particularly after the attacks of September 11, 2001, these old distinctions have been eroded. The military has expanded the meaning of national security to include counterterrorism, interdicting drug traffickers, preparing for natural disasters, and controlling immigration, all areas in which it actively participates. The Department of Defense has drafted operation orders to respond to what it calls a "CIDCON," a "civilian disorder condition." When it declares a CIDCON, it plans to intervene and take control of civilian life. During the Republican Party's convention in Philadelphia in August 2000, for example, the Pentagon placed on alert in case of a large-scale terrorist incident a "Joint Task Force-Civil Support" based at Fort Monroe, Virginia, and "Task Force 250," ready to

go into battle to restore order. Task Force 250 is actually the Army's 82nd Airborne Division based at Fort Bragg, North Carolina.[31]

The United States is obviously not immune to terrorist attacks, including the bombing of the World Trade Center in New York in 1993, the destruction of the Federal office building in Oklahoma City in 1995, and the assaults of September 2001. Some of these incidents reflect blowback from U.S. government activities in foreign countries. The U.S. has also seen instances of state terrorism, as in the FBI's assault on religious dissidents at Waco, Texas, in 1993. It is conceivable that control of such incidents might require the use of U.S. Army troops. But it is equally true that "terrorism" is an extremely flexible concept and that it is open to abuse by the leaders of an ambitious and unscrupulous military. For example, several weeks after September 11, 2001, the FBI was still holding well over 1000 people it had arrested immediately following the attacks but against whom it had filed either no charges or trumped-up charges concerning immigration.

Several civilian agencies, including the FBI, the Public Health Service, and the Federal Emergency Management Agency, have expressed dismay at the growing role of the military in their spheres of responsibility. It is not at all obvious which is a greater threat to the safety and integrity of the citizens of the United States—the possibility of a terrorist attack using weapons of mass destruction or an out-of-control military intent on displacing elected officials who stand in their way.[32]

Notes

1. H. Edward Price, Jr., "The Strategy and Tactics of Revolutionary Terrorism," *Comparative Studies in Society and History*, 19, no. 1 (January 1977), 53.

2. Quoted in Robert Moss, *Urban Guerrillas: The New Face of Political Violence* (London: Maurice Temple Smith, 1972), 13.

3. Alistair Horne, *A Savage War of Peace: Algeria 1954–1962* (Harmondsworth, U.K.: Penguin, 1979), 122–23.

4. See Chalmers Johnson, *Revolutionary Change*, 2nd ed. (Stanford, CA: Stanford University Press, 1982), chapter 8.

5. See James Risen, "Word for Word: ABC's of Coups," *New York Times*, June 18, 2000. Also see Risen, "Secrets of History: The C.I.A. in Iran—A Special Report," *New York Times*, April 16, 2000. For the full text of the original CIA report entitled "Clandestine Service History: Overthrow of Premier Mossadeq of Iran, November 1952–August 1953," see http://cryptome.org/cia-iran-all.htm

6. Robert Michael Gates, *From the Shadows: The Ultimate Insider's Story of Five Presidents and How They Won the Cold War* (New York: Simon & Schuster, 1996), 146–47.

7. Zbigniew Brzezinski, "Les Révélations d'un Ancien Conseiller de Carter: 'Oui, la CIA est Entrée en Afghanistan avant les Russes. . . ,'" *Le Nouvel Observateur* [Paris], January 15–21, 1998; translated by William Blum and David D. Gibbs and published in David D. Gibbs, "Afghanistan: The Soviet Invasion in Retrospect," *International Politics*, vol. 37, June 2000, 233–46.

8. For details, see Chalmers Johnson, *Blowback: The Costs and Consequences of American Empire* (New York: Metropolitan Books, 2000).

9. Quoted in Andrew J. Bacevich and Lawrence F. Kaplan, "Battle Wary," *The New Republic*, May 25, 1998, p. 20.

10. On the Kwangju massacre, see Lee Jae-eui, *Kwangju Diary: Beyond Death, Beyond the Darkness of the Age* (Los Angeles: UCLA Asian Pacific Monograph Series, 1999); and Henry

Scott-Stokes and Lee Jae-eui, eds., *The Kwangju Uprising: Eyewitness Press Accounts of Korea's Tiananmen* (Armonk, NY: M. E. Sharpe, 2000).

11. See Tom Engelhardt, *The End of Victory Culture: Cold War America and the Disillusioning of a Generation* (New York: Basic Books, 1995).

12. Christian G. Appy, *Working-Class War: American Combat Soldiers and Vietnam* (Chapel Hill: University of North Carolina Press, 1993), 5.

13. H. R. McMaster, *Dereliction of Duty: Lyndon Johnson, Robert McNamara, the Joint Chiefs of Staff, and the Lies that Led to Vietnam* (New York: Harper Perennial, 1997), 329.

14. For details, see Frances FitzGerald, *Way Out There In the Blue: Reagan, Star Wars and the End of the Cold War* (New York: Touchstone, 2000).

15. See Chalmers Johnson, "In Search of a New Cold War," *Bulletin of the Atomic Scientists*, September/October 1999, 44–51; and editorial, "China Viewed Narrowly," *New York Times*, June 10, 2001.

16. Kurt M. Campbell, "China Watchers Fighting A Turf War of Their Own," *New York Times*, May 20, 2000. The *Times* nowhere identifies Campbell as a recently departed member of the Pentagon establishment.

17. "Pentagon Lines Up Industry Chiefs for Top Jobs," *Newsday*, June 1, 2001.

18. Richard Gardner, "Foreign Policy on the Cheap," *Financial Times*, June 8, 2001.

19. Gail Kaufman and Gopal Ratnam, *Space News*, June 13, 2001. For earlier efforts to cover up the BMD's failings, see William J. Broad, "Missile Contractor Doctored Tests, Ex-Employee Charges," *New York Times*, March 7, 2000; and Broad, "Pentagon Classifies a Letter Critical of Antimissile Plan, *New York Times*, May 20, 2000.

20. See "Cover-Up Contributed to Osprey Crash, Panel Says," *Los Angeles Times*, April 5, 2001; and James Dao, "Marine Corps Report Links Fatal Osprey Crash to Software Malfunction," *New York Times*, April 6, 2001.

21. *Newsweek*, June 25, 2001.

22. See "Military Escalates Assault on Civilian Schools," Committee Opposed to Militarism and the Draft, *Draft Notices*, May-July 2001, online at www.comdsd.org

23. V. Dion Haynes, "Hollywood Boosts the Military," *Chicago Tribune*, May 27, 2001.

24. Claudia Eller and Richard Natale, "Hit Status Elusive Target for 'Pearl Harbor,'" *Los Angeles Times*, June 17, 2001.

25. John Kifner, "Despite Sub Inquiry, Navy Still Sees Need for Guests on Ships," *New York Times*, April 23, 2001; Tony Perry, "Sub Skipper Is Forced Into Retirement," *Los Angeles Times*, April 24, 2001.

26. Tony Perry, "Morale Likely a Factor in Decision on Sub Crew," *Los Angeles Times*, April 4, 2001.

27. Shigehito Onimura, "Magazine's Okinawa Story Called 'Pentagon Propaganda,'" *Rafu Shimpo*, March 24, 2001. For details on why the United States should leave Okinawa, see Chalmers Johnson, ed., *Okinawa: Cold War Island* (Cardiff, CA: Japan Policy Research Institute, 1999).

28. Mary McGrory, "The Navy Way on Vieques," *Washington Post*, April 26, 2001.

29. Bob Herbert, "Treated Like Trash," *New York Times*, June 14, 2001.

30. Howard W. French, "Dark Side of U.S. Quest for Security; Squalor on an Atoll," *New York Times*, June 11, 2001.

31. Robert Windrem, NBC News, "Military Role Grows on Home Front," online at www.msnbc.com/news/546844.asp?Osp-5b5z1

32. See Kevin Dougherty, "Debate over Revision of Posse Comitatus Act Is Renewed after Attacks," *Stars and Stripes*, October 13, 2001.

CHAPTER 6

Wars of Terror

NOAM CHOMSKY

It is widely argued that the September 11 terrorist attacks have changed the world dramatically, that nothing will be the same as the world enters into a new and frightening "age of terror"—the title of a collection of academic essays by Yale University scholars and others, which regards the anthrax attack as even more ominous.[1]

It had been recognized for some time that with new technology, the industrial powers would probably lose their virtual monopoly of violence, retaining only an enormous preponderance. Well before 9/11, technical studies had concluded that "a well-planned operation to smuggle Weapons of Mass Destruction into the United States would have at least a 90 percent probability of success—much higher than ICBM delivery even in the absence of [National Missile Defense]."

That has become "America's Achilles Heel," a study with that title concluded several years ago. Surely the dangers were evident after the 1993 attempt to blow up the World Trade Center, which came close to succeeding along with much more ambitious plans, and might have killed tens of thousands of people with better planning, the WTC building engineers reported.[2]

On Sept. 11, the threats were realized: with "wickedness and awesome cruelty," to recall Robert Fisk's memorable words, capturing the world reaction of shock and horror, and sympathy for the innocent victims. For the first time in modern history, Europe and its offshoots were subjected, on home soil, to atrocities of the kind that are all too familiar elsewhere. The history should be unnecessary to review, and though the West may choose to disregard it, the victims do not. The sharp break in the traditional pattern surely qualifies 9/11 as a historic event, and the repercussions are sure to be significant.

The consequences will, of course, be determined substantially by policy choices made within the United States. In this case, the target of the terrorist attack is not Cuba or Lebanon or Chechnya or a long list of others, but a state with an awesome potential for shaping the future. Any sensible attempt to assess the likely consequences will naturally begin with an investigation of U.S. power, how it has been exercised, particularly in the very recent past, and how it is interpreted within the political culture.

At this point there are two choices: we can approach these questions with the rational standards we apply to others, or we can dismiss the historical and contemporary record on some grounds or other.

One familiar device is miraculous conversion: true, there have been flaws in the past, but they have now been overcome so we can forget those boring and now-irrelevant topics and march on to a bright future. This useful doctrine of "change of course" has been invoked frequently over the years, in ways that are instructive when we look closely. To take a current example, a few months ago Bill Clinton attended the independence day celebration of the world's newest country, East Timor. He informed the press that "I don't believe America and any of the other countries were sufficiently sensitive in the beginning . . . and for a long time before 1999, going way back to the '70s, to the suffering of the people of East Timor," but "when it became obvious to me what was really going on . . . I tried to make sure we had the right policy."

We can identify the timing of the conversion with some precision. Clearly, it was after September 8, 1999, when the Secretary of Defense reiterated the official position that "it is the responsibility of the Government of Indonesia, and we don't want to take that responsibility away from them." They had fulfilled their responsibility by killing hundreds of thousands of people with firm U.S. and British support since the 1970s, then thousands more in the early months of 1999, finally destroying most of the country and driving out the population when they voted the wrong way in the August 30 referendum—fulfilling not only their responsibilities but also their promises, as Washington and London surely had known well before.

The U.S. "never tried to sanction or support the oppression of the East Timorese," Clinton explained, referring to the 25 years of crucial military and diplomatic support for Indonesian atrocities, continuing through the last paroxysm of fury in September. But we should not "look backward," he advised, because America did finally become sensitive to the "oppression": sometime between September 8 and September 11, when, under severe domestic and international pressure, Clinton informed the Indonesian generals that the game was over and they quickly withdrew, allowing an Australian-led UN peacekeeping force to enter unopposed.

The course of events revealed with great clarity how some of the worst crimes of the late twentieth century could have been ended very easily, simply by withdrawing crucial participation. That is hardly the only case, and Clinton was not alone in his interpretation of what scholarship now depicts as another inspiring achievement of the new era of humanitarianism.[3]

There is a new and highly regarded literary genre inquiring into the cultural defects that keep us from responding properly to the crimes of others. An interesting question no doubt, though by any reasonable standards it ranks well below a different one: Why do we and our allies persist in our own substantial crimes, either directly or through crucial support for murderous clients? That remains unasked, and if raised at the margins, arouses shivers of horror.

Another familiar way to evade rational standards is to dismiss the historical record as merely "the abuse of reality," not "reality itself," which is "the unachieved national purpose." In this version of the traditional "city on a hill" conception, formulated by the founder of realist International Relations theory, America has a "transcendent purpose," "the establishment of equality in freedom," and American politics is designed to achieve this "national purpose," however flawed it may be in execution. In a current version, published shortly before 9/11 by a prominent scholar, there is a guiding principle that "defines the parameters within which the policy debate occurs," a spectrum that excludes only "tattered remnants" on the right and left and is "so authoritative as to be virtually immune to challenge." The principle is that America is a "historical vanguard." "History has a discernible direction and destination. Uniquely among all the nations of the world, the United States comprehends and manifests history's purpose." It follows that U.S. "hegemony" is the realization of history's purpose and its application is therefore for the common good, a truism that renders empirical evaluation irrelevant.[4]

That stance too has a distinguished pedigree. A century before Rumsfeld and Cheney, Woodrow Wilson called for conquest of the Philippines because "Our interest must march forward, altruists though we are; other nations must see to it that they stand off, and do not seek to stay us." And he was borrowing from admired sources, among them John Stuart Mill in a remarkable essay.[5]

That is one choice. The other is to understand "reality" as reality, and to ask whether its unpleasant features are "flaws" in the pursuit of history's purpose or have more mundane causes, as in the case of every other power system of past and present. If we adopt that stance, joining the tattered remnants outside the authoritative spectrum, we will be led to conclude, I think, that policy choices are likely to remain within a framework that is well entrenched, enhanced perhaps in important ways but not fundamentally changed, much as after the collapse of the USSR, I believe. There are a number of reasons to anticipate essential continuity, among them the stability of the basic institutions in which policy decisions are rooted, but also narrower ones that merit some attention.

The "war on terror" re-declared on 9/11 had been declared 20 years earlier, with much the same rhetoric and many of the same people in high-level positions.[6] The Reagan administration came into office announcing that a primary concern of U.S. foreign policy would be a "war on terror," particularly state-supported international terrorism, the most virulent form of the plague spread by "depraved opponents of civilization itself" in "a return to barbarism in the modern age," in the words of the Administration moderate George Shultz. The war to eradicate the plague was to focus on two regions where it was raging with unusual virulence: Central America and West Asia/North Africa. Shultz was particularly exercised by the "cancer, right here in our land mass," which was openly renewing the goals of Hitler's *Mein Kampf,* he informed Congress. The President declared a national emergency, renewed annually, because "the policies and actions of the Government of Nicaragua constitute an unusual and extraordinary threat to the national security and foreign policy of the United States." Explaining the bombing of Libya, Reagan announced that the mad dog Qaddafi was sending arms and advisers to Nicaragua "to bring his war home to the United States," part of the campaign "to expel America from the world," Reagan lamented. Scholarship has explored still deeper roots for that ambitious enterprise. One prominent academic terrorologist finds that contemporary terrorism can be traced to South Vietnam, where "the effectiveness of Vietcong terror against the American Goliath armed with modern technology kindled hopes that the Western heartland was vulnerable too."[7]

More ominous still, by the 1980s, was the swamp from which the plague was spreading. It was drained just in time by the U.S. Army, which helped to "defeat liberation theology," the School of the Americas now proclaims with pride.[8]

In the second locus of the war, the threat was no less dreadful: Mideast/Mediterranean terror was selected as the peak story of the year in 1985 in the annual AP poll of editors, and ranked high in others. As the worst year of terror ended, Reagan and Israeli Prime Minister Peres condemned "the evil scourge of terrorism" in a news conference in Washington. A few days before, Peres had sent his bombers to Tunis, where they killed 75 people on no credible pretext, a mission expedited by Washington and praised by Secretary of State Shultz, though he chose silence after the Security Council condemned the attack as an "act of armed aggression" (U.S. abstaining). That was only one of the contenders for the prize of major terrorist atrocity in the peak year of terror. A second was a car-bomb outside a mosque in Beirut that killed 80 people and wounded 250 others, timed to explode as people were leaving, killing mostly women and girls, traced back to the CIA and British intelligence. The third contender is Peres's Iron Fist operations in southern Lebanon, fought against "terrorist villagers," the high command explained, "reaching new depths of calculated brutality and arbitrary murder" according to a Western diplomat familiar with the area, a judgment amply supported by direct coverage.

Scholarship too recognizes 1985 to be a peak year of Middle East terrorism, but does not cite these events: rather, two terrorist atrocities in which a single person was murdered, in each case an American.[9] But the victims do not so easily forget.

Shultz demanded resort to violence to destroy "the evil scourge of terrorism," particularly in Central America. He bitterly condemned advocates of "utopian, legalistic means like outside mediation, the United Nations, and the

World Court, while ignoring the power element of the equation." His administration succumbed to no such weaknesses, and should be praised for its foresight by sober scholars who now explain that international law and institutions of world order must be swept aside by the enlightened hegemon, in a new era of dedication to human rights.

In both regions of primary concern, the commanders of the "war on terror" compiled a record of "state-supported international terrorism" that vastly exceeded anything that could be attributed to their targets. And that hardly exhausts the record. During the Reagan years Washington's South African ally had primary responsibility for over 1.5 million dead and $60 billion in damage in neighboring countries, while the administration found ways to evade congressional sanctions and substantially increase trade. A UNICEF study estimated the death toll of infants and young children at 850,000, 150,000 in the single year 1988, reversing gains of the early post-independence years primarily by the weapon of "mass terrorism." That is putting aside South Africa's practices within, where it was defending civilization against the onslaughts of the ANC, one of the "more notorious terrorist groups" according to a 1988 Pentagon report.[10]

For such reasons the U.S. and Israel voted alone against a 1987 UN resolution condemning terrorism in the strongest terms and calling on all nations to combat the plague, passed 153–2, Honduras abstaining. The two opponents identified the offending passage: it recognized "the right to self-determination, freedom, and independence, as derived from the Charter of the United Nations, of people forcibly deprived of that right . . . , particularly peoples under colonial and racist regimes and foreign occupation . . ."—understood to refer to South Africa and the Israeli-occupied territories, therefore unacceptable.

The base for U.S. operations in Central America was Honduras, where the U.S. Ambassador during the worst years of terror was John Negroponte, who is now in charge of the diplomatic component of the new phase of the "war on terror" at the UN. Reagan's special envoy to the Middle East was Donald Rumsfeld, who now presides over its military component, as well as the new wars that have been announced.

Rumsfeld is joined by others who were prominent figures in the Reagan administration. Their thinking and goals have not changed, and although they may represent an extreme position on the policy spectrum, it is worth bearing in mind that they are by no means isolated. There is considerable continuity of doctrine, assumptions, and actions, persisting for many years until today. Careful investigation of this very recent history should be a particularly high priority for those who hold that "global security" requires "a respected and legitimate law-enforcer," in Brzezinski's words. He is referring of course to the sole power capable of undertaking this critical role: "the idealistic new world bent on ending inhumanity" as the world's leading newspaper describes it, dedicated to "principles and values" rather than crass and narrow ends, mobilizing its reluctant allies to join it in a new epoch of moral rectitude.[11]

The concept "respected and legitimate law-enforcer" is an important one. The term "legitimate" begs the question, so we can drop it. Perhaps some question arises about the respect for law of the chosen "law-enforcer," and about its reputation outside of narrow elite circles. But such questions aside, the concept again reflects the emerging doctrine that we must discard the efforts of the past century to construct an international order in which the powerful are not free to resort to violence at will. Instead, we must institute a new principle—which is in fact a venerable principle: the self-anointed "enlightened states" will serve as global enforcers, no impolite questions asked.

The scrupulous avoidance of the events of the recent past is easy to understand, given what inquiry will quickly reveal. That includes not only the terrorist crimes of the 1980s and what came before, but also those of the 1990s, right to the present. A comparison of leading beneficiaries of U.S. military assistance and the record of state terror should shame honest people, and would, if it were not so effectively removed from the public eye. It suffices to look at the two countries that have been vying for leadership in this competition: Turkey and Colombia. As a personal aside I happened to visit both recently, including scenes of some of the worst crimes of the 1990s, adding some vivid personal experience to what is horrifying enough in the printed record. I am putting aside Israel and Egypt, a separate category.

To repeat the obvious, we basically have two choices. Either history is bunk, including current history, and we can march forward with confidence that the global enforcer will drive evil from the world much as the President's speech writers declare, plagiarizing ancient epics and children's tales. Or we can subject the doctrines of the proclaimed grand new era to scrutiny, drawing rational conclusions, perhaps gaining some sense of the emerging reality. If there is a third way, I do not see it.

The wars that are contemplated in the renewed "war on terror" are to go on for a long time. "There's no telling how many wars it will take to secure freedom in the homeland," the President announced. That's fair enough. Potential threats are virtually limitless, everywhere, even at home, as the anthrax attack illustrates. We should also be able to appreciate recent comments on the matter by the 1996–2000 head of Israel's General Security Service (Shabak), Ami Ayalon. He observed realistically that "those who want victory" against terror without addressing underlying grievances "want an unending war." He was speaking of Israel-Palestine, where the only "solution of the problem of terrorism [is] to offer an honorable solution to the Palestinians respecting their right to self-determination." So former head of Israeli military intelligence Yehoshaphat Harkabi, also a leading Arabist, observed 20 years ago, at a time when Israel still retained its immunity from retaliation from within the occupied territories to its harsh and brutal practices there.[12]

The observations generalize in obvious ways. In serious scholarship, at least, it is recognized that "Unless the social, political, and economic conditions that spawned Al Qaeda and other associated groups are addressed, the United States and its allies in Western Europe and elsewhere will continue to be targeted by Islamist terrorists."[13]

In proclaiming the right of attack against perceived potential threats, the President is once again echoing the principles of the first phase of the "war on terror." The Reagan-Shultz doctrine held that the UN Charter entitles the U.S. to resort to force in "self-defense against future attack." That interpretation of Article 51 was offered in justification of the bombing of Libya, eliciting praise from commentators who were impressed by the reliance "on a legal argument that violence against the perpetrators of repeated violence is justified as an act of self-defense"; I am quoting *New York Times* legal specialist Anthony Lewis.

The doctrine was amplified by the Bush I administration, which justified the invasion of Panama, vetoing two Security Council resolutions, on the grounds that Article 51 "provides for the use of armed force to defend a country, to defend our interests and our people," and entitles the U.S. to invade another country to prevent its "territory from being used as a base for smuggling drugs into the United States." In the light of that expansive interpretation of the Charter, it is not surprising that James Baker suggested a few days ago that Washington could now appeal to Article 51 to authorize conquest and occupation of Iraq, because Iraq may some day threaten the U.S. with WMD, or threaten others while the U.S. stands helplessly by.[14]

Quite apart from the plain meaning of the Charter, the argument offered by Baker's State Department in 1989 was not too convincing on other grounds. Operation Just Cause reinstated in power the white elite of bankers and businessmen, many suspected of narcotrafficking and money laundering, who soon lived up to their reputation; drug trafficking "may have doubled" and money laundering "flourished" in the months after the invasion, the GAO reported, while USAID found that narcotics use in Panama had gone up by 400 percent, reaching the highest level in Latin America. All without eliciting notable concern, except in Latin America, and Panama itself, where the invasion was harshly condemned.[15]

Clinton's Strategic Command also advocated "preemptive response," with nuclear weapons if deemed appropriate.[16] Clinton himself forged some new paths in implementing the doctrine, though his major contributions to international terrorism lie elsewhere.

The doctrine of preemptive strike has much earlier origins, even in words. Forty years ago Dean Acheson informed the American Society of International Law that legal issues do not arise in the case of a U.S. response to a "challenge [to its] power, position, and prestige." He was referring to Washington's response to what it regarded as Cuba's "successful defiance" of the United States. That included Cuba's resistance to the Bay of Pigs invasion, but also much more serious crimes. When Kennedy ordered his staff to subject Cubans to the "terrors of the earth" until Castro was eliminated, his planners advised that

"The very existence of his regime . . . represents a successful defiance of the U.S., a negation of our whole hemispheric policy of almost a century and a half," based on the principle of subordination to U.S. will. Worse yet, Castro's regime was providing an "example and general stimulus" that might "encourage agitation and radical change" in other parts of Latin America, where "social and economic conditions . . . invite opposition to ruling authority" and susceptibility to "the Castro idea of taking matters into one's own hands." These are grave dangers, Kennedy planners recognized, when "The distribution of land and other forms of national wealth greatly favors the propertied classes . . . [and] the poor and underprivileged, stimulated by the example of the Cuban revolution, are now demanding opportunities for a decent living." These threats were only compounded by successful resistance to invasion, an intolerable threat to credibility, warranting the "terrors of the earth" and destructive economic warfare to excise that earlier "cancer."[17]

Cuba's crimes became still more immense when it served as the instrument of Russia's crusade to dominate the world in 1975, Washington proclaimed. "If Soviet neocolonialism succeeds" in Angola, UN Ambassador Daniel Patrick Moynihan thundered, "the world will not be the same in the aftermath. Europe's oil routes will be under Soviet control as will the strategic South Atlantic, with the next target on the Kremlin's list being Brazil." Washington's fury was caused by another Cuban act of "successful defiance." When a U.S.-backed South African invasion was coming close to conquering newly independent Angola, Cuba sent troops on its own initiative, scarcely even notifying Russia, and beat back the invaders. In the major scholarly study, Piero Gleijeses observes that "Kissinger did his best to smash the one movement that represented any hope for the future of Angola," the MPLA. And though the MPLA "bears a grave responsibility for its country's plight" in later years, it was "the relentless hostility of the United States [that] forced it into an unhealthy dependence on the Soviet bloc and encouraged South Africa to launch devastating military raids in the 1980s."[18]

These further crimes of Cuba could not be forgiven; those years saw some of the worst terrorist attacks against Cuba, with no slight U.S. role. After any pretense of a Soviet threat collapsed in 1989, the U.S. tightened its stranglehold on Cuba on new pretexts, notably the alleged role in terrorism of the prime target of U.S.-based terrorism for 40 years. The level of fanaticism is illustrated by minor incidents. For example, at the present moment a visa is being withheld for a young Cuban woman artist who was offered an art fellowship, apparently because Cuba has been declared a "terrorist state" by Colin Powell's State department.[19]

It should be unnecessary to review how the "terrors of the earth" were unleashed against Cuba since 1962, "no laughing matter," Jorge Dominguez points out with considerable understatement, discussing newly released documents.[20] Of particular interest, and contemporary import, are the internal perceptions of the planners. Dominguez observes that "Only once in these nearly thousand pages of documentation did a U.S. official raise something that resembled a faint moral objection to U.S.-government sponsored terrorism": a member of the NSC staff suggested that it might lead to some Russian reaction. Furthermore, raids that are "haphazard and kill innocents . . . might mean a bad press in some friendly countries." Scholarship on terrorism rarely goes even that far.

Little new ground is broken when one has to turn to House Majority leader Dick Armey to find a voice in the mainstream questioning "an unprovoked attack against Iraq" not on grounds of cost to us, but because it "would violate international law" and "would not be consistent with what we have been or what we should be as a nation."[21]

What we or others "have been" is a separate story. Much more should be said about continuity and its institutional roots. But let's turn instead to some of the immediate questions posed by the crimes of 9/11:

(1) Who is responsible?
(2) What are the reasons?
(3) What is the proper reaction?
(4) What are the longer-term consequences?

As for (1), it was assumed, plausibly, that the guilty parties were Osama bin Laden and his Al Qaeda network. No one knows more about them than the CIA, which, together with U.S. allies, recruited radical Islamists from many countries and organized them into a military and terrorist force that Reagan anointed "the moral equivalent of the founding fathers," joining Angola's Jonas Savimbi and similar dignitaries in that Pantheon.[22] The goal was not to help Afghans resist Russian aggression, which would have been a legitimate objective, but rather normal reasons of state, with grim consequences for Afghans when the moral equivalents finally took control.

U.S. intelligence has surely been following the exploits of these networks closely ever since they assassinated President Sadat of Egypt 20 years ago, and more intensively since their failed terrorist efforts in New York in 1993. Nevertheless, despite what must be the most intensive international intelligence investigation in history, evidence about the perpetrators of 9/11 has been elusive. Eight months after the bombing, FBI director Robert Mueller could only inform a Senate Committee that U.S. intelligence now "believes" the plot was hatched in Afghanistan, though planned and implemented elsewhere. And well after the source of the anthrax attack was localized to government weapons laboratories, it has still not been identified. These are indications of how hard it may be to counter acts of terror targeting the rich and powerful in the future. Nevertheless, despite the thin evidence, the initial conclusion about 9/11 is presumably correct.

Turning to (2), scholarship is virtually unanimous in taking the terrorists at their word, which matches their deeds for the past 20 years: their goal, in their terms, is to drive the infidels from Muslim lands, to overthrow the corrupt governments they impose and sustain, and to institute an extremist version of Islam. They despise the Russians, but ceased their terrorist attacks against Russia based in Afghanistan—which were quite serious—when Russia withdrew. And "the call to wage war against America was made [when it sent] tens of thousands of its troops to the land of the two Holy Mosques over and above . . . its support of the oppressive, corrupt and tyrannical regime that is in control," so bin Laden announced well before 9/11.[23]

More significant, at least for those who hope to reduce the likelihood of further crimes of a similar nature, are the background conditions from which the terrorist organizations arose, and that provide a reservoir of sympathetic understanding for at least parts of their message, even among those who despise and fear them. In George Bush's plaintive phrase, "Why do they hate us?"

The question is wrongly put: they do not "hate *us*," but rather policies of the U.S. government, something quite different. If the question is properly formulated, however, answers to it are not hard to find. Forty-four years ago President Eisenhower and his staff discussed what he called the "campaign of hatred against us" in the Arab world, "not by the governments but by the people." The basic reason, the NSC advised, is the recognition that the U.S. supports corrupt and brutal governments and is "opposing political or economic progress," in order "to protect its interest in Near East oil." The *Wall Street Journal* and others found much the same when they investigated attitudes of wealthy Westernized Muslims after 9/11, feelings now exacerbated by U.S. policies with regard to Israel-Palestine and Iraq.[24]

These are attitudes of people who like Americans and admire much about the United States, including its freedoms. What they hate is official policies that deny them the freedoms to which they too aspire.

Many commentators prefer a more comforting answer: their anger is rooted in resentment of our freedom and democracy, their cultural failings tracing back many centuries, their inability to take part in the form of "globalization" in which the commentators happily participate, and other such deficiencies. More comforting, perhaps, but not too wise.

These issues are very much alive. Just in the past few weeks, Asia correspondent Ahmed Rashid reported that in Pakistan, "there is growing anger that U.S. support is allowing [Musharraf's] military regime to delay the promise of democracy." And a well-known Egyptian academic told the BBC that Arab and Islamic people were opposed to the U.S. because it has "supported every possible anti-democratic government in the Arab-Islamic world. . . . When we hear American officials speaking of freedom, democracy, and such values, they make terms like these sound obscene." An Egyptian writer added that "Living in a country with an atrocious human rights record that also happens to be strategically vital to U.S. interests is an illuminating lesson in moral hypocrisy and political double standards." Terrorism, he said, is "a reaction to the injustice in the region's domestic politics, inflicted in large part by the U.S." The director of the terrorism program at the Council of Foreign Relations agreed that "Backing repressive regimes like Egypt and Saudi Arabia is certainly a leading cause of anti-Americanism in the Arab world," but warned that "in both cases the likely alternatives are even nastier."

There is a long and illuminating history of the problems in supporting democratic forms while ensuring that they will lead to preferred outcomes, not just in this region. And it doesn't win many friends.[25]

What about proper reaction, question (3)? Answers are doubtless contentious, but at least the reaction should meet the most elementary moral standards: specifically, if an action is right for us, it is right for others; and if wrong for others, it is wrong for us. Those who reject that standard can be ignored in any discussion of appropriateness of action, of right or wrong. One might ask what remains of the flood of commentary on proper reaction—thoughts about "just war," for example—if this simple criterion is adopted.

Suppose we adopt the criterion, thus entering the arena of moral discourse. We can then ask, for example, how Cuba has been entitled to react after "the terrors of the earth" were unleashed against it 40 years ago. Or Nicaragua, after Washington rejected the orders of the World Court and Security Council to terminate its "unlawful use of force," choosing instead to escalate its terrorist war and issue the first official orders to its forces to attack undefended civilian "soft targets," leaving tens of thousands dead and the country ruined, perhaps beyond recovery. No one believes that Cuba or Nicaragua had the right to set off bombs in Washington or New York or to kill U.S. political leaders or send them to prison camps. And it is all too easy to add far more severe cases in those years, and others to the present.

Accordingly, those who accept elementary moral standards have some work to do to show that the U.S. and Britain were justified in bombing Afghans in order to compel them to turn over people the U.S. suspected of criminal atrocities, the official war aim announced by President Bush as the bombing began. Or that the enforcers were justified in informing Afghans that they would be bombed until they brought about "regime change," the war aim announced several weeks later, as the war was approaching its end.

The same moral standard holds of more nuanced proposals about an appropriate response to terrorist atrocities. Military historian Michael Howard advocated "a police operation conducted under the auspices of the United Nations ... against a criminal conspiracy whose members should be hunted down and brought before an international court, where they would receive a fair trial and, if found guilty, be awarded an appropriate sentence."[26] That seems reasonable, though we may ask what the reaction would be to the suggestion that the proposal be applied universally. That is unthinkable, and if the suggestion were to be made, it would elicit outrage and horror.

Similar questions arise with regard to the doctrine of "preemptive strike" against suspected threats, not new, though its bold assertion is novel. There is no doubt about the address. The standard of universality, therefore, would appear to justify Iraqi preemptive terror against the U.S. Of course, the conclusion is outlandish. The burden of proof again lies on those who advocate or tolerate the selective version that grants the right to those powerful enough to exercise it. And the burden is not light, as is always true when the threat or use of violence is advocated or tolerated.

There is, of course, an easy counter to such elementary observations: WE are good, and THEY are evil. That doctrine trumps virtually any argument. Analysis of commentary and much of scholarship reveals that its roots commonly lie in that crucial principle, which is not argued but asserted. None of this, of course, is an invention of contemporary power centers and the dominant intellectual culture, but it is, nevertheless, instructive to observe the means employed to protect the doctrine from the heretical challenge that seeks to confront it with the factual record, including such intriguing notions as "moral equivalence," "moral relativism," "anti-Americanism," and others.

One useful barrier against heresy, already mentioned, is the principle that questions about the state's resort to violence simply do not arise among sane people. That is a common refrain in the current debate over the modalities of the invasion of Iraq. To select an example at the liberal end of the spectrum, *New York Times* columnist Bill Keller remarks that "the last time America dispatched soldiers in the cause of 'regime change,' less than a year ago in Afghanistan, the opposition was mostly limited to the people who are reflexively against the American use of power," either timid supporters or "isolationists, the doctrinaire left and the soft-headed types Christopher Hitchens described as people who, 'discovering a viper in the bed of their child, would place the first call to People for the Ethical Treatment of Animals.'" To borrow the words of a noted predecessor, "We went to war, not because we wanted to, but because humanity demanded it"; President McKinley in this case, as he ordered his armies to "carry the burden, whatever it may be, in the interest of civilization, humanity, and liberty" in the Philippines.[27]

Let's ignore the fact that "regime change" was not "the cause" in Afghanistan—rather, an afterthought late in the game—and look more closely at the lunatic fringe. We have some information about them. In late September 2001, the Gallup organization surveyed international opinion on the announced U.S. bombing. The lead question was whether, "once the identity of the terrorists is known, should the American government launch a military attack on the country or countries where the terrorists are based or should the American government seek to extradite the terrorists to stand trial." As we recently learned, eight months later identity of the terrorists was only surmised, and the countries where they were based are presumed to be Germany, the UAE, and elsewhere, but let's ignore that too. The poll revealed that opinion strongly favored judicial over military action, in Europe overwhelmingly. The only exceptions were India and Israel, where Afghanistan was a surrogate for something quite different. Follow-up questions reveal that support for the military attack that was actually carried out was very slight.

Support for military action was least in Latin America, the region that has the most experience with U.S. intervention. It ranged from 2 percent in Mexico to 11 percent in Colombia and Venezuela, where 85 percent preferred extradition and trial; whether that was feasible is known only to ideologues. The sole exception was Panama, where only 80 percent preferred judicial means and 16 percent advocated military attack; and even there, correspondents recalled the death of perhaps thousands of poor people (Western crimes, therefore unexamined) in the course of Operation Just Cause, undertaken to kidnap a disobedient thug who was sentenced to life imprisonment in Florida for crimes mostly committed while he was on the CIA payroll. One respondent remarked "how much alike [the victims of 9/11] are to the boys and girls, to those who are unable to be born that December 20 [1989] that they imposed on us in Chorrillo; how much alike they seem to the mothers, the grandfathers and the little old grandmothers, all of them also innocent and anonymous deaths, whose terror was called Just Cause and the terrorist called liberator."[28]

I suspect that the director of Human Rights Watch Africa (1993–95), now a Professor of Law at Emory University, may have spoken for many others around the world when he addressed the International Council on Human Rights Policy in Geneva in January 2002, saying that "I am unable to appreciate any moral, political or legal difference between this *jihad* by the United States against those it deems to be its enemies and the *jihad* by Islamic groups against those they deem to be their enemies."[29]

What about Afghan opinion? Here information is scanty, but not entirely lacking. In late October, 2001, 1000 Afghan leaders gathered in Peshawar, some exiles, some coming from within Afghanistan, all committed to overthrowing the Taliban regime. It was "a rare display of unity among tribal elders, Islamic scholars, fractious politicians, and former guerrilla commanders," the press reported. They unanimously "urged the U.S. to stop the air raids," appealed to the international media to call for an end to the "bombing of innocent people," and "demanded an end to the U.S. bombing of Afghanistan." They urged that other means be adopted to overthrow the hated Taliban regime, a goal they believed could be achieved without further death and destruction.

A similar message was conveyed by Afghan opposition leader Abdul Haq, who was highly regarded in Washington, and received special praise as a martyr during the Loya Jirga, his memory bringing tears to the eyes of President

Hamid Karzai. Just before he entered Afghanistan, apparently without U.S. support, and was then captured and killed, he condemned the bombing and criticized the U.S. for refusing to support efforts of his and of others "to create a revolt within the Taliban." The bombing was "a big setback for these efforts," he said, outlining his efforts and calling on the U.S. to assist them with funding and other support instead of undermining them with bombs. The U.S., he said, "is trying to show its muscle, score a victory, and scare everyone in the world. They don't care about the suffering of the Afghans or how many people we will lose." The prominent women's organization RAWA, which received some belated recognition in the course of the war, also bitterly condemned the bombing.

In short, the lunatic fringe of "soft-headed types who are reflexively against the American use of power" was not insubstantial as the bombing was undertaken and proceeded. But since virtually no word of any of this was published in the U.S., we can continue to comfort ourselves that "humanity demanded" the bombing.[30]

There is, obviously, a great deal more to say about all of these topics, but let us turn briefly to question (4).

In the longer term, I suspect that the crimes of 9/11 will accelerate tendencies that were already underway: the Bush doctrine on preemption is an illustration. As was predicted at once, governments throughout the world seized upon 9/11 as a "window of opportunity" to institute or escalate harsh and repressive programs. Russia eagerly joined the "coalition against terror," expecting to receive tacit authorization for its shocking atrocities in Chechnya, and was not disappointed. China happily joined for similar reasons. Turkey was the first country to offer troops for the new phase of the U.S. "war on terror," in gratitude, as the Prime Minister explained, for the U.S. contribution to Turkey's campaign against its miserably repressed Kurdish population, waged with extreme savagery and relying crucially on a huge flow of U.S. arms, peaking in 1997; in that single year arms transfers exceeded the entire postwar period combined up to the onset of the counterinsurgency campaign. Turkey is highly praised for these achievements and was rewarded by a grant of authority to protect Kabul from terror, funded by the same superpower that provided the means for its recent acts of state terror, including some of the major atrocities of the grisly 1990s. Israel recognized that it would be able to crush Palestinians even more brutally, with even firmer U.S. support. And so on throughout much of the world.

Many governments, including the U.S., instituted measures to discipline the domestic population and to carry forward unpopular measures under the guise of "combating terror," exploiting the atmosphere of fear and the demand for "patriotism"—which in practice means: "You shut up and I'll pursue my own agenda relentlessly." The Bush administration used the opportunity to advance its assault against most of the population, and future generations, serving the narrow corporate interests that dominate the administration to an extent even beyond the norm.

One major outcome is that the U.S., for the first time, has major military bases in Central Asia. These help to position U.S. corporate interests favorably in the current "great game" to control the resources of the region, but also to complete the encirclement of the world's major energy resources, in the Gulf region. The U.S. base system targeting the Gulf extends from the Pacific to the Azores, but the closest reliable base before the Afghan war was Diego Garcia. Now that situation is much improved, and forceful intervention should be facilitated.

The Bush administration also exploited the new phase of the "war on terror" to expand its overwhelming military advantages over the rest of the world, and to move on to other methods to ensure global dominance. Government thinking was clarified by high officials when Crown Prince Abdullah of Saudi Arabia visited the U.S. in April to urge the administration to pay more attention to the reaction in the Arab world to its strong support for Israeli terror and repression. He was told, in effect, that the U.S. did not care what he or other Arabs think. A high official explained that "if he thought we were strong in Desert Storm, we're ten times as strong today. This was to give him some idea what Afghanistan demonstrated about our capabilities." A senior defense analyst gave a simple gloss: others will "respect us for our toughness and won't mess with us."[31] That stand has many precedents too, but in the post-9/11 world it gains new force.

It is reasonable to speculate that such consequences were one goal of the bombing of Afghanistan: to warn the world of what the "legitimate enforcer" can do if someone steps out of line. The bombing of Serbia was undertaken for similar reasons: to "ensure NATO's credibility," as Blair and Clinton explained—not referring to the credibility of Norway or Italy. That is a common theme of statecraft. And with some reason, as history amply reveals.

Without continuing, the basic issues of international society seem to me to remain much as they were, but 9/11 surely has induced changes, in some cases, with significant and not very attractive implications.

Notes

1. Strobe Talbott and Nayan Chanda, eds., *The Age of Terror.* The editors write that with the anthrax attacks, which they attribute to bin Laden, "anxiety became a certainty."
2. Study cited by Charles Glaser and Steve Fetter, "National Missile Defense and the Future of U.S. Nuclear Weapons Policy," *International Security* 26.1, Summer 2001. Richard Falkenrath, Robert Newman, Bradley Thayer, *America's Achilles Heel: Nuclear, Biological and Chemical Terrorism and Covert Attack* (Cambridge, MA: MIT Press, 1998). Barton Gellman, *Washington Post,* Dec. 20, 2001.
3. Joseph Nevins, "First the Butchery, Then the Flowers: Clinton and Holbrooke in East Timor," *Counterpunch* May 16–31, 2002. On the background, see Richard Tanter, Mark Selden, and Stephen Shalom, eds., *Bitter Flowers, Sweet Flowers: East Timor, Indonesia, and the World Community* (Rowman & Littlefield, 2001); Chomsky, *A New Generation Draws the Line* (Verso, 2001).
4. Hans Morgenthau, *The Purpose of American Politics* (New York: Vintage, 1964); Andrew Bacevich, "Different Drummers, Same Drum," *National Interest,* Summer 2001. Greatly to

his credit, Morgenthau took the highly unusual step of abandoning this conventional stance, forcefully, in the early days of the Vietnam War.

5. Wilson, "Democracy and Efficiency," *Atlantic Monthly*, 1901, cited by Ido Oren, *Our Enemies and Us: America's Rivalries and the Making of Political Science* (Ithaca, NY: Cornell University Press, 2002). For some discussion of Mill's classic essay on intervention, see my *Peering Into the Abyss of the Future* (Delhi: Institute of Social Sciences, 2002, Fifth Lakdawala Memorial Lecture).

6. For further detail on the first phase of the "war on terror," and sources here and below, see Alexander George, ed., *Western State Terrorism* (Polity-Blackwell, 1991), and sources cited.

7. David Rapoport, *Current History, America at War*, Dec. 2001.

8. 1999, cited by Adam Isacson and Joy Olson, *Just the Facts* (Washington, D.C.: Latin America Working Group and Center for International Policy, 1999), ix.

9. See *Current History*, op. cit.

10. 1980–88 record, see "Inter-Agency Task Force, Africa Recovery Program/Economic Commission, *South African Destabilization: the Economic Cost of Frontline Resistance to Apartheid* (New York: UN, 1989), 13, cited by Merle Bowen, *Fletcher Forum*, Winter 1991. *Children on the Front Line* (UNICEF 1989). ANC, Joseba Zulaika and William Douglass, *Terror and Taboo* (New York, London: Routledge, 1996), 12. On expansion of U.S. trade with South Africa after Congress authorized sanctions in 1985 (overriding Reagan's veto), see Gay McDougall, Richard Knight, in Robert Edgar, ed., *Sanctioning Apartheid* (Trenton, NJ: Africa World Press, 1990).

11. Zbigniew Brzezinski, *Guardian Weekly*, Aug. 22–28, 2002. Michael Wines, *New York Times*, June 13, 1999.

12. Bush, Anthony Shadid, *Boston Globe*, Aug. 6, 2002. Ami Ayalon, director of Shabak 1996–2000, interview, *Le Monde*, Dec. 22, 2001; reprinted in Roane Carey and Jonathan Shanin, *The Other Israel* (New Press, 2002). Harkabi, cited by Israeli journalist Amnon Kapeliouk, *Le Monde diplomatique*, Feb. 1986.

13. Sumit Ganguly, *Current History*, op. cit.

14. James Baker, op-ed, *New York Times*, Aug. 25, 2002. On Panama, see my *Deterring Democracy* (Verso, 1991; Hill & Wang, 1992, extended edition), chaps. 4, 5.

15. Ibid., and my *Year 501* (South End, 1993), ch. 3.

16. STRATCOM, "Essentials of Post-Cold War Deterrence," 1995, partially declassified. For quotes and sources, see my *New Military Humanism* (Common Courage, 1999), ch. 6.

17. Acheson, see Ibid., ch. 7. Piero Gleijeses, *Conflicting Missions: Havana, Washington, and Africa, 1959–1976* (U. of North Carolina, 2002; my *Profit over People* (Seven Stories, 1999). Gleijeses writes that JFK asked his brother Robert "to lead the top-level interagency group that oversaw Operation Mongoose, a program of paramilitary operations, economic warfare, and sabotage he launched in late 1961 to visit the 'terrors of the earth' on Fidel Castro and more prosaically, to topple him." The quoted phrase is Arthur Schlesinger's, referring to the goals of Robert Kennedy, for whom the international terrorist operations were "top priority," the declassified record reveals, stopping short only of direct "military invasion." Schlesinger, *Robert Kennedy and His Times* (New York: Ballantine Books, 1978).

18. Gleijeses, op. cit.

19. Alix Ritchie, *Provincetown Banner*, Aug. 29, 2002.

20. "The @@@@#$%& Missile Crisis," *Diplomatic History* 24.2, Spring 2000.

21. Eric Schmitt, *New York Times*, Aug. 9, 2002.

22. Reagan, cited by Samina Amin, *International Security* 26.5, Winter 2001/2. Savimbi was "one of the few authentic heroes of our times," Jeane Kirkpatrick declared at a Conservative Political Action convention where he "received enthusiastic applause after vowing to attack American oil installations in his country." Colin Nickerson, *Boston Globe*, Feb. 3, 1986.

23. Walter Pincus, "The 9-11 masterminds may have been in Afghanistan," *Washington Post Weekly*, June 10–16. Bin Laden, May 1998 interview. PBS *Frontline*, September 13, 2001. Cited by Gilbert Achcar, *The Clash of Barbarisms* (New York: Monthly Review Press, 2002).

24. For sources and background discussion, see my *World Orders Old and New*, 79, 201f.; *9–11* (Seven Stories, 2001).

25. Rashid, *Far Eastern Economic Review*, Aug. 1, 2002. AUC professor El-Lozy, writer Azizuddin El-Kaissouni, and Warren Bass of the CFR, quoted by Joyce Koh, "'Two-faced' U.S. policy blamed for Arab hatred," *Straits Times* (Singapore), Aug. 14, 2002.

26. *Foreign Affairs*, Jan/Feb 2002; talk of Oct. 30, 2001 (Tania Branigan, *San Francisco Bay Guardian*, Oct. 31).

27. Keller, op-ed, *New York Times*, Aug. 24, 2002. McKinley and many others, see Louis A. Pérez, *The War of 1898* (U. of North Carolina, 1998).

28. Ricardo Stevens, Oct. 19; cited in *NACLA Report on the Americas* XXXV. 3, Nov.–Dec. 2001.

29. Abdullahi Ahmed An-Na'im, "Upholding International Legality Against Islamic and American Jihad," in Ken Booth and Tim Dunne, eds., *Worlds in Collision: Terror and the Future of Global Order* (Palgrave, 2002).

30. A media review by Jeff Nygaard found one reference to the Gallup poll, a brief notice in the *Omaha World-Herald* that "completely misrepresented the findings." *Nygaard Notes Independent Weekly News and Analysis*, Nov. 16, 2001, reprinted in *Counterpoise* 5.3/4. Karzai on Abdul Haq, Elizabeth Rubin, *New Republic*, July 8, 2002. Abdul Haq, interview with Anatol Lieven, *San Francisco Bay Guardian*, Nov. 2, 2001. Peshawar gathering, Barry Bearak, *New York Times*, Oct. 25; John Thornhill and Farhan Bokhari, *Financial Times*, Oct. 25, Oct. 26; John Burns, *New York Times*, Oct. 26; Indira Laskhmanan, *San Francisco Bay Guardian*, Oct. 25, 26, 2001. RAWA, web site. The information was available throughout in independent ("alternative") journals, published and electronic, including Znet, www.zmag.org

31. Patrick Tyler, *New York Times*, April 25, 2002; John Donnelly, *Boston Globe*, April 28, 2002.

CHAPTER 7

The Dialectics of Terrorism[1]

PETER McLAREN

The law that authorizes torture is a law that says: "Men, resist pain; and if nature has created in you an inextinguishable self-love, if it has granted you an inalienable right of self-defence, I create in you an altogether contrary sentiment: a heroic hatred of yourselves; and I command you to accuse yourselves, to speak the truth even while muscles are being lacerated and bones disjointed."[2]

We have entered a reality-zone already captured by its opposite: unreality. It is a world where nobody really wanted to venture. It is a world where order has given way to disorder, where reason has given way to unreason, where reality is compromised by truth, where guilt is presumed over innocence, where the once noble search for explanations has been replaced by a dizzying vortex of plastic flags, stars and stripes rhinestone belts, coffee klatch war strategists, Sunday barbecue patrioteering, militant denunciations of war protestors, a generalized fear of whatever lies ahead, xenophobic hostility, and point-blank outrage. Soccer moms in SUVs festooned with images of Old Glory park in dimly-lit alleys and then slink into the local sex shop in search of red, white, and blue thongs for couch potato husbands strangely rejuvenated by daily doses of carnage, courtesy of CNN. Public school teachers across the country eagerly prepare new courses on the glory of Western civilization, elevating the United States to its shining pinnacle. Politicians in the imperial heartland sport American flag lapel pins and compete in advancing the toughest plans for purging domestic political dissent. Hollywood producers hunker down in their studios and plan new Rambo films. Retired generals shine in their new roles as political consultants to the Empire, pronouncing the battle scenes in Afghanistan as invariably 'fluid,' which is a giveaway that they don't know much more than their interviewers, and probably less. Ads for Raditect, "the first affordable radiation detector for your home, car, or office," air on television, boasting of the device's ability to warn homeland families of radiation "long before it's on the news." It costs $149 and we can learn more about it at the Web site www.homelandprotection.net. Scandal-plagued Fifth Amendment capitalists appear in court as defendants, in an ironic reversal of the Fifth Amendment Communists of the McCarthy era. Former Secretary of Education under Bush *padre*, William Bennett, has penned the jeremiad, *Why We*

Fight,[3] charging postmodernized multiculturalists who hawk ethical relativism with being prime enemies of the homeland.

Signalling the fact that Rudyard Kipling's colonial worldview is now in vogue, Max Boot, the *Wall Street Journal's* editorial-features editor, pens *The Savage Wars of Peace*, both a homage to The Great White Father of the American Homeland and a triumphalist assertion that the civilizing mission of the United States must necessarily involve bloody attacks on lands less civilized, for their own good.[4] Harvard Law School Professor Alan Dershowitz basks in the national limelight again, this time advocating the use of "torture warrants" in specified circumstances when the issue of "time" is crucial. Their reason paralyzed by fear and replaced by the logic of mob fury, American citizens eagerly give up their right of habeus corpus for government assurances that terrorists will be tracked down and killed, or if they are captured, for assurances that they will be tried by secret tribunal, and then killed.

The U.S. government proposes a plan to recruit one million domestic spies (euphemistically known as "tipsters") to report any suspicious behavior in our cities, towns, and neighborhoods, not unlike operations once put in place by Joseph Stalin, behind the rust-splotched Iron Curtain. The Bush administration is seeking support for invading Iraq, which it argues has defied international law, while overlooking the fact that "since Bush came into office, the United States government has torn up more international treaties and disregarded more UN conventions than the rest of the world has in 20 years."[5] Once the war on terror was in full throttle, some doyens of the establishment right must have been so thrilled at the prospect of limitless political and military opportunity that they were driven mad, especially after the consent of the public was secured, federal dragnets for rounding up suspicious Arabs were launched across the nation, wiretapping without warrants was put into effect, efforts were made to destabilize the UN convention against torture (in order to keep foreign observers out of the Guantanamo Bay prison camp),[6] and a move to reverse a decades-old ban on government assassination signed by Gerald Ford in 1976 was floated by the Bush administration through Congress so that now the U.S. government "has permitted CIA hit squads to recommence covert operations of the kind that included, in the past, the assassination of foreign heads of state."[7] I can imagine Henry Kissinger in his living room, wickedly brandishing a Clockwork Orange codpiece emblazoned with stars and stripes, and dancing La Macarena in Imelda Marcos's ruby slippers.

The world has been transformed into pure intensity where to seek refuge in the sanctuary of reflection is to engage in an act of unpardonable treason. Where previously silenced realities are now guaranteed never to be heard. Where America is above the law and proud of it. Where a "declaration of war in the name of peace, civilization, and freedom"[8] goes undebated and relatively uncontested. Where America Firsters can celebrate the U.S. attempt to block a new international protocol on torture, where they can champion the recent

Farm Bill that will help U.S. farmers but drive millions of small farmers world-wide into destitution, where they can remain determined to keep America "free of entangling treaties and obligations" and encourage America to "wield its big stick and big wallet abroad because its national interests now span the globe and because the culture war against the Judeo-Christian city on the hill has gone global."[9] Where amidst a recrudescence of jingoistic fervor, the like of which has not been seen since World War II, America can exercise "power unconstrained by laws or norms" and play the role of the "self-deputized enforcer, the final arbiter of good and bad, the Lone Ranger."[10] Where our Commander-in-Chief (or Commander-in-Thief, if we wish to recall how he was "selected" for office) encourages his boys to "smoke 'em out of their caves, to get 'em runnin' so we can get 'em" in order that we can ultimately "save the world from freedom."[11] Where the Emperor of the Free World can hypocritically assert that Palestine will be recognized by the United States only when it has a constitution, while ignoring the fact that Israel itself does not have a written constitution.[12] Where the United States "is now requiring all states to restructure their coercive approaches to fit America's strategic concerns."[13] Where the relatives of those who died in the Twin Towers who refuse to be bought off by a government cash settlement from the Compensation Fund and who, by means of tort lawsuits, seek redress for government and airline company negligence for failing to prevent the attacks, are threatened by government lawyers with lean and hungry looks. Where these legal dobermans of the Bush White House, fearful of further disclosures about how much the government knew about the attacks, seek to limit the scope of discovery and deny the claimants their right to due process and a fair hearing of their legal claims behind the banner of "national security concerns."[14] Where the State Department flagrantly casts aside human rights in favor of strengthening its war on terrorism, this time moving to block a lawsuit by Indonesian villagers (and filed by the International Labor Rights Fund) against Exxon Mobil Corporation that accuses the company of turning a blind eye to the murder, torture, kidnapping, and rape by military guards at Exxon Mobil's gas field in Aceh, Indonesia.[15] Where the Bush administration tries desperately to justify going to war against Iraq by claiming that one of the September 11 hijackers has connections to that country (despite the absence of any CIA or FBI evidence), while in the same breath condemning a Pentagon briefing that accuses Saudi Arabia (where the U.S. has been protecting a ruthless monarchy for over half a century for the sake of U.S. oil interests) of supporting terrorism and attacking U.S. allies.[16] It is truly a world turned, in the words of Eduardo Galeano, "upside down." It is a looking-glass world that "rewards in reverse: it scorns honesty, punishes work, prizes lack of scruples, and feeds cannibalism. Its professors slander nature: injustice, they say, is a law of nature."[17] Within this looking-glass world, that world that exists upside-down, there exists the "looking-glass school" that "teaches us to suffer reality, not to change it; to forget the past, not learn from it; to accept the future, not invent it. In its halls of criminal learning, impotence, amnesia, and resignation are required courses."[18]

As the United States reorganizes itself in a double perspective of praising trade liberalization as the path to freedom while repressing its own popular movements, a disquieting incongruence arises between democracy and freedom. The U.S. as the global steward of benevolence has dropped its mask of civil comity to reveal its spectral Dorian Gray smile. Although the Office of Strategic Security—modelled after Reagan's infamous Office of Public Diplomacy that planted propaganda stories about the Contras in major U.S. media outlets in order to provide misinformation to foreign media organizations— has been shut down, Otto Reich and John Negroponte still lurk in the murky shadows of White House policy. Concerns have surfaced surrounding recent pronouncements from the Bush administration that similar powers given by Ronald Reagan to the Federal Emergency Management Agency (FEMA) with respect to internal dissent in the face of national opposition to a U.S. military invasion abroad (Reagan was considering an invasion of Nicaragua at the time) might be exercised by the Bush administration should there be sufficient opposition to the U.S. plan to invade Iraq. While Reagan's national plan was never fully disclosed, we know from information made public during the Iran-Contra scandal that Oliver North helped FEMA to draft a plan that, on Reagan's executive orders, provided for a suspension of the constitution, internment camps, and the turning over of the government to the president and FEMA. The plan was found to be similar to the one that FEMA director Louis Guiffrida had drafted earlier to combat "a national uprising by black militants" and which provided for the detention "of at least 21 million American Negroes" in "assembly centers or relocation camps."[19] Louis Guiffrida's deputy, John Brinkerhoff, who handled the martial law portion of the planning for FEMA under Reagan and is now with the Anser Institute for Homeland Security, has recently argued for the legality of deploying U.S. military troops on American streets—a position that challenges the Posse Comitatus Act of 1878. Tom Ridge, Director of Homeland Security, insists on a review of U.S. law regarding the use of the military for law enforcement duties. Already in place is the Northern Command to aid Homeland defense, created by the U.S. military.[20] The current retreat of civil liberties is understood not as something imposed by the Bush-Cheney-Rice-Rumsfeld junta, that has rehired many of the participants in the Iran-Contra scandal of Reagan and Bush *padre*, but as something "natural" like the self-regulation of the stock market. Henry Weinstein, Daren Briscoe, and Mitchell Landberg of the *Los Angeles Times* explain it to the public this way:

> American civil liberties are as fixed and steady an influence in national life as the stock market—and every bit as elastic. Like the market, the rights enjoyed by U.S. citizens have grown to an extent that the Founding Fathers probably never

imagined. But in times of danger, civil liberties have shrunk, suffering what market analysts call a correction.[21]

Using the same market logic, our forty-third president, George Bush *hijo*, is looking towards more deregulated, technology-driven wars (that is, employing "adaptive" nuclear capabilities, bunker-busting mini-nukes, and nuclear weapons that reduce "collateral damage") to ensure U.S. geopolitical dominance, so the country can feel secure enough to reverse the "contractions" in civil rights investment that occurred before September 11 and bounce back from our current civil rights recession. But the problem is not simply one of reselling the legacy of Martin Luther King in the language of a brokerage firm, but to pose the question: In an era defined as one of perpetual danger, as one of perpetual war, will we ever regain the rights that we have lost? Will a "hitting first" policy of preemption ever enable the U.S. to assume the moral high ground?

We can now put aside our *fin-de-siècle* existential anxieties about individual mortality and financial worries about stock market investments and lose ourselves in the sheer adrenaline rush of watching the daily carnage that only a new war can bring. As families across the country break out their beer and barbecue chips and sit enthralled in front of their television sets watching bombs drop, rockets fire, and buildings explode, approvingly nodding their heads when the newscaster details (with the aid of computerized illustrations) how the BLU-82 "daisy cutter" bomb incinerates everything in its path while sucking up all the oxygen so that nothing survives its wrath, thousands of Afghan refugees die from hunger, freezing weather, and "collateral damage." Following the war coverage on Fox television feeds the national appetite for death; it's packaged like a 24-hour infomercial produced by the U.S. Army, where images of death and destruction are accompanied by voice-over editorials that legitimize them as the regrettable but necessary price of freedom. And it's not as though our unqualified enthusiasm, rapt attention, and untempered bloodlust go unrewarded. We are generously repaid, for instance, with technical knowledge to which the media is so gracefully attuned. We learn that ordinances the U.S. is dropping on front-line troops defending the poorest country in the world are the size of Volkswagen beetles—even bigger than those deployed by our most famous ex-Gulf War veteran, Holy Ghost warrior, and domestic militia movement patriot:

> The BLU-82 combines a watery mixture of ammonium nitrate and aluminum with air, then ignites the mist for an explosion that incinerates everything up to 600 yards away. The BLU-82 uses about six times the amount of ammonium nitrate that Timothy McVeigh used in the bomb that blew up the Oklahoma City federal building in 1995.[22]

Imagine the limitless opportunities now available for high school science teachers to capture the interest of their freshmen chemistry students. While publishers in Alabama are stamping 40,000 biology textbooks with warning stickers, reminding students that evolution is a controversial theory they should question, and while Bush *hijo* pushes for faith-based programs (which he calls "armies of compassion") to provide social services, and for tax breaks and other benefits for religious charities that would entitle them to be recipients of billions of dollars of government funding, and while Christian talk show hosts prone to lachrymose sermons on the goodness of America continue to bless the war on terrorism "in Jesus' name," one realizes that the U.S. today functions as a covert theocracy.

Those disappointed that the apocalypse was not ushered in at the millennium's end are making up for it in their razor-edged celebration of the war on terror. History has been split down the middle as if it had been sliced by a Taliban cane soaked in water. On the one side, "modernity" houses the transnational ruling class, whose dreams remain unbounded, rewinding time. On the other side, the transnational working class takes refuge in modernity's refuse heap of time unravelled and dreams dehydrated. Understanding how this mighty division has been prepared by capital is the skeleton key that unlocks the bone yard of reason where truth can be found amidst the charred ruins of civilizations past and those yet to come. Once the needs of the ruling class are satisfied, the appetite for other "wants" increases dramatically such that what was once considered excess is now taken for granted and what was once a plaintive longing becomes a fanatical quest.

The specter of world cataclysm is perilously close; it is hiding in the back alley behind Macy's; in the offices of software programmers in Silicon Valley and Bombay; in the Art Deco Reading Room at Claridge's and the bar at George's; in the corporate boardrooms of the international banks; in the factories of Prague; in the Parisian cafes of the Latin Quarter; in the French Quarter of New Orleans; in the *maquiladoras* of Juarez and Mexicali; in the bankrupt offices of Enron; in the shredding rooms of WorldCom; in the shipyards of Gdansk; in the Sky Bar on Sunset Boulevard; in St. Peter's Square; and in the ragged tufts of bin Laden's beard. Here the contradiction we face vastly exceeds the simple choice "between mullahs and the mall, between the hegemony of religious absolutism and the hegemony of market determinism."[23] After all, capitalism is irretrievably contradictory in its own self-constitution, predicated upon a failure to realize its truth in practice. It is a constitutive impossibility for capitalism to create equal access to education, to feed and clothe the poor, and to provide medical assistance to those who are ill. Denys Turner remarks that "Capitalism has to live its own morality ideologically, that is to say, it can sustain its moral convictions only as a way of recognizing the fact that it installs the very conditions under which those convictions are unrealizable. It cannot abandon the moral language it cannot live."[24] In this era of casino capitalism, the house always wins.

Developed and underdeveloped population groups occupying contradictory and unstable locations in a transnational environment, coupled with cultural and religious antagonisms among the capitalist actors, create conditions of desperation and anger among the oppressed, most of them from developing countries. Marable warns: "The question, 'Why Do They Hate Us?' can only be answered from the vantage point of the Third World's widespread poverty, hunger and economic exploitation."[25] The U.S. share of global industrial production is at about 28 percent, while the country accounts for only 4.5 percent of the world population. It continues to be the world's biggest exporter and importer. The U.S. pushes free trade worldwide, not to improve the world's standard of living, but to reap the benefits of unequal exchange, allowing stronger capitalists to appropriate surplus value from weaker parties in the trade and to favor imperialist monopolies by facilitating the cheapening of labor internationally, ensuring debt repayment, asserting intellectual property rights, regulating worldwide production, breaking down remaining barriers to speculation and capital mobility, perpetuating import quotas, restrictions, and export subsidies, and extending the ability of the U.S. to wage war to protect its industrial base.[26]

Most of the populations in Latin America, the Middle East, and Central Asia are poorer today than at the end of the Cold War. The incomes of most Africans are no higher today than they were nearly a half-century ago.[27]

We have entered a world where any linkage between democracy and justice has been irreparably fractured. The Manifest Destiny inscribed in the 1823 Monroe Doctrine and the Truman Doctrine of U.S. interventionism and containment that pushed the view that "the whole world should adopt the American system"[28] find resonance in the Project for the New American Century. An alliance of social and religious conservatives, political neoconservatives, and militarists (including many who were members of the Bush *padre* administration), boasting the likes of Dick Cheney, Donald Rumsfeld, Paul Wolfowitz, Jeb Bush, and William Bennett, the Project for the New American Century aggressively propagandizes its vision of U.S. geopolitical world dominance and unipolar world supremacy and a grim determination to prevent the emergence of any rival superpower.[29] In such a view, the U.S. becomes a raging colonial macrophage, engulfing and consuming all that is foreign.

Of course the U.S. is fully aware of the consequences that will follow the unfettered free trade it so ardently seeks. For instance, in 1999 the National Intelligence Council released an unclassified study on the consequences of globalization that predicted a number of scenarios, including competition among economic blocs located in Europe, Asia, and the Americas; the success of global elites in advanced capitalist nations and continued misery of the majority of the world's population; forced migration; global polarization. The report anticipates dim economic prospects for Eurasia and the Middle East where "populations will be significantly larger, poorer, more urban, and more disillusioned."[30] The U.S. knows that the growing exports from Mexico and the Caribbean basin based on raw materials and cheap labor will lead irrevocably to a "developmental blind alley."[31] The predictions have largely been borne out, with Argentina "enduring the worst peacetime economic crash in history"[32] and with the unregulated juggernaut of market forces "sweeping away many of the gains of job security and a welfare state achieved by 50 years of state-led development."[33]

Like someone raised on but still challenged by checkers, Bush *hijo* is playing a manic endgame on the "global chessboard," and entering the pit of political insanity, by unilaterally maneuvering to control Eurasia's oil reserves,[34] and those of Colombia and West Africa.[35] The events in the U.S. since September 11 despairingly record not only what John Powers calls the "Trumanizing of George W. Bush"[36] but also the remorseless widening of powers by hardliners, revanchists, and hawks over the average citizen, following a constitutional coup d'etat in the form of the USA Patriot Act. Regrettably, the "vestigial spine"[37] developed by the Democrats has done little to stem the tide of political reaction. Bush *hijo* stands under cover of popular political support that is as sturdy as an Augustan arch, even after his business betrothal to "Kenny Boy" came to an embarrassingly abrupt end in the shredding room. His dyslexic comments and bogus sincerity have been shielded from the American public by media punditeers that serve as little more than quislings for the Republican Party, solemnly carrying out their patriotic duty. His gee-whiz-I'm-just-folks bipartisan style has become cruelly calcified in tandem with the autocratic character that his presidency has now assumed. His Enronesque ideology of loathing the little guys who should be squeezed like wet rag dolls if it will wring more profits from their labor-power has permeated the White House. John Powers writes:

> Nobody wants to say it during wartime, but the cozy yet ruthless Texas business culture that produced Enron also produce our president. Bush takes pride in working like a CEO, and if you study his behavior, you find him duplicating, almost exactly, the culture of Enron. He displays the same obsession with loyalty (his number one virtue), the same habit of dishonest, short-term accounting (think of his lies about those tax cuts), the same blithe disregard for ordinary workers (his post-September 11 economic proposals all aimed at helping corporations) and the same pitiless certainty he's on the side of the free-market angels.[38]

The smooth-shaven smile of the impish fraternity brother has given way to the permanent jaw-jutting sneer of the dictator. Bush's increasingly Nixon-like penchant for secrecy and his attempt to keep his and his father's presidential papers from public scrutiny (not to mention his own dealings with Harken) and create drumbeat courts vitiate the very notion of the "open society" he was wont to celebrate before the unforgiving and unforgivable events of September 11. His aw-shucks dyslexic humor and light-minded reveries have given way to imperial declarations of war against all those who oppose his definition of civilization (that is, whatever economic, legal, foreign or domestic policies the U.S. chooses to undertake). As Donald Freed remarked, "He [Bush] looks taller when you are on your knees."[39] What was once thought to be Bush's political autism when it came to foreign policy has now been reevaluated as political psychosis. As Bernard Weiner notes, "The Bush administration is like an Enron alumni reunion, with officials in charge of investigating Enron formerly working for Enron."[40]

We live in a world where it is safer to engage in rehearsed reactions to what we encounter on our television screens; dissent has now acquired a ham-fisted, police state translation that equates it with terrorism. It is safer to react in ways that newscaster/entertainers big on acrimonious scapegoating and short on analysis define for the American public as patriotic: applaud all actions by governmental authorities. CNN has already declared that it is "perverse" to focus on civilian suffering (some reports have already placed the number of civilian Afghan casualties from U.S. bombing raids at 3,500), exercising a racist arithmetic that deems such casualties in the U.S. to be more important than those of Afghan civilian dead. Death and destruction have become as faceless as a smoldering turban on the side of a dirt road.

Those stubborn enough to break away from the media's unvarnished boosterism and frequent mendacity regarding its coverage of the war on terrorism, and who insist on understanding world events in the context of September 11, are implored to submit to explanations provided by carefully chosen "experts" hired by the corporate media, if for nothing else than fear of public humiliation via media-speak, author Susan Sontag and talk-show host Bill Maher being two prominent examples of those so humiliated, although in the case of Maher we have the insight of a *New Times* reader that "Maher isn't Voltaire at the court of the Sun King; he's a corporate lackey who forgot what he did for a living."[41] It is a world best left to television journalist experts to figure out.

Gilbert Achar asks what the reaction around the world might have been if the targets of the terrorist attacks on September 11 had been the two giant Petrona Towers in Kuala Lumpur.[42] He raises the issue of why there wasn't similar worldwide outrage and compassion when the Russians bombed Chechnya, reducing it to "the equivalent of 'Ground Zero'"?[43] Archar asserts that the reason why not only Americans were shocked and moved by the terrorist attacks but also why the rest of the world was so outraged was because the U.S. exercises "absolute hegemony over the media universe of fiction and information" and this results "in a strong tendency for consumers of images the world over to identify with U.S. citizens."[44] He writes that "the intensity of emotion is directly proportional to the proximity of the scene of the crime to the nerve center of the world system and the privileged state of global spectacle."[45] Achar refers to the intensity of emotions elicited worldwide by the destruction of Manhattan's Twin Towers as a result of "narcissistic compassion" by which he means

> A form of compassion evoked much more by calamities striking "people like us," much less by calamities affecting people unlike us. The fate of New Yorkers (in this case) elicits far more of it than the fate of Iraqis or Rwandans ever could, to say nothing of Afghans. Located at the very heart of the premier metropolis of capitalist cosmopolitanism, the towers of the World Trade Center constituted in a certain sense the totem poles of the globalized category of adepts of the "cosmopolitan bourgeois way of life"—a category that massively felt hurt at their destruction.[46]

Achar remarks that the uniqueness of narcissistic compassion displayed by Western elites can be demonstrated by the fact that they "camouflage it as an oceanic humanism indifferent to skin color or religion" when, in fact, it is "nothing more than a masked expression of their own ethnocentrism."[47] He points out that these same elites did not decree a European-wide day of mourning for the 7,000 people massacred in Srebrenica, or the hundreds of thousands of people massacred in Rwanda. Perhaps there should be a day of mourning for those killed by the U.S.-imposed "sanctions of mass destruction" in Iraq and elsewhere which have been reported to have caused more deaths than all the weapons of mass destruction (nuclear, chemical, and biological) used throughout the course of human history (not including the Nazi gas chambers).[48]

A primary ideological vehicle of American empire is Fox News. Owned by Rupert Murdoch, it is rapidly gaining a wide and committed audience on the basis of its appeal to right-wing male viewers, transforming the airwaves into a citadel of paranoia where homeland citizens live in eternal dread, fearful that Al Qaeda might be living next door. Its political catechism spiked with testosterone and rage, Fox News provides hot-air ballast to the logic of transnational capitalism and U.S. militarism. James Wolcott aptly describes this gang as the "Viagra posse":

> Relatively subdued in the first weeks after September 11, Chris Matthews, Geraldo Rivera, and the Viagra posse of Fox News refilled their gasbags and began taking turns on Mussolini's balcony to exhort the mob, their frog glands swelling like Dizzy Gillespie's cheeks. Agitating for the insertion of ground troops, hothead hosts and like-minded guests (many of them retired military officers now getting a chance to coach from the sidelines) scoffed at the overreliance on airpower before doing a nimble backflip and complaining that we weren't bombing enough, or in the right spots. Frustrated, indignant, and irate over the patty-cake pace of the Afghan campaign (talk shows serve strong coffee in the greenrooms), these masters of Stratego escalated their rhetorical heat as if hoping the bombing campaign would follow their lead, sounding riled enough to storm the fighter cockpit and get the job done themselves if these gutless wonders wouldn't.[49]

Fox television's chief "no spin" windbag, commentator Bill O'Reilly—his mind rarely burdened by dialectical thoughts—berates with autocratic homilies those few guests he invites on his show who dare offer an explanation for the events of September 11. The majesty of O'Reilly's self-regard is propped up by a stubborn conviction that unsupported opinions presented in mean-spirited fashion are preferable to complex analysis. Proud of his simple patriotic (that is, warmongering) advice to kill "the enemy" because the enemy is evil, he admonishes anyone offering critical analysis as sanctioning evil and comforting homeland enemies. On a September 17 segment of his show, *O'Reilly Factor*, "no-spin" host Bill put forth a plan for action in case the Taliban did not hand over bin Laden:

> If they don't, the U.S. should bomb the Afghan infrastructure to rubble—the airport, the power plants, their water facilities and the roads. This is a very primitive country. And taking out their ability to exist day to day will not be hard. Remember, the people of any country are ultimately responsible for the government they have. The Germans were responsible for Hitler. The Afghans are responsible for the Taliban. We should not target civilians. But if they don't rise up against this criminal government, they starve, period.[50]

O'Reilly went on to say that the infrastructure of Iraq "must be destroyed and the population made to endure yet another round of intense pain."[51] He also removed himself from any humanitarian sentiments by calling for the destruction of Libya's airports and the mining of its harbors, crying: "Let them eat sand."[52] There is no spectacle of suddenly vanishing competence here, for his reasoning is as inexorably puerile as it is predictable. He is effectively asking for millions more Iraqi children and civilians to die at the hands of the U.S., not to mention the millions of civilian casualties that would result from the kind of utter destruction of the infrastructure he so perversely calls for. We have heard this kind of advice before, underwritten by the same logic that spikes the Taliban's advice to their own followers.

In the weeks following September 11, the print media was hard at work attempting to smear critics by connecting the anti-globalization movement to terrorism. One example from the *National Post* reads as follows: "Like terrorists, the anti-globalization movement is disdainful of democratic institutions. . . . Terrorism, if not so heinous as what we witnessed last week, has always been part of the protesters' game plan."[53]

Attempts to link September 11th to the crisis of global capitalism are left solely in the hands of a few leftist editors whose publications are marked by outlawed academics such as Noam Chomsky and Edward Herman but also modest and diminishing circulation numbers, while the mainstream media is mining the entrails of academia for more comforting oracular theories, such as those offered by Samuel Huntington, who argues that the world is moving from a Cold War bipolar division to more complex multipolar and multicivilization divisions with greater potential conflict. Here Islamic cultures conveniently collide with Western ones with the force of tectonic plates. John Pilger has noted that "Huntington's language relies upon racial stereotypes and a veiled social Darwinism that is the staple of fascism. It is a vision of global apartheid."[54] Against this explanatory backdrop, readers can find conscionable the mirror image, either-or choice between Bush and bin Laden, both of whom betray a profound contempt for the masses that helps support each other's position.

It is not as if the flat-footed storm troopers have already arrived. It is more as if shimmerings of fascism have crossed the political landscape. Ghostly expressions of negative energy are slowly crystallizing into holograms of Joe McCarthy hovering ominously over the White House. We are living in the moist flaps of Richard Nixon's jowls, drowning in the yellow ink of Steve Dunleavy's pen, sleepwalking on a Pirandello stage, discovering ourselves as Ionesco characters in a Rod Serling nightmare. Unlike *The Twilight Zone*, the horror of the human condition will not disappear when we turn off our television sets. The Sword of Damocles that hangs over the "American way of life" glows blood red while the act of patriotism has been shamelessly downgraded as it becomes compulsory. According to novelist John Le Carré,

> it's as if we have entered a new, Orwellian world where our personal reliability as comrades in the struggle [against terrorism] is measured by the degree to which we invoke the past to explain the present. Suggesting there is a historical context for the recent atrocities is by implication to make excuses for them. Anyone who is with us doesn't do that. Anyone who does, is against us.[55]

Edward Said echoes a similar sentiment:

> What terrifies me is that we're entering a phase where if you start to speak about this as something that can be understood historically—without any sympathy— you are going to be thought of as unpatriotic, and you are going to be forbidden. It's very dangerous. It is precisely incumbent on every citizen to quite understand the world we're living in and the history we are a part of and we are forming as a superpower.[56]

James Petras argues that we inhabit a veritable police state, at the cusp of a totalitarian regime. He writes:

> One of the hallmarks of a totalitarian regime is the creation of a state of mutual suspicion in which civil society is turned into a network of secret police informers. The Federal Bureau of Investigation (FBI) soon after September 11 exhorted every U.S. citizen to report any suspicious behavior by friends, neighbors, relatives, aquaintances, and strangers. Between September and the end of November almost 700,000 denunciations were registered. Thousands of Middle Eastern neighbors, local shop owners, and employees were denounced, as were numerous other U.S. citizens. None of these denunciations led to any arrests or even information related to September 11. Yet hundreds and thousands of innocent persons were investigated and harassed by the federal police.[57]

Also forbidding is the current wave of repressive government actions, including the ongoing racial profiling of Muslim U.S. citizens, the clearcutting of constitutional protections of immigrants, and a full-frontal assault on those civil liberties still standing after decades of strip-mining the hard-won gains made by civil rights activists in the 1960s. Bush is transforming the war on drugs in places such as Colombia into counterterrorist laboratories at war with revolutionary movements.

The U.S. government has overrun the waterline of basic constitutional and civil rights, drowning out protests in its assault on immigrants and dangerous classes with creation of the so-called U.S.A. Patriot Act, setting the stage for propaganda "show trials" once reserved for military dictatorships that were formerly U.S. Cold War adversaries. The establishment of military tribunals by Bush *hijo* amounts to little more than legitimizing a network of ad hoc "drumhead" or "kangaroo" courts that can safely bypass both Congress and the judiciary. If, for instance, Bush believes that a long-term resident of the U.S. has aided a terrorist in some way, that resident can be tried in secret by a military commission and sentenced to death on the basis of hearsay and rumor, without appeal to a civilian court. Even the Supreme Court will be out of reach.

The U.S.A. Patriot Act treats Islamic terrorism as a surrogate for Communism and brings to mind the spectacle and ideological intoxication of the Red Menace and historical events burned by fear into the political unconscious of the country. Repressed by guilt and displaced into the crevices of historical memory, these events include: the Espionage and Sedition Acts that were used against socialists, anarchists, and other groups opposed to the U.S. entry into World War I; the 1919–20 Palmer raids that rounded up accused Bolsheviks and those that sympathized with the 1917 Russian Revolution but were used as a device to round up thousands of foreign-born radicals and send them overseas; the 1940 Smith Act designed to go after Nazi sympathizers but also used to imprison Trotskyists and leaders of the U.S. Communist Party; the World War II incarceration of 120,000 Japanese-Americans in concentration camps under the Roosevelt administration; the McCarran Act of 1950 that legitimized secret FBI record-keeping on political "subversives" and deportation of non-citizens who had been Communists at any time in their lives; the McCarthy hearings of the 1950s that functioned as anti-Communist witch hunts targeting reds, union militants, and Hollywood screenwriters that earned the opprobrium of the left for generations that followed; "Operation Wetback" of the mid-1950s that rounded up and deported over one million Mexican men, women, and children; COINTELPRO operations that were put to use against leftists and black militants in the 1960s; the 1980s RICO "anti-racketeering" laws that were developed to target organized crime but were also used to break strikes and exert complete control over unions like the Teamsters; and the creation of a 1984 plan by the Federal Emergency Management Agency to appoint military commanders to run state and local governments in the event of a national "emergency."[58] While it appears a die-casting term reserved for the truly evil, the terrorism of the Patriot Act is actually an extortionate term packed in an aerosol can with a political mistiness enabling the U.S. to declaim against the politics of any country, and to employ lethal force—preemptive strikes rather than defensive maneuvers—against anyone who opposes American vital interests anywhere in the world. Great Britain has been quick to fall in line with whatever foreign policy initiatives come out of the White House. Recently Robert Cooper of the British Foreign Policy Center, an advisor to Tony Blair who represented the British government at the Bonn talks that helped forge the interim Hamid Karzai government in Afghanistan, advocated that Western countries engage in a "defensive imperialism." Basically this means dealing with "old fashioned states outside the postmodern continent of Europe with the rougher methods of an earlier era—force, preemptive attack, deception, whatever is necessary to deal with those who still live in the nineteenth century."[59]

Former CIA director James Woolsey has called for the reversal of the U.S. policy that prohibits the use of foreign "assets" with abusive human rights records, a policy established by CIA director John Deutch in 1996 after it was revealed that CIA informants were involved in kidnapping, torture, and assassination in Guatemala. Without consulting Congress, Bush *hijo* signed executive order 13233 by which he seeks to modify the law and make it more difficult to make presidential papers and records available to the public. In his efforts to rule by executive fiat, he appears to be grasping beyond his executive powers under the Presidential Records Act of 1978, most probably to protect the public from gaining access to information from his father's vice-presidency and presidency. Not only does he want to protect his father but also others (like Dick Cheney) now working in his own administration. Does the Bush administration and its imperial quartermasters want to hide something from the American public now or from now on—or both? And why is this happening just when information is being made public about the connections between the Taliban, the CIA, and Pakistani intelligence, the business dealings of the Bush and bin Laden families through the Carlyle Corporation, the corporate malfeasance of Bush and Cheney before they assumed presidential duties, and the relationship between U.S. oil conglomerates and countries in the Caspian Sea region?

In the face of this particularly fierce, hawkish administration, and in the midst of widespread apprehension about the motives behind the U.S. war on terrorism among Third World peoples, it is a particularly difficult time to call for rethinking the role the U.S. plays in the global division of labor. The recent events of mind-shattering world-historical dimensions, the sudden unfolding nightmare that saw death and destruction unleashed upon thousands of innocent victims in Washington and New York City, such that the gates of hell appeared to have been blown open, have made it difficult for many U.S. citizens to comprehend why their familiar world has suddenly turned upside-down.

The practices of U.S.-backed client regimes in the Middle East, such as Egypt, Algeria, Jordan, Israel, and Saudi Arabia, which are waging brutal campaigns against Islamic opposition, certainly provide a backdrop against which we can begin to analyze—but not justify, rationalize, or legitimize—the events of September 11. The organizing, arming, funding, and training of Islamic groups against working-class rebellion and social revolution has been a cornerstone of U.S. foreign policy.[60] Certainly the alliance that the U.S. has maintained since World War II with the fundamentalist Wahhabist regime in Saudi Arabia has been a particular sore spot among many Islamic groups. We know that the North Vietnamese, who suffered the tragic loss of millions of dead at the hands of the U.S., did not attack the U.S. populace in retaliation.[61] The terrorist attacks required a certain wilful "agency" that served to generate the terrorism—an agency that is context specific. If terrorism is not teleologically inscribed in history as a direct reaction to U.S. foreign and economic policy, it is surely true that U.S. domination of the Third World in general and the Islamic world in particular has created the underlying conditions likely to lead to terrorism. The taproot of terrorism surely lies in the fertile soil of imperialism—both military and economic. It is nourished by the transnationalization of the productive forces and fertilized by the defeated dreams of the vanquished poor. The terrorism of 9/11 was rhizogenic—its roots and filaments interlaced with U.S. foreign policy and practices.

The new Orwellian ambience in the U.S. can be sniffed in the words of prominent right-wing journalist Charles Krauthammer: "America is no mere international citizen. It is the dominant power in the world, more dominant than any since Rome. Accordingly, America is in a position to reshape norms—How? By unapologetic and implacable demonstrations of will."[62] Sound Nietzschean? Readers who are fans of *Zarathustra* might be emboldened by the words uttered by David Rockefeller at the June 1991 Bilderberg meeting in Baden, Germany: a "supranational sovereignty of an intellectual elite and world bankers . . . is surely preferable to the national autodetermination practiced in past centuries."[63] When you put Krauthammer and Rockefeller together, you complete the circuit of totalitarian logic involving "full-spectrum dominance" set in train by the juggernaut of globalized capital. Petras warns that we must start to "recognize the barbarities committed today in the name of Western victories, hegemony, democracy and free markets: the premature death of ten million Russians, twenty million African AIDS victims denied medicine by Western pharmaceutical corporations backed by their governments, the killing of one million Iraqi children by the Anglo-U.S. war and blockade, the 300 million Latin Americans living in poverty, the tens of thousands of Colombians killed thanks to U.S. military training and aid."[64]

While clearly U.S. economic policies and geopolitical strategies are a factor in creating an environment for terrorism—for example, Israeli occupation of the Palestinians and unyielding U.S. support for Israel, support for the repressive regimes of Saudi Arabia and Egypt, as well as the training of military and death squads in numerous Latin American countries that went on to murder hundreds of thousands of peasants—it is also clear that in the case of September 11, other factors are involved, like anti-Semitism, anti-Americanism (as against genuine anti-imperialism), and a reaction against the progressive dimensions of "Western society," such as workers' rights, feminism, gay rights, etc.[65]

Peter Hudis[66] is bracingly forthright in asserting that it is wrong to believe that bin Laden was simply responding to the same injustices as radical leftists, except that he used a method leftists would never condone and would find utterly abhorrent. Bin Laden loathes the masses, whom he is willing to use as cannon fodder in the name of his "holy" war. Steve Niva[67] has rightly pointed out that bin Laden's small, violent, and socially reactionary network—influenced by the reactionary Wahhabi school of Islam—is roundly antagonistic to social justice and differs in important ways from the wider current of Islamic activism in the Arab world and more globally. The wider current of Islamic activism does have a social justice agenda on behalf of the poor and dispossessed, is more involved in party building and mass mobilization, and largely rejects the Islamic doctrines promoted by bin Laden's network. Moreover, Niva stresses that bin Laden's organization is disconnected from wider Islamic activist movements in that they do not locate their struggle in a national context, but rather in a global war on behalf of Muslims worldwide. It is problematic therefore to locate the attacks on September 11 in a natural reflex reaction to U.S. policies and practices. It is much more complicated than that. There is a difference between saying that the U.S. helps to foster conditions in which terrorism thrives and that the terrorist acts of September 11 were a causal reflex of U.S. foreign and economic policy—like billiard balls in a mechanical Newtonian universe. U.S. imperialism creates the potential for and probability of terrorist attacks but it does not ensure that they will occur. Acts of terror are the outcome of an irreducible plurality of causes, and in some cases can be just as regressive as anything done in the service of U.S. imperialism.[68] A great array of crimes can be linked to world capitalism, often going well beyond the participation of the United States. It is important to point out that Islamic fundamentalism is itself an adaptation to world capitalism. As Amin[69] notes, political Islam is in fact not a reaction to the abuses of secularism but little more than an adaptation to the subordinate status of comprador capitalism.

While there surely existed strong left-wing currents across the Muslim world in the 1950s, 1960s, and 1970s, and left-leaning populist leaders (such as Nasser), it is worth remembering that Islam persists today as the official ideology of some capitalist states and as an oppositional force in others. The Islamist movement is multilayered and nuanced, with competing Sunni and Shiite backers. But as Lisa Macdonald notes, "while veiled in religious garb, support for Islam is motivated by the self-interest of the capitalist class of each country."[70] Macdonald asserts that

> Even the most progressive of political Islamists put forward no clear alternative to capitalism. The best they can do is try to insert themselves into the secular national liberation struggles in their countries and point to the sections of the Koran that call for egalitarianism, equality and "brotherhood" to defend their religious flank from attack by traditionalists. Since the basic tenets of Islam also uphold the right of private ownership, individual enterprise and profit, the contradictions are unresolvable. (They are supposedly resolved through the *zaket*— a morally enforced levy on wealth which is given to the poor—but this amounts to no more than charity and is purely cosmetic in a capitalist economy.)[71]

In many cases, Islamic fundamentalist vigilante groups have become a major instrument of counterrevolution for reactionary forces of state imperialism. Islam's popular support has been aided by the failure of local bourgeoisies to provide even basic development in the form of social welfare, public education, and other services and their failure to stem the growing impoverishment of the majority of people in their respective countries.[72]

The Broader Picture

When White House press secretary Ari Fleischer insisted that people now have to "watch what they say, watch what they do," it was not, as some have claimed, a flippant remark. Interestingly but not surprisingly, Cuba is listed as a country that exports terror internationally. Since September 11, some members of Congress have tried to have Cuba removed from the terrorist list but the Cubans in Congress stopped this move in its tracks.

Even though Fidel Castro roundly condemned the terrorist attacks of September 11 and offered to cooperate with Washington in combatting terrorism, the State Department put forward an unconvincing case against Cuba by noting that it harbors Basque separatists. But the truth is that that the separatists are there as the result of an agreement between the Spanish and Cuban governments and are not engaged in terrorist activities of any kind.[73]

The State Department can put forward specious reasons for putting Cuba on the list of countries that harbor terrorists but remains adept at ignoring its own local swamp of terrorist infestation: Florida. As John Pilger notes,

> There is no "war on terrorism." If there was, the SAS would be storming the beaches of Florida, where more terrorists, tyrants and torturers are given refuge than anywhere in the world.[74]

Bertell Ollman echoes similar sentiments when he writes:

> I'm still waiting for [Bush] to declare war on Florida. Miami is a haven for terrorists, it's the terror capital of the world. All these Latin American and Cuban

terrorists go there to refresh, to retire, to conduct their business. If Bush wants to make a war on terror he should start by bombing Miami and arresting the governor of Florida, even if he is his brother. . . . And after he's successfully done away with terrorism in Miami, then we'll talk about the next step.[75]

It is difficult to deny that the U.S. has a calculated penchant for ignoring its own terrorists, including groups and individuals trained and financed either directly or indirectly by the U.S. military; not just the "*gusano*" mafia in Florida,[76] but also fundamentalist Christian mass murderer General Efrain Rios Montt of Guatemala, Savimbi and Renamo in Angola and Mozambique, and the Nicaraguan Contras. Clearly, the U.S. has employed every conceivable tactic to ensure that socialist experiments are doomed to fail. As William Blum writes:

The boys of capital, they also chortle in their martinis about the death of socialism. The word has been banned from polite conversation. And they hope that no one will notice that every socialist experiment of any significance in the twentieth century—without exception—has either been crushed, overthrown, or invaded, or corrupted, perverted, subverted, or destabilized, or otherwise had life made impossible for it, by the United States. Not one socialist government or movement—from the Russian Revolution to the Sandinistas in Nicaragua, from Communist China to the FMLN in [El] Salvador—not one was permitted to rise or fall solely on its own merits; not one was left secure enough to drop its guard against the all-powerful enemy abroad and freely and fully relax control at home.[77]

Many people reject the idea that the U.S. exports terrorism. Some no doubt find it difficult to understand why a powerful nation such as the U.S. needs to employ what are generally considered to be the weapons of the weak. Michael Klare[78] asserts that "Throughout history, the weapon of those who see themselves as strong in spirit but weak in power has been what we call terrorism. Terrorism is the warfare of the weak against the strong: if you have an army you wage a war; if you lack an army you engage in suicide bombings and other acts of terrorism. (Remember: this is exactly what the American Revolution looked like to the British, the strong force in 1775.)"

Chomsky takes issue with this view of terrorism. He explains that, far from being a weapon of the weak, terrorism is primarily the weapon of the strong:

That is the culture in which we live and it reveals several facts. One is the fact that terrorism works. It doesn't fail. It works. Violence usually works. That's world history. Secondly, it's a very serious analytic error to say, as is commonly done, that terrorism is the weapon of the weak. Like other means of violence, it's primarily a weapon of the strong, overwhelmingly, in fact. It is held to be a weapon of the weak because the strong also control the doctrinal systems and their terror doesn't count as terror.[79]

The late Eqbal Ahmad makes the point that the moral revulsion against terrorism is highly selective. He writes that "We are to feel the terror of those groups which are officially disapproved. We are to applaud the terror of those groups of whom officials do approve."[80] In this context it is impossible not to seriously question the odious role of the Western Hemisphere Institute for Security Cooperation, or Whisc, based in Fort Benning, Georgia (until January this year, Whisc was called the "School of the Americas," or SOA). Since 1946, SOA has trained more than 60,000 Latin American soldiers and policemen. Its graduates constitute a veritable rogues gallery of the continent's most notorious torturers, mass murderers, dictators, and state terrorists.

How can the U.S. condemn other countries for human rights abuses and acts of terror and not recognize that it houses, educates, and graduates some of the most notorious butchers in the Americas? If the U.S. really believes that supporting terrorists makes you as guilty as the terrorists themselves, then it would have to put on trial most of its military and political leadership over the last handful of administrations, and more. Alexander Cockburn reports that in recent years the U.S. has been charged by the United Nations and human rights organizations such as Human Rights Watch and Amnesty International with tolerating torture in its prison system. Methods of torture range from putting prisoners into solitary confinement in concrete boxes, twenty-three hours a day, for years on end, to activating 50,000-volt shocks through a mandatory electric stun-belt worn by prisoners.

The U.S. began serious experiments in torture during the Vietnam War. One experiment involved three prisoners being anesthetized and having their skulls opened up. Electrodes were planted into their brains. They were revived, given knives, and put in a room. CIA psychologists activated the electrodes in order provoke the prisoners to attack one another, but the prisoners did not respond as expected. So the electrodes were removed, the prisoners shot, and their bodies burned.[81]

If we want to discuss torture, we have to account for why more than 80 U.S. companies have, over the last decade, been involved in the marketing and export of equipment used to torture—more than any other country in the world.[82] The major recipients of these "exports" were Brazil, Israel, Russia, Taiwan, Egypt, and Saudi Arabia.[83] The U.S., Great Britain, China, France, and Russia are among the main providers of torture training throughout the world.[84] In the case of the United States, we have evidence of intelligence training manuals produced and used at Fort Benning, Georgia, that advocated execution, torture, beatings, and blackmail. And to find examples of known involvement of U.S. agencies in torture, we need look no further than Operation Condor "which coordinated the military intelligence operations against opponents of the regimes of Augusto Pinochet of Chile, Afredo Stroessner of Paraguay, Jorge Videla of Argentina, and Hugo Banzer of Bolivia, and was led by former Secretary of State Kissinger and General Vernon Walters."[85] These operations were discussed in documents discovered by a Paraguayan lawyer who survived torture under the Stroessner regime.

For several months following some of the most heinous crimes ever to occur on U.S. soil, we have been told to remain on high alert, that more terrorist attacks by roving "sleeper" cells are imminent. Nobody seems to know where or when, exactly, the evildoers will strike, or with what arsenal: Dirty bombs? Anthrax? Suitcase-size mini-nukes? Yet we are constantly reminded by the media to be afraid for ourselves and for our family members. After all, citizens who live in fear will give the government a green light to do just about anything, from taking more money from the poor to give to the already filthy rich, to invading more Third World countries to get rid of terrorist cells, to increased racial profiling of Arab Americans, to militarizing the borders in order to seal them off against anyone who even bears a remote physical resemblance to Arab Americans.

Even in times of peace, the average American citizen has vigorously defended the capitalist state, regarded as the "summit" of human achievement. And this has been especially true in recent years, even though the gap in income between wealthiest Americans and the rest of the population—a level of inequality higher than in any other industrialized nation—has witnessed forty-seven percent of the total real income gain between 1983 and 1998 accruing to the top 1 percent of income recipients, 42 percent going to the next 19 percent, and 12 percent accruing to the bottom 80 percent.[86] Of course, this gap now can be conveniently blamed on the terrorist attacks, even though it has been growing steadily for many decades.

If we want to understand the roots of terrorism, we must locate the current war on terrorism within the larger optic of capitalist globalization. When we do, we soon recognize that multinational corporations are still based predominantly in advanced capitalist countries where they exercise enormous political influence. Imperialist countries such as the U.S. wield disproportionate influence within international financial agencies. In contrast, the developing countries are overwhelmingly low-wage areas, interest and profit exporters (not importers), and "virtual captives of the international financial institutions and highly dependent on limited overseas markets and export products."[87] The multinational corporations and banks located in the imperial states constitute the mainspring of transnational flows of capital and commodity trade. The International Monetary Fund and the World Trade Organization define their policies in accordance with imperial imperatives of free trade, free markets, and free flows of capital and serve mainly as staging areas where advanced capitalist states can do business under the leadership of the U.S. While it is true that greater internationally integrated financial markets now exist, it is important to remember that capitalism is not a conglomeration of transnational capitalist corporations—capital is a relation constituted by its contradictory relationship with wage labor. Capitalism has certain conditions of reproduction that set limits to how far its structures can be reformed.[88] Most reforms operate well within the limits set by the requirements of capitalist production. As Petras and Veltmeyer[89] note, the theory of imperialism (as distinct from the idea of globalization) can best explain the relationship between the growth of international flows of capital and the increase of inequalities between states and between CEOs and workers.

Petras[90] has persuasively argued that as the world's leading imperial state, the U.S. plays a predominant role in the world political economy. Petras is correct in claiming that the role of the nation-state is far from over, as we bear witness to numerous U.S. (and EU) practices: interventions to save multinational corporations and world financial systems; bailouts in exchange for opening markets and foreign takeovers of basic industries; the conquest of foreign markets and protection of local markets; negotiation and enforcement of major trade agreements and bilateral and regional multilateral trade pacts; the knocking down of trade barriers and destabilization of nationalist regimes; imposition of protective barriers; the subsidization of industries; limiting of imports through quotas; and preventing exporting countries from entering certain markets. Although we see the appearance of a transnational capitalist elite, we acknowledge that multinational corporations continue to have specific locations in nation-states, where mobility is contingent upon inter-state relations. Clearly, as Petras notes, old nation-state governments have not been superseded by international financial institutions. The so-called information revolution has not eliminated state borders. The new economy remains highly speculative, driven by exorbitant claims of high returns in the absence of profits and sometimes even revenues. The U.S. exercises managed trade that combines protection of home markets with aggressive intervention to secure monopoly market advantages and investment profits. The U.S. continues to operate a "selective" openness in designated product areas (with U.S. affiliates) while Euro-U.S. policymakers and their employees in the IMF-World Bank insist that countries in the Third World eliminate all trade barriers, subsidies, and regulations for products and services in all sectors. The U.S. preaches market fundamentalism to the Third World while protecting its own domestic economic sectors. The U.S. operates as the Alpha Male of a neo-mercantilist imperialism and uses its military might to back itself up. Petras notes that

> So-called globalization grew out of the barrel of a gun—an imperial state gun. To further protect overseas capital, the U.S. and the EU created a new NATO doctrine which legitimates offensive wars outside of Europe against any country that threatens vital economic interests (their MNCs). NATO has been expanded to incorporate new client states in eastern Europe and new "peace associates" among the Baltic states and the former republics of the USSR. In other words, the imperial state military alliances incorporate more states, involving more state apparatuses than before—to ensure the safe passage of Euro-U.S. MNCs into their countries and the easy flow of profits back to their headquarters in the U.S. and western Europe.[91]

It is clear now that the spread of globalization has not helped the world's poor: from 1960 to 1980, the gross domestic product in Latin America grew by

75 percent per person, but from 1980 to 2000—a period of massive globalization, market liberalization, and international investment—the gross domestic product rose only 6 percent. In Africa, the gross domestic product rose by a third from 1960 to 1980 but over the next twenty years lost nearly half of that gain.[92] Ted Fishman comments:

> The lethal double dynamic begins with the dirt poor whom the spread of global capitalism has not helped. Half the planet lives on less than two dollars a day, a billion people on half of that. For them, globalization has meant little in terms of real income gain. Oxfam recently recalculated the statistics in the World Bank study on developing countries, this time not weighted for population, and determined that incomes for people in countries that are pursuing a global program grew just 1.5 percent. For one in three of these countries, incomes actually rose more slowly than in states that resisted reforms.[93]

The influx of capital and liberalization measures brings some countries closer to war, decimating large impoverished sections of the population. Fishman notes that most of the world's battles involve groups of capitalist profiteers struggling for competitive advantage, using offshore bank accounts and dummy corporations—that is, behaving like Enron—and fighting each other with cheap soldiers. He asks:

> Should we be surprised, then, that the freeing up of world financial markets and world trade has spread an epidemic of violence? The dictators, warlords, corporate partners, banks, law firms, and nations that thrive on deadly business have known it all along.[94]

The U.S. is the largest arms dealer in the world, and its weapons manufacturers stand to—forgive the metaphor—"make a killing" in the current war on terrorism. Currently, about 85,000 private firms profit from the military contracting system. The Carlyle Group (which removed its web site after the September 11 attacks), a privately owned American $12-billion dollar international merchant bank or equity firm, and the eleventh largest military contractor in the country, invests heavily in the arms sector and makes its money from military conflicts and weapons spending. It retains Bush *padre* as a senior consultant (Bush has been allowed to buy into Carlyle's investments, which involve at least 164 countries). Carlyle's chairman and managing director is former U.S. Secretary of Defense Frank Carlucci (and former roommate of Donald Rumsfeld) and its partners include former U.S. Secretary of State James A. Baker III, George Soros, Richard Darman (Reagan aide and GOP operative), and Fred Makek (Bush *hijo*'s campaign manager). The Carlyle Group has in the past done business with the bin Laden family, including deals involving the aerospace industry.

Joseph Stiglitz, awarded the Nobel Prize in economics in 2001, admitted:

> Clearly, terrorists can be people like bin Laden who come from upper-income families. Nevertheless, abject poverty and economies without jobs for males be-

tween the ages of 18 and 30 are particularly good breeding grounds for extremism. Solving the economic problems doesn't eliminate the risk of terrorism, but not solving them surely enhances it.[95]

Michael Klare situates the current danger facing the world as one that puts the U.S. economy at the service of hypothetical future enemies—or actually creates those enemies by producing a climate of fear and hostility in anticipation of those enemies one day arising:

> The question facing all Americans, therefore, is whether the expenditure of hundreds (later thousands) of billions of dollars to defend against hypothetical enemies that may not arise until thirty or forty years from now is a sensible precaution, as contended by the President and Defense Secretary, or whether it eventually will undermine U.S. security by siphoning off funds from vital health and educational programs and by creating a global environment of fear and hostility that will produce exactly the opposite of what is intended by all these expenditures.[96]

But what about the new technologies supposedly bringing about what has been described as the "information economy"—an economy characterized as qualitatively different from the industrial capitalism theorized by Marx. It can be argued that the new technologies have not changed the basic reproductive principles of advanced capitalism, since they remain embedded in preexisting classes and nation states and within the structural dynamics of the capitalist system. The international division of labor has not been transformed by these new technologies, since most of the industrial output in both Third World and imperial countries is for domestic consumption and is produced by domestic owners.[97] These information technologies have been good at bombarding people with the message that there is no alternative to capitalism, that any attempts to replace capitalism with an alternative will bring about rampant destruction. But what about possible alternatives to the globalization of capital—especially to the voracious binge capitalism that currently engulfs us? Socialist planning has been discredited after the collapse of the bureaucratic command economies of the Soviet Union, what Callinicos calls "economic statism."[98] The only alternatives seemingly available are economic statism, neoliberalism, and the more progressive Rhineland model of regulated capitalism.[99] I don't believe capitalist social relations can be "transformed" such that they will serve the interests of those who live in developing countries, or those who live in relations of economic servitude in advanced capitalist countries.

The contemporary project of corporate power resembles Hannah Arendt's "omnipresent center" where the logic of capital accumulation is internalized as public value-set.[100] In this context, the war on terror exemplifies what John McMurtry calls the logic of "the extortion racket of the neighborhood" writ large, "the symbolic male gangs in corporate logos."[101] McMurtry writes that "transnational corporations have marketed and financed these political leaders to ensure that captive states serve them rather than the peoples governments are elected by, guaranteeing through state plenipotentiaries and transnational trade edicts that governments can no longer govern them in common interest without infringing the new trade and investment laws in which transnational corporations alone are granted rights."[102] He points out that the "permanent war against 'terrorists' of the Third World is the cap of a continuous and historically unprecedented financial deregulation of markets and hemorrhages of transnationally mobile capital in and out of nations leading to meltdowns from Brazil and Mexico and Russia and Asia."[103] The invisible hand of the market is now a clenched fist wielding the sword of civilization, mercilessly punishing those who disobey its laws.

McMurtry claims that the U.S. has created a new form of totalitarianism: the old totalitarian culture of the "Big Lie" is marked by "a pervasive overriding of the distinction between fact and fiction by saturating mass media falsehoods."[104] This Big Lie "is disseminated by round-the-clock, centrally controlled multi-media which are watched, read or heard by people across the globe day and night without break in the occupation of public consciousness instead of national territories."[105] McMurtry writes that "in the old totalitarian culture of the Big Lie, the truth is hidden. In the new totalitarianism, there is no line between truth and falsehood. The truth is what people can be conditioned to believe."[106] And conditioned they certainly are.

The culture of the new totalitarianism and the international division of labor produced by the globalized capital cannot fully account for a climate of terrorism, for the terrorist attacks against the U.S. The remaining challenge is to understand how the new totalitarianism and globalization of capital are causally related to the foreign policies and military activities undertaken by imperial nations. We inhabit a world in which one can identify certain kinds of "terrorism from below" along with examples of "terrorism from above." Joel Kovel clarifies the distinction thusly:

> For the oppressed, terror is the restitution of identity through violence against the oppressor; while for the latter, it becomes a "collateral damage." In this respect the suicide bomber striking on behalf of a ravaged people has a certain moral advantage over the powerful nation who impersonally bombs a helpless population. The former may falsely deny that he is doing evil, but at least he knows he is being violent, and that he is willing to take violence to the limit of giving his own life. The terrorism from below is undoubtedly evil, because it strikes back at innocents to get back at an oppressor; but its evil is refracted through the objective reality of that oppressor. The terror from above, on the other hand, is nakedly of the oppressor himself, hurled down from the great heights of the Command and Control Center while its perpetrator looks forward to an evening at the mall, or thinks, if he is the President and has to give a press conference, of how good we are.[107]

A Global Culture of Terror

The U.S., and the capitalist West in general, reproduces a global culture that nourishes and sustains the virus of terrorism. But historical denial and elite arrogance helped put blinkers on public awareness that America was anything other than America the Good. As Lewis Lapham remarks, "We didn't see the planes coming because we didn't think we had to look."[108] It is striking how terrorism is sanctioned, condemned, and by whom. In 1990, Bush *padre* released from house arrest the notorious Orlando Bosch, after Bosch had served two years for illegally entering the United States. Government officials believed Bosch was involved in the bombing of a Cuban civilian airliner that killed 73 people and the Justice Department linked him to at least 30 acts of sabotage. The *New York Times* called Bosch "one of the hemisphere's most notorious terrorists."[109] It turns out that Bush's son, Jeb, who was at the time a burgeoning Republican leader trying to curry favor with Miami's anti-Castro Cubans, had lobbied for Bosch's release.[110]

President Bush's central position, around which his justification for the war pivots—the preservation of democracy and civil liberties—is plagued by a profound contradiction. In a speech before Congress he piously intoned that terrorists "hate what they see right here in this chamber: a democratically elected government." He went on to say: "They hate our freedoms: our freedom of religion, our freedom of speech, our freedom to vote and assemble and disagree with each other. They want to overthrow existing governments in many Muslim countries such as Egypt, Saudi Arabia, and Jordan." He ended by saying: "This is the fight of all who believe in progress and pluralism, tolerance and freedom."

But how could this be true, since any coalition that includes the bonapartist rulers and corrupt monarchs of countries in the Muslim Crescent such as Egypt, Saudi Arabia, and Jordan cannot seriously abide by the principles stated by Bush. Each of these countries restricts freedom of speech, the press, assembly, association, religion, and movement. Jordan is a monarchy in which the security forces engage in torture and "extrajudicial" killings. The establishment of political parties is prohibited in Saudi Arabia, which has a religious police force—the *mouttawa*—to enforce a very conservative form of Islam. Egyptian security forces regularly arrest and torture people under the banner of fighting terrorism. Clearly, Bush's characterization of the U.S. as the pinnacle of civilization and every country that fails to support the U.S. war in Afghanistan as evil barbarians is absurd. Has Bush been educated in a capitalist *madras*? One would think so after listening to what he said at an October 11 press conference:

> How do I respond when I see that in some Islamic countries where is vitriolic hatred for America? I'll tell you how I respond: I'm amazed. I'm amazed that there's

such misunderstanding of what our country is about that people would hate us. I am—like most Americans, I just can't believe it because I know how good we are" (cited in Kovel, 2001, page 17).[111]

Of course, Bush's simplistic rhetoric is to be expected; it is, in fact, politically de rigueur. Instead of listening to the incredulous comments made for television cameras by Bush, the public would be better served by feminist Muslim voices of women such as Nawal El Saadawi, Asma Jahangir, Fatema Mernissi, and the Revolutionary Association of Women in Afghanistan (RAWA) who condemn the attacks of September 11 and urge the Muslim world to promote a culture of democracy and tolerance within their own countries but who also implore the U.S. government to consider the root causes of terrorism.[112]

The world has become more attuned to the hypocritical and pernicious exercise of U.S. double standards, to what, in the words of Eqbal Ahmad, could be termed "a new pathology of power."[113] American concepts of justice are riven with a perfidiously stage-managed spin. How else to explain how the U.S. can celebrate democracy within its own borders and lay waste to it outside of them? How can the U.S. justify its economical, logistical, and military support of undemocratic regimes, some of which are involved in the worst atrocities? And how can the U.S. government pillory those critics who raise such questions for the public record? How can the U.S. overlook its complicity in forty years of support for terrorist military dictatorships in Guatemala after the CIA overthrew the democratically elected Arbenz regime in 1954? What kind of racist arithmetic makes U.S. casualties more important than, for instance, the 250,000 dead of indigenous Guatemala, cruelly tortured and executed by the U.S.-backed Guatemalan military? How can the U.S. overlook infamous operations like JM Wave and Mongoose that killed innocent Cuban civilians, with operations that included the placing of cement powder by U.S. agents operating in Cuba in the tankers transporting milk from the countryside to Havana?[114] How can it escape its support of military dictatorships—and the rivers of blood that ensued—throughout the Americas? Can it forget its support of the murderous Contras? The world will judge the U.S. not solely in terms of its payback against the odious actions of Osama bin Laden and his followers but in terms of its own past actions, such as the "collateral damage" resulting from its regular bombing campaigns against "rogue" nations. Former UN weapons inspector Scott Ritter admitted that the U.S. does not want to disarm Iraq because that would mean a lifting of sanctions; in fact, the U.S. deliberately put pressure on weapons inspectors to provoke a confrontation with Iraqi officials so that weapons inspectors could be pulled out—in other words, they weren't kicked out by Iraq but pulled out by the U.S. The targets bombed by the U.S. after the Gulf War were those developed through the inspection process, adding weight to the Iraqi claim that the weapons inspectors were involved in espionage.[115]

Under the sign of the Stars and Stripes the war against terrorism unchains the attack dogs of the New World Order in defense of homeland civilization. In the process, the U.S. has crossed the threshold of militant authoritarianism and goose-stepped onto the global balcony of neofascism, befouling the Constitution along the way. As long as the nation keeps cheering, and Bush's impish jaw juts ever forward, the stench goes unnoticed.

Among the Bush administration, there is a concerted effort to meld political rhetoric and apocalyptic discourse within a larger politics of fear and paranoia. Like a priest of the black arts, Bush has successfully disinterred the remnants of Ronald Reagan's proto-fascist rhetoric from the graveyard of chiliastic fantasies, appropriated it for his own interests, and played it in public like a charm. Self-fashioning one's image through the use of messianic tropes works best on the intended audience when the performance is disabused of shrillness, devoid of mincing while remaining confident and sometimes allegorical. Bush met with rescued Quecreek coal miners for a photo-op session, observing: "It was their determination to stick together and to comfort each other that really defines kind of a new spirit that's prevalent in our country, that when one of us suffers, all of us suffer."[116] He lectured on the imperatives of "responsibility" and not asking "where am I going to get my next paycheck from."[117] His opportunistic move to link the heroic rescue to the renewed spirit of post-September 11 America and his "war on terrorism" camouflaged the fact that earlier this year the Bush administration proposed to cut the federal Mine Safety and Health Administration by six percent or seven million dollars (even though coal miner fatalities have gone up for three years in a row) while proposing to decrease funding for occupational safety and health.[118] Bill Vann aptly notes:

> If Bush had been prepared to speak frankly, he might have told his assembled audience: "I'm glad you fellows were rescued. But the fact remains, you and your kind have to work at dirty and unsafe jobs for a pittance so that I and my kind can live in luxury."[119]

Fascist plainspeak is a discursive rendering that is straightforward and unapologetic, and, like an iceberg, does most of the damage beneath the surface. It conceals the value form of labor that produces wage and power hierarchies under a veil of platitudes (in Bush's case, silver spoon platitudes). Bush's handlers are masters of right-wing spin, and Bush is a perfect candidate since he hardly needs ideological persuasion to get on board the reactionary bandwagon. He is the perfect vehicle for collapsing the distinction between religious authoritarianism and politics. Bush's war on terrorism works largely through archetypal association, and operating in the crucible of the structural unconscious. Bush may believe that Providence has assigned him the arduous yet glorious task of rescuing America from the Satanic forces of evil, as if he, himself, were the embodiment of the generalized will and the unalloyed spirit of the American people. Evoking the role of divine prophet who identifies with the sword arm of divine retribution, Bush reveals the eschatological undertow to the war on terrorism, perhaps most evident in his totalizing and Manichean pronouncements where he likens bin Laden and his Al Qaeda warriors to absolute evil and the United States to the apogee of freedom and goodness.

A Holy Ghost Warrior does not forestall reprisal but acts swiftly and unhesitatingly. Violence seeks shelter in religion, and the violence unleashed by Commander Bush under the banner of Lord Jesus is likely to beget only more violence. Carlos Fuentes writes:

> One could be tempted by an easy Babylonian vengeance—the Code of Hammurabi, Lex talionis; an eye for an eye, a tooth for a tooth. It's the easy way out. It is the useless way out. It is retaliation that provokes more retaliation, an uncontrollable spiral of violence that could engulf us all. It's the U.S. retaliation against a faceless enemy that encourages and justifies Russian retaliation against Chechnya and Chinese repression against its northern ethnic groups. It's the retaliation that, like Macbeth's spot of blood, expands until it drowns all, even our sleep.[120]

Placing a veil of righteousness over the exercise of mass destruction and the quest for geopolitical dominance, Bush has been accorded nearly sacerdotal status by the vast majority of the American people, at least according to opinion polls. Bush might be seen as offering metaphysical hope for rebirth of the American Spirit that has wasted away in a morally comatose state within what is perceived by conservatives as the debauched interregnum of the Clinton years.

Bush strides into the international theater with both Bible and sword. Commander-in-Chief of the most powerful armed forces ever assembled in history, he wields his sword arm to protect and expand U.S. interests worldwide; with the Bible of Christian fundamentalism he blesses this very expansionism. His confidant, Robert Kaplan, author of *The Coming Anarchy*, a neoconservative vision of a world divided between the civilized and unmolested regions of the rich and the battered wastelands of the chaos-riven poor, advises in his new book, *Warrior Politics*, that the rich employ military brutality to crush all soldiers of anarchy that might spring up from the deserts of hopelessness.

No doubt Bush is following Kaplan's advice. Bush was raised an Episcopalian but after marriage he became a Methodist. In 1985, Billy Graham's famously genteel God-power channeled by a fire-and-brimstone rhetoric was apparently strong enough to sear into oblivion even the most minute grains of cocaine from Bush *hijo*'s unsaved heart. After accepting Jesus as Lord, Bush was later inspired to make "Jesus Day" an official holiday in Texas. Announcing to Texas evangelist James Robinson that God wanted him to be President, Bush went on record that non-Christians would not make it into heaven. According to a recent *Washington Post* article, Bush now stands at the head of the Protestant fundamentalist movement in the United States.

> For the first time since religious conservatives became a modern political movement, the president of the United States has become the movement's de facto leader—a status even Ronald Reagan, though admired by Christian conservatives, never earned. Christian publications, radio, and television shower Bush with praise, while preachers from the pulpit treat his leadership as an act of providence. A procession of religious leaders who have met with him testify to his faith, while Web sites encourage people to fast and pray for the president.[121]

Mark Crispin Miller warns that worldviews such as those endorsed by Bush and Ashcroft always lead to war, both beyond our borders and among ourselves. The same crusading spirit that impelled the drive to nail the Antichrist, Bill Clinton, also motivated Bush to seek the presidential chalice for the GOP. "It's Redemption Time!" he cried when he decided to reclaim the White House for his father. Such piety spells trouble for the Constitution—just as it did when Bush's dad was in the White House. "Sometimes you just have to obey a higher law," as Fawn Hall put it in her blunt defense of the illegalities of Iran-Contra.[122]

Ever since the myth of America as God's chosen nation entered the collective unconscious of the American people, U.S. politics has been primed for the appearance of national saviors and sinners. Without skipping an opportunistic beat, Bush has assumed the mantle of *jefe* global warlord, taken up the Hammer of Thor, and is continuing to wield it recklessly in blatant disregard of world opinion. Bush appears to believe that God's elect—the Amercian *übermenschen*—in their potent attempt to realize Bush *padre*'s vision of making America the iron-fisted steward of a New World Order—must not be compromised by the liberal ideas of negotiation and compromise. It is not as though Bush *hijo* is trying to remake the U.S. into a New Jerusalem; more likely he believes that the U.S. is *already* the New Jerusalem and therefore must be protected by leaders ordained by the Almighty. Of course, the civilization versus chaos myth is a rewrite of the myth of white racial superiority over people of color. Instead of the echoes of Wagner, we have the music of *Rocky*, instead of Wotan serving as our favorite media action hero, we have Conan the American chasing Marxists through the jungles of Colombia, instead of *Triumph of the Will* we have Fox news shots of Geraldo in Afghanistan fudging locations where particular events were supposed to have occurred.[123]

What is key to remember about Bush is that he fluctuates from the Anti-Terrorist Warlord to the Business Buffoon with greased rapidity. After the Enron and WorldCom scandals, Bush gave a televised address to the nation in which he assumed a posture that Lewis H. Lapham aptly described as "guileless as the unicorn and innocent as Forrest Gump."[124] Here Bush feigned a naïveté as insincere as it was convincing, where he "adopted the familiar persona of the idiot CEO—the President of the United States revealed as just another good-natured, holy fool, a block of polished wood at the head of the boardroom table, helpless in the hands of charlatans (irresponsible and un-American) who mystified the SEC [Stock Exchange Commission] with numbers that not even Vice President Dick Cheney could understand."[125] Here Bush was able to condemn the moral lapse of American CEOs while at the same time affirming "the great truth that every true American is entitled to everything he or she can get away with."[126]

We need to ask ourselves how, exactly, the rhetoric of postmodern fascism works, assuming that the infrastructure for a transition to a fascist state is already in place—we have the Patriot Act, we have the military tribunals, we have the Office of Homeland Security, we have the necessary scapegoats, we have the Office of Strategic Influence working hand in hand with the U.S. Army's Psychological Operations Command (PSYOPS) operating domestically, we have the strongest military in the world, we have the military hawks in control of the Pentagon, we have pummeled an evil nation into prehistory while turning Central Asia into a zone of containment, and shown that we can kill mercilessly and control media reporting in the theater of operations, burying stories of civilian atrocities. (According to a UN report, unarmed women and children were pursued and killed by American helicopters in the village of Niazi Kala in Afghanistan, even as they fled to shelter or tried to rescue survivors.)[127] And we have a "leader" who is little more than a glorified servant of the military industrial complex—and one who is able to admit this publicly while arousing little opposition. In fact, such an admission wins him the glowing admiration of the American people. The Bush administration's scheduled release of documents under the Presidential Records Act of 1978, which includes Ronald Reagan's papers, has successfully been placed in lockdown. So far Cheney's much publicized legal stonewalling has prevented full disclosure of the extent of Enron-National Energy Policy Development Group contacts. Government secrecy and withholding of information available to the public by law has beome a guiding axiom of government practice.

The consequence of Bush's mystic vengeance is the death of thousands of innocent civilians. As Carlos Fuentes remarks:

> We can recall the blindness, bordering on oligophrenia, of the U.S. government when it fed milk to vipers who responded with venom. Saddam Hussein is a product of U.S. policy to limit and fence in the triumphant and intolerant Ayatollahs of Iran. Osama bin Laden is a product of forceful U.S. diplomacy to counter the Soviet presence in Afghanistan. From Castillo Armas in Guatemala to Pinochet in Chile, it was U.S. diplomacy that imposed the bloodiest dictatorships in Latin America. In Vietnam, even though armies faced armies, the civilians were the greatest casualty, transforming yesterday's exceptions—Guernica,

Coventry, Dresden—to today's rule: the main and sometimes only victims of modern conflicts are innocent civilians.[128]

While Bush rhapsodizes about "freedom and democracy" at home, the truth is that such values have effectively been put on hold. The Office of Homeland Security (a "properly Teutonic-sounding word," according to former CIA officer and now critic of the CIA, David MacMichael[129]) is dedicated to ensuring domestic safety; yet at the same time it is designed to promote what conservative scholar James M. Rhodes calls "ontological hysteria," summarized by Michael Grosso[130] as follows: "Ontological hysteria consists of a prolonged fear of imminent annihilation, panic over the insecurity of existence. People experience it in disastrous, disorienting times." A key tactic of the Bush elites is to take advantage of this ontological terrorism to keep the public disoriented and in a sustained feeling of dependence on Bush the Crusader to protect them. Whenever the public seems ready to let down its guard, we receive an announcement from the CIA or other sources that a terrorist attack is expected soon, perhaps in a matter of days.

The terrorist attacks—real and anticipated—have given Bush a cloak of Teflon; criticism cannot stick. All Bush has to do is make bold proclamations, bereft of complexity. Apocalyptic overkill is the prophylactic gel that kills criticism on contact. The point is that it is profoundly more effective to hide complex geopolitics in the simplistic, infantilizing language of religious apocalypse and millennial logic. Here Manichean dualisms abound uncontested: good vs. evil, civilized values vs. tribal barbarism, warlords vs. elected officials, and so forth. Within such a scenario, the act of critique itself is seen as intemperate. Critique is tolerated in the opinion pages of newspapers, but not as editorial commentary. It can appear in local television venues with relatively small viewing audiences but cannot be tolerated on major televised news shows. Those who would criticize a President in the midst of directing a global war against terrorism could only be seen by the public at large as self-interested, as "spoilers" at best and traitors at worst. We saw what happened to Bill Maher and Susan Sontag.

Seemingly, all that Bush has to do is to remain militantly forthright: the U.S. has now geographically ordained a new global partnership bent on mass destruction, a new axis of evil (North Korea, Iran, and Iraq) that must be eliminated. You cannot name something as "evil" and then work out a compromise without you, yourself, being implicated in the very evil you ostensibly oppose. You cannot say: "America will not permit the world's most dangerous regimes to threaten us with the world's most destructive weapons,"[131] without somehow backing up the threat. This is why the special operations AC-130 Spectre gunship, used since the Vietnam war to pulverize any and every opponent of civilization that dares stand in its path, is now being fitted with a laser that can bring down missiles, melt holes in aircraft, and destroy ground radar stations.

A key factor here is that it might take years to defeat an evil regime but decades to defeat an axis of evil—even with laser-equipped gunships.

In effect, what Bush did in his 2002 State of the Union Address was to formalize in both temporal and spatial terms the new Cold War. Of course, when you talk about an axis there is always room for more players: thus we should never count out either China or Russia. While Bush was touring South Korea, a U.S. soldier pointed out that an axe used to kill two American soldiers in the 1970s was now ensconced in a museum just across the border in North Korea. Bush responded, "No wonder I think they're evil."[132] During a meeting of the Senate Judiciary Committee in early December, Attorney General John Ashcroft took conservative phrasemongering to new heights. In a rabid, sermon-like tone, Ashcroft issued a warning so politically toxic it spiked the air like aerosolized anthrax: "To those who scare peace-loving people with phantoms of lost liberty, my message is this: Your tactics only aid terrorists, for they erode our national unity and diminish our resolve. They give ammunition to America's enemies, and pause to America's friends. They encourage people of goodwill to remain silent in the face of evil."[133]

These are ringing statements for someone whose nomination as Attorney General was surrounded by controversy. Ashcroft, a devout evangelical Pentecostal, once proclaimed at Bob Jones University that the U.S. has "no king but Jesus." He proclaimed with ecclesiastical certainty that "When you have no king but Caesar, you release Barabbas—criminality, destruction, thievery, the lowest and the least. . . . When you have no king but Jesus, you release the eternal, you release the highest and best, you release virtue, you release potential. . . . If America is to be great in the future, it will be if we understand that our source is not civic and temporal, but our source is godly and eternal."[134] An open admirer of the Confederacy, Ashcroft had to defend himself against numerous allegations of racism during confirmation hearings in the Senate in January, 2001. Also an avowed opponent of desegregation, abortion, contraception, and gay rights, Ashcroft is clearly relishing his new duties, which include undermining the Constitution. Unmoored from reason and set adrift in the lagoon of repressed rage, Ashcroft's deft machinations of legal priestcraft employed in developing draconian anti-terrorism legislation in the wake of September 11 serve to eviscerate civil liberties and the Constitution in one fell swoop. Ashcroft's comments echo those made by former FBI Director William Webster in 1982, when he argued that groups which "produce propaganda, disinformation and 'legal assistance' may even be more dangerous than those who actually throw the bombs."[135] The admonitions of both Webster and Ashcroft are underwritten by the logic of what Alexander Cockburn calls "comic-book advisories" reflected in Bush *hijo*'s statements such as "You're for us or against us."[136]

The cartoon-like authoritarianism and pugnaciousness slowly settling into place is generously assisted by Ashcroft. Consider his recent remarks on the struggle against terrorism: "Civilized people—Muslims, Christians and Jews—all understand that the source of freedom and human dignity is the Creator."[137] Ashcroft made these remarks in front of a group of Christian broadcasters. At the same event he proclaimed: "Civilized people of all religious faiths are called to the defense of His creation. We are a nation called to defend freedom—a freedom that is not the grant of any government or document, but is our endowment from God."[138] Lewis H. Lapham writes that "the country's war-making powers serve at the pleasure of people who seem more sympathetic to the religious enthusiasms of John Ashcroft than to the secular concerns of the United Nations—true believers, secure in the knowledge of their own virtue, quick to issue the writs of moral censure and add another 40,000 names to the list of the world's evildoers."[139] Kovel observes that as globalization moves across borders, Bush's outlook becomes all the more curious: "From a purely logical standpoint, the idea that any particular people would be special, or good, or chosen by a higher power, is a pathetically childish illusion, with no greater claim on the truth than a four-year-old's belief that his mommy prefers him over all others. Yet one can make this interpretation until the end of time, and nothing will change."[140]

And while the Attorney General exiles Orpheus into the political hinterland by covering the breasts of the statues in the lobby of his workplace, he offers the wrath of Jehovah as a libidinal replacement to Christian fundamentalists embarking on their torchlit rallies and declaring that "united we stand." Recently Cheney told Orange County Republicans gathered at the Richard Nixon Library in Yorba Linda, California, that "the United States must accept the place of leadership given to us by history."[141] Clearly, his peace through strength of message was a secular rewrite of a divine mandate to destroy the infidel. Reverend Jerry Falwell who, in the 1980s, was told by President Ronald Reagan that Armageddon was fast approaching, invoked a God of vengeance and destruction when he blamed feminists, civil libertarians, abortion rights advocates, and gays and lesbians for the terrorist attacks of September 11. He echoed a belief shared by other evangelicals that divine protection is summarily withdrawn from nations who have followed in the footsteps of the inhabitants of Sodom and Gomorrah and have irredeemably become steeped in sin. Bush, Cheney, Ashcroft, and Falwell express similar sentiments, but Falwell has failed where the others have succeeded because their attack demonizes "them" rather than splitting "us" into an "us and them" (good Americans versus bad Americans).

Bush *hijo* believes that by challenging the interminable evil engulfing the globe, he can transform the evil violence of the terrorists into the sacred benevolence of America the Beautiful, promoting unanimity and redemption of secular culture and its vile moral chaos. Bush's behavior can be seen in the light of mimetic desire, a reaffirmation of the spirit of the traditional values of civilization that emerges from the fault line separating the barbarians from the saved during moments of volcanic upheaval. Bush's bombastic odes dedicated to the military machine, defining war as a way of cleansing the world of evil—an evil projected onto others so we can have our own sins expiated—are helping to prepare the socio-cultural cornerstone of our new surrogate victim: the Muslim. Since 9/11 Muslims have become ritual vehicles for catharsis, purification, purgation, and exorcism. Rene Girard notes that "the working basis of human thought, the process of 'symbolization,' is rooted in the surrogate victim."[142] And while the act of generative unanimity vomited up immediately after September 11—symbolized in the phrase "United We Stand"—does not appear to be backed with the same resolve now that we have had time to engage with more digested reactions to the horror and bring to it a more critical stance, Bush is still crafty enough to serve up to his potential voters what they want to hear: the U.S. is the world's only superpower and that gives us the right to rewrite the rules of the game.

Christian fundamentalists see nuclear annihilation as a sign that Jesus Christ is about to return to Earth to prevent humankind from destroying itself; only those who heed God's Word are to be protected from the holocaust. In February 2002, the Doomsday Clock—on which midnight marks the onset of widespread nuclear destruction—was adjusted by physicist Leon Lederman to two minutes before midnight as a result of tensions between Pakistan and India. Once Jesus returns to earth after a hard-fought battle against the Axis of Evil, and sets up headquarters in Disneyland, He promises to all the faithful a holographic version of the Elysian Fields, accompanied by muzak versions of John Ashcroft singing pentecostal hymns. When Nathan Lewin wrote in the on-line magazine *Sh'ma* that families of Palestinian suicide bombers should be executed as a deterrent, citing the biblical destruction of the tribe of Amalek as a precedent,[143] many Christian fundamentalists would nod their heads in agreement. This is precisely why John Le Carré admonishes the Manichean rivals that God is better left out of this debate:

> To imagine that God fights wars is to credit Him with the worst follies of mankind. God, if we know anything about Him, which I don't profess to, prefers effective food drops, dedicated medical teams, comfort and good tents for the homeless and bereaved, and, without strings, a decent acceptance of our past sins and a readiness to put them right. He prefers us less greedy, less arrogant, less evangelical and less dismissive of life's losers. It's not a new world order, not yet, and it's not God's war.[144]

When Mark Twain wrote that "Patriotism means being loyal to our country all the time and to its government when it deserves it," he made this statement in opposition to U.S. conquest of the Philippines—a conquest that turned out to be one of the most infamous acts of genocide in U.S. history.[145] One can only wonder what that great architect of the American Revolution, Thomas Paine, a fighter against class privilege and entitled aristocracy, would make of today's Republican administration. The propertied class that decried Paine for penning *The Rights of Man*, the British government that charged him with treason, the preachers throughout the country who, during the nineteenth century, made his name synonymous with the Devil, would no doubt feel comfortable in the current White House. No doubt Paine would be in trouble. Lapham remarks: "Were Paine still within reach of the federal authorities, Attorney General John Ashcroft undoubtedly would prosecute him for blasphemy under a technologically enhanced version of the Alien and Sedition Acts."[146] Moreover:

> Paine would have recognized the government now situated in Washington as royalist in sentiment, "monarchical" and "aristocratical" in its actions, Federalist in its mistrust of freedom, imperialist in the bluster of its military pretensions, evangelical in its worship of property. In the White House we have a President appointed by the Supreme Court; at the Justice Department, an Attorney General believing that in America "we have no king but Jesus"; in both houses of Congress, a corpulent majority that on matters of tax and regulatory policy votes its allegiance to the principles of hereditary succession and class privilege.[147]

By any reckoning, the Bush presidency has enjoyed a very successful war. Bush has adhered to the "three grand imperatives of geostrategy" as put forward by Zbigniew Brzezinski: "to prevent collusion and maintain security among the vassals, to keep tributaries pliant and protected, and to keep the barbarians from coming together."[148] The mapping of the globe is proceeding apace and the conquest of other parts of the globe are in the planning stages. But Bush and his hawk-headed advisors are really part of the larger political will of global market agents and the logic of transnational capital. It is not surprising to read in a 1995 *Harper's Roundtable* discussion by *Wall Street Journal* editorialist David Frum an argument that the government should "get rid of" Medicare, Medicaid, and all other social programs for children, the poor, the elderly, and the racially or otherwise disadvantaged, at the same time William Kristol rails against the Roosevelt New Deal, proclaiming that "you cannot have a federal guarantee that people won't starve."[149] It is as if the transnationalization of the productive forces and the emergence of the transnational capitalist class carries an ethnocidal *logos* within its structural unconscious.

The logic behind the drive to accumulate capital is what trumps all other motives, and is what makes it likely that regardless of who is in the White House the search for geostrategic advantage in the struggle for resources such as oil will be the primary agenda. While it is difficult to argue against George Monibot's assertion that "the greatest threat to world peace is not Saddam Hussein, but George Bush,"[150] it is safe to assume that strategies for geopolitical dominance similar to those of Bush *hijo* would have been put into motion by any U.S. administration that was in power.

As of this writing (October 2002), the oil triumvirate of Bush, Cheney, and Rice, and their "wartime *consigliere*" Ashcroft are preparing to invade Iraq. Bush desperately needs a diversion from the economic crisis afflicting the U.S.—a crisis for which his administration has no solution. War seems to be the only answer. In order to make his case for war against Iraq, Bush sets himself up as a modern-day Churchill, holding fast against the barbarous threat of Saddam Hussein, a posture meant to contrast in the minds of the public with the infamous betrayal of Munich in 1938 when British Prime Minister Neville Chamberlain succumbed to Hitler's aggressive politics and placed Czechoslovakia in the hands of the Nazis. The comparison of Bush's challenge to Hussein with Churchill's challenge to Hitler, however, "attains a degree of mendacity that no other administration has ever achieved."[151] In fact Bush's clarion call for a war with Iraq "recalls the methods employed by the Nazi regime in its wilful fabrication of the Czech crisis and its conduct of the negotiations in Munich in September, 1938." The Bush foreign policy "is being shaped by ruthless and reckless sections of the U.S. ruling elite who are aggressively demanding the use of war as a means of realizing the global geostrategic and economic ambitions of American imperialism."[152]

The Bush administration is worried about the stability of Saudi Arabia, especially given that many September 11 terrorists were recruited from that country. Since Saudi Arabia is the principal supplier of Persian Gulf oil to the U.S., and since Cheney's recent *National Energy Policy Report* made it abundantly clear that future U.S. oil supplies would have to come from the Persian Gulf region, the Bush administration is seeking a backup should instability in Saudi Arabia lead to a drop in oil production, triggering a global recession.[153] As Michael Klare notes, the only country that possesses the capacity to substantially increase oil production in the event of a Saudi collapse is Iraq.[154] Control of Iraqi oil would enable the U.S. to ignore to an even greater extent than it already does Saudi demands for U.S. assistance to the Palestinians. Such control would also weaken OPEC's ability to set oil prices. Klare points out that Iraq harbors the world's largest remaining reservoir of untapped and unclaimed petroleum, so whoever controls this reservoir will influence global energy markets of the twenty-first century. Hussein has begun to provide contracts for these untapped fields to oil firms in Europe, Russia, and China in an attempt to win allies in his confrontation with the Bush regime. Iraqi dissidents chosen by Washington to lead a new regime in Baghdad have said they will cancel all contracts awarded to countries refusing to assist the U.S. in overthrowing Hussein. As Klare indicates, most Hussein-era contracts to be voided by any new regime set up by Washington are expected to be awarded to U.S. oil firms, in a move Klare calls potentially "the biggest oil grab in modern history."[155]

Bush has condemned Iraq for flouting numerous UN resolutions (conveniently ignoring the fact that Israel has done so for the last thirty-five years), and for developing weapons of mass destruction (again, conveniently ignoring the fact that the sale of U.S. hardware to Iraq during the Reagan and Bush *padre* administrations helped fund Iraq's chemical and biological arsenals). When Bush offers to examine Iraq's war crimes of the past, he can count on the fact that the American public will be largely ignorant of the fact that these crimes occurred with the tacit approval of the Reagan and Bush *padre* administrations—a condition of social amnesia we can attribute largely to the success of the corporate media. This clears the way for Bush *hijo*'s role as avenging angel. But history has taught us, warns Robert Scheer, "to beware the firepower of the angels of death, for they are never restrained by uncertainty of purpose."[156]

The author wishes to thank Carl Boggs for his suggestions on earlier drafts of this chapter.

Notes

1. This is a revised draft of several papers that have been previously published or that are now in press: "The Dialectics of Terrorism: A Marxist Response to September 11. (Part One: Remembering to Forget)" *Cultural Studies/Critical Methodologies*, (vol. 2, no. 2, May, 2002), 169–190; "The Dialectics of Terrorism: A Marxist Response to September 11. (Part Two: Unveiling the Past, Evading the Present)" *Cultural Studies/Critical Methodologies*, December, 2002; "George Bush, Apocalypse Sometime Soon, and the American Imperium." *Cultural Studies/Critical Methodologies*, (vol. 2, no. 3, 2002), 327–333.
2. Cesare Beccaria, *On Crimes and Punishment*. Translated and with an introduction by Henry Paolucci. (New York: Macmillan, and London: Collier Macmillan, 1963), 1. (Originally published in 1764.)
3. William Bennett. *Why We Fight: Moral Clarity and the War on Terrorism* (New York: Doubleday, 2002).
4. Max Boot, *The Savage Wars of Peace: Small Wars and the Rise of American Power* (New York: Basic Books, 2002).
5. George Monibot, "The Logic of Empire," *The Guardian*, Tuesday, August 6, 2002, 1. See http://www.guardian.co.uk/comment/story/0,3604,769699,00.html
6. Ibid.
7. Ibid.
8. Leo Panitch, "Violence as a Tool of Order and Change: The War on Terrorism and the Antiglobalization Movement." *Monthly Review*, vol. 54, no. 2 (June, 2002), 20.
9. Tom Barry, "Frontier Justice: A Weekly Chronicle," *The Progressive Response*. Vol. 6, No. 22, July 25, 2002, 3. Also available online: http://www.fpif.org/progresp/volume6/v6n22.html
10. Ibid.
11. Cited in Elayne Tobin, "Dubyaspeak," *The Nation*, Vol. 275, no. 5, August 5–12, 2002, 42.
12. See Michael Elliot, "George W. Kipling," *Time*, 8 July 2002, 35.
13. Leo Panitch, "Violence as a Tool of Order and Change: The War on Terrorism and the Antiglobalization Movement." *Monthly Review*, vol. 54, no. 2 (June, 2002), 21.
14. Walter Gilberti, "Bush Administration Moves to Stifle Discovery in 9/11 Lawsuits," *World Socialist Web Site*, August 2, 2002, 1–3. See http://www.wsws.org/articles/2002/aug2002/bush-a02.shtml
15. Responding to Exxon Mobil lawyers' request for State Department intervention on foreign-policy grounds, the State Department argued that the lawsuit could hurt business interests in Indonesia, discouraging foreign investment as well as impeding its joint-venture war on terrorism with Indonesia's infamous military forces. See Tom Wright, "US Moves to Block Human-Rights Lawsuit Against Exxon Mobil." *Dow Jones Business News*, Tuesday, August 6, 2002. http://story.news.yahoo.com/news?tmpl=story&u=/dowjones/20020806/bs_dowjones/2002080601343000163
16. See "US Disavows Report on Saudis," *Los Angeles Times*, Wednesday August 7, 2002, A6. See also Carol J. Williams, "Allies Cool to Striking Baghdad," *Los Angeles Times*, Wednesday August 7, A1, A8.

17. Eduardo Galeano, *Upside Down: A Primer for the Looking-Glass World* (New York: Metropolitan Books) 7.
18. Ibid., 8.
19. Ritt Goldstein, "Foundations are in Place for Martial Law in the US." *The Sydney Morning Herald* (July 27, 2002), 2. Also available online: http://smh.com.au/articles/2002/07/27/1027497418339.html
20. Ibid.
21. Henry Weinstein, Daren Briscoe, and Mitchell Landberg, "Civil Liberties take a back seat to safety." *Los Angeles Times*, March 20, 2002, A1.
22. "Response to Terror: in Brief," *Los Angeles Times*, Tuesday, November 16, 2001, A10.
23. Benjamin Barber, "Beyond Jihad vs. McWorld: On Terrorism and the New Democratic Realism," *The Nation*, Vol. 274, no. 2, January 21, 2002, 17.
24. Denys Turner, *Marxism and Christianity* (Oxford: Basil Blackwell, 1983), 151.
25. Manning Marable, "The Failure of U.S. Foreign Policies." *Along the Color Line*. November, 2001. http://www.manningmarable.net, 1.
26. Wadi'h Halabi, "Who's Afraid of Globalization?" *Political Affairs*, Vol. 81, no. 6, June, 2002, 7–9.
27. David Eisenhower, "The Forever War: Globalization and the New World Order." *Political Affairs*, Vol. 81, no. 6, June, 2002, 11.
28. Cited in Peter Schwab, *Cuba: Confronting the U.S. Embargo* (New York: St. Martin's Press, 1999).
29. David Eisenhower, ibid., 12.
30. David Eisenhower, ibid., 11.
31. Duncan Green, "Let Latin America Find its Own Path," *The Observer*, August 4, 2002, 1.
32. Ibid.
33. Ibid.
34. See Zbigniew Brzezinski, *The Global Chessboard: American Primacy and Its Geostrategic Imperative.*
35. David Eisenhower, ibid. 13.
36. John Powers, "Rank and Yank at Enron, or, the Fine Art of Bankruptcy," *LA Weekly*, Vol. 24, no. 3, January 11–17, 2002, 24. Also available online, http://www.laweekly.com/ink/02/08/on-powers.php
37. Ibid.
38. Ibid.
39. Steven Mikulan, "A Small Universe of People," *LA Weekly*, Vol. 24, no. 4, Nov. 30–Dec. 6, 2001, 23. Also available online, http://www.laweekly.com/archives
40. Bernard Weiner, "The OEWar on Terrorism for Dummies," *Counterpunch*. March 3, 2002. Available online, http://www.counterpunch.org/archives, 6.
41. Alfredo Tryferis, "Bill's Blather," *Los Angeles New Times*, Dec. 6–12, 2001, 7.
42. Gilbert Achar, "The Clash of Barbarisms," *Monthly Review*, Vol. 54, no. 4 (September 2002), 24.
43. Ibid.
44. Ibid., 25.
45. Ibid.
46. Ibid., 26.
47. Ibid., 27.
48. Ibid., 23.
49. James Wolcott, "Terror on the Dotted Line," *Vanity Fair*, January 2001, 54.
50. Peter Hart, "No Spin Zone?" *Extra*, Vol. 14, no. 6, December, 2001, 8.
51. Ibid.
52. Ibid.
53. Aaron Lukas, "America Still the Villain," *National Post*, 18 September 2001, quoted in Leo Panitch, "Violence as a Tool of Order and Change: The War on Terrorism and the Antiglobalization Movement." *Monthly Review*, Vol. 54, no. 2 (June, 2002), 12–32.
54. John Pilger, *Hidden Agendas* (London: Vintage, 1999), 36.
55. John Le Carré, "A War We Cannot Win," *The Nation*, Vol. 273, no. 16, November 19, 2001, 15.
56. David Barsamian, "Edward Said Interview," *The Progressive*, November, 2001. Available online, http://www.progressive.org/0901/intv1101.html
57. James Petras, "Signs of a Police State are Everywhere," *Z*, Vol. 15, no. 1, January 2002, 10.
58. See "'Anti-Terror' Law: Shredding Your Rights," *Workers Vanguard*, No. 770, December 7, 2001, 1, 8–10.

59. Cited in Jean Bricmont, "Why We Should Still be Anti-Imperialists," *What Next?* No. 23 (2000): http://mysite.freeserve.com/whatnext/

60. Lisa Macdonald, "The Nature of Islamic Fundamentalism," *Links*, No. 21, May to August 2002. Available online http://www.dsp.org.au/links/back/issue21/Macdonald.htm

61. Peter Hudis, "Terrorism, Bush's Retaliation Show Inhumanity of Class Society," *News and Letters*, Vol. 46, no. 8, October 2001, 1, 10–11.

62. Cited in John McMurtry, "Why is there a War in Afghanistan?" Opening address, *Science for Peace Forum and Teach-In, University of Toronto*, December 9, 2001, 1–13.

63. Ibid.

64. James Petras, "Notes Towards an Understanding of Revolutionary Politics Today," *Links*, No. 19, September to December 2001, 14. Available online http://www.dsp.org.au/links/back/issue19/petras.htm

65. Hudis, *News and Letters*, 2001.

66. Ibid.

67. Steve Niva, "Fight the Roots of Terrorism," *Common Dreams News Center*. Friday, Septermber 21, 2001. Available online http://commondreams.org/views01/0921–06.htm

68. Hudis, *News and Letters*, 2001.

69. Samir Amin, "Political Islam," *Covert Action Quarterly*, No. 71, Winter 2001, 3–6.

70. Macdonald, "The Nature of Islamic Fundamentalism."

71. Ibid., 17.

72. Ibid.

73. JoAnn Kawell, "Terror's Latin American Profile", *NACLA Report on the Americas*, Vol. XXXV, no. 3, 2001, 50–53.

74. John Pilger, "There Is No War on Terrorism. If There Was, the SAS Would be Storming the Beaches of Florida," *New Statesman*, Vol. 14, Issue 680, October 29, 2001, 2–3.

75. Bertell Ollman. As cited in Tony Monchinski, "Capitalist Schooling: An Interview with Bertell Ollman," *Cultural Logic*. Vol. 4, no. 1 (2002), 7. http://eserver.org/clogic/4–1/monchinski.html

76. See Peter McLaren and Jill Pinkney-Pastrana, "Cuba, Yanquizacion, and the Cult of Elian Gonzales: A View from the 'Enlightened' States," *International Journal of Qualitative Studies in Education*, Vol. 14, no. 2, March-April 2001, 201–219.

77. William Blum, *Killing Hope: U.S. Military and CIA Interventions Since World War II*. (Monroe, ME: Common Courage Press, 1995), 8.

78. Michael T. Klare, "Asking 'Why,'" *Foreign Policy in Focus*, September 2001, available online http://www.fpif.org/commentary/0109why.html

79. Noam Chomsky, "The New War Against Terror," *Counterpunch*, October 24, 2001, 11. Also available online http://www.counterpunch.org/chomskyterror.html

80. Ahmad, Eqbal. "Terrorism: Theirs and Ours." A presentation at the University of Boulder, Colorado, October 12, 1998. Association of Tamils of Eelam & Sri Lanka in the U.S. http://www.sangam.org/ANALYSIS/Ahmad.htm

81. Alexander Cockburn, "The Wide World of Torture," *The Nation*, Vol. 273, no. 17, November 26, 2001, 10.

82. Orlando Tizon, "Torture: State Terrorism vs. Democracy." *CovertAction Quarterly*, no. 73 (Summer 2002), 7.

83. Ibid.

84. Ibid.

85. Ibid.

86. Bill O'Brien, "Say Anything," *Slate Online Magazine*, Saturday, December 15, 2001. Available online http://slate.msn.com/?id=2059793

87. James Petras and Henry Veltmeyer, *Globalization Unmasked: Imperialism in the 21st Century* (London and New York: ZedBooks and Halifax, Canada: Fernwood Publishing, 2001), 30.

88. Petras and Veltmeyer, ibid.

89. Petras and Veltmeyer, ibid.

90. Petras, "Signs of a Police State Are Everywhere," *Z Magazine*, September 2002.

91. Ibid., 5.

92. Ted Fishman, "Making a Killing: The Myth of Capital's Good Intentions," *Harper's*, Vol. 1850, no. 1827, August 2002, 33–41.

93. Ibid., 34.

94. Ibid., 41.

95. Eyal Press, "Rebel with a Cause: The Re-Education of Joseph Stiglitz," *The Nation*, Vol. 274, no. 22, June 10, 2002, 16.
96. Michael Klare, "Endless Military Superiority," *The Nation*, Vol. 275, no. 3, June 15, 2002, 15.
97. Petras and Veltmeyer, *Globalization Unmasked: Imperialism in the 21st Century*.
98. Alex Callinicos, *Against the Third Way* (Cambridge, U.K.: Polity Press, 2001), 119.
99. Ibid.
100. McMurtry, "Why is there a War in Afghanistan?"
101. Ibid., 3.
102. Ibid., 4.
103. Ibid., 9.
104. Ibid., 9.
105. Ibid., 9.
106. Ibid., 9–10.
107. Joel Kovel, "Ground Work," *Tikkun*, Vol. 17, no. 1, January/February 2002, 17. Also available online http://www.tikkun.org/magazine/index.cfm/action/tikkun/issue/tik0201/article/020111d.html
108. Lewis Lapham, "Drums Along the Potomac," *Harper's*, Vol. 303, no. 1818, November 2001, 41.
109. Cited in Joey Bortfeld and Jim Naureckas, *Extra!* Vol. 14, no. 3, June 2001, 14.
110. Ibid.
111. Cited in Kovel, "Ground Work," 17.
112. Fawzia Afzal-Khan, "Here are the Muslim Feminist Voices, Mr. Rushdie!" *Television and News Media*, Vol. 3, no. 2, May 2002, 139–142.
113. Cited in Chellis Glendinning, "Re-membering Decolonization," *Tikkun*, Vol. 17, no. 1, January/February, 2002, 42.
114. David MacMichael, "CIA and RIT. Fundamentally Incompatible: 'Intelligence' and Higher Education," *CovertAction Quarterly*, no. 73, (Summer, 2002), 15.
115. Steve Rendall, "'We've Made it Impossible to Talk About Iraq': Interview with Former U.N. Weapons Inspector Scott Ritter," *Extra!*, Vol. 15, no. 4 (August, 2002), 16–18.
116. David Corn, "W. and the Coal Miners: Photo-Op Cover for Anti-worker Policies," *The Nation*, August 9, 2002. http://www.thenation.com/capitalgames/index.mhtml?bid=3&pid=90
117. Bill Vann, "Bush Rubs Shoulders with the Pennsylvania Miners," World Socialist Web Site (8 August, 2002). http://www.wsws.org/articles/2002/aug2002/mine-a08.shtml
118. See David Corn, ibid.; and Bill Vann, ibid.
119. Bill Vann, ibid.
120. Carlos Fuentes, "New Reality, New Legality," *El Andar*, Vol. 12, no. 3, Fall/Winter 2001, 33.
121. Dana Milbank, "Religious Right Finds Its Center in Oval Office," *Washington Post*, December 24, 2001. As cited in Gilbert Achar, "The Clash of Barbarisms," *Monthly Review*, Vol. 54, no. 4 (September, 2002), 21–22.
122. Mark Crispin Miller, *The Bush Dyslexicon: Observations On a National Disorder* (New York and London: Norton, 2002), 148.
123. John L. Hess, "Indirect from the Battlefield," *Extra! Update*, February 2002, 4.
124. Lewis H. Lapham, "Notebook: Compass Bearings," *Harper's*, Vol. 305, no. 1828 (September): 9–11.
125. Ibid.
126. Ibid.
127. Rachel Coen, "New York Times Buries Stories of Airstrikes on Civilians," *Extra! Update*, February, 2002, 3.
128. Fuentes, "New Reality, New Legality," 33.
129. David MacMichael, op. cit., 15.
130. Michael Grosso, *The Millennium Myth: Love and Death at the End of Time* (Wheaton, IL: Quest Books, 1995), 197.
131. Cited in Eric Umansky, "Eyeing the Axis," *Slate Online Magazine*, Wednesday, February 20, 2002. http://slate.msn.com/?id=2062284
132. Ibid.
133. Cited in John Powers, "On Wyatt Earp and theWitchfinder General," *LA Weekly*, December 14–20, 2001, 18. Also, available online, http://www.laweekly.com/ink/02/04/on-powers.php
134. Cited in Mark Crispin Miller, op. cit. 147–148.
135. *New York Times*, 24 June 1982, as cited in "'Anti-Terror' Law: Shredding Your Rights," *Workers Vanguard*, No. 770, December 7, 2001, 8–10.

136. Alexander Cockburn, "Sharon or Arafat: Which is the Sponsor of Terror?" *The Nation*, Vol. 273, no. 21, December 24, 2001, 10.
137. Cited in Umansky, op. cit.
138. Ibid.
139. Lewis Lapham, "Notebook: Dues Lo Volt," *Harper's*, Vol. 304, no. 1824, May 2002, 9.
140. Kovel, "Ground Work," 17.
141. Jean O. Pasco, "Cheney Hits Right Notes for Nixon Library Audience," *Los Angeles Times*, February 20, 2002, Section B, 6.
142. Rene Girard, *Violence and the Sacred*, translated by P. Gregory (Baltimore: Johns Hopkins University Press, 1977), 306.
143. Alexander Cockburn, "Terrorism as Normalcy," *The Nation*, Vol. 275, no. 1, July 1, 2002, 9. See also Dennis Bernstein, "Strangling the Messengers: Palestine and the High Price of Truth-Telling." *CovertAction Quarterly*, no. 73 (Summer, 2002), 4.
144. John Le Carré, "A War We Cannot Win," *The Nation*, Vol. 273, no. 16, November 19, 2001, 17.
145. David MacMichael, op. cit., 15.
146. Lewis H. Lapham, "Notebook: Uncommon Sense," *Harper's*, Vol. 305, no. 1826, July 2002, 7.
147. Ibid., 9.
148. Doug Lorimer, "Imperialism in the 21st Century," *Links*, No. 21, May to August 2002, http://www.dsp.org.au/links/
149. Cited from *Harper's*, March 1995, 42, in John McMurtry, *Value Wars: Moral Philosophy and Humanity* (London: Pluto Press) in press.
150. Monbiot, "The Logic of Empire," ibid., 3.
151. David North, "The Bush Administration Wants War," *World Socialist Web Site*, September 18, 2002. http://www.wsws.org/articles/2002/sep2002/iraq-s18.shtml
152. Ibid.
153. Michael T. Klare, "Oiling the Wheels of War," *The Nation*, vol. 275, no. 11 (October, 2002), 6–7.
154. Ibid.
155. Ibid., 7.
156. Robert Scheer, "Bush Jumps the Gun With Preemptive Strikes," *Los Angeles Times*, September 24, 2002, B13.

CHAPTER 8

Outlaw Nation

The Legacy of U.S. War Crimes

CARL BOGGS

Consistent with the general political mythologies that shroud American foreign and military policies, namely that the U.S. has historically been a force behind human rights, democracy, and lawful behavior in global affairs, any serious public discourse around U.S. culpability for terrible abuses of democratic practice and international law—much less for war crimes or crimes against humanity—has always been taboo, outside legitimate debate. As far as the established media, political system, and academic world are concerned, the nation's international presence has been a taken-for-granted benevolent one, motivated by good intentions and dedicated to human progress despite occasional flaws or mistakes in carrying out its policies. War crimes are demonic, barbaric actions carried out by others—Nazis, Serbs, Iraqis, Rwandans, Chinese, Japanese, and of course terrorists. Even where the U.S. and its allies or surrogates have been clearly shown to commit atrocities of one sort or another, these are justified within the larger humanitarian design of Western values and interests, or they simply wind up obscured to the point of vanishing from public view. This phenomenon has been deeply reinforced in the post-9/11 atmosphere in which Hobbesian chaos produced by the terrorist menace requires ever-harsher police, intelligence, and military responses in defense of an embattled society. Yet, if the war on terrorism has exacerbated already strong trends toward expansion of the security state and war machine, it has also pointed toward a different set of concerns: the need for universal laws and principles to restrain military forces in their violent pursuit of political ends.

The historical reality is that the U.S. drive for economic, political, and military domination has led to massive and horrific war crimes, to repeated and flagrant violations of international law—a legacy easily documented but one which has been obscured, covered up, or simply ignored within the national ethos of denial. The U.S. record of war crimes has been, from the nineteenth century to the present, a largely invisible one with no government, no political leaders, no military officials, no lower-level operatives held accountable for criminal actions. A culture of militarism has saturated the public sphere, including academia, endowing *all* U.S. interventions abroad with a patina of patriotic goodness and democratic sensibilities beyond genuine interrogation. Anyone challenging this mythology is quickly marginalized, branded a traitor or Communist or terrorist or simply a lunatic beyond the pale of reasonable discussion. After 9/11 this situation has worsened: a nominally liberal-democratic system has moved ever more ominously along the road of corporatism, authoritarianism, and narrowing public discourses. American society today exhibits every sign of ideological closure, one-dimensionality, and erosion of civic culture accompanied by the rise of national chauvinism and hostility to foreign influences, exacerbated by the spring 2003 invasion and occupation of Iraq. Recent ideological trends involve a steadfast refusal to confront the larger context of U.S. foreign policy or to reflect upon the far-reaching consequences of U.S. empire, as if the terrorist attacks occurred in a historical void. Of course psychological denial has profound ramifications, for with it a siege mentality can readily appear—and such a mentality seems to have gripped much of American public life. As Chalmers Johnson writes in *Blowback*: "What we have freed ourselves of . . . is any genuine consciousness of how we might look to others on this globe. Most Americans are probably unaware of how Washington exercises its global hegemony since so much of this activity takes place either in relative secrecy or under comforting rubrics. Many may, as a start, find it hard to believe that our place in the world even adds up to an empire."[1] Nowhere is this proposition more evident than in the sphere of war crimes discourse.

In their ambitious and far-ranging volume, *Crimes of War*, Roy Gutman and David Rieff follow this ethnocentric pattern exactly, detailing a vast assemblage of military atrocities from every corner of the globe—the blame always squarely placed on *others*: Russians, Serbs, Iraqis, Rwandans, South Africans. References to war crimes attributed to U.S. allies or client states are careful to avoid any mention of American complicity, whether in furnishing arms, training, material and logistical supports, or political backing. Where reference to U.S. involvement could simply not be avoided, as in the Indochina War and the use of nuclear weapons against Japan, ethical and political issues are treated in a rather ambiguous fashion. The authors of this comprehensive text merely *assume*, contrary to all historical evidence, that U.S. foreign and military policies have been guided by noble ambitions: democracy, human rights, rule of law. As for the canons of international law, here again the U.S. and its allies are presented as standing at the forefront in the struggle for universal principles of rights and obligations, valiantly striving to extend liberal ideals to a generally messy, violent, and recalcitrant world—as in the recent case of Iraq. Thus: "In the well-off Western countries, the canons of international law took hold. . . ."[2] The historic shift toward codification of worldwide humanitarian law, say the authors, was triggered by the awful events in the Balkans during the 1990s, when Serbs under Slobodan Milosevic embarked upon their program of "ethnic cleansing."[3] In his brief introduction to the volume, Lawrence Wechsler exults that we are presently in the midst of an important historical development—reflected in the Hague Tribunal for the Former Yugoslavia—toward expansion and codification of international law applied to crimes of war. We have reached a conjuncture where new global procedures, norms, laws, and conventions can be firmly established, thanks to the bold initiatives of Western powers.[4] That the 79 days of NATO bombing of Yugoslavia, with its massive destruction of the public infrastructure and terrible civilian toll, was itself a gross violation of the United Nations Charter (Article 2-4) which obliges member states to "refrain in their international relations from the threat or use of force against the territorial integrity or political independence of any state" is never mentioned. Nor is the fact that the Hague Tribunal, obsessed with prosecuting mainly Serbs, has not indicted any NATO leaders for war crimes in the face of abundant evidence.

As I argue in this essay, the "rules of engagement" for U.S. economic, political, and military intervention are shaped far less by any ethical or humanitarian concerns than by sheer geopolitical *power* interests that, in the New World Order, seem to recognize no limits, as we have abundantly seen in Iraq. Indeed American national interests, even with increasing globalization, have increasingly come to be asserted over the canons of international law—most starkly visible in Bush junior's formulation of a military strategy based upon the doctrine of "preemptive strike." The rules of U.S. military action today have little to do with customs or morality or laws that might in any way infringe upon national interest or the transnational corporate power it supports. It is probably fair to say that, for the U.S., "ethics" has little meaning once we reach the water's edge. From this standpoint, international law exists only to protect the most powerful. What Sven Lindqvist writes seems especially relevant to the American modus operandi: "The laws of war protect [those] of the same race, class, and culture. The laws of war leave the foreign and the alien [and one might add weak] without protection."[5]

Today perhaps more than ever, U.S. foreign policy revolves around a harsh, brutal ("realistic") principle—that its military can intervene virtually anywhere in the world (or indeed in space) outside the jurisdiction of international justice, beholden to no higher authority, while suffering minimal negative consequences for its desperado politics. Moreover, given the advent of high-tech weaponry, aerial and space-based surveillance, new sophisticated aircraft, and enhanced battlefield flexibility, the empire has presumably entered a comfortable zone of "safe wars." Never in history has a nation established such global hegemony, with military bases scattered worldwide, a huge nuclear arsenal, widespread covert action made more efficient by new technology, and a military budget larger than the next eight nations combined. U.S. military action has led, directly and indirectly, to terrible loss of human life since World War II, much of it the result of deliberate, planned, callous strategies.[6] Aerial bombardment in particular has been devastating, but artillery, infantry, armor, death squads, and economic sanctions have taken an unspeakable toll. American crimes of war have been overt and brutally direct as in the cases of Indochina, Panama, Iraq, and Yugoslavia, or mediated through proxy wars carried out in such locales as Central America, Indonesia, Turkey, Israel, and Colombia, although the agents of such crimes have usually managed to escape culpability.

NATO's Hague Tribunal

By the 1990s, after a full century of treaties, conventions, and tribunals designed to establish legal criteria for governing the military behavior of nations, no truly universal structure for this purpose had been established. Principles embodied in the various Hague and Geneva Protocols along with the Nuremberg and Tokyo courts set up after World War II—much of which found its way into the UN Charter of 1948—had never become internationally binding in legal or political terms. The great promise of Nuremberg to hold political and military leaders responsible for war crimes and crimes against humanity did not come to fruition. Finally, in 1998, a majority of nations (139 in all) met in Rome to ratify a treaty creating an International Criminal Court that would allow for binding global jurisdiction. The Court would be a professional, impartial body charged with bringing leaders and others to justice for assorted war crimes, genocide, and crimes against humanity. In July 2002, the Court became a reality, confirming the long-held hopes of human-rights partisans around the world. Unfortunately, however, the U.S. took a fiercely hostile stance to the Court from the outset, first refusing to sign the treaty and then setting out to sabotage the body's operations. The U.S. government, first under Clinton and then under Bush, insisted upon "guarantees" that no American officials or military personnel could be brought before the Tribunal; the nation with the only truly global military presence wanted immunity.

The U.S. was threatening to paralyze UN peacekeeping operations in Bosnia and elsewhere if it could not receive assurance that Americans would be insulated from Criminal Court prosecution—conditions that backers of the Court found politically and legally untenable. Having refused to endorse the Tribunal, the U.S. now demanded special exemption from possible charges, arguing that it might be the target of "politically-motivated" legal actions. Despite broad support for the Court, Bush was able to say (in early July 2002): ". . . the one thing we're not going to do is sign on to the Criminal Court." Within a week of this statement, the U.S. was able to muscle through the Security Council a resolution granting U.S. troops and officials a renewable one-year exemption from investigation or prosecution by the International Court. But the U.S. exemption turned out to be outrageously illegal not to mention politically corrupt. As one long-time observer at the UN remarked: "We do not think it is the business of the Security Council to interpret treaties that are negotiated somewhere else."[7] The resolution was not only in flagrant opposition to the world consensus, it effectively validated the idea that the U.S. is free to stand outside the canons of international law. Such exceptionalism renders the Court and its procedures a mockery, since laws and procedures clearly require universality to be legitimate and effective. At precisely the time all this was taking place, Secretary of Defense Donald Rumsfeld outlined a series of sweeping proposals that would drastically weaken Congressional oversight of the Pentagon—the idea being to provide the military with more freedom than ever to conduct its domestic and global business, a move justified by the war against terrorism. Further, U.S. efforts to subvert the Criminal Court while expanding the scope of Pentagon power coincided with Bush's aggressive new strategy of "preemptive strike" directed, for the moment, against Iraq.

Yet even as the U.S. government refuses the jurisdiction of international law for its own behavior, its political elites remain ever vigilant in seeking to bring *others* to justice—notably those (like the Serbs) who have had the audacity to stand in the way of American geopolitical interests. The International Criminal Tribunal for the Former Yugoslavia (ICTY), set up by NATO powers in May 1993, has been convened in the Hague to try Milosevic and other Serb leaders for monstrous crimes supposedly carried out during a near-decade of bloody civil wars in the Balkans. Milosevic was indicted in May 1999, at the very height of the NATO attack on Yugoslavia, on 61 counts that included genocide, crimes against humanity, and war crimes associated with Serb policies of "ethnic cleansing" in Bosnia, Croatia, and Kosovo. Milosevic was arrested in March 2001, and then delivered to the Hague Tribunal in June 2001, after the U.S. simultaneously threatened and bribed the new Serb government with millions in cash. The Western powers, with the U.S. taking the lead, portrayed Milosevic and the Serbs as modern-day Nazis responsible for an unspeakable holocaust filled with acts of mass murder, mass rapes, torture, and ethnic cleansing that left the entire region devastated, in ruins. These atrocities were so horrific as to demand immediate "humanitarian" intervention by NATO military forces. Once the bombing was finished, the NATO-supported and financed Hague Tribunal would finally bring the Serb leaders to justice.

In the U.S., both the media and politicians eagerly embraced the new war crimes trials, celebrating the ICTY as an inspiring "triumph of the civilized world."[8] By holding Serb leaders accountable for such terrible crimes the Tribunal was said to have opened up a new era of international law. Former Secretary of State Madeleine Albright referred to the Hague as the "mother of all tribunals" where it would now be possible to try, in the manner of Nuremberg, some of the greatest monsters in European history.[9] Caricatured as a Hitler-like dictatorial figure obsessed with building an ethnically pure Greater Serbian state, Milosevic was deemed the kind of war criminal the world desperately needed to bring to trial in order to avoid a condition of "international anarchy."

Serbs were regularly demonized in the mass media, referred to by columnist Anthony Lewis and others as "beasts" and "monsters." The mainstream text *Indictment at the Hague* (2002) is subtitled "The Milosevic Regime and Crimes of the Balkans Wars." In it, authors Norman Cigar and Paul Williams set out to present a case for war crimes against the Serbs, replete with documents from the Hague Tribunal and U.S. State Department; there is no mention of other parties to the Balkans civil wars, nor to the role of NATO and the U.S. (in the context of war crimes). "No matter how he personally meets his end," write the authors, "Milosevic shall remain one of the most villainous figures in the history of the South Slavs." They add: "The atrocities committed by Serbian forces were part of a planned, systematic, and organized campaign to secure territory for an ethnically 'pure' Serb state by clearing it of all non-Serb populations." The Tribunal represents a historical breakthrough, they remind us, since by "attacking liability for war crimes [it] will serve as a reminder to other prospective war criminals that their actions will not be granted *de facto* immunity by the world community."[10]

Despite the overblown rhetoric denouncing genocidal Serb Nazis on the march, it takes little effort to reveal the ICTY as a first-rate fraud. From the very outset this Tribunal was totally biased and one-sided, hardly the product of universal jurisprudence—inevitable given that the Tribunal was set up and financed by the NATO powers (above all the U.S.) and received the bulk of its investigative and informational resources from these same powers, the very powers that carried out seven weeks of intensive military aggression against the Serbs. The fraudulence is quickly shown by the obvious one-sidedness of the indictments: after many years of violent civil wars involving not only Serbs but Croatians, Bosnian Muslims, Kosovar Albanians, and myriad paramilitary groups of varying ideological and ethnic makeup, not to mention the intense period of covert and armed intervention by NATO powers, we are told to believe that only the Serbs were guilty of atrocities, that all others were simply victims of a singular evil force, that others were victims *only* while Serbs themselves were *never* victimized. This scenario, constructed mainly by Western public relations firms and the mass media, defies all logic. Indeed the Serbs could be said to have suffered *most*, especially when the calculations of merciless NATO/U.S. bombings are taken into account. Without doubt Serbs were responsible for atrocities, but historical evidence from the field, unfiltered by propaganda, shows convincingly that atrocities were committed on all sides and that Serbs too were abundantly on the receiving end of war crimes. The Hague Tribunal has completely ignored this complex history, dismissing those instances where Serbs experienced the horrors of civil war—for example, several thousand killed and at least 500,000 displaced in Croatia alone, yet another 330,000 displaced in Kosovo in the wake of U.S.-backed Kosovo Liberation Army terrorism and NATO aerial attacks. In August 1995, the U.S.

and Germans supported a bloody Croatian military offensive in the Kraijina region, killing thousands of Serbs and forcing another 200,000 from their homes.[11] Yet when looking at such atrocities, the moral outrage over "ethnic cleansing" that so consumed NATO elites as they targeted Serbs suddenly vanishes. The failure of ICTY to address this terrible anomaly, to investigate and prosecute war crimes across the board, to pursue *all* combatants involved in the civil wars, demonstrates ipso facto its moral and political bankruptcy.

In reality the Hague proceedings do little more than conceal the long sordid involvement of the U.S. and its NATO allies in the Balkans; by now the self-righteous ruminations concerning "genocide" and "ethnic cleansing" should ring hollow. Nowhere has it been shown that Milosevic's supposed drive toward a "Greater Serbia" was motivated explicitly by goals of ethnic purity. Was "ethnicity" more a factor in Serbian politics than for the Croatians or Bosnians, or for the Kosovar Albanians? Belgrade itself was and remains an extremely diverse, cosmopolitan city, with Muslims, Albanians, and others by the hundreds of thousands living peacefully in close proximity. In no military operation of the civil wars was anything resembling a genocidal policy actually designed or carried out. The propaganda campaign focused on Serb atrocities was in fact not too far removed from the narrative contained in the film *Wag the Dog*. Such propaganda totally ignored the role of Western powers in the post–Cold War disintegration of Yugoslavia, the U.S. role in supporting the fascist Tudjman regime in Croatia, the horrors of the right-wing Islamic fundamentalist Izetbegovic regime in Bosnia, and the rampant terrorism of such groups as the KLA that was organized and funded by the U.S. Also ignored was the increased NATO *military* presence in regions of Yugoslavia after 1995, not to mention longstanding U.S. geopolitical interests in the Balkans.[12] To believe that *only* the Serbs could have committed war crimes within such a complex historical scenario is so preposterous on its face that, for this reason alone, the credibility of ICTY should be roughly zero.

In fact the most egregious crimes of war in the Balkans can be laid at the doorstep of the U.S./NATO military forces, guilty of carrying out 79 days of high-tech aerial terrorism with its wanton destruction of civilian targets and population, including virtually all of the Serb infrastructure. Belgrade alone suffered upwards of 10,000 casualties, with thousands more scattered throughout the country. The attacks destroyed power plants, factories, apartment complexes, bridges, water plants, roads, hospitals, schools, and communications networks. NATO targets in Yugoslavia were roughly 60 percent civilian, including 33 hospitals, 344 schools, and 144 industrial plants. The "humanitarian" air squadrons, relying on the comfort and safety of techno-war, dropped cluster bombs and delivered missiles tipped with depleted uranium, spewing thousands of tons of toxic chemicals and radiation into the air, water, and crops that will surely produce long-term health and ecological disasters. Beneath the rhetoric of human-rights intervention, a small, poor, weak, relatively defenseless nation of eleven million people was pulverized by the largest military machine in history. NATO Commander General Wesley Clark boasted that the aim of the air war was to "demolish, destroy, devastate, degrade, and ultimately eliminate the essential infrastructure of Yugoslavia."[13] This of course was no "war" but rather an aerial massacre of defenseless human beings, most of them civilians. Not only did this assault violate the UN Charter prohibiting offensive war against a sovereign nation, it willfully abrogated the whole tradition of Hague and Geneva Protocols declaring illegal the wanton destruction of civilian populations. Whatever the crimes of Milosevic, they would pale in comparison with the U.S./NATO reign of death and destruction in Yugoslavia. NATO leaders were indeed charged with monstrous war crimes in 1999, in a suit that named President Clinton, Defense Secretary William Cohen, Secretary of State Albright, and General Clark along with British leader Tony Blair. With massive evidence at their disposal, including calculated policies of mass murder, the plaintiffs took their case to the Hague Court, hoping for an audience before chief prosecutor Carla Del Ponte—but the case was summarily thrown out after U.S. leaders protested vehemently, convinced of the mystical (but iron) principle of American immunity. As for Milosevic, Hague prosecutors were admitting (in September 2002) that the case against him—once trumpeted with arrogant confidence—was more flawed than earlier believed owing to difficulty in proving the Serb leader's actual connection with the atrocities in question.

As in the Persian Gulf during 1991, there was never in fact a "war" between NATO and Serb forces in the Balkans—simply a protracted, one-sided campaign of aerial annihilation carried out in direct violation of international law. As Michael Parenti writes: "In sum, NATO's aerial aggression accomplished nothing, except to deliver a magnitude of death and destruction across Yugoslavia far greater than any it claimed to arrest."[14] It has become clear that the U.S. targeted the Milosevic government not because of terrible crimes against humanity—the ideologically charged nature of such claims made them bogus from the outset—but rather because it was seen as an impediment to U.S. domination of the Balkans, strategically close to the rest of Europe, Russia, the Middle East, and the Caspian Sea, a region rich in oil, natural gas, and other valuable resources.[15] U.S. plans were clearly laid out in a 46-page Pentagon document,[16] stating that the U.S. is prepared to militarily challenge any nation that stands in the way of U.S. policies and interests.[17]

In this context the Hague Tribunal can be seen as nothing more than a recycled form of victor's justice, where the entire proceedings are so politically biased and legally one-sided as to deny their very legitimacy. Here it represents not so much a new era of international law as a great retreat from its promises and a return to the earlier colonial ethos where the Western powers could dictate everything by means of crude military superiority.[18] Reflecting on the conflicted legacy of Nuremberg, Telford Taylor wrote: "To punish the foe—especially the vanquished foe—for conduct in which the enforcing nation has engaged, would be so grossly inequitable as to discredit the laws themselves."[19]

Crimes Against Peace

Even setting aside forms of intervention such as proxy wars, CIA-sponsored covert action, attempts at economic or political subversion, and blockades, the U.S. record of military aggression waged against sovereign nations since World War II stands alone for its criminality and barbaric outcomes. Immersed from the outset in a logic of seemingly perpetual warfare, the American nation-state first achieved imperial status as it expanded westward and outward, then reached maturity through development of the permanent war economy during and after World War II. Since 1945, the U.S. has initiated dozens of military attacks on foreign nations resulting in a gruesome toll: at least eight million deaths, tens of millions wounded, millions more made homeless, and ecological devastation impossible to measure. In the post-9/11 milieu, with the brazen military aggression against Iraq and new U.S. interventions on the horizon, there is sadly no end in sight to this imperial onslaught. With just two possible exceptions (the U.N.-backed Korean venture and recent operations in Afghanistan) these interventions violated commonly held principles of international law.

At the end of World War II, the Germans and Japanese were tried for "crimes against peace"—that is, unprovoked military aggression waged against sovereign nations. Eventually 15 Germans and 24 Japanese were convicted of such offenses, with U.S. prosecutors the most adamant in pursuing guilty verdicts. Nazi elites were prosecuted and convicted of planning and waging war against Poland, the USSR, Norway, Denmark, Holland, Yugoslavia, and Greece. The Charter of the International Military Tribunal at Nuremberg defined illegal warfare as "planning, preparation, initiation, or waging a war of aggression, or a war in violation of international treaties, agreements, or assurances, or participation in a common plan or conspiracy [for war]." Drawing on the Nuremberg principles, the nascent UN banned the first use of force, stating that "All members shall refrain in their international relations from the threat or use of force against the territorial integrity or political independence of any state." According to Steven Ratner, "the illegality of aggression is perhaps the most fundamental norm of modern international law and its prevention the chief purpose of the United Nations."[20] The Charter provides a definitive list of acts of military aggression: invasion, occupation, bombardment, blockade, attack on a nation's armed forces, using territory for aggression, supporting groups to carry out aggression. Such prohibitions are contained in many treaties, convention protocols, and organizational charters drawn up in the several decades since Nuremberg.

At one time or another, the U.S. has violated every one of these principles, holding itself (then as now) above the most hallowed norms of international law. Its acts of military aggression have, for the most part, been planned, deliberate, systematic, and brutal, with its massive firepower directed against weak, small, underdeveloped, and militarily inferior countries. Such acts were *always* carried out in the absence of serious military threat to the U.S. arising from the nations targeted for attack; the U.S. took the first move, sidestepping or ignoring serious diplomatic initiatives. The American military has conducted both selective and strategic bombing, attacked civilian populations and infrastructures, mined harbors, invaded and occupied foreign territories, set up blockades, organized massive population relocation programs, and set up paramilitary groups for proxy wars on behalf of U.S. interests—and has done so across the globe. In most cases U.S. military assaults have been blatantly unilateral, in others it has come under cover of a UN or NATO coalition where U.S. military (and political) resources were all-decisive. Rhetorical justifications for military adventure are offered for public consumption with regularity—"humanitarian" agendas, human rights, defense of national security, protection of American lives, arrest of drug traffickers, defeat of Communism or terrorism, support for democracy—none of which, however, enjoy much credibility outside the U.S. Economic and geopolitical interests have consistently driven U.S. military intervention in the postwar years.

A comprehensive list of U.S. military actions, direct and indirect, through 2001 can be found in William Blum's *Rogue State*.[21] The flimsy use of a human rights crusade to justify military aggression in the Balkans has already been mentioned. In the case of Vietnam, American leaders looked to a military solution from the first breakout of Vietnamese nationalism, purportedly to halt the spread of Communism in Southeast Asia. President Kennedy and his circle (Dean Rusk, Robert McNamara, McGeorge Bundy, Walt Rostow, Maxwell Taylor, and others) set forth an ambitious war plan according to which Indochina was to be a major testing ground in the Cold War. The foundation of everything that would unfold later—large-scale deployment of troops, aerial bombardments, strategic hamlets, free-fire zones, chemical warfare—was already in place under JFK.[22] War as counterinsurgency was immediately and energetically taken up as vital to the global contest between Communism and democracy. The logic of military intervention meant rapid expansion of U.S. operations, starting with teams of "advisers," from South to North Vietnam by 1965 and then to Laos and Cambodia, ignoring diplomatic overtures as spelled out in the 1954 Geneva Accords not to mention the UN Charter prohibition against military aggression. What JFK and his planners had set in place was further intensified during the Johnson and Nixon presidencies even though war was never formally declared against Vietnam, Laos, or Cambodia. The U.S. mercilessly bombed North Vietnam (after 1965), Laos (after 1965), and Cambodia (1969–70) with the deadliest aerial onslaught in history, leaving vast regions of utter destruction. For one of the most flagrant violations of international law ever, three U.S. presidents and their war managers ought to be held criminally accountable for crimes against peace just as the Nazis and Japanese were at Nuremberg. Christopher Hitchens has correctly identified Henry Kissinger as a mass murderer and war criminal for his role in Indochina, but Hitchens fails to explain why the list should stop with Kissinger.[23]

Turning to the Caribbean region, the U.S. has a long and well-known legacy of unprovoked military aggression there, designed to protect American economic and strategic interests. Leaving aside covert action and proxy wars, recent decades have witnessed one-sided warfare launched against five sovereign nations: Haiti, the Dominican Republic, Nicaragua, Grenada, and Panama. In April 1965, a popular revolt broke out in the Dominican Republic with the aim of restoring to power reformist Juan Bosch (earlier overthrown with U.S. help), whereupon the U.S. sent in 23,000 troops to crush the rebellion and keep a military dictatorship in power. Waging proxy warfare in Central America for many decades, U.S. operations became more "direct" at times—for example, with the mining of Nicaraguan harbors in the early 1980s. Nicaragua filed suit in the World Court in 1984 asking for relief, whereupon the Court ruled (in 1986) that the U.S. was in violation of international law, should cease its intervention, and should pay reparations. The Reagan government dismissed the charges and the verdict summarily, refusing to accept the Court's jurisdiction. In October 1983, the U.S. invaded tiny Grenada, killing hundreds of people (including 84 Cubans) with the intent of overthrowing the reformist Maurice Bishop government—ostensibly to "restore democracy." A decade later, in Haiti, President Clinton sent U.S. troops to bring Jean-Bertrand Aristide back to power under the diktat (enforced by occupying soldiers) that he adopt neoliberal economic policies.

Perhaps the most brazen U.S. military attack came against Panama on December 20, 1989, when air and ground forces invaded and then took over the country, ousting supposed drug-trafficker Manuel Noriega and installing its own friendly regime at the cost of at least 4,000 Panamanian lives (mostly civilian) and the crushing of opposition political groups. The working-class section of Panama City, El Chorillo, was largely demolished, with 14,000 people left homeless. The Bush presidency justified the totally unprovoked attack on several grounds—arresting Noriega for drug trafficking, restoring democracy, protecting American lives—none of which carried much weight relative to the pull of U.S. strategic interests in the Canal region. Bush never declared war, nor did he secure the endorsement of the Organization of American States or the United Nations.[24]

In the case of Iraq, U.S.-organized and managed crimes against peace must be considered among the most egregious of the twentieth century—and, sadly, they are ongoing. Dismissing all negotiating initiatives after the Iraqi attack on Kuwait in 1990, the U.S. mobilized a coalition of military forces, largely by means of bribes and threats, to carry out a fiercely efficient technowar against Iraq, destroying the country's frail infrastructure and killing at least 200,000 people, including 30,000 troops in retreat along the "highway of death" as operations were ending. The U.S. inflicted more damage on Iraq than on any other country in the twentieth century, excepting Vietnam. (Although the U.S. was able to buy participation of coalition partners, such as granting $7 billion in loans to Russia, *military* action remained mostly the province of Americans, with British help.) After the Gulf War the U.S. created "no-fly" zones over Iraq, continued regular bombing missions, and enforced draconian sanctions that UN agencies report have cost about 500,000 lives.[25] While the Security Council endorsed *political* efforts to contain Iraqi foreign ambitions, there were no stipulations allowing the kind of *military* carte blanche so eagerly pursued by the U.S. War crimes visited upon Iraq include some of the most barbaric in modern history. Even with the blessing of UN cover, the U.S. was guilty of planning and carrying out a brutal war of aggression intended to crush a sovereign nation.

Other less flagrant or horrendous cases of U.S. military aggression have taken place during the postwar years—for example, four aerial bombardments of Libya in the 1980s, troop deployments to Somalia in 1993, and the "war against terrorism" in Afghanistan beginning in October 2001. (The Afghan operations to destroy Al Qaeda base camps and overthrow the Taliban regime can be justified as strictly *defensive* responses to 9/11, permitted under the UN Charter, but the excessive cost in human lives there, reaching well over 3,000, raises questions of proportionality.) In early November 2002, a CIA-operated unmanned Predator aircraft struck a target in Yemen with a laser-guided Hellfire missile, killing six people in a vehicle—part of the increasingly bold military response to terrorism. This attack, coinciding with Bush's doctrine of "preemptive strike," expands the boundaries of warfare: the U.S. has given itself the right to intervene militarily in any country, at any time, in flagrant violation of international law.[26] In these and other cases a few generalizations regarding U.S. military intervention stand out: the casualty toll is mainly civilian, the military option is unprovoked, justifications are bogus, reliance on aerial technowar minimizes American casualties while creating more bloodshed on the ground, attacks are waged against rather small, weak, defenseless nations that deviate in some way from U.S. global priorities. In all cases (again with the possible exception of Afghanistan) U.S. militarism stands in direct, increasingly dangerous violation of international law, the very essence of crimes against peace.

U.S. leaders might try to argue that a breakdown in negotiations, due to the unreasonable stubbornness of adversaries, is enough to warrant military response. For the most part, however, U.S. "diplomacy" when confronting much weaker rivals has not been very serious, providing mainly a pretext for warfare. At no time has U.S. intervention met the conditions stipulated in the UN Charter—namely, that armed attack cannot proceed except in cases of national defense, or without efforts to negotiate in good faith. Indeed the very requirement for diplomacy has typically been problematic: international "crises" are more often than not contrived phenomena, as the cases of Vietnam, Iraq, and Panama reveal. When it takes place, U.S. diplomacy usually involves laying down a set of demands treated as ironclad and nonnegotiable, presented as the basis of "agreements." The other side is naturally reluctant to concede every point or yield to every condition (such as allowing foreign occupation troops or "weapons inspectors" to roam freely around the country). The predictable lack of cooperation is seized upon by U.S. "negotiators" as a clear sign of obstructionism, a failure to negotiate in good faith. Ultimatums are issued, followed by massive use of firepower extending from days to months and even years. Such maneuvers are doubly criminal insofar as they are deliberately fraudulent and a cynical cover for militaristic intent.

Aerial Terrorism—from Hiroshima to Baghdad

Since the final months of World War II, the U.S. military has dropped tens of millions of tons of bombs on several mostly defenseless countries with casualties (mostly civilian) also running into the tens of millions. Since the 1920s war managers have placed overriding faith in the efficacy of aerial warfare: planes were seen as awesome destructive machines capable of bringing "order" to the general chaos and unpredictability of ground and naval operations. Bombing from high altitudes was indeed a nascent form of technowar. By 1944 and 1945 this faith assumed new dimensions as first the British and then the U.S. embraced prospects of "strategic" or area bombing in Germany and Japan, ostensibly to end the war more quickly but in reality for purposes of revenge, weapons-testing, and political statement. With the incendiary assaults on German cities (Hamburg, Dresden, Berlin) by the Royal Air Force, U.S. General Curtis LeMay saw in this new model of aerial warfare vast possibilities for punishing the Japanese, literally burning cities to the ground while minimizing American casualties. This legacy remains a cornerstone of U.S. imperial power to the present day.

One problem with aerial combat is that it obliterates the time-honored distinction between combatants and noncombatants, between military and civilian targets—a maxim especially applicable to strategic bombing which, by definition, rains death and destruction indiscriminately across wide parcels of territory. Article 25 of the Fourth Hague Convention in 1907 stated that "bombardment, by whatever means, of towns, villages, dwellings, or buildings which are undefended, is prohibited"—still a valid principle of international law.[27] Efforts to deepen and further codify these provisions have been, predictably, fiercely resisted by the U.S. and Britain, nations that refused to prosecute the Germans and Japanese after World War II for bombing civilian populations, knowing they were even more guilty of the same crimes. Such rejectionism continued into the Geneva Conventions of 1949, with the U.S. especially opposed to any restraints on aerial bombing (including use of nuclear weapons). Above all the two countries worked diligently to block any reference to aerial "war crimes." As Lindqvist notes: "The victorious powers could hardly forbid bombing of civilians without incriminating themselves for what they had already done and planned to continue doing."[28]

Finally, in 1977, Protocol One of the Geneva Conventions was signed by 124 countries, despite continued U.S. resistance to any laws guaranteeing protection of civilians. The basic rule states: "In order to ensure respect for and protection of the civilian population and civilian objects, the parties to the conflict shall at all times distinguish between the civilian population and combatants and between civilian objects and military objectives and accordingly shall direct their operations only against military objectives." Article 52 further states that "attacks shall be limited strictly to military objectives." Article 54 contains additional references—for example: "It is prohibited to attack, destroy, remove, or render useless objects indispensable to the survival of the civilian population, such as foodstuffs, agricultural areas, . . . crops, livestock, drinking water installations and supplies and irrigation works. . . ." Article 57 warns those planning military attacks to "refrain from deciding to launch any attack which may be expected to cause incidental loss of civilian life, injury to civilians, damage to civilian objects, or a combination thereof."

If strictly adhered to, such provisions would rule out aerial warfare directed against populated areas or civilian infrastructures—precisely the methodology most favored by the Pentagon since 1945, and precisely why the war planners vehemently object to the provisions. In July 1945, American planes, with the Pacific war virtually ended, raided 66 defenseless Japanese cities with no military purpose in mind, burning most of them to ashes and killing up to 500,000 civilians. On March 9–10, 1945, hundreds of U.S. planes attacked Tokyo with incendiary bombs, killing 100,000 and making another one million homeless—again, without real military intent. As is well known, on August 6 and 9, 1945, the U.S. dropped atomic bombs on Hiroshima and Nagasaki, unprotected urban centers with little military import, killing at least 200,000 civilians. LeMay and his aides celebrated these raids as wonderful testimonials to the awesome power of aerial bombardment. Douglas MacArthur aide General Bonner Fuller, on the other hand, described the raids as "one of the most ruthless and barbaric killings of noncombatants in all history."[29] They were in stark violation of the Fourth Geneva Convention. In 1946 to 1948 the International Military Tribunal for the Far East tried Japanese political and military elites for war crimes, but in reality the U.S. was a much bigger offender—but of course as victor none of its officials were ever brought to justice nor was the very *discourse* of U.S. war crimes ever broached.

The end of World War II brought a new era in the history of military combat—aerial warfare without limits; strategic bombing, with the inevitable annihilation of civilian populations and infrastructures, was now (above all for the U.S.) perfectly legitimate, indeed preferred and celebrated. If World War II provided a testing ground for massive area bombing, for widespread use of incendiary devices including napalm, and for nuclear weaponry, the Korean War offered new opportunities for refinement: aerial terrorism was pushed to new levels. In three months of 1951 alone, the USAF used B-52s to systematically destroy every significant North Korean city and town, not only slaughtering hundreds of thousands of defenseless civilians but creating widespread homelessness, starvation, disease, and other miseries. No laws of warfare were adhered to. By the end of the war the Korean death toll (North and South) reached nearly three million, mostly from U.S. aerial bombardments. Visiting Korea in summer 1952, Supreme Court Justice William O. Douglas said: "I had seen the war-battered cities of Europe, but I had not seen devastation until I had seen Korea."[30] As in the case of Japan (and later Indochina), civilian populations were deliberately and brutally targeted, the massive death and destruction celebrated by its perpetrators. Referring to Korea and China, Lindqvist writes: "In American eyes, the yellow and red perils had now been united, and a half-billion people had suddenly become America's enemies."[31]

Two decades later, the U.S. had (between, roughly, 1965 and 1973) dropped eight million tons of bombs on Vietnam—by far the largest air assault in history, the equivalent of one hundred Hiroshima-sized atomic bombs. The goal was to conduct massive counterinsurgency mainly through saturation bombing carried out by B-52s, with no attempt whatsoever to distinguish between civilian and military objects. As William Gibson writes, Vietnam marked the real beginnings of technowar, involving a strategy explicitly designed to minimize ground combat and U.S. casualties, though it would not achieve full expression until Desert Storm in 1991.[32] Aside from nuclear weaponry itself (actually considered at one point), the U.S. military employed everything in its arsenal with the aim of bombing a poor, underdeveloped country into total submission: saturation attacks with 2000-pound bombs, napalm, white phosphorous, cluster bombs, chemical defoliants like Agent Orange, sophisticated missiles, and regular ordnance. Laos and Cambodia also became targets of much the same strategy, in more concentrated dosages. The war left some 10 million bomb craters in Vietnam alone.[33] Commenting on such aerial terrorism, Marilyn Young wrote: "In the South 9000 out of 15,000 hamlets, 25 million acres of farmland, 12 million acres of forest were destroyed and 1.5 million farm animals had been killed; . . . all six of the industrial cities in the North were badly damaged, as were the provincial and district towns and 4000 out of 5,800 agricultural communes. North and South, the land was cratered and planted with tons of unexploded ordnance."[34]

Honing merciless assaults against civilian targets, the U.S. manufactured new types of napalm designed to adhere more closely to the skin, burn more deeply, and cause more horrific injury. During World War II the U.S. had dropped 14,000 tons of napalm, mainly against the Japanese. During the Korean War the total was 32,000 tons. But in Vietnam, from 1963 to 1971, the total was about 373,000 tons of the new, more effective napalm—eleven times the total used in Korea. Napalm was especially preferred by the military since it could destroy wide target areas while incapacitating human beings with only peripheral hits.[35]

During the Gulf War the USAF flew 11,000 sorties that dropped 88,000 tons of bombs, more than half of them on densely populated urban centers like Baghdad and Basra. There was deliberate intent to destroy the Iraqi infrastructure, with the stated objective of leaving the country of 23 million people in a preindustrial state. This meant destroying targets essential to human life: water and electrical plants, transportation, communications, agriculture, factories, even residential dwellings. The U.S. brought debilitating aerial weapons, including 15,000-pound "daisy cutter" bombs, CBU-87 cluster bombs with random killing effects over hundreds of square meters, 2.5-ton superbombs, a variety of bombs and missiles tipped with depleted uranium (DU). The human and ecological consequences of such weapons of wanton destruction will persist for decades, exacerbated by continued bombing raids *after* 1991 and draconian economic sanctions legitimated by the UN Security Council but maintained and enforced by American power.[36] For acts of military aggression against Iraq the first Bush administration was charged with massive war crimes by the independent Commission for Inquiry for the International War Crimes Tribunal. Indictment four states: "The U.S. intentionally bombed and destroyed civilian life, commercial and business districts, schools, hospitals, mosques, churches, shelters, residential areas, historical sites, private vehicles, and civilian government offices." Indictment five adds: "The U.S. intentionally bombed indiscriminately throughout Iraq." Volumes of evidence were brought forward in support of these charges.[37] Such wanton aerial destruction violates every canon of international law and morality.

In spring 1999, the U.S. and some of its NATO allies initiated bombing raids over Yugoslavia for seven weeks, visiting similarly terrible destruction upon Belgrade and other Serb cities and towns. The attacks destroyed public and residential buildings, water and electrical works, transportation, communications, bridges, hospitals, schools, and food production as well as military targets, leaving the Serb civilian infrastructure in ruins, killing up to 10,000 people, and leaving hundreds of thousands displaced. Civilian objects were deliberately and systematically hit, in accordance with General Clark's ruthless edict mentioned above. The U.S. reliance on technowar again favored deployment of especially fearsome weapons: bombs and missiles tipped with DU, cluster bombs, napalm, mines dropped from parachutes, and toxic chemicals sprayed on cropland and water supplies.[38] All this against a nation virtually devoid of an air force or even air defenses—that is, defenseless, as revealed by the fact the U.S. military suffered *no* casualties while producing its endless carnage. As in Iraq, of course, this was really no "war" but rather an organized, planned, criminal massacre orchestrated from the skies. As Parenti observes:

"Such a massive aggression amounts to a vastly greater war crime than anything charged against Milosevic,"[39] and indeed wanton destruction of this sort is clearly prohibited by the Hague and Geneva Protocols.

After the events of 9/11, Bush II launched a massive bombing campaign in Afghanistan directed against Al Qaeda and the Taliban regime, resulting in at least 3000 civilian deaths. Previous missions were carried out in Afghanistan and the Sudan, with fewer casualties. Insofar as these actions can be seen as a defense against terrorism, their status as war crimes is more ambiguous—though deliberate assaults on civilian objects *under any circumstances* is a violation of international law. Other instances of U.S. aerial terrorism—for example, Panama and the more recent bombardment of Iraq—deserve serious attention. Since World War II the U.S. has defended its military atrocities—above all the systematic destruction of civilian objects—as a necessary means of undermining enemy morale, blunting the capacity of its workforce, creating social and psychological havoc, and destroying the basis of its arms production. Barbarism for any of these reasons, however, is totally unjustified and must be placed in the category of war crimes or even, in many cases, of crimes against humanity.

Warfare Against Civilians

Contrary to popular mythology, civilian populations have always been the main victims of U.S. military ventures and, more often than not, such victims were clearly *intended*. Tariq Ali is not exaggerating when he writes: "The massacre of civilian populations was always an integral part of U.S. war strategy."[40] Nor is Edward Herman overstating the case when he observes that "U.S. military policy has long been based on strategies and tactics that involve a heavy civilian toll."[41] This is patently true of aerial warfare, as we have seen, but the perpetual, bloody onslaught against civilians goes far beyond this to include ground operations.

The record of European settler military assaults on native peoples, as Ward Churchill documents, spans at least four centuries, part of a "vicious drive toward extermination" that killed tens of millions. Upon its founding the U.S. became a decisive force behind exterminism. Carried out within a matrix of capitalism, imperialism, and racism, massacres of Indian tribes were often systematic, planned, and accompanied by utter destruction of peoples' land and culture—war crimes and crimes against humanity by any reckoning.[42] So much of the American tradition of war—savage, total, racist—was inherited from the Indian wars, then given ideological meaning through Manifest Destiny and the Monroe Doctrine. It was a tradition that generally allowed for merciless attacks on civilian populations.[43] The legacy was continued during wars with Mexico and Spain, turning outward with colonial expansion in the twentieth century. Not surprisingly, the U.S. has consistently rejected international treaties and protocols for protecting civilians against the horrors of war.

As Caleb Carr observes, the U.S. was historically adept at constructing an "evangelical military" bereft of any respect for other nations and cultures which, thoroughly devalued in a context of imperial arrogance, were readily demonized and offered up for destruction.[44] Americans have pursued their global ambitions through every conceivable barbaric method: wars of attrition, carpet bombing, free-fire zones, massacres of unarmed civilians, support for death squads, forced relocations, destruction of public infrastructures, the burning down of cities, use of weapons of mass destruction including atomic bombs. Filled with an imperial contempt for others and a sense of moral supremacy, U.S. leaders have predictably established themselves as beyond the reach of international law, immune to any moral or legal rules of engagement.

Had such rules of engagement ever come into play historically—as seemed to be the case in World War I, when civilians were spared the brunt of the carnage—they were mercilessly transcended by the end of World War II when large urban areas became targets of military action. In the Pacific, this was not simply a matter of aerial terrorism. Ground and naval combat was also devoid of limits, on both sides. For its part, the U.S. carried out military operations with unbelievable savagery: prisoners were regularly tortured and shot, soldiers and civilians were massacred by the hundreds and thousands, prisoners were buried alive in mass graves, survivors of sunken ships were strafed and killed at sea, towns and cities were annihilated with wanton disregard for human life. Savagery of this sort was hardly incidental to larger military goals and modus operandi or a simple product of "collateral damage"; it was in large part de rigueur, accepted within the virtually nonexistent rules of engagement in the Pacific theater. Thus officers of the U.S. Army were proud to say, for example, that "the 41st [unit] didn't take prisoners."[45]

The Korean War of 1950–53 took an even more horrendous toll in civilian life: aside from the torrent of bombs dropped by U.S. planes, ground forces conducted themselves with extreme cruelty in what became a terrible war of attrition. During a period of retreat in fall 1950, General MacArthur ordered a total scorched-earth campaign, whereupon the U.S. Army destroyed everything in its path—factories, homes, farms, hospitals, sources of water and electricity, irrigation dams, roads, animals. Hundreds of towns and villages were destroyed with no regard for the civilian inhabitants, who were dismissed as the "enemy" or otherwise useless in the anti-Communist crusade. As in the Pacific, prisoners were routinely tortured and killed. Large-scale massacres, such as the well-known incident at Nogun Ri in 1951, were as common as they had been during World War II and would later be in Vietnam. Referring to the entire debacle of Korea, Stephen Endicott and Edward Hagerman write: "American military culture accepted the World War II standpoint that mass destruction of civilians was a legitimate military target in an expanded war of attrition."[46] Flagrant war crimes were committed by the highest-ranking military officers down to the lowest ranks, but no one was ever charged much less convicted of such crimes.

U.S. military policy and conduct was even more brutal throughout Indochina, spanning an entire decade rather than three years as in Korea. Carnage in Vietnam resulted not only from aerial bombardments but ground warfare of all types: free-fire zones, search-and-destroy missions, defoliation, soldiers prepared to kill anything that moved. More than 10 million persons were displaced while hundreds of thousands were relocated in "hamlets" that served as concentration camps. Herbicides destroyed millions of acres of jungle and crop land. More than 1200 square miles of land was bulldozed. Towns and villages were bombed, torched, and bulldozed, their inhabitants slaughtered. An entire society was pulverized in the name of "pacification" and "nation-building," codewords for the most ruthless counterinsurgency program ever undertaken.

The standard modus operandi in Vietnam, as in Korea, was to destroy *any* impediment to military success in the field—to "kill 'em all," as the title of a BBC documentary on U.S. war crimes in Korea conveys. "Search and destroy" meant attacking not only combatants but civilians, animals, the whole ecology, as part of effective counterinsurgency operations. When troops came upon any village, they usually came in opening fire, often with support of helicopter gunships. U.S. troops were rewarded according to the well-known "body count," never limited simply to identifiable combatants. As one GI put it: "We're here to kill gooks, period." A common GI refrain in Vietnam went: "Bomb the schools and churches. Bomb the rice fields too. Show the children in the courtyards what napalm can do."[47] Still another refrain: "Kill one, they call you a murderer. Kill thousands, and they call you a conqueror. Kill them all, and they won't call you anything."[48] Units that routinely engaged in murder, rape, and mutilation made sure that no soldier would press charges, and few did. Under these conditions prisoners were rarely taken; if so, they were tortured and then executed. At the Dellums Committee hearings in April 1971, several veterans testified as to how military training prepared them for savage, unrestrained killing in the field: above all it was crucial to dehumanize the enemy so that it would be possible to "kill without mercy."

As in Korea, the U.S. military pursued a relentless war of attrition in Vietnam, as well as in Laos and Cambodia. The use of American firepower was nothing short of hysterical, resulting in the loss of three million lives (mostly civilians) across Indochina. The crimes were unspeakable and endless, carried out with a fierce chauvinistic animus, but no political officials or military personnel were ever charged—with the famous exception of Lieutenant William Calley for his role in the My Lai massacres of March 1968, when more than 200 innocent civilians were shot to death. Calley was court-martialed and given a light sentence, serving less than three years for crimes that deserved much harsher punishment. The problem was that My Lai was hardly an aberration;

massacres of this sort were common, but never reported or, if reported, covered up by military personnel. As the Bertrand Russell Tribunal made clear at the time, U.S. war crimes were of such a magnitude and implicated so many high-level political and military officials that only a Nuremberg-style international tribunal could have brought justice. Since the perpetrators of mass murder and other crimes of war were able to hide under the cloak of a superpower, there was no Nuremberg and no justice. Indeed one of the leading criminals of the period, President Richard Nixon, would have the last word: "When the President does it, that means it is not illegal"—a maxim that, sadly for Nixon, pertained only to foreign affairs.

Compared to the Indochina carnage that continued well over a decade, the U.S. invasion of Panama in December 1989 was a relatively minor, brief incursion with only moderate casualties. Quick as it was, however, the operation was intense, high tech, and deadly, revealing again the utter contempt of U.S. military forces for local populations. Ostensibly to arrest Noriega and protect American lives, the invasion produced (in just a few days) at least 4000 civilian deaths and 50,000 homeless, according to the 1990 Independent Commission of Inquiry. A working-class district in Panama City, El Chorillo, was mostly burned to the ground; oppositional political groups were destroyed or banned; people were arrested and detained for weeks, even months, with no formal charges; many others (both military and civilian) "disappeared."[49] The Pentagon strategy for a quick and total victory meant using heavy firepower over a small territory. According to one eyewitness report: "Before reaching the street, we saw a group of some 18 U.S. soldiers coming down the street. We saw them entering each house and the residents coming out followed by the soldiers and then we saw houses one-by-one going up in smoke. The U.S. soldiers were burning our houses."[50] Commenting on the horrors of technowar in Panama, Chu Chu Martinez said: "The volume of U.S. firepower and the refinement of their weapons is incredible. They did in Panama more or less what Hitler did in Spain, using it as a practice ground for the weapons he would use during World War II."[51] In this case, the dress rehearsal happened to be for the Gulf War little more than a year later.

It was during Desert Storm that the U.S. military was first able to unveil technowar in its full glory: Iraq became a "free-fire" zone over which 110,000 sorties were flown, dropping some 88,000 tons of bombs on a country with minimal air defenses. As we have seen, the USAF was able to pulverize the Iraqi infrastructure while suffering few casualties of its own (until later, when the terrible health effects of DU and other toxic agents became visible). At the very end of combat, with nothing left in doubt, U.S. planes bombed and strafed retreating Iraqi troops, killing at least 30,000—clearly a violation of the Hague and Geneva Protocols. The bombings continued regularly after the main warfare concluded. The U.S. employed thousands of weapons tipped with DU, ensuring that radioactive substances would be left in the water, soil, and food chain for decades.[52]

The harshly punitive and inhuman policy of economic sanctions, enforced mainly by the U.S. and Britain under UN cover, cost at least 500,000 civilian lives after 1991—maintained on the hypocritical insistence that Iraq dispose of its "weapons of mass destruction." The embargo cruelly blocked vital imports such as medical supplies, water-treatment technology, even certain foodstuffs that, under the excessively broad definition of "dual use," might be considered useful to the military. Sanctions policies of this sort have been employed regularly by the U.S., using its economic clout, as a foreign policy tool since the 1950s. The main victims have been civilians, mostly children. The 1977 Additional Protocols to the Geneva Conventions prohibit measures that deprive the civilian population of goods indispensable to survival, with Article 18 mandating *relief* operations to aid civilians suffering "undue hardships owing to lack of supplies essential for its survival, such as foodstuffs and medical supplies." In fact the U.S. alone had obstructed every humanitarian effort, mounted by NGOs as well as members of the UN Security Council, to lift the sanctions. Writing in *Harper's*, Joy Gordon characterized the sanctions as a "legitimized act of mass slaughter." She added: ". . . epidemic suffering is needlessly visited on Iraqis via U.S. fiat inside the UN Security Council. Within that body, the U.S. has consistently thwarted Iraq from satisfying its most basic humanitarian needs, using sanctions as nothing less than a deadly weapon."[53]

With new generations of high-tech weaponry, aerial and space-based surveillance, sophisticated aircraft, and general battlefield flexibility, the U.S. military has theoretically entered an era of "safe wars." This produces a profound "asymmetry" of warfare, meaning that superior force can expect fewer risks and casualties while inflicting even greater damage on targeted foes. The inevitable atrocities resulting from such warfare in the U.S. will go largely unreported or, if reported, quickly swept aside in the midst of wartime media spectacle. Thus in Afghanistan it became known that U.S. planes frequently attacked and destroyed civilian targets: bombers saturated large areas with devastating impact, while heavy AC-130 gunships armed with howitzers, cannons, and machine guns had carte blanche throughout the country. The main targets were Al Qaeda base sites, Taliban military positions, and bunker hideouts, yet civilian areas were hit with loss of life estimated (by the Red Cross) to be upwards of 3000. On December 29, 2001, U.S. aircraft destroyed an entire village, killing dozens of civilians and injuring many more, after flying several quick sorties in early-morning darkness. Taliban leaders were said to be "concealed" in the village of Qualaye Niazi, but most of the people hit were part of a large wedding party. According to the UN, unarmed women and children were chased and killed by helicopters as they fled to shelter or tried to rescue survivors.[54] After nearly three months of sustained bombing of one of the poorest countries on earth, various aid agencies made desperate pleas for a bombing halt so that food and medicine could be delivered to hundreds of thousands of refugees, but the U.S. flatly refused. The U.S. may have been involved in the mass murder (possibly more than a thousand) of Taliban prisoners rounded up by the U.S. and Northern Alliance forces near Konduz in later November 2001. According to many reports from different sources, prisoners were herded into container trucks on the journey from Konduz to Sheberghan, condemned to slow and painful death, and then dumped into mass grave sites, all while U.S. Special Forces—working closely with the ruthless General Abdul Rashid Dostum—remained in the area. As Red Cross and UN representatives expressed "grave concern" about the atrocities, the Pentagon stonewalled any investigation.[55] If a cardinal principle of international law is to protect both civilians and prisoners of war from wanton or indiscriminate military attack, the U.S. has failed this test dismally.

The long U.S. record of war crimes against civilians, far beyond combat miscalculations or "collateral damage" here and there, is the result of several combined factors: unprecedented global reach and ambitions, the advent of technowar, a deepening culture of violence and militarism, a xenophobic patriotism and ethnocentrism devaluing the life of human beings from other (especially non-European) territories and cultures. These factors take on greater weight in the context of yet another condition—sheer imperial arrogance. As Phyllis Bennis comments: "This American-style law of empire exuded extraordinary arrogance, the arrogance of absolute power unchallenged by any other global force."[56] Viewed culturally, it is part of a "sacralization of war" that erupts through what Barbara Ehrenreich characterizes as a "burst of nationalist religiosity" where foreign populations become faceless, dehumanized, and demonized, always with a powerful assist from the jingoistic mass media.[57] Military training stresses all this and more, producing a kind of conversion process leading to what Richard Rhodes defines as a "brutalization ethos" with a quick willingness to kill, especially from a distance. Such killing is often accompanied by pleasure, even celebration, resembling ancient Roman spectacles.[58] Here the military prepares its recruits for a comfortable escape from all moral restraints. The harsh consequences of militarism become more or less normalized. This helps explain why the endless U.S. legacy of war crimes—repeated with callous indifference throughout the postwar era—has been so systematically ignored, denied, and (when necessary) covered up, even meeting with silence from reputed ethical forces that one might expect to speak out: religious leaders, political officials, intellectuals, the mass media. Silence is made all the easier when even the most horrendous crimes are carried out under cover of "democracy," "human rights," and of course "social progress."

Weapons of Mass Destruction

Contrary to popular mythology, the development of weapons of mass destruction includes not only nuclear, chemical, and biological technology but extends to conventional weaponry (for example, saturation bombing) as well as economic sanctions. These weapons have awesome destructive power in at least three respects: the boundary separating combatants and civilians is *by definition* obliterated, the potential for casualties is typically *massive*, and the environmental impact can be both terrible and long-term. Of these five types only chemical and biological warfare have been explicitly outlawed; the use of nuclear and conventional weapons, as well as sanctions, violates international law only in the sense it is deemed "wanton destruction," where civilians are directly targeted. The U.S. alone among all nations has employed *all* these weapons of mass destruction and, since 1945, is the only country to develop and use these weapons in ways that must be regarded as war crimes. At a time when U.S. leaders are threatening nations such as Iraq and North Korea for their WMD "violations," this picture should not be forgotten.

We know that the U.S. dropped two atomic bombs on Japan at the end of World War II, causing unnecessary wanton destruction of civilian targets. With the onset of the Cold War the U.S. rushed to develop its nuclear arsenal and laid out a strategic doctrine tied to first-strike capability.[59] By the 1950s the Pentagon was on perpetual ready-alert, prepared to rain more than 800 Hiroshimas on the USSR, refining its power to destroy human civilization on earth several times over. In Lindqvist's view, the threat of nuclear annihilation was partly an expression of certain white-male ruling-class fantasies with roots in Wild West mythology.[60] In any event, the Armageddon-style policies established during the Cold War have remained in force, backed by ever greater nuclear power, ever since. There is evidence that the U.S. has *threatened* use of nuclear weapons on several occasions in the postwar years. In 1968, the nations of the world signed the Nonproliferation Treaty, but this did not stop the U.S. from increasing its warhead total from 4500 to nearly 10,000 within a decade, a deployment that has been continuously modernized since. Far from renouncing nuclear warfare as inherently barbaric, the U.S. has been dedicated to unfettered domination in this area, one reason it rejects antiballistic and other arms-control treaties and is moving full-speed toward the weaponization of space.[61] As of 2002, the U.S. had manufactured and deployed more nuclear weapons than all other nations combined.

In 2002, President Bush and Russian leader Vladimir Putin signed the Moscow Treaty ostensibly to control production and deployment of nuclear weapons by the two powers. The Treaty, however, was essentially a fraud: in the process the U.S. wound up scrapping an agreement that is *binding*, involving regular inspections and strict limits, replacing it with one that is largely unilateral and *voluntary*. With the new accords all categories of nuclear warheads and delivery systems are left uncontrolled—precisely what the U.S. wanted all along. Meanwhile, Bush had already rejected the Comprehensive Test Ban Treaty and had withdrawn from the 1972 Anti-Ballistic Missile Treaty.

Over the past decade, moreover, the U.S. has been the only country to use depleted uranium in its bombs and missiles. The Pentagon has at least one billion pounds of nuclear waste available, much of it converted to strengthen conventional weaponry in the Gulf and the Balkans, with deadly results. Tens of thousands of DU-enhanced rounds were released in both these "wars," producing radioactive effects upon explosion that have long-term effects on people, crops, animals, and the ecology. Widespread use of DU in Iraq gave rise to "Gulf War Syndrome" among both Iraqis and U.S. military forces.[62] Upon impact with a target, DU becomes a widespread mist of particles which, once inhaled or ingested, can lead to cancer, kidney disease, and genetic defects. By 1995 Iraqi health officials reported alarmingly high increases in rare diseases, especially among children.[63] Such weapons inevitably cause wanton destruction and therefore must be considered criminal. In 1996 a UN subcommission passed a resolution condemning DU, but the U.S. simply ignored it, refusing any legal or moral restraints on its conduct of warfare.

In the realm of chemical weapons, the U.S. has been the world leader by far in the production, dissemination, and military use of highly toxic liquids, sprays, incendiary devices, powders, and explosives. The American military first experimented with napalm in World War II, refined its usage in Korea, employed it on a massive scale in Vietnam, and has kept it as part of its arsenal ever since; incendiary bombs follow a similar pattern. It is well known that the U.S. sprayed tens of thousands of tons of herbicides over three million acres in Vietnam from 1965 to 1971, intended to wipe out jungle foliage and crops. The use of Agent Orange polluted Vietnam with 500 pounds of the deadly chemical dioxin, impacting several million Vietnamese along with tens of thousands of American troops. There have been many reports of high levels of cancer and birth defects in regions saturated with Agent Orange. The U.S. Army also employed such toxic chemicals as CS, DM, and CN gasses, designated by the Pentagon as "riot control" agents.[64] According to the Hatfield Report, the legacy of chemical warfare left behind by the U.S. in Indochina would have health and ecological consequences for many decades. For all this the U.S. never offered any apologies, any reparations, anything for cleanup. The U.S. has not shrunk from later use of chemical warfare, including its widespread adoption in Plan Colombia to defoliate coca plantations—nor has it been reluctant to share its scientific knowledge and resources with other nations. In Colombia the U.S. has begun spraying a new Monsanto-produced fungus, glyphosate, an herbicide that causes lethal infections in humans. In its lengthy discussion of chemical weapons as violations of international law, the volume *Crimes of War*[65] scandalously omits any reference whatsoever to the extensive history of U.S. chemical warfare. The main culprit identified is Iraq, with Russia getting honorable mention. The volume does mention that 111 states (including the U.S.) signed the Chemical Weapons Convention in Paris in 1993, taking legal force in 1997, but fails to mention U.S. efforts to subvert the treaty by denying *inspection* provisions to any external body.

In January 1998, President Clinton emphasized that the world must "confront the new hazards of chemical and biological weapons, and the outlaw states, terrorists, and organized criminals seeking to acquire them." Anticipating Bush's later rhetoric, he particularly castigated Iraq for acquiring "weapons of mass destruction." Yet it was the U.S. government that initially furnished the Iraqis with a wide variety of chemical and biological agents, exported to Iraq by private American companies licensed by the Department of Commerce, an arrangement going back to at least 1985. Shipments included materials related to anthrax and botulinum toxin, vital to development of whatever program Iraq might still have.[66] It was recently learned that the U.S. military tested a variety of bioweapons in and near local civilian populations, off the coast of such states as California, Florida, Maryland, and Hawaii, exposing millions of people unknowingly to deadly agents between 1962 and 1973. The report makes clear that such weapons tests (including sarin nerve gas) were held to experiment with both offensive and defensive weaponry.[67]

Earlier reports of widespread U.S. military deployment of biological warfare in Korea have been recently documented with some degree of certainty.[68] Bioweapons were an officially sanctioned part of Pentagon strategy in the early 1950s and surely much later, as the above reports suggest. Both Koreans and Chinese complained about large death tolls resulting from plague, smallpox, anthrax, scarlet fever, encephalitis, and other diseases unleashed by bombs and artillery shells from U.S. military operations. We know that the U.S. Medical General Lab, Far East, had become a center for researching insect vectors for such lethal diseases as smallpox, cholera, and encephalitis.

As mentioned, the U.S. strategy in Korea—carried over from World War II—was to wear down and ultimately annihilate the enemy. Under such circumstances, any "rules of engagement" were jettisoned. Atrocities were routinely committed from the air and on the ground. The USAF bombing campaigns were nothing short of barbaric. Prisoners of war were killed en masse. Endicott and Hagerman write: "These acts in Korea indicated again that the U.S. subscription to laws of war and treatment of prisoners was no check on its political and military leaders' use of whatever methods and weapons were considered necessary to achieve their goals."[69] Faced with seemingly endless stalemate on the battlefield through 1951 and 1952, the U.S. looked desperately for new solutions. One answer was to expand the war further into civilian population centers, to which end the USAF demolished eleven hydroelectric plants along the Yalu River in June 1952. Another response was President Eisenhower's resurrection of President Truman's earlier threat to use atomic bombs in order to break the deadlock. A third response, evidently carried out with vigor, was biological warfare. In the words of Endicott and Hagerman: "The U.S. had substantial stocks of biological weapons on hand. Moral qualms about using biological or atomic weapons had been brushed aside by top leaders, and biological warfare might dodge the political bullet of adverse public and world opinion if it were kept secret enough to make a plausible denial of its use. If it were uncovered, a last resort could be to fall back on the fact the U.S. had not signed the 1925 Geneva Protocol on biological warfare."[70]

Evidence of U.S. biowarfare came not only from Korean and Chinese government archives but from the testimony of American flyers (soon forced to recant under pressure) and, later, from independent scholarly research. In the end, however, the resort to bioweaponry achieved only limited results: thousands of people were hospitalized and scores killed during 1951 and 1952, but the overall impact on Korean-Chinese military efforts was negligible.

For several decades the U.S. war machine, swollen through expanded national quest for imperial domination, has built its strategic capability around weapons of mass destruction—nuclear, conventional, and economic (sanctions) above all. Chemical weapons have been used widely in counterinsurgency while biological weapons, ostensibly retired from the arsenal, have not been the desired option in the wake of the Korean fiasco. In 1972 the U.S., along with 140 other nations, signed the Biological Weapons Convention treaty prohibiting the production, development, and use of germ warfare agents. There were still, however, provisions needed for compliance and verification. Discussions aimed at strengthening the treaty continued throughout the 1990s, with the U.S. dead set against inspections that would be considered an infringement on the commercial rights of American chemical and pharmaceutical labs. Finally, even the watered down draft favored by the U.S. was rejected by the Bush administration in July 2002, leaving the world without viable biological weapons prohibitions. Here too the U.S. insisted upon concessions from all other parties but refused any for itself.

Given their strategic centrality to the logic of empire—their very *threat* constitutes a fearsome military force—WMD today represent a *nonnegotiable* part of the U.S. arsenal. This helps explain why American leaders (Democrats and Republicans alike) have strongly opposed virtually all efforts by nations of the world to establish treaties and conventions limiting production and deployment of WMD. Because of its overwhelming superiority in this area, moreover, the U.S. possesses greater flexibility than ever to pursue aggressive militarism worldwide, which only further reinforces a Hobbesian global anarchy where brute military and economic power obliterates any prospect for binding laws, treaties, ethics, and rules of engagement.

War Crimes by Proxy

An especially shameful U.S. violation of international law and human rights principles has been its support of terrorist regimes and paramilitary groups around the world since the late 1940s, often with the aim of setting up proxy wars, insurgencies, and other forms of mayhem to advance imperial designs. Brutal governments have been aided in Israel, Colombia, Turkey, Chile, and Indonesia, rebellions have been financed in Nicaragua, Yugoslavia, and

Afghanistan, and death squads have been created in El Salvador and Guatemala. Governments have been overthrown through covert and/or direct intervention, as in Chile and, earlier, in Iran and Guatemala. Proxy activities where U.S. military forces remain in the background while atrocities are carried out mainly by local groups are often the preferred method. Support has taken many forms: direct material assistance, military equipment and weaponry, training and recruitment, intelligence, and political supports within international bodies like the UN. For many decades the U.S. has trained thousands of operatives within the country who would later become members of governments, militias, and death squads complicit in horrendous war crimes. Such crimes by proxy, where perpetrators are knowingly and deliberately provided the resources to carry out their barbaric deeds, make the U.S. just as guilty as the providers and ought to be held just as accountable. Within international law this is known as "aiding and abetting war crimes." Indeed this is one of the major charges against Milosevic at the Hague, where he is accused of helping paramilitary groups in the Balkans (Arkan's Tigers, for example) by means of financial aid, training, weapons shipments, and logistical support. Prosecutors argue that Milosevic is just as culpable of war crimes as if he had taken over formal leadership of the groups involved.[71] Such a proxy relationship to regimes and organizations has been a stock in trade of U.S. foreign and military policy since World War II—yet no U.S. leader has ever been held accountable.

From 1980 to the mid-1980s the Central Intelligence Agency recruited, trained, and supported a well-armed Contra network, a made-in-America insurgency set up to overthrow the reformist Sandinista government in Nicaragua. Based in Honduras, the Contras did everything possible to destabilize the system: economic sabotage, mining of harbors, assassination of political officials, and above all the large-scale massacre of civilians as part of subverting public morale. The death toll will never be known, but probably ran well into the thousands.[72] Later, during the 1990s, the U.S. helped recruit, train, and equip local rebellions in Yugoslavia—most notably the right-wing Kosovo Liberation Army (KLA)—operating alongside fascistic governing forces in Croatia and Bosnia, all intended to destabilize the elected rulers of Serbia. During 1995–98 the KLA moved freely throughout Kosovo, killing hundreds of local Serb officials with the goal of liberating the province from Serb control. (The Serb military response to KLA actions was defined as "ethnic cleansing," but the KLA was naturally exempted from such labels in the U.S.) In early August 1995, Croatian military forces, armed by the U.S., launched what turned out to be the most brutal offensive of the Balkan civil wars, destroying huge Serb regions in the province of Krajina, killing several thousand civilians and forcing more than 200,000 from their homes. Trapped Serbians pouring into Bosnia were massacred in large numbers by Croatian and Bosnian military forces, supported by Germany and the U.S. It was a bloody offensive that Clinton's Secretary of State, Warren Christopher, had openly endorsed.[73] While the

Hague Tribunal has been quick to charge Milosevic and other Serbs with "ethnic cleansing" and war crimes, nothing has been said about this criminal military aggression directed against civilians nor about U.S. involvement in the very type of proxy war crimes laid at the doorstep of Milosevic.

The U.S. has supported, indeed *created*, dozens of paramilitary terrorist groups in Latin America alone since the early 1980s. At the School of the Americas, renamed Western Hemisphere Institute for Security Cooperation, located in Fort Benning, Georgia, the U.S. military has trained thousands of terrorists in the methods of bloody guerrilla warfare directed at legitimate nation-states or local civilian organizations—methods including assassination, torture, murder, and death-squad intimidation of specific targets. Graduates of SOA include Roberto d'Aubuisson, who organized a death-squad network in El Salvador during the 1980s, reportedly killing upwards of 10,000 people as part of U.S. and Salvadoran elite campaigns to destroy leftist opposition. Massacres were common, with scores of villages burned to the ground. Death squads were comprised of both civilians and members of the armed forces, trained and supported by the U.S. According to the UN Truth Commission on Salvadoran Death Squads, former Major d'Aubuisson helped organize and maintain the paramilitary groups, bringing together American interests, Miami-based exiles, and right-wing Salvadoran forces.

In Guatemala, the CIA and Pentagon have supported death-squad activity and governmental repression since the U.S. engineered the overthrow of Jacobo Arbenz in 1954. The killings, presided over by a series of brutal U.S.-backed dictators, have been estimated at over 200,000—made possible by American weapons, equipment, training, money, and logistical aid. Throughout the 1980s and 1990s the Guatemalan death squads were organized primarily by two organizations, the G2 and Archivo, both funded by the CIA and run by CIA-paid Guatemalan military and police officers trained at the SOA and elsewhere. According to witnesses, the G2 has maintained a web of torture centers, secret body dumps, and crematoria.[74] This is nothing less than an ongoing, brutal, criminal U.S. military action by proxy.

U.S. assistance to governing regimes guilty of long-term war crimes against targeted civilian populations struggling for independence and/or human rights has been one of the darkest features of American foreign policy. The Guatemalan repression and murder of tens of thousands of indigenous peoples is just one case in point. The arming and financing of the Iraqi military throughout the 1980s during its brutal war with Iran, including the use of chemical weapons, provides another example.

Between 1965 and 1969, the Indonesian military regime massacred some 500,000 people, virtually anyone linked to the left opposition, with full U.S. diplomatic and military support—surely one of the great atrocities of the postwar years, but one that was met with silence in the Western media. A decade later Indonesia invaded East Timor, killing perhaps another 100,000 people for the sin of wanting national self-determination, all while the U.S. continued to arm the regime and block UN measures to halt the carnage. The Suharto regime was one of the favorites of the CIA and the Pentagon owing to its ruthless efficiency. After the 1975 invasion of East Timor, U.S. weapons sales to Jakarta exceeded one billion dollars.

In the case of Turkey, its repression of the huge Kurdish population has continued for decades while the nation remains a close U.S. ally and a major recipient of its financial and military aid. Repression worsened throughout the 1990s as the Turkish Army devastated Kurdish regions, sending hundreds of thousands of poor civilians into flight. Perhaps two million were left homeless while death squads murdered thousands more. Napalm was used on villages, dropped by U.S.-made planes. At this point Turkey had become the single largest importer of U.S. military goods, including F-16 fighter-bombers, M-60 tanks, Cobra gunships, and Blackhawk helicopters in large numbers, all used against the mostly defenseless Kurds.

The Israeli occupation of Palestine with its ruthless political and military actions over many decades is perhaps the most egregious case of U.S. war crimes by proxy. In many respects the state of Israel has been an American outpost in the Middle East, replete with every conceivable form of financial, political, diplomatic, and military backing; it is a relationship sui generis. With the fourth largest army in the world, Israeli militarism has ensured perpetuation of a harsh apartheid system marked by ongoing violations of international law: forced settlement of the land, illegal arrests, torture, relocation of civilian populations, massacres, harsh curfews, assault on cultural institutions, the wanton bulldozing of homes and property, depriving people of basic services. All of this constitutes a blatant violation of the Fourth Geneva Convention along with the UN Charter, but efforts to hold the Israelis accountable have been blocked by the U.S., which helps guarantee the occupation of Gaza and the West Bank through its repeated vetoes of UN resolutions. Furthermore, there are 5.5 million Palestinian refugees housed in 59 camps, denied the right to return to their homes in contravention of UN Resolution 194 and international law. The issue of war crimes here cannot be addressed in the U.S. since, as Edward Said notes, "the systematic continuity of Israel's 52-year-old oppression and maltreatment of the Palestinians is virtually unmentionable, a narrative that has no permission to appear." It is the "last taboo."[75] From 1949 to 2000, the U.S. gave more than $90 billion in foreign aid and other grants to Israel, including $5.5 billion in 1997 alone. There were 18 arms sales to Israel in the year 2000. Thanks to American largesse, the Israelis have the largest fleet of F-16s outside the U.S., an integral part of their vast war machine. The regime of Ariel Sharon is fully backed by the U.S., although Sharon was responsible for horrific attacks against Palestinians, including the 1982 invasion of Lebanon and the massacre of several thousand unarmed civilians in the refugee camps of Sabra and Shatila in September 1982.

The very charges leveled against Milosevic at the Hague—the aiding and abetting of war crimes—could be brought against the U.S. hundreds of times over as it uses its preponderant economic, political, and military power to wage deadly proxy wars around the globe.

The Routinization of Mass Murder

One of the more tragic parts of the U.S. war crimes legacy has been its almost total absence from the public discourse: mass media, politics, academia, intellectual life. This can be seen as the result partly of civic ignorance, partly collective denial, partly a matter of what Gilbert Achcar refers to as "narcissistic compassion," the indifference to suffering of others.[76] However understood, there is little question about the degree to which the horrible costs and consequences of American Empire have become routinized within both elite and popular consciousness; the very idea of U.S. culpability for terrible atrocities, including war crimes, human rights violations, and crimes against humanity, is generally regarded as too far off the normal spectrum of discourse to be taken seriously.

Given the postwar historical record, we are dealing here with nothing less than callous insensitivity to mass murder. The U.S. has become such a dominant world superpower that its crimes become more or less invisible, that is, they appear as an integral, acceptable, indeed predictable element of imperial power. Never a loser in war, the U.S. has not had to confront the grievances of those who have been wronged. This condition is exacerbated by the advent of technowar which, since World War II, has largely removed any sense of immediate *personal* involvement in warfare, meaning that feelings of guilt, shame, and moral outrage that normally accompany acts of mass murder are more easily sidestepped, repressed, forgotten—much easier yet where such acts are carried out by proxies. Long experience tells us that large numbers of people, having completed military training, can more or less calmly plan and implement the killing of unknown, faceless, innocent, defenseless human beings, whether by firing missiles, dropping bombs from 30,000 feet, shooting off long-distance artillery shells, or simple ground combat (increasingly rare for the U.S. military). Once the "enemy" is portrayed as sinister beasts and monsters, dehumanized as worthless "others," then the assault becomes a matter of organization, technique, and planning, part of the day to day routine of simply obeying commands, carrying out assigned tasks, fitting into a bureaucratic structure. Within this universe the human targets of military action are virtually *always* defined as barbaric, subhuman, deserving of their fate and possibly even complicit in it: Native Americans, Filipinos, Japanese, Guatemalan peasants, Koreans, Vietnamese, Iraqis, Serbs. As on the Frontier, mass killing may be understood as necessary, a moral imperative to ensure survival and save "civilization." Viewed thus, the forces of racial supremacy, imperialism, and xenophobia converge with a cult of violence to form an ideological cauldron where crimes of war may come to seem natural, logical.

Within the culture of militarism, large-scale massacres, authorized and legitimated by political and military commands, take on the character of the *ordinary*, where guilt and culpability are routinely evaded.[77] Actions viewed from outside this culture as heinous and criminal appear rather normal, acceptable, even laudatory *within* it, part of a taken-for-granted world. Ethical discourses are silenced, jettisoned. Surveying U.S. war crimes, one can see that taken-for-granted barbarism assumes many forms: saturation bombing of civilian habitats, free-fire zones, chemical warfare, relocations, search-and-destroy massacres, torture and killing of prisoners—all sanctioned through an unwritten code of regular military operations. In technowar especially, all human conduct becomes managerial, clinical, distant, impersonal, rendering the carnage technologically "rational"; individual feelings, including the pain and suffering of victims, disappear from view. Even the most ruthless, bloody actions have no villains insofar as all "initiative" vanishes within the organizational apparatus and the culture supporting it. War managers' ideology contains specialized military/technical discourses with their own epistemology, devoid of any moral criteria. As Gibson writes in the context of Vietnam: "Technowar as a regime of mechanical power and knowledge posits the high-level command positions of the political and military bureaucracies as the legitimate sites of knowledge."[78] Here bureaucratic jargon serves to obscure militarism and its victims with familiar references to the primacy of "national security," the need for "surgical strikes," the regrettable problem of "collateral damage," and "self-inflicted" casualties. Words like "incursion" substitute for real armed attacks, "body counts" for mass slaughter, "civilian militias" for death squads. Here structure of language helps to establish a gulf between perpetrators and victims, between war criminals and the crimes they commit. In general those who plan do not kill, and those who kill are merely following orders—and they too are usually shielded from the psychological immediacy by the mechanism of technowar.

Yet not all war crimes are extensions of technowar: in Vietnam and other locales massacres were indeed authorized and carried out in the midst of ground combat. The My Lai atrocities are well known, but others like them occurred with some frequency in Vietnam and elsewhere. My Lai in fact was part of a search-and-destroy mission by U.S. troops, with standing orders to obliterate any resistance or "suspicious" activity and whose incentives were high body counts. After troops used machine guns and grenades to slaughter innocent people in the village, the operation was defined as a "great victory" for Charlie Company. In reality neither Lieutenant Calley nor other participants expressed much regret for what they did, echoing previous responses of U.S. military personnel after such atrocities as Wounded Knee and Hiroshima. Said

Calley: "I was just ordered to go in there and destroy the enemy. That was my job on that day. That was the mission I was given."[79] Similarly, former U.S. Senator and now president of the New School in New York, Robert Kerrey, expressed few misgivings over having led a Commando raid that slaughtered 14 unarmed civilians at the hamlet of Thanh Phong in February 1969. When finally compelled to face the atrocity 22 years later, after reports began surfacing in the media, Kerrey expressed some anguish over his involvement but refused to accept moral accountability, pleading bad memory.[80] Kerrey, of course, remained president of a major American university while life on campus routinely went on (after the Faculty Student Union unsuccessfully called on Kerrey to step down) and the mass media largely ignored the massacre while sympathizing with Kerrey's own "travails."

In the end, the normalcy of Kerry's life was hardly disturbed, consistent with the embellishment of his persona as just another dedicated, hardworking, distinguished citizen who fought for his country and might have made a mistake along the way—far from the image of a war criminal. Kerry looked and acted "normal" enough, then and now. So too did the vast majority of U.S. political and military elites who in some way were involved in the endless crimes of war discussed in this essay: the Pentagon war machine is led and staffed by ordinary folks with good educations, solid family backgrounds, nice manners, and benevolent ways. Indeed the Vietnam War itself was the work not of revolting thugs or Hannibal Lecter-type maniacs—or even xenophobic right-wingers—but mainly of liberal, highly educated, literate, humane people, many of them even celebrated academics like McGeorge Bundy, Walt Rostow, and Henry Kissinger. Robert Persico writes that the Nazi defendants at Nuremberg looked and acted in every respect "ordinary," with the exception of the massive, gruff, red-faced Ernst Kaltenbrunner, a Nazi from central casting. Few Nazis looked like sadistic monsters. "It would be hard to pick out most of these men as war criminals from a gathering of Rotarians or accountants."[81] In fact Albert Speer came across as just another intelligent, successful businessman, someone who could have been a manager at General Motors—although Speer at least confessed to war crimes.

Given the immense size and scope of the U.S. war machine, no one should be surprised to find the most horrific human deeds engulfed and camouflaged by vast bureaucratic structures that readily appear ordinary and rational on the surface. Obedience, violence, imperial arrogance, even racism are built into the logic of the system—and covered up by that same system. This recalls Hannah Arendt's famous analysis of the Eichmann trial and Nazism. The Nazis too were viewed as "normal" in their killing operations, and most indeed led "normal" lives. Writes Arendt: "The trouble with Eichmann was precisely that so many were like him, and that many were neither perverted nor sadistic, that they were . . . terribly and terrifyingly normal."[82] As would later be the case in Hiroshima, Vietnam, Panama, and other theaters of U.S. war crimes,

the people committing atrocities—from top to bottom—with very few exceptions believed they were doing the right, patriotic thing.

Conclusions

The experience of two disastrous World Wars gave rise to an unprecedented
global commitment to international law that would presumably curtail the worst
features of human warfare, reflected in the Nuremberg and Tokyo Tribunals, the
UN Charter, the Geneva Protocols, and more recently the International Criminal
Court set up in Rome. Ideally all states and political actors would have strict
obligations to follow moral and legal principles, including definite rules of engagement in warfare. The UN Charter, above all, clearly prohibits military force
as an instrument of statecraft except in clear-cut examples of self-defense. Of
course the very notion of such a paradigmatic shift in relations among nations
always depended upon the emergence of an international community of interests. Despite references here and there to a growing "culture of human rights,"
however, this pacifistic dream has turned into a Hobbesian nightmare as imperial aggression and armed violence have come to dominate the global scene. In
such a milieu, moral and legal criteria, following the "realist" outlook championed by Western powers, have seemingly vanished from the political landscape.

There can be no universally valid tenets and practices of international law
so long as the U.S. carries out its relentless pursuit of global domination in
support of its economic and geopolitical interests. The expansion of U.S. militarism, now reaching every corner of the globe as well as space, is incompatible
with a regimen of international law and human rights—as is the neoliberal
corporate order that militarism sustains.[83] We are at the point where U.S.
global hegemony supersedes all hope for shared norms, laws, customs, and
treaties.[84] The deadly cycle of militarism and terrorism, involving perpetual
war waged from the White House and the Pentagon, can only exacerbate this
predicament. Revelations about U.S. blueprints for world domination, for an
extended global "Pax Americana," are scarcely reassuring. An "American grand
strategy" is projected for "as far into the future as possible," calling on the U.S.
to "fight and decisively win multiple, simultaneous major theater wars" as a
"core mission." The document reveals that the Bush clique will tolerate no
powerful rival and, to that end, has intended to gain control of the Gulf region
since well before the 2000 election.[85]

The implications of all this for the future of international relations are depressing indeed: as imperial rogue state with few restraints on its power, the
U.S. will be increasingly emboldened to subject the world to its economic and
military agendas. Now more than ever, American elites will feel empowered to
disregard and then violate laws and treaties even as they proclaim their allegiance to "human rights" and peaceful resolution of conflicts—while expecting other nations to obey those same laws and treaties. As in its scandalous
rejection of the War Crimes Tribunal, the U.S. posture today remains one of

exceptionalism, even moral supremacy, placing the most powerful, aggressive military force on earth beyond the reach of controls and sanctions. This is hardly shocking for, as Noam Chomsky notes: "Contempt for the rule of law is deeply rooted in U.S. practice and intellectual culture."[86] Meanwhile, as U.S. imperial domination expands in the face of shrinking obstacles, thriving on the cycle of militarism and terrorism, the superpower capacity to wreak havoc across the globe widens dramatically. A Hobbesian world feeds into the militaristic impulse. Writing even *before* the events of 9/11, Lindqvist observes: "Wars will not disappear—instead they will be longer, bloodier, and more terrible."[87] The refinements of technowar, while perhaps shortening military episodes, are bound to make them ever more terrible. For the American public, however, warfare visited upon other countries has become an entertaining spectacle, profitable and at the same time a mechanism for satisfying masculine power and imperial egos.[88]

As for the legacy of war crimes, the very discourse has become obliterated under the weight of U.S. imperial and military power. The Nuremberg principles, adopted by the UN in 1950, state that any person committing an act that constitutes a war crime under international law is legally accountable and subject to punishment, as was the case with German and Japanese defendants. Such principles were regarded as universal, transcending national laws, traditions, and ideologies, binding for all persons whatever their place in the chain of command. No heads of state, no political or military officials, were seen as immune to criminal prosecution. Throughout the postwar years, unfortunately, the U.S. has done everything possible to subvert the Nuremberg principles, which makes its ringing endorsement of human rights and rule of law abstract, hypocritical, meaningless. Indeed the horrific legacy of war crimes and human-rights abuses stemming from unfettered U.S. global power has its roots in historical *continuity*, the result of a deliberate, planned, and systematic pattern of imperial aggrandizement. From this standpoint, war crimes have been a predictable outcome of U.S. relations with other nations and the world, virtually a matter of institutional necessity—easy to get away with, moreover, in the absence of media, political, or intellectual scrutiny. Hiding behind the veneer of "democracy" and "human progress," ruling elites have never come to grips with this criminal history: no apologies, no self-reflection, no reparations, no sense of accountability. The superpower accepts no moral or legal restraints on its ambitions. It would be foolhardy to expect otherwise so long as the U.S. imperial behemoth, championing doctrines of "humanitarian intervention" and "preemptive strike," continues to seek world domination.

Notes

1. Chalmers Johnson, *Blowback: The Costs and Consequences of American Empire* (New York: Henry Holt, 2000), 7.
2. Roy Gutman and David Rieff, *Crimes of War* (New York: W.W. Norton, 1999), 8.

3. *Crimes of War*, 9.
4. Lawrence Wechsler, "International Humanitarian Law: An Overview," in *Crimes of War*, 19.
5. Sven Lindqvist, *A History of Bombing* (New York: The New Press, 2000), 2.
6. See William Blum, *Rogue State* (Monroe, ME: Common Courage Press, 2000).
7. *Los Angeles Times* (July 13, 2002).
8. *New York Times* (February 11, 2002).
9. Gary Jonathan Bass, *Stay the Hand of Vengeance* (Princeton, NJ: Princeton University Press, 2000), 282.
10. Norman Cigar and Paul Williams, *Indictment in the Hague* (New York: New York University Press, 2002), 17, 21.
11. Sara Flounders, "Bosnia Tragedy: The Unknown Role of the Pentagon," in *NATO in the Balkans* (New York: International Action Center, 1998), 63. See also Diana Johnstone's excellent account in *Fool's Crusade: Yugoslavia, NATO, and Western Delusions* (New York: Monthly Review, 2002), 40–64.
12. See Sean Gervasi, "Why is NATO in Yugoslavia?" in *NATO in the Balkans*, 29–46.
13. Michael Parenti, *To Kill a Nation* (London: Verso, 2000), 124.
14. Parenti, 164.
15. See Gervasi, in *NATO in the Balkans*.
16. *New York Times* (March 8, 1992).
17. Flounders, in *NATO in the Balkans*, 71.
18. David Chandler, "'International Justice,'" *New Left Review* (November–December 2000), 65.
19. Telford Taylor, *Nuremberg and Vietnam* (Chicago: Quadrangle Books, 1970), 39.
20. Steven R. Ratner, "Aggression," in *Crimes of War*, 25.
21. Blum, *Rogue State*, 125–67.
22. On President Kennedy's involvement in the Vietnam War planning and escalation, see Bruce Miroff, *Pragmatic Illusions* (New York: David McKay, 1976), 142–66, and Marilyn B. Young, *The Vietnam Wars* (New York: HarperCollins, 1991), 60–105.
23. Christopher Hitchens, *The Trial of Henry Kissinger* (London: Verso, 2001).
24. See Philip E. Wheaton, *Panama Invaded* (Trenton, NJ: The Red Sea Press, 1992), 143–58.
25. Anthony Arnove, ed., *Iraq Under Siege* (Boston: South End Press, 2000), especially chs. 1–3 and 11–13.
26. On the attack in Yemen, see the *Los Angeles Times* (November 5, 2002).
27. Lindqvist, *A History of Bombing*, 26.
28. Lindqvist, 121.
29. John Dower, *War Without Mercy* (New York: Pantheon, 1986), 41.
30. Cited in Lindqvist, 128.
31. Lindqvist, 121.
32. James William Gibson, *The Perfect War* (New York: Atlantic Monthly, 1986), 327.
33. Gibson, 327.
34. Young, *The Vietnam Wars*, 301–02.
35. Lindqvist, 162.
36. See *Iraq Under Siege*, chs. 1, 4.
37. Ramsey Clark, et al., *War Crimes* (Washington D.C.: Maisonneuve Press, 1992), parts 1–3.
38. Clark, "Indictment of the US/NATO," in John Catalinotto and Sara Flounders, eds., *Hidden Agenda: U.S./NATO Takeover of Yugoslavia,* (New York: IAC, 2002), 33–45.
39. Parenti, *To Kill a Nation*, 124.
40. Tariq Ali, *The Clash of Fundamentalisms* (London: Verso, 2002), 267.
41. Edward Herman, "'Tragic Errors' in U.S. Military Policy," *Z* (September 2002), 27.
42. Ward Churchill, *A Little Matter of Genocide* (San Francisco: City Lights, 1997), 188.
43. Caleb Carr, *The Lessons of Terror* (New York: Random House, 2002), 172–73.
44. Carr, 255.
45. Dower, *War Without Mercy*, 69.
46. Stephen Endicott and Edward Hagerman, *The United States and Biological Warfare* (Bloomington: University of Indiana Press, 1998), 89.
47. Cited in Gibson, *The Perfect War*, 141–42.
48. Gibson, 199.
49. Wheaton, *Panama Invaded*, 115–16.
50. Wheaton, 31.
51. Wheaton, 53.

52. See the anthology, *Metal of Dishonor* (New York: International Action Center, 1999), especially chs. 1, 3, and 8.

53. Joy Gordon, "Cool War," *Harper's* (November 2002), 43.

54. *Los Angeles Times* (January 4, 2002).

55. See *Newsweek* (August 6, 2002).

56. Phyllis Bennis, *Before and After: U.S. Foreign Policy and the September 11 Crisis* (New York: Olive Branch, 2003), 104.

57. Barbara Ehrenreich, *Blood Rites* (New York: Henry Holt, 1997), 222–23.

58. Richard Rhodes, *Why They Kill* (New York: Vintage Books, 1999), 287.

59. Robert Aldrich, *First Strike!* (Boston: South End Press, 1983), ch. 1.

60. Lindqvist, *A History of Bombing*, 126.

61. Karl Grossman, *Weapons in Space* (New York: Seven Stories, 2001).

62. Michio Kaku, "Depleted Uranium: Huge Quantities of Dangerous Waste," in *Metal of Dishonor*, 111–15.

63. Blum, *Rogue State*, 96–97.

64. Ibid., 105–06.

65. See Peter Pringle, "Chemical Weapons," in *Crimes of War*, 74–75.

66. Blum, op. cit., 121–22.

67. *Los Angeles Times* (October 9, 2002).

68. See Endicott and Hagerman, *The United States and Biological Weapons*.

69. Ibid., 100.

70. Ibid., 103.

71. Cigar and Williams, *Indictment at the Hague*, 96–97.

72. On the Contra wars against Nicaragua and the U.S. role, see Noam Chomsky, *Turning the Tide* (Boston: South End Press, 1986), 127–46.

73. See Gregory Elich, "The Invasion of Serbian Krajina," in *NATO in the Balkans*, 130–140.

74. Richard Stutsman, "CIA Death Squads in Guatemala" (online April 7, 1995).

75. Edward Said, "America's Last Taboo," *New Left Review* (November–December 2000), 47.

76. Gilbert Achcar, "After September 11," *Monthly Review* (September 2002).

77. See Henry T. Nash, "The Bureaucratization of Homicide," in E.P. Thompson and Dan Smith, eds., *Protest and Survive* (New York: Monthly Review Press, 1981), 149–62.

78. Gibson, *The Perfect War*, 464.

79. Herbert Kelman and V. Lee Hamilton, "The My Lai Massacre," in David Newman, ed., *Sociology: Readings* (Newbury Park, CA: Pine Forge, 1995).

80. See Richard Falk's account in the *Nation* (July 9, 2001).

81. Joseph E. Persico, *Nuremberg* (New York: Penguin Books, 1995), 188.

82. Hannah Arendt, *Eichmann in Jerusalem* (New York: Penguin Books, 1963), 276.

83. Richard Falk, *Human Rights Horizons* (New York: Routledge, 2000), ch. 10.

84. Chandler in *New Left Review*, 63.

85. *The Sunday Herald* (October 15, 2002).

86. Noam Chomsky, *Rogue States* (Boston: South End Press, 2000), 17.

87. Lindqvist, *A History of Bombing*, 184.

88. Douglas Kellner, *The Persian Gulf TV War* (Boulder, CO: Westview Press, 1992).

PART **III**
The Militarized Society

CHAPTER **9**

Postmodern Military and Permanent War[1]

DOUGLAS KELLNER

The U.S. Commission on National Security for the Twenty-First Century maintained that "Outer Space and cyberspace are the main arteries of the world's evolving systems. Through technical and diplomatic means, the U.S. needs to guard against the possibility of 'breakout' capabilities in space and cyberspace that would endanger U.S. survival or critical interests."[2] In his first speech on military affairs after announcing his candidacy for president in 1999, George W. Bush affirmed the concept of a "Revolution in Military Affairs" (RMA) and was soon touting the virtues of a National Missile Defense (NMD) shield. Upon obtaining the presidency through a highly controversial electoral process, Bush called for a dramatic increase in military spending and pushed the space missile NMD program, popularly known as Star Wars II. The Bush administration also undermined collective security based on multilateral negotiations and treaties over weapons control by renouncing nuclear weapons treaties and attempts to regulate nuclear testing, biological and chemical weapons, small arms trading, land mines, and environmental treaties, which had been carefully nurtured by decades of diplomacy.

In this essay, I chart the genealogy and development of new trends in high-tech warfare which have emerged in the past decade and explore its challenges and dangers. I discuss the Bush administration's military program and foreign policy moves, highlighting the ways that the Bush II group intensifies the dangers of high-tech war, while undermining efforts at collective security, environmental protection, and global peace. My argument is that the volatile mixture of a highly regressive, unilateralist, and militarist government with development of high-tech weapons provides a clear and present danger of a protracted and frightening period of war. The mixture of right-wing unilateralism and militarism dramatically erupted with Bush's military response to the terrorist attacks of September 11 and it has increased dangers to world peace in the campaign against terrorism some have labeled "World War III."

Cyberwarriors and Cyberwar: Military Postmodernization

In 1983, the Defense Advance Research Projects Agency (DARPA), responsible for development of the Internet, published a document outlining a "Strategic Computing Program" (SCP).[3] The SCP was a five-year, $600,000,000 plan to produce a new generation of military applications for computers. The proposal included a thousand-fold increase in computing power and an emphasis on artificial intelligence. It envisioned "completely autonomous land, sea and air vehicles capable of complex, far-ranging reconnaissance and attack missions." These vehicles would have human abilities, such as sight, speech, understanding natural language, and automated reasoning. The SCP promoted the view that the human element in many critical decision-making instances could be largely or totally taken over by machines.[4] In this momentous process, just as humans are becoming like machines, machines are ever more taking on human qualities.[5]

The Persian Gulf TV war indicated the extent to which computer and information systems were of primary importance in the planning and execution of the war, the ways that new fusions of humans and technologies engendered a cyberwarrior, and how military media spectacles can promote weapons systems and project national power.[6] The development is part of a process of creating soldiers better able to integrate themselves into technological systems and to fight increasingly complex battles. This involves cultivating high-tech skills in future soldiers. It requires disciplinary training to fit into technical apparatuses and use of psychotechnologies and drugs to enhance human abilities, while providing prostheses and implants that will produce technological amplification of human powers and abilities.[7]

The accelerated role of information technologies in postmodern war has led some theorists to talk of new "Network-Centric Warfare" and a "revolution in military affairs" (RMA). These changes have been produced "by the co-evolution of economics, information technology, and business processes and organizations." They are, in the words of military authorities, linked by three themes: shifts from platform to network; a change from viewing actors as independent to viewing them as "part of a continuously adapting military-techno ecosystem"; and the "importance of making strategic choices to adapt or even survive in such changing ecosystems."[8]

The postmodernization of war thus pertains to the increasing displacement of humans by technology with ever more "smart machines" supplementing and even replacing human beings. The 1991 Gulf intervention, 1999 NATO war against Serbia, and 2001 Afghan war saw a widespread exploitation of drones, pilotless planes engaged as decoys and as instruments of surveillance, in addition to Cruise missiles and other "smart" weapons. The U.S. military is developing "unmanned" technologies for ground, air, and undersea vehicles.[9] Smart tanks are already under production and as Gray notes:

There are projects to create autonomous land vehicles, minelayers, minesweepers, obstacle breachers, construction equipment, surveillance platforms, and anti-radar, anti-armor and anti-everything drones. They are working on smart artillery shells, smart torpedoes, smart depth charges, smart rocks (scavenged meteors collected and then "thrown" in space), smart bombs, smart nuclear missiles and brilliant cruise missiles. Computer battle-managers are being developed for AirLand battle, tactical fighter wings, naval carrier groups, and space-based ballistic-missile defense. . . . The Army even hopes to have a robot to "decontaminate human remains, inter remains, and refill and mark the graves."[10]

Exotic high-tech military devices include MEMS (Micro Electrono-Mechanical Systems) that will produce tiny airplanes or insect-like devices that can gather intelligence or attack enemies. MARV (Miniature Autonomous Robotic Vehicle) technologies and various other automated military systems would guide robot-ships, disable landmines and unexploded arms, and provide more effective sensors, stabilization, navigation, control, and maintenance devices. These technologies would ultimately construct cyborg soldiers who will incorporate such devices into their own bodies and equipment.[11] Such miniature machines and cyberwarriors would be capable of gathering information, processing it, and then acting upon it, thus carrying through a technological revolution based on new intelligent machines.

Military spokespeople also claim that the next generation of Army vehicles will be "Net-ready." The Army plans to pursue a battlefield digitization project while it develops and fields a new family of lightweight, easily deployable combat vehicles with digital technology built into them, rather than bolting it on as the Army has had to do with older tanks and Bradley Fighting Vehicles.[12] Cyborg soldiers can utilize the Global Positioning Satellite system (which can be accessed from a computerized helmet) for precise mapping of the "enemy" and terrain. With the complex communications systems now emerging, all aspects of war—from soldiers on the ground and thundering tanks to pilotless planes overhead—are becoming networked with wireless computers providing information and exact locations of all parties. Robot scouts can roam the terrain sending back data instantaneously to commanders. SIPE (Soldier Integrated Protection Ensemble) is an army software program designed to merge all military digital technologies into one integrated data system. Even the physical state of the soldier can be monitored by computers, and one can imagine surgeons operating on wounds from continents away by using robots and the technology of "telemedicine."

The autonomization of warfare and ongoing displacement of humans by technology creates the specter of technology taking over and the greater possibility of military accidents. A fierce argument is raging in military circles between those who want to delegate more power and fighting to the new "brilliant" weapons opposed to those who want to keep human operators in charge of technical systems.[13] Critics of cyberwar worry that as technology supplants human beings, taking humans out of decision-making loops, the possibility of the accidental firing of arms at inappropriate targets, and even nuclear war, increases. Manuel De Landa fears nuclear accidents and technology out of control in fully automated cyberwar and calls for the manufacture of weapons over which humans maintain authority and interact creatively with technology, rather than being its object and servomechanism.[14] Eugene Rochlin also cites dangers of possible accidents on automated battlefields and cyberwar where humans are forced to react more quickly to high-speed systems.[15] To support his arguments, Rochlin presents case studies of accidents in automated milieux over the past decade, warning that humans must attempt to maintain control over their technology.

In this unprecedented situation, new technologies are creating frightening types of technowar that require rethinking the very nature of military conflict and the dangers of military solutions to current problems in the face of such dangers. Theorists of novel modes of war focus both on the transformations of conventional warfare owing to incorporation of computer technologies into the warfare state, as well as new phenomena like information war; threats of hacker disruption of the economy, transportation, and communication systems; and exotic modes of biological, genetic, and chemical warfare (easier and cheaper to obtain than nuclear weapons).

There is growing apprehension over evolving types of chemical and biological warfare, involving virulent and deadly forms of mass destruction.[16] Lethal weapons, such as a stolen nuclear bomb or weapons using radiation exposure alone, could destroy vast urban areas, or poison water and food supplies. Biological weapons, such as anthrax, the plague, and many other disease-carrying biological agents, can be readily produced and distributed and could be extremely toxic, as films such as *Outbreak* (1995) have warned and the anthrax attacks of fall 2001 have demonstrated. Chemical weapons, which some think were deployed, or released by U.S. bombing, in the war against Iraq, are also extremely toxic and relatively easy to procure and deploy. The Internet makes the production of such armaments available to large numbers of groups and individuals.

Cyberwar was previewed in the 1991 war against Iraq and was an important component of the Kosovo war that was planned, programmed, and orchestrated through computer networks, as well as the 2001 war against the Al Qaeda network and Taliban in Afghanistan. While the Persian Gulf war was arguably the most spectacular military campaign of the TV Global Village, the war in Yugoslavia was perhaps the first Internet war. Not only was computerization deployed to plan and execute high-altitude bombing, but the Internet became a primary source of information and debate for the public. The volatile situation on the ground in Yugoslavia, with heavy NATO bombing, brutal retaliation against the Kosovar Albanians by the Serbs, swarms of refugees in the region, and the ensuing lawlessness made it extremely difficult for the major broadcasting and news corporations to bring in their employees. Instead, freelance reporters wrote on-the-ground testimonials and accounts, sent to leading web-based zines like *Salon* and *Slate*, or in some cases newspapers. In addition, there was a tremendous amount of information from the region transmitted over the Internet via list-serves, e-mail, and web sites. The NATO war was intensely debated over the Internet, if not the mainstream broadcasting and print media, bringing the Internet to the fore of political communication and debate.

Emergent forms of postmodern war would include new modes of netwar fought in cyberspace wherein warring nations, or terrorists, attempt to destroy information and communications systems.[17] This type of netwar was previewed in what might be called the "hacker wars." The term "hacker" initially meant someone who made creative innovations in computer systems to facilitate the exchange of information and construction of new communities.[18] But it came to refer to a mode of "terrorism" whereby malicious computer nerds either illegally invade closed computer systems, or breed viruses or worms that will disable computers and even entire computer networks.[19] During the 1990s and into the Third Millennium, panic emerged whenever a new virus was discovered and the national security apparatuses began preparing for an information war that might disable important computer systems, disrupting the world economy, a nation's defense establishment, or any aspects of the system of production, transportation, and communication.[20]

Such new modes of military conflict have evoked much discussion of "cyberwarriors," an "electronic Pearl Harbor," and dire threats to the world economy and individual security. In this scenario, information guerrilla warriors could disrupt or dismantle every vital infrastructure system of the military and civilian sectors, creating problems ranging from power outages and airline crashes to the shutdown of banks, the stock market, and the growing realm of electronic commerce. Quite unlike hand-to-hand combat, cyberwarriors can attack a nation from continents away. Dispensing with guns, tanks, and airplanes, cyberwar takes place through computers and modems. While cyberwar may unfold as abstract and bloodless, it too can have deadly "collateral damage" by damaging institutions like hospitals, emergency services, and air traffic control systems. Hackers and infowarriors employ new weapons such as viruses, logic bombs, trojan horses, and worms, all designed to replicate within and destroy the systems they penetrate.[21]

After the bombing of the Chinese Embassy in Belgrade by NATO forces in May 1999, hackers broke into the NATO web site, protesting the action. There are also many examples of hackers breaking into Pentagon and Defense Department sites to post critical messages and deface government bulletin boards. Hacker campaigns have been organized against the governments of

Mexico, Indonesia, and others, protesting against unpopular policies by defacing official web sites or bombarding government sites and servers with spam or logic bombs, attempting to shut them down. One of the more spectacular hacker attacks against commercial e-business sites occurred in February 2000, when hackers temporarily blocked access to the popular Internet sites Yahoo, Amazon.com (an Internet book company), CNN, and Buy.com, an e-business retail site. Attacks followed on the news site ZDNet and E-Trade, an online brokerage. Demonstration of the ease with which commercial Internet sites can be disabled sent jitters through the stock market, put the FBI and law enforcement agencies in motion, and set off a flurry of discussions regarding the need for better cybersecurity.

In July 2001, the White House web site was attacked by the "Code Red" virus that allegedly infected more than 225,000 computer systems around the world. U.S. Attorney General John Ashcroft announced the government would be forming nine special units to prosecute hacking and copyright violations.[22] Meanwhile, a Sircam virus infected countless computer systems and personal computers, and once again hacking, worms, and viruses were being perceived as a serious threat to the digital economy and culture. And in May 2001, after a Chinese plane crashed in a skirmish with a U.S. intelligence plane, Chinese hackers launched several days of attacks at U.S. web sites.

The possibility of new forms of cyberwar, along with terrorist threats from chemical, biological, or nuclear weapons, creates new vulnerabilities in the national defense of the overdeveloped countries and provides opportunities for weaker nations or groups to attack stronger ones. Journalist William Greider, author of *Fortress America*, claims that: "A deadly irony is embedded in the potential of these new technologies. Smaller, poorer nations may be able to defend themselves on the cheap against the intrusion of America's overwhelming military strength"[23]—or exercise deadly terrorism against civilian populations. Hence, the more technologically advanced a society is, the more vulnerable it is to cyberwar.

Realizing such dangers, the Pentagon is in the first stages of assembling something like a digital Manhattan Project with multi-billion dollar investments. Alarmed by threats to the national information infrastructure, the U.S. is organizing a Federal Intrusion Detection Network, or Fidnet, to monitor computer networks and attempt to block intrusions and other illegal acts.[24] Jeffrey Hunter, the National Security Council director of information in charge of the initiative, stated that: "Our concern about an organized cyberattack has escalated dramatically. We do know of a number of hostile foreign governments that are developing sophisticated and well-organized offensive cyber attack capabilities, and we have good reason to believe that terrorists may be acquiring similar capabilities." The initiative is currently under review with civil libertarians concerned that the project might compromise privacy and threaten civil liberties while increasing exponentially the power of the state.[25]

Ever scarier, theorists are worrying about new biotechnology and nanotechnology military instruments that might miniaturize weapons of mass destruction in as yet unforeseeable forms.[26] Following the logic of miniaturization characteristic of advanced bio- and information technology, some observers imagine that weapons could become nearly invisible and release destructive forces in unimaginable ways. The coming stage of military technology could thus involve microscopic nanotechnologies in which what were envisaged as "engines of creation" could become "engines of destruction."[27]

Postmodern war is thus part of the dangerous side of the new millennium, increasing global insecurities and the prospects of world destruction. Postmodern war exhibits a continuation of the worst features of modernity, threatening to take the development of new technologies to a catastrophic endgame. Yet within the global restructuring of capital, the form of military capitalism dominant since World War II appeared during the Clinton administration to have been overshadowed by a more user-friendly digital capitalism. In this mode, new entertainment and information technologies would reproduce an infotainment society where war would be irrelevant and even harmful to the pursuit of profit and human well-being. The Internet itself, originally conceived and funded as a multi-point communications system for the military after a nuclear attack, was restructured into an instrument for communication and information-sharing, commerce, and politics.

The information and communications technologies produced by the military might conceivably be refunctioned and restructured for peace, human purposes, and empowerment, rather than destruction and war. Cyborg systems can perform dangerous industrial labor, or simple household labor, as well as generate electronic battlefields. Conversion from warfare state to welfare state was a rational expectation at the end of the Cold War, although current trends of dismantling the welfare state and continued proliferation of a military-technowar establishment run counter to such expectations. Developments within the Bush administration and the ensuing militarization of the world after the 9/11 terrorist attack on the U.S. suggest a new era of military conflict with frightful consequences for the human adventure.

The Bush Administration and Terror War

Reflections on economic conversion and the transformation of a war economy into a peace economy are utopian in the context of George W. Bush's theft of the presidency in Election 2000 and the war against terrorism that arose as a response to the September 11 events.[28] Bush's ascent to the presidency suggests a return to a harder, more militarist, predatory capitalism. The Cold Warriors from Bush's father's circles who surround the figurehead and control policy are key representatives of the virulent military-industrial complex and are promoting a plethora of new weapons systems, as well as unparalleled expansion of the U.S. military budget and scope of military intervention.

The Bush administration initially proposed $310 billion in military spending for 2001, with much more expected for a missile-defense system that was the pet project of his Secretary of Defense, Donald Rumsfeld. In mid-February 2001, Bush announced he was seeking an additional $2.6 billion for high-tech weapons and by the end of the month would detail further requests for hikes in the Pentagon budget beyond the $310 billion already targeted. By summer 2001, the Pentagon budget was up to $324 billion, while Bush's 2002 budget proposed a 6 percent boost in spending to raise the Pentagon budget to $330 billion, eventually going up to $355 billion. And for fiscal year 2003, Bush proposed a record $48 billion increase, with Congress eventually passing in October 2002 a record $355.1 billion budget.[29]

The dramatically increased military spending to develop a space-based "National Missile Defense" system (Reagan's "Star Wars" program reborn) threatened not only to expand the military budget but to accelerate both a new arms race and the militarization of space.[30] Before assuming office Bush spoke of "American responsibilities" and the "promise of America," while promising a "humble" U.S. foreign policy that eschewed "nation-building." Once in office, however, Bush pursued a highly irresponsible politics of unilateralism that renounced global environmental treaties, rejected arms limitations treaties, pushed ahead to build a missile defense system strongly opposed by U.S. allies, and accelerated tensions with Iraq, Iran, North Korea, China, and Russia, generating "enemies" that would justify a missile defense system and increased military spending.

During its first nine months the Bush administration pursued a hardline foreign policy reminiscent of the Cold War at its peak. In the opening weeks Bush bombed Iraq and heightened tensions in the Middle East, threatened China, told Russia to expect reduced aid, and alienated Japan when a Navy submarine giving Republican financial supporters a demonstration sank a Japanese fishing boat, killing nine people. The Bush administration worried much of Europe due to its aggressive approach to national missile defense (NMD), making it clear that it does not intend to pursue constructive negotiations with North Korea. Even before September 11, the Bush administration returned the world to the Cold War paranoid universe of the military-industrial complex, while Dr. Strangelove seemed to be alive and well in the U.S. Defense Department, concocting Star Wars missile systems that will cost trillions of dollars and have yet to be proved functional.

Bush, Cheney, and Rumsfeld had also resurrected the concept of "rogue state," a concept jettisoned by the Clinton administration that was sure to increase tensions and the possibility of war. Dangers of an aggressive new Bush foreign policy were soon evident. On March 24, 2001, the *Washington Post* published a report that Bush had had a meeting two days before with Defense

Secretary Rumsfeld who was preparing a report that China had supplanted the USSR as its Number One Enemy and should be the focus of U.S. military policy. Some days later, an "accident" occurred when a Chinese plane and a U.S. spy plane off the Chinese coast collided and the U.S. plane, loaded with high-tech surveillance equipment and the latest military computers, crash-landed on a Chinese off-shore island, after which the crew was held hostage for eleven tense days while its release was negotiated.

Critics claim that "corporate payback" is the "defining trait" of the Bush administration and a major force in determining its hard-right policies. Abrogation of the Kyoto Treaty and the Bush-Cheney energy policy were payback for the more than $50 million contributed by the oil and energy industries. The former director of the Star Wars program under Reagan, Dr. Robert M. Bowman, makes a similar argument in terms of Bush's military policy. Star Wars II, Bowman argues, will "line the pockets of weapons manufacturers for decades" at the expense of "optional" programs like health, education, the environment, and welfare. Moreover, it gives "the multinational corporations and banks absolute military superiority for their 'gunboat diplomacy around the world.'"[31]

The militarization of space constitutes yet another troubling dimension of Bush administration pursuit of a space-based missile program and unilateral foreign policy.[32] UN treaties have called for the demilitarization of space and the renunciation of space-based military programs. The Bush administration, however, has made clear that it plans to deploy weapons in space with a land-, sea-, air-, and space-based Star Wars II system. The Pentagon has revived the Reagan-era plan for "Brilliant Pebbles," a scheme that would place thousands of missile interceptors in space, raising the possibility of space wars and accidental mishaps. Another piece of Reagan's SDI, "Brilliant Eyes," has been resurrected, consisting of a series of low-flying satellites geared to tracking missiles or presumed weapons.

Maintaining a weapons-free space, however, is crucial to a high-tech economy that depends on communications satellites for its functionality, as well as increasing the hopes of global peace. The more weapons there are flying around in space, the greater chance of their misuse or an accident. It is also tragic that the militarization of space has supplanted efforts for the scientific exploration of space, as the Star Wars II budget is now twice that of the entire NASA budget. The destiny of the human race depends on the peaceful exploration of space, while its militarization could threaten the very survival of the human species.[33]

The Bush administration has undermined every single arms control treaty it has faced since coming to power. When it rejected a pact to enforce a biological weapons ban in July 2001, a British commentator noted: "America's lone, wanton wrecking of long-running negotiations to enforce the 1972 treaty banning biological or germs weapons is an insult to the pact's 142 other signatories, a body-blow for the treaty itself and a major setback for international efforts to agree to practical curbs on the proliferation of weapons of mass destruction."³⁴ Bush stood condemned as "proliferator-in-chief" of dangerous weapons, whose presidency "confirms a pattern of reckless, unilateralist behavior on arms control, as on environmental and other issues."³⁵

Once again Bush carried out the wishes of his main campaign supporters, as it was the biotech and pharmeceutical industries that opposed the inspection program called for in the biological weapons treaty. Although biological weapons are deemed a disturbing threat to the entire world, the U.S. found itself in a minority of one in opposing the treaty, putting U.S. corporate interests before those of global security. Similarly, the U.S. was the sole nation out of 178 to renounce ratification of the Kyoto treaty to combat global warming during a July 2001 meeting in Bonn.

For several weeks following September 11 the global community appeared to be building an effective multilateral strategy to fight terrorism by arresting suspected members of the Al Qaeda network, tracking and blocking their financial support, and developing internal and global mechanisms and policies to fight terrorism. Suddenly, however, the campaign against terrorism turned to war. On Sunday, October 7, just short of one month after the terrorist attacks on the U.S., the Bush administration unleashed a full-scale military assault on Afghanistan, purportedly to annihilate the bin Laden network and the Taliban regime that had been hosting it. The unilateralism of the U.S. response was striking. Leading American newspapers provided a rationale for U.S. rejection of a UN-led or NATO-led coalition against international terrorism:

> In the leadup to a possible military strike, senior administration and allied officials said Mr. Rumsfeld's approach this week made clear that the United States intends to make it as much as possible an all-American campaign.
>
> One reason, they said, is that the United States is determined to avoid the limitations on its targets that were imposed by NATO allies during the 1999 war in Kosovo, or the hesitance to topple a leader that members of the gulf war coalition felt in 1991.
>
> "Coalition is a bad word, because it makes people think of alliances," said Robert Oakley, former head of the State Department's counter-terrorism office and former ambassador to Pakistan.
>
> A senior administration official put it more bluntly: "The fewer people you have to rely on, the fewer permissions you have to get."³⁶

In his September 25, 2001, speech to Congress declaring the war on terrorism, Bush announced what his administration would describe as "the Bush doctrine." Calling the crusade against terrorism a war between freedom and fear, between "those governed by fear" who "want to destroy our wealth and freedoms," and those on the side of freedom, Bush asserted that "you're either with us, or against us." Bush also said that his administration held accountable those nations that supported terrorism, and in his October 7 speech announcing a bombing campaign against the Taliban, he claimed that the Taliban leadership had sustained the Al Qaeda network and would be subject to military retaliation. Bush warned that his administration was planning to go after other targets later, and there was talk that the war against terrorism and resultant Jihad of Islam against the West could lead to World War III.

As the U.S. continued its bombing campaign in Afghanistan through the end of 2001 and into 2002, threatening to expand its military actions to states like Iraq, worries circulated that U.S. military intervention might create more problems than it could ever hope to solve. When Rumsfeld compared the war on terror to the Cold War, which lasted roughly forty years, the specter of endless war was invoked—which is perhaps what the Pentagon had in mind when they first named their military intervention "Operation Infinite Justice." Jokes circulated through the Pentagon that an endless war on terrorism would drag them into "Operation Infinite War."

"Endless war" would no doubt be a hard project to sell to the public for the long term and one wonders how long it would take for costs to overwhelm benefits. Although war throughout the new millennium would keep America's troops fully employed and the Pentagon budget escalating, it would also keep U.S. citizens in a state of fear over terrorist retaliation, for endless war would no doubt generate endless terrorism in the form of blowback. Moreover, it was not clear how the U.S. could afford to finance an endless war against terrorism, nor how the global economy could function in a situation of perpetual fear and war.

Preemptive Strikes, Permanent War, and the New American Empire

In a speech to West Point cadets on June 1, 2002, George W. Bush proclaimed a new "doctrine" that the U.S. would strike first against enemies. It was soon apparent that this was a major shift in U.S. military policy, replacing the Cold War doctrine of containment and deterrence with a new policy of preemptive strikes, one that could be tried out in Iraq. U.S. allies were extremely upset with this shift in U.S. policy. In an article "Bush to Formalize a Defense Policy of Hitting First," David E. Sanger wrote in the *New York Times* (June 17, 2002) that: "The process of including America's allies has only just begun, and administration officials concede that it will be difficult at best. Leaders in Berlin, Paris and Beijing, in particular, have often warned against unilateralism. But Mr. Bush's new policy could amount to ultimate unilateralism, because it reserves the right to determine what constitutes a threat to American security and to act even if that threat is not judged imminent."[37]

After a summer of limited debates on the prospects of the U.S. going to war against Iraq to destroy its weapons of mass destruction, on August 26, Cheney applied the new preemptive strike and unilateralist doctrine to Iraq, arguing: "What we must not do in the face of a mortal threat is to give in to wishful thinking or willful blindness. . . . Deliverable weapons of mass destruction in the hands of a terror network or murderous dictator or the two working to-gether constitutes as grave a threat as can be imagined. The risks of inaction are far greater than the risks of action." Cheney was responding to many for-mer generals and high-level members of the first Bush administration who had reservations about the sort of unilateralist U.S. attack against Iraq that hawks in the Bush administration were urging.

Bush and others in his circle regularly described Terror War as World War III, and Cheney, speaking like a true militarist, said it could go on for a "long, long time, perhaps indefinitely." Such an Orwellian nightmare could plunge the world into a new millennium of escalating war with unintended conse-quences and embroil the U.S. in endless wars, normalizing war as conflict reso-lution and creating countless new enemies for the would-be American hegemon. Indeed, as Chalmers Johnson writes in *Blowback*, empire has hidden costs.[38] Becoming hegemon breeds resentment and hostility and when the em-pire carries out aggression it elicits anger and creates enemies, intensifying the dangers of perpetual war.

On September 20, 2002, it was apparent that the hawks' position in the Bush administration had triumphed, at least on the level of official military doctrine, when the Bush administration released a document signaling some of the most important and far-ranging shifts in U.S. foreign and military pol-icy since the end of the Cold War. Titled "The National Security Strategy of the United States," the 33-page report outlined a new doctrine of U.S. military su-premacy, providing justifications for the U.S. to wage unilateral and preemp-tive strikes in the name of "counterproliferation." This clumsy Orwellian concept was offered as a replacement for the concept of nonproliferation and in effect would legitimate unilateral destruction of a country's presumed weapons of mass destruction. The document, in effect, renounced the global security, multilateralism, and rule by international law that to some degree had informed U.S. thinking since World War II, and that appeared to be an emerg-ing consensus among Western nations during the era of globalization.

The Bush administration's language of "preemptive strikes," "regime change," and "anticipatory self-defense" is purely Orwellian, presenting eu-phemisms for raw military aggression. Critics assailed the new "strike first, ask questions later" policy, the belligerent unilateralism, and dangerous legitima-tion of preemptive strikes.[39] Israel, Pakistan, Russia, China, and lesser powers had already used the so-called "Bush doctrine" and "war against terrorism" to legitimate attacks on domestic and external foes, and there were looming dan-gers that it could legitimate a proliferation of wars and make the world more unstable and violent. As William Galston states:

> A global strategy based on the new Bush doctrine of preemption means the end
> of the system of international institutions, laws and norms that we have worked
> to build for more than half a century. What is at stake is nothing less than a fun-

damental shift in America's place in the world. Rather than continuing to serve as first among equals in the postwar international system, the United States would act as a law unto itself, creating new rules of international engagement without the consent of other nations. In my judgment, this new stance would ill serve the long-term interests of the United States.[40]

The Bush doctrine of preemptive strikes could indeed unleash a series of wars that would plunge the world into the sort of nightmare militarism and totalitarianism sketched out in George Orwell's *1984*. The Bush policy is highly barbaric, taking the global community to a Darwinian battleground where decades of international law and military prudence will be put aside in perhaps the most dangerous foreign policy doctrine in U.S. history. It portends a militarist future and an era of perpetual war in which a new militarism generates a cycle of unending violence and retribution of the sort evident in the Israel and Palestine conflict.

Around the time the Bush administration was pushing its new strategic doctrine and seeking to apply it in a war against Iraq, a 2000 report circulated titled "Rebuilding American Defense: Strategies, Forces and Resources for A New American Century." Drawn up by the neoconservative think-tank Project for a New American Century (PNAC) for a group that now comprises the right wing of the Bush administration, including Cheney, Rumsfeld, and Paul Wolfowitz, the document spelled out a plan for U.S. world hegemony grounded in U.S. military dominance of the world and control of the Persian Gulf region with its oil supplies.[41] Its upfront goals were a "Pax Americana" and U.S. domination of the world during the new millennium. The document shows that core members of the Bush administration had long envisaged taking military control of the Gulf region, with the PNAC text stating: "The United States has for decades sought to play a more permanent role in Gulf regional security. While the unresolved conflict with Iraq provides the immediate justification, the need for a substantial American force presence in the Gulf transcends the issue of the regime of Saddam Hussein."

The PNAC document argues for "maintaining global U.S. pre-eminence, precluding the rise of any great power rival, while shaping the international security order in accordance with American principles and interests." The vision is long-range, urging U.S. domination of the Gulf "as far into the future as possible." It also calls for the U.S. to "fight and decisively win multiple, simultaneous major theatre wars" as a "core mission." U.S. armed forces would serve as "the cavalry on the new American frontier," with its military power blocking the emergence of other countries challenging U.S. domination. It would enlist key allies such as Britain as "the most effective and efficient means of exercising American global leadership," and would place the U.S., and not the UN, as leader of military interventions and peacekeeping missions. It envisions taking on Iran after Iraq, spotlights China for "regime change," and calls for the creation of "U.S. Space Forces" to dominate outer space, positioning the U.S. to totally control cyberspace and prevent "enemies" from using the Internet against the U.S.

The outcome of U.S. military intervention against Iraq and other states in the "axis of evil," or countries that possess weapons of mass destruction, is far from certain and will perhaps play itself out for years in sharpening conflicts between the West and radical Islam. If the Bush administration pursues its military ambitions it could easily isolate the U.S. as a rogue nation attempting to manage an empire constantly under attack. While technological revolution and the postmodernization of war are probably inevitable, it is clear that in today's increasingly dangerous world there must be multilateral agreements to control weapons proliferation and to enforce collective global peace and security.

It is doubtful that the human species can survive the dual forces of terrorism and militarism. Human survival depends upon the ability to institutionalize peaceful means of resolving conflict, to criminalize and reduce the worldwide threat of terrorism, and to renounce unilateralist militarism as a dangerous force giving rise to more problems than it can ever hope to solve. The Bush administration military doctrine of preemptive strikes and plans for world domination threatens to plunge the world into an Orwellian nightmare of perpetual wars, creating conditions for totalitarian government and a Hobbesian world in which life is nasty, brutish, and short. Only by understanding the clear and present dangers of the Bush doctrine and by organizing to oppose them can the future and survival of life on earth be guaranteed.

Notes

1. The first part of this study draws upon work with Steven Best published in *The Postmodern Adventure. Science, Technology, and Cultural Studies at the Third Millennium* (Best and Kellner, 2001). The second part draws on material from my *Grand Theft 2000* (Kellner, 2001) and my forthcoming book *September 11 and Terror War: The Dangers of the Bush Legacy*. For helpful comments on the text and sustained discussion of the issues involved I would like to thank Carl Boggs, Steve Best, and Rhonda Hammer.
2. See Mark Steel, "The Secret Plans of the World's Most Dangerous Rogue State," June 19, 2001, *The Independent*.
3. See Chris Hables Gray, *Postmodern War*. (New York: Guilford Press, 1997).
4. See the critique of SCP in Gray, *Postmodern War*.
5. See Steven Best and Douglas Kellner, *The Postmodern Adventure*. (London and New York: Routledge and Guilford Press, 2001), Chapter 4.
6. See Douglas Kellner, *The Persian Gulf TV War*. (Boulder, CO: Westview Press, 1992) and Best and Kellner, *The Postmodern Adventure*.
7. See Chris Hables Gray, "The cyborg soldiers: The U.S. military and the post-modern warrior," in Levidow and Robins, 1989: 159–178; *Postmodern War*; and *Cyborg Citizen*. (London and New York: Routledge, 2001).
8. See the account by Vice Admiral Arthur K. Cebrokswky and John J. Garistka at www.usni.org/Proceedings/Articles98/PROcebrowski.htm. Michael Ignatieff in *Virtual War: Kosovo and Beyond* (New York: Henry Holt, 2000, 164ff.) describes the "revolution" in terms of the deployment of precision targeting at a distance and use of computers, also noting conservative military resistance to calls for dramatic transformation of the military (171f.).
9. See "Pilotless Plane Pushes Envelope for U.S. Defense," *Los Angeles Times*, May 14, 2000: A-1 and A-30, and "Robots with the Right Stuff," *Wired* (March 1996). See also James Adams, *The Next World War*. (New York: Simon and Schuster, 1998).

10. See Gray, *Postmodern War*, 54.

11. See Adams, *The Next World War*, 122–137.

12. See Gray, *Postmodern War*, Adams, *The Next World War*, and www.cnn.com/2ready.combat.vehicle.idg/index.html

13. See Peter Arnett, *Live From the Battlefield*. (New York: Simon and Schuster, 1994); Adams, *The Next World War*, and Ignatieff, *Virtual War*.

14. See Manuel de Landa, *War in the Age of Intelligent Machines*. (New York: Zone Books).

15. See Eugene Rochlin, *Trapped in the Net*. (Princeton, NJ: Princeton University Press, 1997).

16. On biowarfare, see Judith Miller, Stephen Engelberg, and William J. Broad, *Germs: Biological Weapons and America's Secret War*. (New York: Simon & Schuster, 2001).

17. Some analysts use "information war" to cover all the modes of new high-tech war; see Winn Schwartau, *Information Warfare* (New York: Thunder's Mouth Press, 1996). Rand theorists David Arquilla and David Ronfeldt focus on "netwar" and "cyberwar" in *The Advent of Network*. (Santa Monica, CA: Rand Corporation, 1996).

18. Steven Levy, *Hackers* (New York: Dell Books, 1985) and Katie Hafner and John Markoff, *Cyberpunk. Outlaws and Hackers on the Computer Frontier*. (New York: Simon and Schuster, 1991).

19. See Hafner and Markoff, *Cyberpunk*, and Bruce Sterling, *The Hacker Breakdown. Law and Disorder on the Electronic Frontier*. (New York: Bantam, 1992).

20. Schwartau, *Information Warfare*, and Adams, *The Next World War*.

21. The Department of Defense estimates that its 2.1 million computer networks were infiltrated 250,000 times in 1995 (www.fas.org/irp/eprint/snyder/infowarfare.htm). The National Security Association (NSA) calculates that more than 120 countries now have "computer attack capacities" that could overtake Pentagon computers in a way that would "seriously degrade the nation's ability to deploy and sustain military forces" (www.govexec.com/dailyfed/0497/042297b1.htm). Moreover, teenage hackers, or "script kiddies," can develop programs that will disable electronic commerce and invade computer systems and destroy programs, as has happened regularly in recent years (see Best and Kellner, 2001, Chapter 4). With summer 2000 virus attacks of the "Lovebug" and "resume," and summer 2001 Code Red and Sircam attacks, it appears that netwar is now spreading throughout all domains of society, targeting citizens as well as businesses and governments.

22. See "Ashcroft Aims at Cyber-Criminals," *Associated Press*, July 20, 2001, and "Inept Virus Hits White House," *Wired News*. July 20, 2001.

23. Greider was cited at www.abcsnew.com, 11/01/99.

24. Cited in *New York Times*, July 28, 1999.

25. For discussion of the earlier October 1997 Marsh report for the President's Commission on Critical Infrastructure Protection and subsequent U.S. policy initiatives to protect the information infrastructure, see Adams, 182ff. The October 2001 USA Patriot Act gave the U.S. government the right to survey without a warrant e-mail and Internet usage, telephone and cell phone communication, and other restrictions on privacy and civil liberties that greatly alarmed civil libertarians; see Declan McCullagh, "Terror Law Foes Mull Strategies," (www.wired.com, Nov. 3, 2001).

26. Bill Joy, "Why the Future Doesn't Need Us," *Wired*, 8.07 (July 2000): 238–246.

27. See Joy, "Why the Future Doesn't Need Us," and the discussion of nanotechnology and Joy's critique in Best and Kellner, *The Postmodern Adventure*, Chapter 4.

28. See Douglas Kellner, *Grand Theft 2000*. (Lanham, MD: Rowman and Littlefield, 2001) and *September 11 and Terror War: The Dangers of the Bush Legacy*. (Lanham, MD: Rowman and Littlefield, 2003).

29. On Bush administration military budgets, see articles in *Los Angeles Times*, February 14, 2001: A14; *Washington Post*, June 23, 2001; *Los Angeles Times*, Sept 18, 2002; and *Washington Post*, October 10, 2001. In February 2002 testimony to the House Budget Committee, Lawrence J. Korb of the Council on Foreign Relations and Business Leaders for Sensible Priorities noted that the Bush military budget represented a 30 percent increase over the previous year. If approved, U.S. military spending would exceed the total defense outlays "of the next 15 countries in the world combined." Furthermore, the proposed "increase of $48 billion alone is more than the total military budgets of every nation in the world." Lawrence Korb, cited in James Carroll, "Bush's radical shift in military policy." *Boston Globe*, Feb. 19, 2002.

30. See "Missile Shield Analysis Warns of Arms Buildup. U.S. System could lead other nuclear powers to enhance arsenals, spread technology, report says." *Los Angeles Times*, May 19,

2000: A1 and A22, and "Risk of Arms Race Seen in U.S. Design of Missile Defense," *New York Times*, May 27, 2000. For a damning critique of the Star Wars/missile shield programs, see Frances FitzGerald, *Way Out There in the Blue: Reagan, Star Wars, and the End of the Cold War.* (New York: Touchstone Books), and Steven Weinberg, "Can Missile Defense Work?" *The New York Review of Books*, February 14, 2002. On the militarization of space, see Karl Grossman, *Weapons in Space.* (New York: Seven Stories Press, 2001). Finally, for critique of excessive Pentagon and the "iron triangle" of the defense industry, the military, and Congress which perpetuates this obscenity, see Greider, *Fortress America.*

31.   Dr. Robert M. Bowman, "Wounding National Security. Star Wars II Endangers the American people." *The News Insider*, July 23, 2001. Bowman criticizes his own participation in the earlier Star Wars program that he now terms "military lunacy." He argues that the new Star Wars II would seriously harm U.S. national security by increasing the arms race, isolating the U.S., eating up resources, and violating treaties, while presenting no real protection against nuclear terrorism. Bowman and many other critics also argue convincingly that the Star Wars II shield just cannot work.

32.   Secretary of State Donald Rumsfeld, popularly referred to as "Dr. Strangelove" in light of his obsession with space and missiles, announced on May 8, 2001, a sharply increased interest in outer space in U.S. strategic military planning. See James Dao, "Rumsfeld Plans to Seek a Military Strategy Using Outer Space," *New York Times*, May 8, 2001, and the critique of the proposed militarization of space, "The Risks of a New Space Race," *New York Times*, Op-Ed, May 13, 2001. The post-September 11 Terror Wars temporarily postponed confrontation over the missile defense program that is proceeding apace without serious debate or opposition.

33.   See Best and Kellner, *The Postmodern Adventure.*

34.   Leader, "Proliferator-in-Chief," *The Guardian*, July 26, 2001.

35.   Ibid.

36.   Cited in the *New York Times*, October 7, 2001.

37.   See also Thomas E. Ricks and Vernon Loeb, "Bush Developing Military Policy of Striking First," *Washington Post*, June 10 , 2002: A1. For a sharp critique of Bush's new preemptive strike policy, see "Werther Report: Is Preemption a Nuclear Schlieffen Plan?" at www.d-n-i.net/fcs/comments/c453.htm

38.   See Chalmers Johnson, *Blowback. The Costs and Consequences of American Empire.* (New York: Henry Holt, 2000).

39.   See William Saletan, "Shoot First. Bush's whitewashed national security manifesto," *Slate*, Sept. 20, 2002; Peter Slevin, "Analysts: New Strategy Courts Unseen Dangers. First Strike Could Be Precedent for Other Nations," *Washington Post*, Sept 22, 2002; and Paul Krugman, "White Man's Burden," *New York Times*, Sept. 24, 2002.

40.   William Galston, "Perils of Preemptive War," *The American Prospect* (Vol. 13, Issue 17, Sept. 23, 2002).

41.   An article by Neil Mackay, "Bush planned Iraq 'regime change' before becoming president" (*The Sunday Herald*, Sept. 15, 2002), widely circulated through the Internet, called attention to the sort of lunatic global strategic vision that informed Bush administration policy. The 2000 plan is available at http://www.newamericancentury.org/RebuildingAmericasDefenses.pdf

CHAPTER 10

Mass Media

Aiding and Abetting Militarism

NORMAN SOLOMON

Propaganda Machinery

"The greatest triumphs of propaganda have been accomplished, not by doing something, but by refraining from doing," Aldous Huxley observed long ago. "Great is truth, but still greater, from a practical point of view, is silence about truth." Despite the media din about "9/11," a silence—rigorously selective—has largely pervaded mainstream news coverage. For policymakers in Washington, the practical utility of that silence is huge. In response to the mass murder committed by hijackers, the righteousness of U.S. military action remains clear—as long as double standards go unmentioned.

On the morning of September 11, 2001, while rescue crews braved intense smoke and grisly rubble, ABC News analyst Vincent Cannistraro helped to put it all in perspective for millions of TV viewers. Cannistraro is a former high-ranking official of the Central Intelligence Agency who was in charge of the CIA's work with the Contras in Nicaragua during the early 1980s. After moving to the National Security Council in 1984, he became a supervisor of covert aid to Afghan guerrillas. In other words, Cannistraro has a long history of assisting terrorists—first, Contra soldiers who routinely killed Nicaraguan civilians; then, mujahideen rebels in Afghanistan—like Osama bin Laden.

How can a longtime associate of terrorists now be credibly denouncing "terrorism"? Easy: all that is required is for media coverage to remain in a kind of history-free zone that has no use for any facets of reality that are not presently convenient to acknowledge. In his book *1984*, George Orwell described the mental dynamics: "The process has to be conscious, or it would not be carried out with sufficient precision, but it also has to be unconscious, or it would bring with it a feeling of falsity and hence of guilt. . . . To tell deliberate lies while genuinely believing in them, to forget any fact that has become inconvenient, and then, when it becomes necessary again, to draw it back from oblivion for just so long as it is needed, to deny the existence of objective reality and all the while to take account of the reality which one denies—all this is indispensably necessary."

Secretary of State Colin Powell denounced "people who feel that with the destruction of buildings, with the murder of people, they can somehow

245

achieve a political purpose." He was describing the terrorists who had struck his country hours earlier, but Powell was also aptly describing a long line of top officials in Washington. Surely U.S. policymakers believed they could "achieve a political purpose"—with "the destruction of buildings, with the murder of people"—when launching missiles at Baghdad or Belgrade. But media scrutiny of atrocities committed by the U.S. government is rare. Only some cruelties merit the spotlight. Only some victims deserve empathy. Only certain crimes against humanity are worth American tears.

"This will be a monumental struggle of good versus evil," President Bush proclaimed. The media reactions to such rhetoric were overwhelmingly favorable. Yet the heart-wrenching voices heard on the nation's airwaves were, in human terms, no less or more important than those voices we have never heard. The victims of terrorism in America have been deserving of our deep compassion. So have the faraway victims of American foreign and military policies—human beings whose humanity has gone unrecognized within the U.S. media.

With the overwhelming bulk of news organizations accustomed to serving as amplification systems for Washington's warriors in times of crisis, the White House found itself in a strong position to retool and lubricate the machinery of domestic propaganda after September 11, 2001. When confronted with claims about "coded messages" that Osama bin Laden and his henchmen might be sending via taped statements (as though other means like the Internet did not exist), TV network executives fell right into line.

Tapes of Al Qaeda leaders provided a useful wedge for the administration to hammer away at the wisdom of (government-assisted) self-censorship. Network execs from ABC, CBS, NBC, Fox, and CNN were deferential in an October 10 conference call with Condoleeza Rice. The conversation was "very collegial," Ari Fleischer told the White House press corps.[1] The result was an agreement, the *New York Times* reported, to "abridge any future videotaped statements from Osama bin Laden or his followers to remove language the government considers inflammatory."[2] It was, the *Times* added, "the first time in memory that the networks had agreed to a joint arrangement to limit their prospective news coverage." News corporation magnate Rupert Murdoch, speaking for Fox, promised: "We'll do whatever is our patriotic duty."[3] CNN, owned by the world's largest media conglomerate, AOL Time-Warner, was eager to present itself as a team player: "In deciding what to air, CNN will consider guidance from appropriate authorities."[4]

"Guidance" from the "appropriate authorities" was exactly what the president's strategists had in mind—brandishing a club without quite needing to swing it. As longtime White House reporter Helen Thomas noted in a column, "To most people, a 'request' to the television networks from the White House in wartime carries with it the weight of a government command. The major networks obviously saw it that way. . . ."[5] The country's TV news behemoths snapped to attention and saluted. "I think they gave away a precedent, in effect," said James Naughton, president of the Poynter Institute for Media Studies. "And now it's going to be hard for them not to do whatever else the government asks."[6]

Some ominous steps were underway. "The U.S. State Department contacted the Voice of America, a broadcast organization funded by the federal government, and expressed concern about the radio broadcast of an exclusive interview with Taliban leader Mullah Mohammed Omar," according to the Committee to Protect Journalists, based in New York.[7] As a follow-up, VOA head Robert Reilly "distributed a memo barring interviews with officials from 'nations that sponsor terrorism.'" In early October, while the U.S. government prepared for extensive bombing of Afghanistan, efforts increased to pressure media outlets—both domestically and globally. Colin Powell urged the Emir of Qatar to lean on the Qatar-based Al Jazeera satellite TV network. A correspondent for the *San Francisco Chronicle*, reporting from Cairo, remarked on "the sight of the United States, the defender of freedom and occasional critic of Arab state repression, lobbying one of the most moderate Arab leaders to rein in one of the region's few sources of independent news."

What was the global impact of such measures? The Committee to Protect Journalists included this assessment in its "Attacks on the Press" annual report: "The actions taken by the Bush administration seemed to embolden repressive governments around the world to crack down on their own domestic media. In Russia, a presidential adviser said President Vladimir Putin planned to study U.S. limitations on reporting about terrorists in order to develop rules for Russian media."

While the bombing of Afghanistan continued, the U.S. proved to be quite a role model for how avowedly democratic nations can serve rather explosive notice on specific news outlets. The Pentagon implemented a devastating November 13 missile attack on the Al Jazeera bureau in Kabul. Months later, the Committee to Protect Journalists expressed skepticism about the official explanations: "The U.S. military described the building as a 'known' al-Qaeda facility without providing any evidence. Despite the fact that the facility had housed the Al Jazeera office for nearly two years and had several satellite dishes mounted on its roof, the U.S. military claimed it had no indications the building was used as Al Jazeera's Kabul bureau."

That is one of many ways for governments to "dispatch" news.

Terrorism and New Media

During the first two days of October 2001, CNN's web site displayed an odd little announcement: "There have been false reports that CNN has not used the word 'terrorist' to refer to those who attacked the World Trade Center and Pentagon," the notice said. "In fact, CNN has consistently and repeatedly referred to the attackers and hijackers as terrorists, and it will continue to do so." The CNN disclaimer was accurate—and, by conventional media standards, reassuring. But it bypassed a basic question that festers beneath American media coverage: Exactly what qualifies as "terrorism"?

For this country's mainstream journalists, that turns out to be a non-question about a no-brainer. More than ever, the proper function of the "terrorist" label seems obvious. "A group of people commandeered airliners and used them as guided missiles against thousands of people," said NBC News executive Bill Wheatley. "If that doesn't fit the definition of terrorism, what does?" True enough. At the same time, it is noteworthy that American news outlets routinely define terrorism the same way that U.S. government officials define it. Editors usually assume that reporters have no need for any formal directive because the appropriate usage is simply understood. The *Wall Street Journal* does provide some guidelines, telling its staff that the word terrorist "should be used carefully, and specifically, to describe those people and nongovernmental organizations that plan and execute acts of violence against civilian or noncombatant targets." In newsrooms across the U.S., media professionals would agree.

But, in sharp contrast, Reuters has adhered to a distinctive approach for decades. "As part of a policy to avoid the use of emotive words," the global news service says, "we do not use terms like 'terrorist' and 'freedom fighter' unless they are in a direct quote or are otherwise attributable to a third party. We do not characterize the subjects of news stories but instead report their actions, identity and background so that readers can make their own decisions based on the facts." During autumn 2001, the Reuters management took considerable heat for maintaining this policy—and for reiterating it in an internal memo, which included the observation that "one man's terrorist is another man's freedom fighter." In a clarifying statement, released on October 2, 2001, the top execs at Reuters explained: "Our policy is to avoid the use of emotional terms and not make value judgments concerning the facts we attempt to report accurately and fairly."

Reuters reports from 160 countries, and the "terrorist" label is highly contentious in quite a few of them. Behind the scenes, many governments have pressured Reuters to flatly describe their enemies as terrorists in news dispatches. From the vantage point of government leaders in Ankara or Jerusalem or Moscow, for example, journalists should never hesitate to describe their violent foes as terrorists. But why should reporters oblige by pinning that tag on Kurdish combatants in Turkey, or Palestinian militants in the occupied territories, or rebels in Chechnya? Unless we buy into the absurd pretense that governments never engage in "terrorism," the circumscribed use of the term by U.S. media makes absolutely no sense. Turkish military forces have certainly terrorized and killed many civilians, while the same is true of Israeli forces and Russian troops. As a result, a large number of Kurds, Palestinians, and Chechens are grieving.

American reporters could plausibly expand their working definition of terrorism to include all organized acts of terror and murder committed against civilians, but of course such consistency would meet with fierce opposition in high Washington places. During the 1980s, with a non-evasive standard for terrorism, news accounts would have routinely referred to the Nicaraguan Contra guerrillas—in addition to the Salvadoran and Guatemalan governments—as U.S.-backed "terrorist" organizations. Today, for instance, such a standard would require news coverage of terrorism in the Middle East to include Israeli assaults with bullets and missiles that take the lives of Palestinian children and other civilians.

It's entirely appropriate for news outlets to describe the September 11 hijackers as "terrorists"—if those outlets are willing to utilize the "terrorist" label with integrity across the board. Evenhanded use of the "terrorist" label would mean sometimes affixing it directly on the U.S. government. During the past decade, from Iraq to Sudan to Yugoslavia, and Afghanistan, Pentagon missiles have destroyed the lives of civilians just as innocent as those who perished on September 11, 2001. If journalists dare not call that "terrorism," then maybe the word should be retired from the media lexicon.

In the spring of 2002, Thomas Friedman won a Pulitzer Prize for commentary. The award came after many months when the syndicated *New York Times* columnist appeared on television more than ever, sharing his outlooks with viewers of *Meet the Press, Face the Nation, Washington Week in Review,* and other programs. "In the post-9/11 environment, the talk shows cannot get enough of Friedman," a *Washington Post* profile noted.[8] Another media triumph came for Friedman in early 2002 with the debut of "Tom's Journal" on the *NewsHour with Jim Lehrer.* A news release from the influential PBS program described it as a "one-on-one debriefing of Friedman by Lehrer or one of the program's senior correspondents." Friedman was scheduled to appear perhaps a dozen times per year, after returning from major trips abroad. If he were as fervent about stopping wars as starting them, it is hard to imagine that a regular feature like "Tom's Journal" would be airing on the *NewsHour.*

Friedman has been a zealous advocate of "bombing Iraq, over and over and over again" (in the words of a January 1998 column).[9] When he offered a pithy list of prescriptions for Washington's policymakers in 1999, it included: "Blow up a different power station in Iraq every week, so no one knows when the lights will go off or who's in charge."[10] But in an introduction to the book *Iraq Under Siege,* editor Anthony Arnove points out: "Every power station that is targeted means more food and medicine that will not be refrigerated, hospitals that will lack electricity, water that will be contaminated, and people who will die." Yet Friedman-style bravado goes over big with editors and network producers who share his complete disinterest in taking into account such human costs. Many journalists seem eager to fawn over their stratospheric colleague. "Nobody understands the world the way he does," NBC's Tim Russert claims.

At various times Friedman has become fixated on four words in particular. "My motto is very simple: Give war a chance," he told Diane Sawyer in late 2001 on *Good Morning America*.[11] It was the same motto he had used two and a half years earlier in a Fox News interview. Different war; different enemy; different network; same solution. In the spring of 1999, as bombardment of Yugoslavia went on, Friedman recycled "Give war a chance" from one column to another. "Twelve days of surgical bombing was never going to turn Serbia around," he wrote in early April. "Let's see what 12 weeks of less than surgical bombing does. Give war a chance."[12] Another column included this gleeful approach for threatening civilians in Yugoslavia with protracted terror: "Every week you ravage Kosovo is another decade we will set your country back by pulverizing you. You want 1950? We can do 1950. You want 1389? We can do 1389 too."[13] In November 2001, his column returned to a similar groove. "Let's all take a deep breath and repeat after me: Give war a chance. This is Afghanistan we're talking about."[14]

Friedman seems to be crazy about wisps of craziness in high Washington places. He has a penchant for touting insanity as a helpful ingredient of U.S. foreign policy—some kind of passion for indications of derangement among those who call the military shots. During an October 13, 2001, appearance on CNBC, he said: "I was a critic of Rumsfeld before, but there's one thing . . . that I do like about Rumsfeld. He's just a little bit crazy, OK? He's just a little bit crazy, and in this kind of war, they always count on being able to out-crazy us, and I'm glad we got some guy on our bench that's our quarterback—who's just a little bit crazy, not totally, but you never know what that guy's going to do, and I say that's my guy."[15]

And Friedman does not simply talk that way. He also writes that way. "There is a lot about the Bush team's foreign policy I don't like," a Friedman column declared in mid-February 2002, "but their willingness to restore our deterrence, and to be as crazy as some of our enemies, is one thing they have right."[16] Is Thomas Friedman clever? Perhaps. But not nearly as profound as a few words from W.H. Auden: "Those to whom evil is done / Do evil in return."

In the fall of 2001, Pentagon reporters sought—and received—more frequent news conferences. "Let's hear it for the essential daily briefing, however hollow and empty it might be," Secretary Rumsfeld said in the middle of October. "We'll do it."[17] After that, Rumsfeld regularly helped with the propaganda chores. Airing live on such cable networks as MSNBC, CNN, and Fox, his performances won profuse media accolades. A news report by CNN called him "a virtual rock star." A *Wall Street Journal* essay by TV critic Claudia Rosett, a member of the newspaper's editorial board, described Rumsfeld as "a gent who in our country's hour of need has turned out to be one [of] the classiest acts on camera." Published on the last day of 2001, Rosett's article was a fitting climax to a media season of slathering over the well-heeled boots of the man in charge of the Pentagon. During the closing weeks of the year, she noted approvingly, "in print and on the air, we've been hearing about Don Rumsfeld, sex symbol, the new hunk of home-front airtime."

Deep into the mass-media groove, the *Wall Street Journal* article declared: "The basic source of Mr. Rumsfeld's charm is that he talks straight. He doesn't expend his energy on spin. . . ." Now there is an outstanding example of some prodigious spinning. Actually, Rumsfeld—who excels at sticking to the lines of the day—is a fine practitioner of spin in the minimalist style, with deception accomplished mostly by what's left unsaid. Yet for some, Rumsfeld's dissembling style has been a source of continual delight. "These briefings, beamed out live, have become, to my mind, the best new show on television," Rosett gushed. "It's a rare one that doesn't contain, at some point, some variation on his wry trademark reply when asked to discuss matters he'd rather not go into: 'I could, but I won't.'"

One of the subjects that Rumsfeld would "rather not go into" was civilian deaths in Afghanistan. Just before 2001 ended, University of New Hampshire professor Marc Herold released a report calculating that 3,767 Afghan civilians had been killed by the bombing from October 7 to December 10. (That figure was later revised to between 2,650 and 2,970 civilians.) Ignored by major U.S. media, the report got considerably more attention in Britain. "The price in blood that has already been paid for America's war against terror is only now starting to become clear," an editor at the *Guardian* in London wrote on December 20. Seumas Milne explained that Herold's research was "based on corroborated reports from aid agencies, the UN, eyewitnesses, TV stations, newspapers and news agencies around the world." Milne added: "Of course, Herold's total is only an estimate. But what is impressive about his work is not only the meticulous cross-checking, but the conservative assumptions he applies to each reported incident. The figure does not include those who died later of bomb injuries; nor those killed in the past 10 days (December 10–20); nor those who have died from cold and hunger because of the interruption of aid supplies or because they were forced to become refugees by the bombardment."

But the civilian deaths resulting from American military action held little interest among the people in charge of major U.S.-based media outlets. After the first weeks of bombing, CNN chair Walter Isaacson sent a memo to the network's international correspondents telling them that it "seems perverse to focus too much on the casualties or hardship in Afghanistan." Interviewed by a *Washington Post* reporter on October 30, Isaacson explained: "I want to make sure we're not used as a propaganda platform." He added: "We're entering a period in which there's a lot more reporting and video from Taliban-controlled

Afghanistan. You want to make sure people understand that when they see civilian suffering there, it's in the context of a terrorist attack that caused enormous suffering in the United States."

Meanwhile, a separate memo went out to CNN anchors from the network's head of standards and practices, Rick Davis, who supplied helpful examples of appropriate language to use on the air: "'We must keep in mind, after seeing reports like this from Taliban-controlled areas, that these U.S. military actions are in response to a terrorist attack that killed close to 5,000 innocent people in the U.S.' or, 'We must keep in mind, after seeing reports like this, that the Taliban regime in Afghanistan continues to harbor terrorists who have praised the September 11 attacks that killed close to 5,000 innocent people in the U.S.,' or 'The Pentagon has repeatedly stressed that it is trying to minimize civilian casualties in Afghanistan, even as the Taliban regime continues to harbor terrorists who are connected to the September 11 attacks that claimed thousands of innocent lives in the U.S.'" The memo was clear about the mandatory nature of the instructions: "Even though it may start sounding rote, it is important that we make this point each time."

Agenda-Setting for War against Iraq

To fend off the threat of peace, determination is necessary. Elected officials and high-level appointees must work effectively with reporters and pundits. The summer of 2002 was no time for the U.S. government to risk taking "yes" for an answer from Iraq. Guarding against the danger of peace, the Bush administration moved the goal posts, quickly pounding them into the ground. In early August, a State Department undersecretary swung a heavy mallet. "Let there be no mistake," said John Bolton. "While we also insist on the reintroduction of the weapons inspectors, our policy at the same time insists on regime change in Baghdad—and that policy will not be altered, whether inspectors go in or not."

A sinister cloud appeared over the sunny skies for war when the U.S. Congress got a public invitation. A letter from a top Iraqi official "said Congressional visitors and weapons experts of their choice could visit any site in Iraq alleged to be used for development of chemical, biological or nuclear weapons," USA Today reported. Summing up this diplomatic overture, the front page of the New York Times informed readers that the letter "was apparently trying to pit legislators against the Bush administration" (a pithy phrase helping to quash a dastardly peace initiative). Later on, the article noted that "the letter said members of Congress could bring all the arms experts they wanted and should plan to stay three weeks."

There may have been a moment of panic in Washington. On the face of it, the August 5 invitation was unequivocally stating that members of the Senate and House—along with some of the best and most experienced weapons inspectors in the world—could go to Iraq and engage in a thorough inspection process. The news had ominous potential: it could derail the war train then gaining so much momentum. But U.S. media coverage matched the bipartisan refusal by leaders in Congress to do anything but scorn the offer. Even before describing the invitation from the Iraqi government, the first words of the *USA Today* news story on August 6 called it "the latest Iraqi bid to complicate U.S. invasion plans." With our most powerful politicians hell-bent on starting a war, complete with human misery and death of unfathomable proportions, the last thing they wanted was complications before the bloodshed got underway. Why should anyone in Washington try to defuse the crisis when there was such a clear opportunity to light an enormous fuse in the Middle East?

On the domestic scene, there are always some people eager to unleash the dogs of peace. Not content to pray, they actually believe in a fanciful ideal: Blessed be the peacemakers. They refuse to acquiesce to the machinery of war that grinds human beings as if they were mere sausage. They refuse to make peace with how determined the Executive Branch must be—and how sheepish and even cowardly the members of Congress must be—so that the bombs can fall in all their glory.

One of the people trying to impede the war drive was Scott Ritter, a former chief weapons inspector for the UN in Iraq. "The Bush administration," he said, "has been unable—or unwilling—to back up its rhetoric concerning the Iraqi threat with any substantive facts." Meanwhile, in Britain, the press failed to welcome the oncoming war. On August 4, 2002, in the *Observer*, foreign affairs editor Peter Beaumont wrote: "The question now appears to be not whether there will be a war, but when. The answer is that in war, as other matters, timing is all. For President George W. Bush that timing will be dictated by the demands of a domestic political agenda."

A news story in the July 30 edition of the *Financial Times* began this way: "Rolf Ekeus, head of United Nations weapons inspections in Iraq from 1991–97, has accused the U.S. and other Security Council members of manipulating the UN inspections teams for their own political ends. The revelation by one of the most respected Swedish diplomats is certain to strengthen Iraq's argument against allowing UN inspectors back into the country." Such reporting, if widely pursued on this side of the Atlantic, could have seriously undermined the war planners. But they had little cause for worry: the threat of peace was up against good ol' professional news judgment in the USA.

Some people were suspicious that President Bush would go for a "wag the dog" strategy—boosting Republican prospects with a military assault on Iraq shortly before Election Day. But a modified approach was underway, something that might be called "wag the puppy."

After a number of GOP luminaries blasted his administration's war scenarios, Bush claimed to appreciate "a healthy debate." The president offered assurances that he would consult with Congress rather than take sudden action. But his handlers were simply adapting to circumstances that made it impractical for the Pentagon to kill large numbers of Iraqis prior to Election Day. Before initiating vast new carnage abroad, the White House wanted its propaganda siege to take hold domestically. Countless hours of airtime and huge vats of ink were needed to make this work. Like safecrackers trying first one combination and then another, the Bush team continued to twirl the media dials until their warmaking rationales somehow clicked.

The most widely publicized critics of attacking Iraq were hardly inclined to withstand the hot rhetorical winds that would accompany the first U.S. missile strikes. Objections from the likes of Dick Armey and Brent Scowcroft were apt to swiftly morph into pseudo-patriotic deference once Bush gained momentum for the initial terrorizing launch of missiles against Iraqi cities. And history gave the president ample reasons to believe that most hand-wringing punditry would turn into applause once the Pentagon began its mass slaughter.

Delaying war is of course very different than preventing it. In fact, many of the arguments marshaled in the mainstream media against a precipitous attack on Iraq appeared to be accepting the need for the U.S. government to afflict that country with massive violence, only at a later time. Whether on Capitol Hill or in media venues, most of this criticism seemed largely concerned with style, timing, and tactics. Enormous amounts of flak also came from pro-war commentators who wanted Bush to get his militaristic act together. The bloodthirsty editor of *The Atlantic* magazine, Michael Kelly, used his August 21 column on the *Washington Post*'s op-ed page to lament "the president's refusal to wage a coherent campaign to win public—and, let's force the issue, Congressional—approval for the war."

While President Bush huddled with hawks at the top of the pecking order at his ranch in Crawford, Texas, war enthusiasts were on the offensive across the nation's media landscape. Their efforts added to a sustained volume of valuable news coverage. The mid-summer media obsession with Iraq offered tangible benefits for Shrub's party—including real progress in changing the subject. The more that Iraq dominated front pages, magazine covers, news broadcasts, and cable channels, the less space there was for such matters as the intensifying retirement worries of many Americans, the Wall Street scandals, and specific stories about entanglements that linked Bush or Dick Cheney with malodorous corporate firms like Enron, Harken, and Halliburton.

During late summer and into the fall, the "healthy debate" over Iraq displaced a range of negative economic stories from the top of the news. Of course Bush's advisers hardly minded the strong prospect that a similar pattern would hold through early November. For months the president had plenty of domestic political incentives to keep "wagging the puppy" while floating a variety of unsubstantiated claims—like references to wispy dots that implausibly claimed to connect the Iraqi dictatorship with Al Qaeda. Meanwhile, sending more ships and aircraft to the Persian Gulf region could be calculated to evoke plenty of televised support-our-troops spectacles. With Old Glory in the background as tearful good-byes were exchanged at U.S. military ports and bases, how many politicians or journalists would challenge the manipulative tactics of the commander-in-chief?

Even without unleashing the Pentagon on Iraqi people before the November elections, White House efforts to boost pre-war fever promised to have an enormous media impact with big dividends at the polls. The American public observed something short of a "wag the dog" extravaganza provided by leading officials of the Bush administration. But the full-grown dogs of war were not far behind.

For a news watcher, coverage of the United Nations is liable to be confusing at times. Is the UN a vital institution or a dysfunctional relic? Are its Security Council resolutions profoundly important for international relations—or beside the point because global leadership now winds up coming from the world's only superpower?

Americans kept hearing that the United States would need to launch a full-scale attack on Iraq because Saddam Hussein had violated UN Security Council resolutions—at the same time that we were told the U.S. government must reserve the right to take military action unilaterally if the Security Council failed to make appropriate decisions about Iraq. To clarify the situation, here are three basic guidelines for understanding how to respond in sync with America's leading politicians and pundits:

• The UN resolutions approved by the five permanent members of the Security Council are hugely important, and worthy of enforcement with massive military force—if the White House says so. Otherwise, the resolutions have little or no significance, and they certainly can never be allowed to interfere with the flow of American economic, military, and diplomatic support to any of Washington's allies.

Several countries have continued to ignore large numbers of resolutions approved by the UN Security Council since the early 1990s. Morocco remains in violation of more than a dozen such resolutions. So does Israel. And Turkey continues to violate quite a few. But top officials in Rabat, Jerusalem, and Ankara are not really expecting ultimatums from Washington anytime soon.

• Some UN resolutions are sacred. Others are superfluous.

To cut through the media blather about Security Council resolutions that have been approved in past years, just keep this in mind: In the world according to American news media, the president of the United States has Midas-like powers in relation to those UN resolutions. When he confers his holy touch upon one, it turns into a golden rule that must be enforced. When he chooses not to bless other UN resolutions, they lose all value.

• The United Nations can be extremely "relevant" or "irrelevant," depending on the circumstances.

When the UN serves as a useful instrument of U.S. foreign policy, it is a vital world body taking responsibility for the future and reaffirming its transcendent institutional vision. When the UN balks at serving as a useful instrument of U.S. foreign policy, its irrelevance is so obvious that it risks collapsing into the dustbin of history while the USA proceeds to stride the globe like the superpower colossus that it truly is.

"There's a lot of lofty rhetoric here in Washington about the UN," said Erik Leaver of the Institute for Policy Studies. Pretty words function as window-dressing for warmaking. While the president claimed the right to violently enforce UN Security Council resolutions, Leaver added, "there are almost 100 current Security Council resolutions that are being ignored, in addition to the 12 or so resolutions that Iraq is ignoring. What the U.S. is saying here is that it has the right to determine which Security Council resolutions are relevant and which are not."

Leaver was outside the usual media box when he brought up a key question: "If the U.S. takes military action using the cover of the United Nations, what is to prevent other countries from launching their own military attacks in the name of enforcement of UN resolutions—against Turkey in Cyprus, or Morocco in Western Sahara, or Israel in Palestine? This is precisely the reason why the doctrine of preemptive force is a dangerous policy for the United States to pursue." When Leaver maintained that "We can't uphold the U.N. at one moment and then discard it the next," he was up against powerful media spin that hails such hypocrisy as a mark of great American leadership on the world stage. From the vantage point of Washington's reigning politicians and most of the journalists who cover them, it is quite proper to treat the United Nations as a tool for U.S. diplomacy—war by another means, useful until the time comes for the bloody real thing.

Spinning Public Opinion toward War

Before decisions get made in Washington—and even before most politicians open their mouths about key issues—there are polls. Lots of them. Whether splashed across front pages or commissioned by candidates for private analysis, the statistical sampling of public opinion is a constant in political life. We may believe that polls tell us what Americans are thinking, but polls also gauge the effectiveness of media spin—and surely contribute to it. Opinion polls do not simply *measure*; they also manipulate, helping to shape thoughts and tilt our perceptions of how most people think. Polls routinely invite the respondents to choose from choices that have already been prepared for them. Results hinge on the exact phrasing of questions and the array of multiple-choice answers, as candid players in the polling biz readily acknowledge.

"Slight differences in question wording, or in the placement of the questions in the interview, can have profound consequences," Gallup executive David Moore wrote in his book *The Superpollsters*. He observed that poll outcomes "are very much influenced by the polling process itself." And in turn, whatever their quality, polling numbers "influence perceptions, attitudes and decisions at every level of our society."

In the process, opinions are narrowed into a few prefabricated slots: the result is likely to be mental constriction in the guise of illumination. "Opinion-polling as practiced in the United States ... presents itself as a means of registering opinions and expressing choices," media critic Herbert Schiller noted in the early 1970s. His assessment of polling remains cogent today: "It is a choice-restricting mechanism. Because ordinary polls reduce, and sometimes eliminate entirely, the ... true spectrum of possible options, the possibilities and preferences they express are better viewed as 'guided' choices."

Mainstream polls are so much a part of the media wallpaper that we are apt to miss how arbitrarily they limit people's sense of wider possibilities. And we may simply forget that those who pay the pollsters commonly influence the scope of ideas and attitudes deemed worthy of consideration. In his book *The Mind Managers*, Herbert Schiller pointed out: "Those who dominate governmental decision-making and private economic activity are the main supports of the pollsters. The vital needs of these groups determine, intentionally or not, the parameters within which polls are formulated."

When the U.S. government takes military action, instant polls help to propel the rapid-fire cycles of spin. After top officials in Washington have engaged in a well-coordinated media blitz during the crucial first hours of warfare, the TV networks tell us that most Americans approve—and the quick poll results may seem to legitimize and justify the decision to begin the bloodshed. During late 2002, in the case of the Bush administration's planned launch of an all-out attack on Iraq, the U.S. military build-up in the Persian Gulf region was running parallel to a sustained propaganda campaign for domestic consumption. Even so, the extent of public support was foggy.

At the end of September 2002, a murky picture emerged from an article in the *Washington Post* by the director of the big-bucks Pew Research Center for the People and the Press. "Almost all national surveys this year," Andrew Kohut wrote, "have found a broad base of potential support for using military force to rid the world of Saddam Hussein." Yet such generalities could be deceiving. Kohut reported that a Pew Center poll "found that 64 percent generally favor military action against Iraq, but that withers to 33 percent if our allies do not join us." Meanwhile, according to a CBS News poll, 51 percent of Americans said that Hussein was involved in the 9/11 attacks. But there was no evidence for that assertion. So, as in countless other cases, the failures of news media to clearly convey pivotal matters of fact—and the unwillingness of journalists to challenge deceptive claims from the White House—boosted the poll numbers for beliefs lacking a factual basis.

Polls may seem to provide clarity in a confusing world. But all too often they amount to snapshots taken from slanted angles.

Marketing a war is serious business, and no product requires better brand names than one that squanders vast quantities of resources while intentionally killing large numbers of people. Euphemistic fog for such enterprises began several decades ago. It is now very old news that the federal government no longer has a department or a budget named "war." At present it is called "defense," a word with a strong aura of inherent justification. The sly effectiveness of the labeling switch can be gauged by the fact that many opponents of reckless military spending nevertheless constantly refer to it as "defense" spending.

The intersection of two avenues, Pennsylvania and Madison, has given rise to media cross-promotion that increasingly sanitizes organized mass destruction known as warfare. Along the way, the first Bush administration enhanced the public relations techniques for U.S. military actions by "choosing operation names that were calculated to shape political perceptions," linguist Geoff Nunberg recalled. The invasion of Panama in December 1989 went forward under the name Operation Just Cause—an immediate media hit. "A number of news anchors picked up on the phrase Just Cause, which encouraged the Bush and Clinton administrations to keep using those tendentious names."

As Nunberg pointed out, "it's all a matter of branding. And it's no accident that the new-style names like Just Cause were introduced at around the same time the cable news shows started to label their coverage of major stories with catchy names and logos." The Pentagon became adept at supplying video-game-like pictures of U.S. missile strikes at the same time that it began to provide the big-type captions on TV screens.

Ever since the Gulf War in early 1991, people across the political spectrum have commonly referred to that paroxysm of carnage as Operation Desert Storm—or, more often, just Desert Storm. To the casual ear, this sounds kind of like an act of nature or, perhaps, an act of God. Either way, according to the vague spirit evoked by the label Desert Storm, men like Dick Cheney, Norman Schwarzkopf, and Colin Powell may well have been assisting in the implementation of divine natural occurrences, with high winds and 2,000-pound laser-guided bombs raining down from the heavens. Soon after the Gulf War a.k.a. Desert Storm ended, the Army's chief of public affairs, Major General Charles McClain, commented: "The perception of an operation can be as important to success as the execution of that operation."[18] For guiding the public's perception of a war—while it is happening and after it has become history—there is nothing quite like a salutary label that sticks.

In October 2001, while launching missiles at Afghanistan, the Bush team came up with Operation Infinite Justice, only to swiftly scuttle the name after learning it was offensive to Muslims because of their belief that only Allah can provide infinite justice. The replacement, Enduring Freedom, was well received in U.S. mass media, an irony-free zone where only the untowardly impertinent might suggest that some people had no choice other than enduring the Pentagon's freedom to bomb.

It was a candid slip of the tongue in late summer 2002 when the White House chief of staff, Andrew Card, told the *New York Times*: "From a marketing point of view, you don't introduce new products in August." Not coincidentally, the main rollout of new-and-improved rationales for an upcoming war on Iraq did not take place until September. Meanwhile, some media spinners at the White House were undoubtedly devoting considerable energy to sifting through potential brand names for the expected U.S. war on Iraq.

The War Road Ahead

Overall, the systems of mass media in the United States are well suited to boosting the war agendas of the White House. Contradictions and nuances are always present in news coverage, but the large-scale repetition of key themes and phrases—the essence of propaganda—has huge ongoing effects on public perceptions. The media walls of U.S. society have numerous cracks, and sometimes those fissures are politically significant; yet the media industry's structural constraints mitigate against wide-ranging public discourse. Those constraints tighten during times of U.S. military action.

The United States was moving into a new era of militarism during the autumn of 2001, with 9/11 serving as a catalyst. By late 2002, the concept of a "pre-emptive war"—in effect, the proclaimed right to launch a war of aggression against Iraq—had gained sufficient momentum to win support from most members of Congress and most of the U.S. news media. In such a context, the well-established dynamics of news manipulation for war were undergoing great acceleration. The media road ahead looked to be filled with war and rationalizations for more war.

Shaped by the political economy of the United States, this media terrain could only be disheartening for people convinced that social justice and peace are essential for the future of the nation and the world. Out of necessity, efforts to meet the daunting challenges ahead must include vigorous analysis of present-day propaganda—and willingness to confront the manipulations of news media in all their deadly expressions.

Notes

1. Fleischer quoted in *San Francisco Chronicle*, "Networks to use caution with tapes from al Qaeda," Oct. 11, 2001.
2. *New York Times*, "Networks Agree to U.S. Request To Edit Future bin Laden Tapes," Oct. 11, 2001.
3. Murdoch quoted by Agence France Presse, "Media mogul Murdoch labels US strikes in Afghanistan 'short term,'" Oct. 11, 2001.
4. CNN quoted by the Associated Press, "Powell says terror network may be using public statements to convey hidden message," Oct. 10, 2001.
5. Helen Thomas, "Networks Wrong to Censor Bin Laden," *Seattle Post-Intelligencer*, Oct. 16, 2001.
6. Naughton quoted in *San Diego Union-Tribune*, "News media stuck between a rock and the White House," Oct. 19, 2001.
7. Quotes from the Committee to Protect Journalists (New York) are in its annual report "Attacks on the Press in 2001."

8. Friedman profile, *Washington Post*, "The Op-Ed Force; Thomas Friedman Comes Out Swinging In His Columns on The Middle East," Dec. 6, 2001.
9. *New York Times*, Jan. 31, 1998.
10. *New York Times*, Jan. 19, 1999.
11. ABC TV's *Good Morning America*, Oct. 29, 2001, and Fox News, April 7, 1999.
12. *New York Times*, April 6, 1999.
13. *New York Times*, April 23, 1999.
14. *New York Times*, Nov. 2, 2001.
15. CNBC interview with Tim Russert, Oct. 13, 2001.
16. Feb. 13, 2002.
17. Rumsfeld quoted in *New York Times*, "Reporters Want More Access, But Are Careful to Ask Nicely," Oct. 22, 2001.
18. Quoted in *Virginian-Pilot* (Norfolk, VA), "No Game in Naming Military Ops," Sept. 26, 2001.

CHAPTER 11

Patriarchal Militarism

R. CLAIRE SNYDER

When the United States was attacked on September 11, 2001, it was the target of groups not only opposed to American foreign policy in the Middle East but also seemingly committed to a religious state, the rule of force, and the total subordination of women. From a progressive democratic standpoint, the U.S. response to this crisis might be expected to be twofold: bringing those responsible to justice while preventing further attacks, but in a way that safeguards the democratic values it claims to represent—secular government, the rule of law, and civic equality for all citizens, including women—because these are the values that make the country worth protecting in the first place.

While the fight against terrorism arguably has a legitimate military component, the Bush Administration's turn toward *militarism* constitutes an inappropriate and dangerous response to 9/11. That is to say, militarism—glorification of the military as the most important state institution and primary tool of foreign policy—threatens fundamental democratic principles for which the U.S. ostensibly stands. Nevertheless, since September 11th, both the neoliberal and social-conservative wings within the Republican party have been deliberately fueling the forces of militarism in order to advance their longstanding political agendas—protecting corporate interests and reconsolidating male dominance—with precious little resistance from the Democratic party. While militaristic policy and jingoistic rhetoric may help assuage the insecurity felt by many Americans in the wake of the terrorist attacks on New York City and Washington, they endanger democratic practices by undermining pluralistic, participatory values at home and fueling anti-Americanism abroad. It is a manifestly counterproductive response to the crisis of 9/11.

Democratic Anti-Militarism and the Citizen-Soldier Tradition

In determining how to balance military agendas with the democratic priorities, the early American tradition of the citizen-soldier can provide some guidance.[1] Growing out of the civic republicanism theorized by Machiavelli and Rousseau and actualized during the American and French Revolutions, the citizen-soldier tradition presents a rich vision of democracy, in which both popular sovereignty and rule of law are fundamental principles.[2] In order to protect liberty, citizens participate in governing themselves for the common good through the rule of law and take up arms to defend their ability to do so. By linking military service to republican self-government, the tradition maintains that the decision to wage war should be decided by those who will actually have to fight. This strong conception of participatory democracy cannot be reduced to market relations and electoral politics of the liberal or neoliberal models, nor does it accept the decisions of corrupt and unaccountable elites as legitimate.[3]

Recognizing the unavoidable tension between military imperatives and democratic values, the normative tradition of the citizen-soldier addresses this paradox: a democratic society requires a military for defense, yet the military itself can easily pose a threat to the workings of democratic institutions. Antithetical to democracy, military values affirm obedience over liberty, hierarchy over equality, authority over accountability, and force of arms over the "force of the better argument" (i.e., deliberation, rational discourse, and open debates). Thus while a democratic society must have armed protection to defend itself from enemy attack, the military itself potentially constitutes a negation of principles underlying democratic self-government. While part of the solution to this conundrum includes civilian control over the military—the liberal approach—the citizen-soldier tradition of civic republicanism emphasizes other modalities as well.

The citizen-soldier tradition maintains that all citizens share responsibility for military service, for three reasons. First, a military comprised of temporary citizen-soldiers helps prevent the emergence of a distinct warrior class that could impose tyranny upon an unarmed populace. Second, it assumes that ordinary citizens generally do not want to serve and will only go to war when it is absolutely urgent. Finally, it is simply unfair and antidemocratic to expect only the economically disadvantaged to risk their lives in the context of violent warfare. Shared responsibility for military service helps protect ordinary citizens from both elite power and elite irresponsibility, while also backing popular sovereignty with the force of arms.

While tensions between military imperatives and democratic values can never be eliminated, the citizen-soldier tradition seeks to *contain* threats posed by militarism within a set of democratic parameters.[4] It strives to create a military that has no vested interest in prolonging war or advancing the agenda of illegitimate rulers. The tradition does this by requiring all citizens to share responsibility for the military as a temporary obligation, instead of relying on professional warriors whose very livelihoods depend upon waging war. Thus it would be misleading to say the tradition advocates "militarized citizenship"[5] since at its core it seeks to control and regulate the impetus toward militarism—the warrior ethic—and establish a military fully under the control of ordinary citizens.

In the sixteenth century, Machiavelli viewed *hired mercenaries* as a fundamental threat to republican self-government.[6] Professional soldiers could not be trusted, he argued, because they "are obliged either to hope that there will be no peace, or to become so rich in time of war that in peace they can support themselves."[7] Because they do not profit from war-making, citizen-soldiers do not expect anything from war "except labor, peril, and fame." Instead of wanting to remain at war, they wish "to come home and live by their profession." In Machiavelli's words, the citizen-soldier "when he was not soldiering, was willing to be a soldier, and when he was soldiering, wanted to be dismissed."[8] A citizen-soldier "will gladly make war in order to have peace," but "will not seek to disturb the peace in order to have war."[9] Thus, a military comprised of citizen-soldiers should *decrease* the possibility of war.

Writing in the eighteenth century, Rousseau feared the existence of *a standing army* that could help maintain the illegitimate power of the king.[10] In his words:

> Regular armies have been the scourge and ruin of Europe. They are good for only two things: attacking and conquering neighbors, and fettering and enslaving citizens. . . . The state's true defenders are its individual citizens, no one of whom should be a professional soldier, but each of whom should serve as a soldier as duty requires.[11]

Rousseau argued that because a republic is fundamentally concerned with protecting liberty, "offensive power is incompatible with [a republican] form of government. Those who will freedom must not will conquest as well."[12] Furthermore, "he who tries to take away the freedom of others nearly always ends up losing his own."[13] From this standpoint, citizen-soldiers constitute the best defense against both tyranny and war.

The American founders agreed that *a standing army detached from the citizenry* posed a strong danger to republican self-government. Only a military comprised of temporary citizen-soldiers would be willing and able to maintain peace, preserve liberty, and minimize the omnipresent possibility of tyranny.[14] The Second Amendment grew directly out of this fear of a standing army: "A well-armed militia being necessary to the security of a free state, the right of the people to keep and bear arms shall not be infringed." While contemporaneously interpreted as protecting individual rights, this amendment actually protected the right of *the people* (a collective) to bear arms to protect republican self-government, thus defending popular sovereignty by working against a potentially tyrannical state from gaining a monopoly on "legitimate violence." In addition, the founders passed the Militia Act of 1792, establishing the *principle* that all fully enfranchised citizens must share responsibility for military service.[15] And while the founders recognized the need for some full-time troops to supplement part-time local militias, they specifically subordinated those troops to civilian control, assuming such a safeguard would help prevent the emergence of an autonomous warrior class disconnected from civil society, interested in prolonging war, and capable of disregarding the will of the people.[16]

In the present milieu, an additional threat exists: *civilian elites who espouse militarism in order to advance their own economic interests and political power.* In this sense militarism can be seen as serving the interests of two sectors of the New Right coalition: neoliberal elites seeking to wage war in order to protect and profit the military-industrial-petroleum complex,[17] and social conservatives who favor militarism because they want to reconsolidate male dominance. Both constituencies, of course, expect that militarism will benefit the Republican party at the polls, while many Democratic politicians apparently believe that supporting aggressive war will help secure their own political careers.

Traditional critiques of militarism do not fully recognize the threat posed by self-serving civilian leaders because such critiques focus mainly on how the military endangers democratic society. Thus Chalmers Johnson argues that "the three prime indicators of militarism [are] a military class, the predominance of the military in the administration of the state, and an obsession with military preparedness." After 9/11, he argues, "the military is in the process of *passing beyond civilian control* and is acting as a separate corporate body in order to preserve and enlarge its diverse spheres of influence."[18] Clearly Johnson sees the military as an imminent threat to peace and democracy.

In the wake of September 11th, however, the push toward militarism comes less from the military than from the *civilian leadership* of the Bush Administration. The problem is not that the military is "passing beyond civilian control," but rather that civilian control is scarcely functioning to decrease the possibility of war; indeed many military leaders have publicly criticized the Bush administration's eagerness to wage war on Iraq.[19] Ironically, under the administration of Bush II, it is General Colin Powell who works to *minimize* the chances of war, while the civilian leadership—President Bush, Vice President Dick Cheney, and Secretary of Defense Donald Rumsfeld—actively spearheads the most bellicose military policy in U.S. history, including the Bush Doctrine of "preemptive strike."[20] While no necessary opposition exists between military and civilian elites, my point is that the role of civilian elites in fueling the dynamics of militarism cannot be underestimated.

Militarism and Neo-Patriarchy

Militarism serves diverse interests within the New Right coalition, above all those of the social conservatives and the neoliberals. While several other essays in this volume address the connections between militarism and neoliberalism, few explore the ways militarism helps to systematically establish and secure male dominance in American society. Social conservatives actively oppose gender equality in all areas of society, including of course the military. They argue that gender differences are natural, the creation of God and/or the result of evolutionary biology.[21] Their attacks on the elevated status of women in the military rely on the contention that "there is something uniquely male about the warrior,"[22] and that the integration of women into the necessarily masculine military has produced a "kinder, gentler military" that can never win wars.[23] Because military service in the U.S. has always been conceptualized as the responsibility of "first-class citizens," an attack on women in the military inevitably constitutes an attack on women's *civic* equality. Moreover, insofar as militarism becomes the driving force of American politics and only men are naturally suited to become warriors, women's status will be correspondingly diminished.

The extent to which women should be integrated into the military is controversial (even among feminists[24]), and the New Right has repeatedly used opposition to women in the military as a cornerstone of its fight against gender equality. During the 1970s, conservative opponents of the Equal Rights Amendment (ERA) were able to mobilize support by arguing that the ERA would require the conscription of women. This rhetorical move was quite successful, and in fact the combat issue played a major role in the amendment's defeat.[25] The New Right, which began its rise in 1965, finally consolidated its base in opposition to gender equality.[26] And while the principle of legal equality for women has largely been implemented through the courts, despite defeat of the ERA, the idea of drafting women remains controversial. In the wake of September 11th, two congressmen introduced the "Universal Military Training and Service Act of 2001" in the House that would "require the *induction into the Armed Forces of young men* registered under the Military Selective Service Act, and to *authorize young women to volunteer*, to receive basic military training and education for a period of up to one year."[27] Regardless of one's view of conscription, the question remains: If women are really the civic equals of men, why should they have the option of not serving in the military?

Social conservatives are using the crisis of 9/11 to bolster their already burgeoning movement to secure patriarchal dominance. By 2000, the neo-patriarchal fatherhood movement had generated a burgeoning literature blaming "feminism" and single mothers for social problems caused by men and teenaged boys. While the packaging of their arguments varies slightly, advocates of this school of thought generally make a similar claim: refusing to respect natural gender differences, feminists have pathologized masculinity and futilely attempted to change the behavior of men and boys. They have undermined the rightful authority of men as heads of the household, attempted to change the natural division of labor between mothers and fathers, and propagated the idea that a woman can fulfill the role traditionally played by a man, rendering fathers superfluous to family life. Social conservatives insist that men have lost interest in fulfilling their traditional family responsibilities, so that boys have no male figures to teach them how to become responsible men.

Detached from the "civilizing influence" of the traditional patriarchal family, males are seen as creating a wide array of social problems, with everybody suffering in the end.[28]

Lionel Tiger relates his anthropological version of this argument directly to the question of women in the military: men are innately aggressive, bellicose predators, naturally suited to martial exploits. While contemporary feminists demonize man's essential nature, he argues, in a more natural society both men and women would recognize and value "male" characteristics. Although the development of civilization led to domestication of men via the patriarchal family, the indelible imprint of evolutionary biology can never be fully transcended, nor should it be. Tiger asserts that natural sex differences are hardwired to ensure the reproduction of the species, so that natural male aggression always remains, only needing to be properly channeled in order to ward off festering social problems. Here traditional military institutions played a central role in harnessing male aggression for the good of society. At the same time, according to Tiger, the integration of women into this conventional male province has disrupted male bonding, introduced sexual desire into military ranks, and lowered training standards—all weakening combat effectiveness, endangering lives, costing the government money, and making men less willing to serve.[29] Robert Bork, Christina Hoff-Sommers, and Stephanie Gutmann have fashioned similar arguments.[30]

Anti-Feminism and the Attack on DACOWITS

In the face of Bush's vision of an unending war on terrorism and the impending war on Iraq, one might expect that elites would welcome the skills of all citizens for military service. Yet right-wing groups have actually seized upon the crisis of 9/11 as an opportunity to subvert the position of women in the military, justifying their agenda by appealing to the military ethos of "wartime" mobilization. Michelle Easton, president of the Claire Booth Luce Policy Institute, argues that

> since the horror of the terrorist attacks on Sept. 11, the feminization of the military is no longer just an interesting debate point for talk shows. If we continue to allow the social engineers, the feminists and the politicians to experiment with women in the military, our nation will not have the security and preparation that it needs for the future.[31]

Washington Times columnist Mona Charen concurs: "Now that there's a real war on, isn't it time to tell the truth? The United States military exists to win our wars, not to serve as the tool of a bunch of noisy feminists."[32] Likewise, Sandy Rios, president of the Christian Right group Concerned Women for America, insists that "this is no longer a power game where ambitious female officers try to advance their careers. This is a matter of life and death."[33] Finally, Phyllis Schlafly asks: "Will the Bush Administration . . . be man enough

. . . to tell Clintonista feminists that their days of unchallenged influence ended on January 20, 2001?"[34]

Right-wing women's groups have long targeted the Defense Advisory Committee on Women in the Services (DACOWITS) for elimination. DACOWITS was created by Congress in 1951 to serve "as the advisory arm for the Pentagon on issues pertaining to the recruitment and retention of women" in the military, and it functioned as "a key government-based advocacy organization for developing women's roles and opportunities in the forces."[35] The committee came under intense fire during the 1990s, when it pushed for the repeal of combat exclusion laws after the Gulf War and because of pressure it exerted on the Pentagon to deal with increasing reports of sexual harassment in the military.[36] However, the Right charges that "the committee supports policies that compromise training standards, weaken morale, worsen deployment problems, hurt recruiting and retention and forces women into land combat"[37] and functions as a "tax-funded feminist lobby."[38] Meanwhile, the Independent Women's Forum suggested a link between DACOWITS's advocacy of women's issues and the terrorists attacks: "As the terrorists prepared to hit the World Trade Center towers and the Pentagon itself, our military leaders were directed 'to engage in open dialogue' on lactation tactics."[39] This position clearly ridicules the legitimate concerns of soldiers who are also mothers, implying that somehow their needs endanger national security.

Within six months after 9/11, anti-feminist groups finally succeeded in their longstanding goal of undermining the civilian-governed DACOWITS, when Bush refused to renew its charter. While the Bush Administration did not jettison the committee altogether, it instituted a new charter ostensibly to "revitalize" DACOWITS. The organization will now advise the Secretary of Defense on matters related not to women but to "highly qualified professional women," it will include an emphasis on "family issues" in its mission statement, and its previously civilian appointees will now be "selected on the basis of their experience in the military, as a member of a military family, or with women's or family-related workforce issues."[40] Center for Military Readiness (CMR) president Elaine Donnelly hopes the new committee will work to get rid of maternity, childcare, healthcare, and family benefits for military personnel that "subsidize and encourage single parenthood, poverty, and a demand for food stamps."[41] A wide array of conservative organizations support Bush's attack on DACOWITS, including Christian Right groups like Focus on the Family, Concerned Women for America, the Culture & Family Institute, and the anti-feminist women's group Eagle Forum. Bush's decision was praised by the Heritage Foundation, the *National Review*, and the *Washington Times*. Interestingly enough, neither the *New York Times* nor the *Washington Post* so much as *mentioned* this development.

With the attack on DACOWITS, the Right combines its opposition to gender equality with its criticism of civilian oversight of military affairs. For example, the *National Review* argues that "to have a powerful taxpayer-funded team of *civilian women* go around checking up on fully integrated bases—complete with three-star protocol status—is simply an embarrassing and needless expense." One has to wonder which is the larger "insult": civilian oversight or the authority of women?[42] Donnelly's comment that "Secretary of Defense Donald Rumsfeld had every right to abolish the high-budget, *insubordinate*, self-discredited committee" because "at its 50th Anniversary (and last) meeting last year, members *defied* combat experts once again" does not clarify the issue.[43] However, Woody West says "the reformation of DACOWITS is at best a beginning to restore the appropriate *masculine* component of soldiering as U.S. troopers battle the al-Qaeda fanatics in the Afghani mountains."[44] Here again male dominance and militarism are inextricably linked in the eyes of the Right.

Return of the Manly Warrior

Social conservatives argue that gender equality in the military has gone too far, having eroded combat effectiveness. According to Stephanie Gutmann, during the course of the 1990s, in the wake of Tailhook, Aberdeen Proving Ground, and other sexual harassment scandals, "the thinking seemed to be 'If the warrior culture frightened away women, then the warrior culture had to be changed.'"[45] While few conservatives explicitly advocate a complete purging of women from the military, they clearly want to turn back the clock to a time before gender integration—an opening that began in 1967 with the lifting of the 2 percent cap, continued with the 1973 transition to an All Volunteer force after Vietnam, and accelerated in the late 1970s. Now, in the aftermath of September 11th, the Right seems to have much greater justification for its neo-patriarchal agenda.

Social conservatives often attack women in the military by virtue of claiming an essential connection between man and warrior. In doing so, the Right does *not* lay claim to the "citizen-soldier" tradition but rather appeals to the alternative vision within American culture: the "warrior mythology"[46] of the "the fighter"[47] or the "manly warrior."[48] This powerful narrative has played an important role in American history alongside the citizen-soldier tradition, yet the warrior ideal unleashes precisely the type of militaristic passions the citizen-soldier tradition attempts to contain by means of the democratic safeguards mentioned above.[49] Those who posit a natural connection between maleness and war-making inevitably depart from the citizen-soldier ethos, which understands both masculinity and soldiering as produced through certain practices. That is to say, despite the thoroughly masculine character of the citizen-soldier, this ideal and the tradition it embodies implicitly contain a *performative* understanding of identity,[50] where male individuals *become* masculine citizen-soldiers through the *performance* of civic and martial practices. If men were naturally warriors and women were not, then the argument that all citizens must share responsibility for military service would mean that only men were capable of full citizenship. In contrast, the citizen-soldier tradition does not assert that men are *naturally* warriors; biological males become warriors only through engagement in martial practices. This of course allows for the possibility that female individuals could become citizen-soldiers alongside men.[51]

Before gender integration, the goal of basic training was to *produce* not simply soldiers but *manly warriors.* Despite attempts of conservative ideologues to portray men as natural-born warriors, a review of the literature on military socialization contradicts this assertion.[52] New recruits, both then and now, must undergo an intensive training process in order to *become* soldiers. Both recent scholarly studies of the military and interviews with current and former soldiers clearly demonstrate that one of the main purposes of basic training is the *transformation* of the individual into a warrior ready for combat.[53] The process of military socialization entails an actual *change of identity*, during which the individual *becomes* a soldier. Hence the first phase of basic training involves not only intensive physical training to prepare recruits for combat but also purposeful exhaustion, psychological intimidation, and personal humiliation, all aimed at breaking down feelings of individualism among new recruits. A sense of group identity emerges out of the imposition of matching uniforms and haircuts, the use of group punishments, and the denial of privacy even during the most intimate personal moments. The introduction of weapons traditionally marks the key transition from the first disintegrative phase of boot camp to the second reconstitutive phase, during which harassment lets up and recruits actually *become* soldiers.[54]

Before gender integration, moreover, the military was unabashedly concerned with producing an ethos of masculinity. As Melissa Herbert puts it, "prior to the elimination of the draft, the military represented a part of traditional sex-role identity for American men, as well as a primary socialization agent for this identity."[55] Traditionally "young males have either been lured or drafted into the military with the promise of becoming a man: 'Join the army, Be a man'; 'The army will make a man out of you';. . . Overall, socially and personally joining the military is viewed as not only an opportunity for boys to become men but the opportune time for the military to make men out of boys."[56] Thus while biological maleness formed a necessary prerequisite for military service, young recruits were considered manly only after military training. In other words, masculinity in the ideal sense was not a necessary prerequisite for military training but rather its ideal outcome.[57]

In the time before the "political intimidation by radical feminists" laid the groundwork for the "feminization of the U.S. military,"[58] misogyny and homophobia openly played a central role in all dimensions of the boot camp experience, as evidenced by the literature on Vietnam-era basic training. Thus drill instructors commonly referred to recruits as feminine for the purpose of degrading them and breaking down their civilian identity. According to a Vietnam Marine veteran interviewed by Richard Moser, "especially in the earlier stages of boot-camp, when people are real confused and real disorganized, they always said, 'Girls—you cunts—pussies.'"[59] Christian Appy's study reveals that recruits were routinely called names like "pussies," "faggots," and "candy-asses."[60] Drill instructors used misogynistic and homophobic ridicule to shame new recruits into acting like men. For example, Appy reveals that "any evidence of weakness or fatigue (or simply failure to conform) was typically attributed to a lack of manhood. Failure as a soldier constituted failure as a man and left the recruit inhabiting the status of a woman."[61] Similarly, Moser found that "both gay and feminine sexuality were used as threats and negative examples."[62] Platoon sergeants used sexism to facilitate male bonding. During training exercises, soldiers often marched together in accordance with cadence counts ("jodies") that ranged from the sexist[63] to the sexually aggressive[64] to the downright misogynistic.[65] In short, during the Vietnam era, basic training deliberately portrayed both women and gay men in negative terms, using them "interchangeably as the epitome of all that is cowardly, passive, untrustworthy, unclean, and undisciplined."[66]

Even today such practices continue, despite their official prohibition. For example, in 1997 the Federal Advisory Committee on Gender-Integrated Training observed that in all four branches of the armed forces, "the training cadre is transmitting attitudes of sexual discrimination (for example, by telling recruits 'you run like a bunch of women') and that it is being tolerated as motivational."[67] While such practices might seem trivial and their critics hypersensitive, criticizing male recruits by comparing them to "a bunch of women" communicates the message that strong, combat-ready soldiers can only be men. Such a motivational strategy obviously undermines the credibility of female soldiers and negates the possibility of women's equality not only within the military but within the larger society.

During the Vietnam era, drill instructors openly facilitated the process of creating manly warriors by encouraging their young male recruits—mostly still teenagers—to identify their weapons with their genitalia and to view war "as a substitute for sex or as another form of sex."[68] Appy found that "sexual talk permeated the distribution and handling of weapons. Recruits were instructed to call their weapons rifles, not guns. To emphasize the point, drill instructors might order their men to run around the barracks with their rifle in one hand, their penis in the other chanting, 'This is my rifle, this is my gun; one is for fighting, the other's for fun.'"[69] While this strategy may produce male bonding, it also encourages violence against women. To quote one Vietnam vet, "a perfectly regular guy could come into the Army, and before he knew it, he was doing things he'd never done before. . . . Talking about what it would be like to get a gang together and take the cafe waitress out in the alley."[70] Thus, while the identification of weapons with genitalia aims to teach young soldiers to desire rather than fear combat, this type of training strategy explicitly encourages young male recruits to link anger, aggression and sexuality in a way that creates hostility toward women (and effeminate men).[71]

Homophobic hazing and initiation rituals that fuel hatred and contempt for gay men are also rife in a military ostensibly charged with protecting American society and its democratic values. Consider the homophobic homoeroticism of Marine and Navy "initiation rituals involving cross-dressing, spanking, simulated oral and anal sex, simulated ejaculation, nipple piercing, and anal penetration with objects or fingers."[72] While obviously homoerotic, such hazing rituals are simultaneously homophobic because they deploy homoeroticism in the context of degradation. Or consider the Marine tradition of "applying burning chemicals to the penises and anuses of initiates."[73] In this particular ritual the genitalia of new recruits are simultaneously stimulated and punished, no doubt producing aggressive hostility and anger. And while that anger can be functionally channeled into a desire for combat, it also fuels contempt and hatred toward gay men—as well as toward women. That is to say, being on the receiving end of such routines during initiation clearly has degrading connotations—which is largely the point. By extension, however, those seen as enjoying penetration as part of their sexual orientation, specifically women and gay men, come to be viewed as essentially degraded as well. Viewed thusly, homophobic hazing rituals, while problematic in the lessons they teach about gay men, should also be understood as fundamentally misogynistic.

Employing misogynistic and homophobic methods to construct bonds among soldiers creates a particularly unstable masculine identity predicated on denigration of femininity and homoeroticism. While masculinity always forms in opposition to femininity, the type of martial masculinity created through misogynistic and homophobic hazing defines itself as *hostile* toward what it perceives as the homoerotic and the feminine. Such masculinity not only yields a hatred and fear of women and gay men, but also requires that soldiers strongly repress the "feminine" parts of themselves,[74] as well as any homoerotic feelings that will necessarily arise during the intense and intimate activities of the military.[75] This gives rise to a precarious form of masculine machismo that, for the warrior, must be constantly reestablished. As Moser puts it, "the obsessive drive to create and maintain machismo drew upon an insatiable insecurity that may be momentarily slaked only by a display of domination against some threat."[76]

Defenders of military tradition focus on the allegedly negative impact of gender integration on military cohesion and effectiveness, yet they express little concern about how misogynistic and homophobic training methods undermine humane and democratic values, including citizen equality. But that is exactly what misogynistic and homophobic elements of military culture do: they fuel and justify feelings of *heterosexual male dominance* within soldiers and lay the groundwork for hatred and contempt of women and gay men—the majority of the American population. Put differently, since the main justification for a democratic society to establish a military force in the first place is *to protect democracy and its values from any antidemocratic enemies*—whether aristocrats, tyrants, or religious fundamentalists—it makes little sense to *undermine democracy from within* by military personnel in a way that makes them hostile toward the majority of American citizens and contemptuous of attempts to foster civic equality and respect for human dignity.[77]

The U.S. military has made considerable strides towards eliminating the misogyny that formed the centerpiece of Vietnam era basic training. But right-wing ideologues mock these recent attempts to reform traditional practices in accordance with democratic principles as simply the "social engineering schemes" of "noisy homosexual and feminist activists."[78] While critics of women in the military insist they are simply concerned about military effectiveness, their claim seems disingenuous in light of the unexpectedly swift victory in Afghanistan. Is there any reason to believe that the U.S. armed forces have become a "kinder, gentler military" that cannot win wars? When seen within the larger right-wing backlash against feminism, histrionics about the "feminization of the military" seem to be more about gender relations and sexuality than about combat readiness as such.

The Citizen-Soldier Tradition Revisited

While social conservatives argue that the warrior ethic has been undermined by the pervasive influence of feminism, they fail to recognize that the citizen-soldier tradition developed precisely *to prevent the warrior ethic from gaining strength because of the threat it poses to democratic values.* Unfortunately, the militarism of the Bush Administration in the wake of September 11th bolsters those very militaristic tenets that most threaten democratic institutions and practices. The demand that all Americans and their elected officeholders support the President with "one voice" while taking his agenda at face value clearly prioritizes *obedience* to the executive over the freedom of citizens to form their own opinions and make their own decisions. The construction of an Office of Homeland Security and the removing of protections for federal employees emphasizes *hierarchy* over equality (as does the redistribution of advantages to the airlines and other wealthy corporations). The secretiveness of the Bush administration and its demand that Congress give the President absolute power to wage war how and when he chooses affirm the role of executive *authority* over democratic accountability. Finally, the arrogant unilateralism and complete contempt for international laws and treaties repeatedly demonstrated by the U.S. under Bush exemplifies a preference for "*might makes right*" over rational deliberation and the rule of law.

While the military arguably thrives on antidemocratic values and practices to operate effectively, the bleeding of that authoritarian mindset into ordinary politics and civil society illustrates the ways patriarchal military values can totally overwhelm democratic ones. The citizen-soldier tradition recognizes the omnipresent threat of militarism, striving to prevent its flourishing by giving responsibility for the military not to those seeking war for glory or profit but to those (ordinary citizens) who want neither. Thus, while patriotic rhetoric can surely fan the flames of militarism among mass publics, we know on the basis of survey research data that the majority of American people do not support a unilateral U.S. military attack on Iraq.

The citizen-soldier legacy does insist that if people want various rights and liberties that come with living in a democratic society, they must share the obligations of defending that society from military attack. Since the terrorist attacks of September 11th, Bush has called upon the U.S. military to protect American society from radical Islamic terrorists who reject gender equality and uphold male dominance, who scorn secularism and desire religious law, and who shun rational discourse in favor of violence. At the same time, however, the Bush forces have allowed Christian Right groups—fully opposed to equality and religious freedom—to use the crisis of 9/11 to push harder for their own antidemocratic agendas of xenophobic superpatriotism, militarism, and male dominance.

Notes

1. James Burk argues that mature democracies need a theory of civil-military relations that both protects society and helps sustain democratic values. See "Theories of Democratic Civil-Military Relations," *Armed Forces & Society* 29, no. 1 (2002).

2. For a fuller exploration of the political theory of the citizen-soldier, see R. Claire Snyder, *Citizen-Soldiers and Manly Warriors: Military Service and Gender in the Civic Republican Tradition* (Lanham, MD: Rowman & Littlefield, 1999). For a discussion of the civic republican tradition, see Maurizio Viroli, *Republicanism* (New York: Hill & Wang, 2002).

3. The citizen-soldier has historically been understood as fundamentally masculine. For a discussion of how women can be integrated into this tradition, see Snyder, op. cit.

4. While the term "militarism" did not appear until the 1860s, the threat of military dominance dates back to the beginning of recorded history.

5. Ilene Rose Feinman, *Citizenship Rites: Feminist Soldiers & Feminist Antimilitarists* (New York: New York University Press, 2000), 201.

6. This theme comes up repeatedly in both the *Prince* and the *Discourses*. For a full discussion of the citizen-soldier ideal in Machiavelli, see Snyder, *Citizen-Soldiers*, chapter 2.

7. *Machiavelli: The Chief Works and Others*, trans. A. Gilbert (Durham, NC: Duke University Press, 1965), *Art of War*, I, 574.

8. Ibid., 576.

9. Ibid., 578.

10. For a full discussion of the citizen-soldier ideal in Rousseau, see Snyder, *Citizen-Soldiers*, chapter 3.

11. Jean-Jacques Rousseau, *The Government of Poland*, tr. Willmoore Kendall (Indianapolis: Hackett Publishing Co., 1985), 80–81.

12. Ibid., 80.

13. Ibid., 85.

14. See anti-federalist arguments in J. R. Pole, *The American Constitution For and Against: The Federalists and Anti-Federalist Papers* (New York: Hill and Wang, 1987), 52, 84, 120; see also Allan R. Millett and Peter Maslowski, *For the Common Defense: A Military History of the United States of America* (New York: The Free Press, 1984), 57; David R. Segal, *Recruiting for Uncle Sam: Citizenship and Military Manpower Policy* (Lawrence, KS: University of Kansas Press, 1989), 3; and J. G. A. Pocock, "The Americanization of Virtue," in *The Machiavellian Moment: Florentine Political Thought and the Atlantic Republican Tradition* (Princeton, NJ: Princeton University Press, 1975).

15. While never universally required in practice, military service was understood to be a fundamental responsibility of all fully enfranchised citizens.

16. For a more in-depth discussion of the citizen-soldier tradition in America, see Snyder, *Citizen-Soldiers*, chapter 4.

17. See Carl Boggs, "Overview: Globalization and the New Militarism" and Douglas Kellner, "Postmodern War in the Age of Bush II," *New Political Science: A Journal of Politics and Culture* 24, no. 1 (March 2002), 66–71.

18. Chalmers Johnson, "American Militarism and Blowback: The Costs of Letting the Pentagon Dominate Foreign Policy," *New Political Science: A Journal of Politics and Culture* 24, no. 1 (March 2002), 34, emphasis added.

19. Elizabeth Kline and Mosi Secret, "The Generals Speak," *The Nation*, October 21, 2002. http://thenation.com/doc.mhtml?i=20021021&s=secret

20. A *New York Times* article recently made this point: "Now it is uniformed commanders scarred by Vietnam and politicians shaped by its legacy who most urge caution, while civilian Pentagon officials and a president who saw no combat as a home-front National Guard pilot seem more disposed toward military force." Todd S. Purdum, "The Missiles of 1962 Haunt the Iraq Debate," *New York Times*, October 13, 2002, "Week in Review," 1.

21. For a discussion of how these two types of arguments work together, see Linda Kintz, *Between Jesus and the Market: The Emotions That Matter in Right-wing America* (Durham, NC: Duke University Press, 1997).

22. Richard Rayner discusses this view in "Women in the Warrior Culture," *New York Times Magazine*, 22 June 1997.

23. Stephanie Gutmann, *The Kinder, Gentler Military: Can America's Gender-Neutral Fighting Force Still Win Wars?* (New York: Scribner, 2000).

24. Feinman, *Citizenship Rites*.

25. Feinman, *Citizenship Rites*, 128.

26. Jane Mansbridge, *Why We Lost the ERA* (Chicago: Chicago University Press, 1986), 110.

27. H.R. 3598 IH, emphasis added.

28. For examples of this argument see Lionel Tiger, *The Decline of Males: The First Look At An Unexpected New World For Men and Women* (New York: St. Martin's Griffin, 2000); Christina Hoff Sommers, *The War Against Boys: How Misguided Feminism is Harming Our Young Men* (New York: Simon & Schuster, 2000); and James Dobson, *Bringing Up Boys: Practical Advice and Encouragement For Those Shaping the Next Generation of Men* (Wheaton, IL: Tyndale House Publishers, Inc., 2000).

29. For his discussion of the military, see Tiger, *Decline of Males*, 208–230.

30. Robert Bork, *Slouching Towards Gomorrah: Modern Liberalism and American Decline* (New York: Regan Books, 1997), 218–223; Sommers, *War Against Boys*, 134–136, 210; and Gutmann, *Kinder, Gentler Military*.

31. "Women Urge Abolition of Feminist Defense Panel DACOWITS," NewsMax.com Wires, February 1, 2002. http://www.newsmax.com/cgi-bin/printer_friendly.pl. NewsMax.com is affiliated with the Center for Military Readiness, the leading organization in the fight against gender equality in the military.

32. Mona Charen, "Misguided Military Advisory Vehicle," *Washington Times*, March 18, 2002. http://asp.washingtontimes.com/printarticle.asp?action=print&ArticleID=20020318-1319140

33. Martha Kleder, "DACOWITS Down . . . But Not Out," Culture & Family Institute Report, March 6, 2002. http://cultureandfamily.org/report/2002–03–06/n_dacowits.shtml?print

34. Phyllis Schlafly, "Special-Interest Lobbyists Overlooked By The Media," March 13, 2002. http://www.eagleforum.org/column/2002/mar02/02–03–13.shtml

35. Feinman, *Citizenship Rites*, 98.

36. Linda Bird Francke, *Ground Zero: The Gender Wars in the Military* (New York: Simon & Schuster, 1997), chapter 1.

37. Reported in Sgt. Stacy Wamble, "Women's Equality or National Defense? Where Does One Begin and the Other End," *Pentagram*, February 8, 2002. http://www.dcmilitary.com/army/pentagram/7_05/commentary/14021–1.html

38. "Homosexual and Feminist Agendas Weaken Military," NewsMax.com, August 9, 2000. http://www.newsmax.com/articles/print.shtml?a=2000/8/8/201248

39. Charmaine and Jack Yoest, "Booby Traps at the Pentagon," *The Women's Quarterly*, Winter 2002. http://server1.griffinsg.net/iwf/printit.cfm

40. Charter, Defense Advisory Committee on Women in the Services, filed April 17, 2002. http://www.dtic.mil/dacowits/charter.html

41. "Demise of DACOWITS: Will New Charter Signal Rejection of Committee's Radical Past?" Center for Military Readiness, April 15, 2002. http://cmrlink.org/dacowits.asp?docID=142

42. Kathryn Jean Lopez, "D-Day for DACOWITS: Should a civilian feminist bastion in the Pentagon remain?" *National Review Online*, February 28, 2002, emphasis added. http://www.nationalreview.com/nr_comment/nr_commentprint022802.html

43. "Demise of DACOWITS," emphasis added.

44. Woody West, "U.S. Military Has a New Strategy in the Battle of the Sexes," *Insight Magazine*, April 15, 2002, emphasis added.

45. Gutmann, *Kinder, Gentler Military*, 14.

46. James William Gibson, *Warrior Dreams: Paramilitary Culture in Post-Vietnam America* (New York: Hill & Wang, 1994).

47. See Richard R. Moser, *The New Winter Soldiers: GI and Veteran Dissent During the Vietnam Era* (New Brunswick, NJ: Rutgers University Press, 1996).

48. See Snyder, *Citizen-Soldiers*.

49. Interestingly, Judith Youngman notes that she attended a conference at which a split developed among attendees, with the older men using the discourse of the citizen-soldier and the younger men embracing the warrior ideal. Comment made at the Women in Uniform Conference, sponsored by WREI, November 30, 2000, in Arlington, Virginia.

50. Judith Butler, *Gender Trouble: Feminism and the Subversion of Identity* (New York: Routledge, Chapman & Hall, Inc., 1990).

51. For the full theoretical argument see Snyder, *Citizen-Soldiers*.

52. For the arguments of those who assert that males are naturally warriors, see Carlson Tucker, "Emasculating the Marines: The Hysteria Over Hazing," *The Weekly Standard*, 17 February 1997, 29; Rayner, "Warrior Culture," 26; and Gutmann, *Kinder, Gentler Military*.

53. See Christian G. Appy, *Working-Class War: American Combat Soldiers and Vietnam* (Chapel Hill & London: University of North Carolina Press, 1993); Moser, *New Winter Soldiers*; and Steven Zeeland, *The Masculine Marine: Homoeroticism in the U.S. Marine Corps* (New York & London: Harrington Park Press, An Imprint of The Haworth Press, Inc., 1996). See also Gutmann, *Kinder, Gentler Military*, chapter 2. However, studies of other contexts cite similar socialization processes. For a discussion of traditional military academies, see Sanford M. Dornbusch, "The Military Academy as an Assimilating Institution," *Social Forces* 33 (1955). For a historical account, see Richard Holmes, *Acts of War: The Behavior of Men in Battle* (New York: The Free Press, 1985). For a description of nearly identical processes in the Canadian Airborne, see Donna Winslow, "Rites of Passage and Group Bonding in the Canadian Airborne," *Armed Forces & Society* 25, no. 3 (Spring 1999), 429–457.

54. Appy, *Working-Class War*, 104–5.

55. Melissa Herbert, *Camouflage Isn't Only For Combat: Gender, Sexuality, and Women in the Military* (New York: New York University Press, 1998), 8.

56. William Arkin and Lynne R. Dobrofsky, "Military Socialization and Masculinity" in *Making War/Making Peace: The Social Foundations of Violent Conflict*, edited by Francesca M. Cancian and James William Gibson (Belmont, CA: Wadsworth Publishing Company, 1990), 70.

57. See Gibson, *Warrior Dreams*.

58. Bork, *Slouching Towards Gomorrah*, 223.

59. Moser, *New Winter Soldiers*, 26.

60. Appy, *Working-Class War*, 100.

61. Appy, *Working-Class War*, 101.

62. Moser, *New Winter Soldiers*, 27.

63. "I don't know but I've been told, Eskimo pussy is mighty cold." Arkin and Dobrofsky, "Military Socialization and Masculinity," 74.

64. "Climbed all out with his dick in his hand/Said, 'Looky here, ladies, I'm a hell of a man.'/. . . Fucked ninety-eight till his balls turned blue/Then he backed off, jacked off, and fucked the other two." Francke, *Ground Zero*, 162.

65. "Who can take a chain saw/Cut the bitch in two/Fuck the bottom half/And give the upper half to you?" Jean Zimmerman, *Tailspin: Women at War in the Wake of Tailhook* (New York: Doubleday, 1995), 236–7.

66. Appy, *Working-Class War*, 101.

67. *Report of the Federal Advisory Committee on Gender-Integrated Training*, 19.

68. Appy, *Working-Class War*, 102; Arkin and Dobrofsky, "Military Socialization and Masculinity," 74; Holmes 1985, 56–7. For an interesting discussion of the eroticization of weapons in popular culture, see James William Gibson, *Warrior Dreams*, chapter 5.

69. Appy, *Working-Class War*, 102.

70. Quoted in Appy, *Working-Class War*, 99. Compare to the real-life account of Paula Coughlin, a victim of the Tailhook gathering: "I was practically gang-banged by a group of fucking F-18 pilots." See Zimmerman, *Tailspin*, 23.

71. Arkin and Dobrofsky, "Military Socialization and Masculinity," 75.

72. Zeeland, *Masculine Marine*, 5.

73. Ibid., 8.

74. Gibson, *Warrior Dreams*, 36.

75. Zeeland, *Masculine Marine*, 65.

76. Moser, *New Winter Soldiers*, 28.

77. For a more extended version of this argument, see R. Claire Snyder, "The Citizen-Soldier Tradition and Gender Integration of the U.S. Military," *Armed Forces & Society* 29, no. 2 (2002).

78. Elaine Donnelly, "Military voters due an agenda for change," *Washington Times*, 4 February 2001.

CHAPTER 12

Empire of Death
and the Plague of Civic Violence

DARRELL Y. HAMAMOTO

"I am what you have made of me and the mad dog devil killer fiend leper is a reflection
of your society."
—Charles Manson[1]

"Isn't killing just killing, regardless if it's in Vietnam or Jonesboro, Arkansas?"
—Marilyn Manson[2]

Within the human group, violent death at the hand of another is a startlingly
mundane social fact that transcends historical epoch, geography, and culture.
Whether murder is committed by one individual against another out of jeal-
ousy, anger, revenge, or material necessity; whether murder is committed at
the state level for reasons of territorial expansion, political advantage, or pro-
fessed self-defense, regular intraspecies killing is consistent with the 13,000
years of sociocultural evolution since the last Ice Age. The romantic myth of
the nonviolent peaceable kingdom of band and tribal societies once held dear
by both anthropologists and the lay public has proven to be little more than
the collective fantasy of those in advanced civilizations seeking relief from the
sophisticated barbarism of the modern age. Killing, in all its grisly variations
(despite the finely wrought legal-juridical rationalizations that often attend its
exercise), stands at the core of what it means to live in human society. The
charnel house is the true temple of civilization.

Just as the more joyous and virtuous aspects of communal life—love,
friendship, fraternity—vary considerably across cultures and through history, murder and killing as expressive behavior also take different forms,
characteristics, and stem from varying motivations according to time, place,
and circumstance. A recent popular history of murder by Colin Wilson cata-
logues all manner of violent crime committed over the past five hundred
years.[3] Although largely restricted to Western societies, the epic scope of this
study makes it clear that the *kinds* and *types* of murder and killing are determined to a significant degree by the sociocultural milieu in which they occur.
Prior to the mid-nineteenth century, for example, the struggle for subsistence

meant that most murders were "economic" in nature. With the subsequent maturation of the industrial capitalist social order and its vast population of polyglot peoples in urban concentrations, the "sex crime" murder began to proliferate.[4] By the 1970s, law enforcement agencies and criminologists began to discern a disturbingly novel pattern of homicide that linked multiple unrelated victims with a single perpetrator; the so-called serial killer.

The Phenomenon of Serial Murder

The term "serial killer" was coined by Robert K. Ressler in the mid-1970s while serving as an instructor at the FBI National Academy in Quantico, Virginia. In applying a label to this relatively new criminal phenomenon, Ressler was inspired by the Saturday afternoon cliff-hangers of his childhood. These short, episodic movies would leave the audience anxious and in a state of suspenseful tension from week to week, thus ensuring regular return visits to the theater.[5] To Ressler, this seemed like the perfect analogy to characterize the murderer whose psychopathology compels him to satisfy a thirst for killing that is never quite slaked. But whereas the generalized fantasies of the average moviegoer are benign and rarely translate into actual behavior, the serial killer acts upon violent fantasies of death that never quite live up to his expectations.

Ressler contends that serial murder can be traced back 125 years, appearing in tandem with the rise of interpersonal violence beginning in the mid-nineteenth century. "It is connected to the increasing complexity of our society," he explains, "to our interconnectedness via the media, and to the alienation many of us feel."[6] While Ressler's summary account of the historical roots and the etiology of serial murder is woefully lacking in explanatory force, it remains beyond dispute that the number of such crimes committed in the U.S. has risen precipitously during the second half of the twentieth century. More specifically, serial murder increased in frequency beginning in the late 1960s and 1970s. This upward trend continued unabated in the years that followed. According to a noted criminologist, "More offenders were identified in the 20-year time frame between 1975 and 1995 than during any previous 25-year span."[7] The documented increase in serial murder might be due in part to the redefinition of what were once called "stranger killings" and the heavy emphasis given such spectacular crimes by the Violent Criminal Apprehension Program (VICAP) at the FBI's National Center for the Analysis of Violent Crime (NCAVC).

The classic profile of the serial killer is found in Theodore Robert Bundy. From 1973 to February 1978, "Ted" Bundy, "normal" in appearance, even "attractive" by some accounts, murdered between thirty and forty young women and one girl. Like his fellows in the elite fraternity of serial killers, Bundy had a morbid fascination with death. The process of selecting his prey, stalking, and then killing her brought him a sense of complete power, mastery, and control. "As evidence of his morbidity," wrote an investigator who spent many hours personally interviewing the notorious killer, "Ted readily admitted that he was preoccupied with the cyanotic hue of a corpse's fingernails, discoloration of the skin after death, necrophilia, and possession of the female corpse."[8] Despite the nature and scope of his crimes, a significant number of seemingly sensible women devotedly pined for Ted Bundy during the years preceding his long delayed execution on January 24, 1989. Famed author Ann Rule, who coincidentally had worked alongside Bundy as a telephone counselor at the Seattle Crisis Clinic in 1971, often was pestered by calls from female devotees who had read the book she had written on the object of their perverse affection. After his execution, Rule reported on the effect Bundy had on women even in death: "There were so many calls," she writes, "so many crying women. Many of them had corresponded with Ted and fallen in love with him, each devoutly believing that she was his only one. Several told me they suffered nervous breakdowns when he died."[9]

Mass Murder

Similar to (but distinct from) the serial killer, the mass murderer is predominantly white (70 percent) and male (95 percent). Like serial murder, the number of mass killings has escalated in recent times. During the fifteen years between 1976 and 1991, there were 350 mass murders that claimed almost 2,000 victims.[10] Supervisors, co-workers, family members, and strangers alike might incur the lethal wrath of the mass murderer. Economic uncertainty, the decline in real income, emasculation by routinized and tenuous jobs, and resentment against non-white minorities have caused more than a few middle-aged and vengeful white men to explode in paroxysms of violent rage against those seen as responsible for their plight:

> He sees little opportunity for finding another job, and he suspects that all the breaks are going to younger competitors—or even to blacks, women, and foreigners. Having grown up in the 1950s and 1960s, an era of unparalleled prosperity, he feels entitled to a well-paying, meaningful job. Rudely awakened from the American dream, he resents that his birthright has been snatched from him, and he looks for someone to blame.[11]

Sniper Culture

On August 1, 1966, a veteran of the U.S. Marine Corps studying engineering at the University of Texas, Austin, lived up to the sharpshooter rating he had earned in the military by proceeding to pick off unsuspecting human targets as they walked below the landmark clock tower wherein he held strategic position. He had brought along his personal arsenal of weapons and enough ammunition to hold off his perceived enemies. Before climbing to his post in the tower, Charles Joseph Whitman had killed both his mother and wife with a bayonet. By the time a police officer stormed the sniper's position and shot him dead, Whitman had killed a total of fifteen people.[12] The "gun fetishism" (common among mass murderers) of Whitman had been bequeathed him by his equally firearms-obsessed father. Whitman's love for guns was refined and channeled during his stint with the Marines.

The sudden death visited upon the University of Texas campus by Whitman ushered in a new era in the history of mass murder. By 1966, the U.S. was deeply entrenched in its genocidal war against the people of Southeast Asia. The parallel between the Texas Tower mass murder and the routine killing of civilians in Vietnam and neighboring countries is not merely historical coincidence. It will be argued in these pages that there is a strong causal connection between an increasingly militarized society and the attendant rise of serial and mass murder over the past few decades. More specifically, it is hypothesized that this causal relationship has its material origins in the Vietnam War era, during which organized and sustained violence against human beings reached a scale virtually unprecedented in world history. U.S.-sponsored military violence resulted in at least four million deaths in Laos, Cambodia, and Vietnam; the killing due largely to the routine carpet bombing of civilian population centers on a level far exceeding that of World War II.[13] Tens of millions more became medical, social, and psychological casualties of the war.

An exhaustive empirical study by Archer and Gartner of cross-national homicide rates points to the causal relationship between the rise in civilian murder and state "legitimation" of violence during the Vietnam War.[14] Researchers Archer and Gartner write:

> If wartime killing does legitimate homicidal violence in some lasting or general way, as this model suggests, then one would expect increases in violent crime in postwar societies. In addition, since civilians and soldiers alike could be influenced by the legitimation process, this model predicts that homicide increases will occur among both veterans and nonveterans.[15]

That the homicide rate in the U.S. continued to climb each year of the Vietnam War serves as compelling proof that the militarist imperatives of the imperial state have given rise to "blowback" in the form of violent crime within civilian society.

Operation Domestic Storm

Thirty-six years after the Texas Tower killing spree by Whitman, John Allen Muhammad and his lover John Lee Malvo were alleged to have killed ten people by sniping at them with a Bushmaster XM-15 .223-caliber rifle, a civilian version of the M-16.[16] (It is worth noting that Richard Dyke, the owner of Bushmaster Firearms of Windham, Maine—the manufacturer of the weapon employed by Muhammad and Malvo—was the chief fundraiser in the state of Maine for presidential candidate George W. Bush in 2000 until a "controversy erupted over the fact that his firm makes assault weapons."[17]) Before being apprehended on October 24, 2002, the pair had terrorized those living in Washington, D.C., and surrounding areas for twenty-two days. As in the case of Whitman, the military background of Muhammad and his anti-American politics was underplayed in the mainstream media, which instead chose to portray him as a loser with no agenda other than taking out his personal frustrations on innocent victims. An article in the *Los Angeles Times* characterized Muhammad as a "former soldier who'd gone to war but earned no glory, who couldn't keep a job or a wife. . . ."[18]

In truth, John Allen Williams (he changed his name to Muhammad in 2001) had an extensive military career that began with his 1978 enlistment in the Louisiana Army National Guard. In 1985, the year of his conversion to Islam, Williams left the National Guard and joined the Army. Like convicted serial killer Robert Lee Yates, Jr., Williams was stationed at Fort Lewis, Washington, near Tacoma. Like convicted mass murderer Timothy McVeigh, Williams served in the Gulf War as a combat engineer in 1990. After a relatively undistinguished career save for the expert marksmanship skills he acquired while in the service, Williams remained in the Army until April 1994.[19] Despite being charged with insubordination in one case and assaulting a noncommissioned officer in another, Williams was in his element while in the Army. After leaving the service, he brought into civilian society the specialized arts of concealment, stealth, evasion, and the deadly sniper skills he had learned during his military career.

"A Few Good Men"

The influence of the U.S. military and its allied institutions on the larger American society and culture runs deep. It began with the holocaust of forced removal and exterminationist wars against Native Americans that continued until the latter part of the nineteenth century and soon thereafter expanded overseas into Asia with the conquest and colonization of the Philippines, where an estimated 200,000 civilians were killed.[20] Not until World War II and the period immediately following, however, did the militarization of civilian society begin in earnest, as powerful political and economic interests combined to realize the vision of a world capitalist order led by the U.S. and sustained mainly by force both at home and abroad. Since the end of World War II, more than fifty major military interventions have been staged both directly and through client states in every region of the world.[21] The retaliatory bombing raids against Afghanistan following the terror attacks launched on U.S. homeland on September 11, 2001, are but the latest in a succession of military strikes in support of the permanent warfare state.

Prior to his April 19, 1995, demolition of the nine-story reinforced concrete Alfred P. Murrah Federal Building (reportedly the "largest act of domestic terrorism in our nation's history" up to that time), Timothy James McVeigh served as gunner on a Bradley Fighting Vehicle with the First Infantry Division of the U.S. Army.[22] The future murderer of 168 fellow Americans in Oklahoma City served with distinction during Operation Desert Storm in 1991 and was awarded the Bronze Star for his contribution to the war effort. Part of his assignment was to shoot Iraqi soldiers trying to escape being buried alive in their trenches by U.S. tanks equipped with plow attachments. McVeigh apparently enjoyed his foreign duty, even having "boasted of blowing off an Iraqi soldier's head with his cannon at 1,100 meters."[23]

After returning Stateside and failing to qualify for the Special Forces, McVeigh plunged more deeply into the anti-government gun-toting survivalist politics that eventually compelled him to take revenge for the 1993 government slaughter of more than eighty innocent civilians (including children) at the Branch Davidian compound in Waco, Texas.[24] McVeigh already was angered by the 1992 all-out federal government assault on the home of white racial separatist Randy Weaver at Ruby Ridge, Idaho. On that fateful day, FBI sniper Lon Horiuchi of the Hostage Rescue Team shot and killed Weaver's defenseless wife Vicki and fourteen-year-old son Samuel. In a 542-page report issued by the U.S. Department of Justice over a year after the fiasco, the FBI was criticized severely for its pivotal role in a case that confirmed the dark suspicions of those who warn against the further encroachment by the federal government on constitutionally-protected freedoms.[25]

Race Murder

The act of murder does not take place in a social vacuum. Just as the *type* of murder varies through time, the *method* employed in the dispatch of victims is determined by larger historical forces. Mass murder of the over-the-top sort witnessed in recent years, for example, becomes possible only with the proliferation of semiautomatic weapons in a hyper-militarized civilian society. Similarly, the mobility, anonymity, and sometimes wide territorial range of the serial killer is facilitated by an extensive interstate highway system funded by the Federal government that began construction during the early years of the Cold War with the intention of providing a rapid and efficient means of transporting military vehicles.

Once having established the historicity of the type, method, and means of killing, it remains to consider variations in the *kind* of victims preferred by serial and mass murderers. Ted Bundy specialized in white female college students, while Randall Woodfield favored impressionable teenagers and single young women susceptible to the charms of the physically prepossessing murderer. John Wayne Gacy, Jr. murdered a total of thirty-three young men, many of whom were male prostitutes. In the early 1970s, Edmund Emil Kemper III began picking up young female hitchhikers who were then killed for post mortem sex and subsequent dissection. The women thought to have fallen prey to Roger Kibbe, observed rookie homicide detective Kay Maulsby, "all had long hair and most had seemed to be busty."[26]

Among the few women who meet the definition of "serial killer," Aileen "Lee" Carol Wuornos shot to death at least seven "johns" who had paid her for sex. (Unlike her male counterparts who thrill in their acts of sexual predation, it is more likely that Wuornos "lashed out against her victims in a rage that originated in decades of abusive and debilitating encounters with men that began in her early childhood."[27]) One of only fifty-two women on death row in the United States, Wuornos was executed at Florida State Prison on October 10, 2002 via lethal injection of potassium chloride. She actively sought execution for herself despite legal and moral appeals to the Florida Supreme Court to overturn the death signed by Governor Jeb Bush the previous September. "If I have to spend life in prison," Wuornos once told a judge, "I will kill again."[28] Understanding the *kind* of victim produced by serial killers and mass murderers is crucial in reaching a deeper understanding of these historically specific forms of violent crime.

Like genocide, mass murder and serial killing are highly "racialized" expressions of violent behavior. But beyond the easily observable generalization that the overwhelming majority of perpetrators in the U.S. are of Euro-American descent, both the "true crime" literature and scholarly studies fail to fully explore the significance of racial identity among killers and victims. Moreover, any explanatory model that pretends to articulate the underlying motivations, impulses, and predilections of the modern mass murderer or serial killer must confront at some point the history of white supremacist systematic violence against people of color. Only then is it possible to understand what otherwise might be dismissed as aberrant behavior and little else.

The holocaust of African slavery and the genocidal destruction of Native America are the twin tributaries of the mighty river that feeds into the racist imagination of many mass murderers and serial killers. The loss of life resulting from four centuries of enslaved Africans brought to the Americas is estimated conservatively at 50 to 100 million deaths.[29] Within North America alone, an aboriginal population that stood at an estimated fifteen million in 1492 systematically had been reduced by as much as 99 percent within five hundred years.[30]

But in the latter half of the twentieth century, it was the race wars waged against yellow people first in Korea and then in Southeast Asia that have had a decided influence on the preferred victims of the contemporary "sociopath."[31] In addition to the hundreds of thousands of civilians killed or wounded during the Vietnam War, the "body count" for combatants numbered 250,000 from the U.S.-supported South and about 900,000 Northern enemy troops. The U.S. invested more than $200 billion in prosecuting its Asian exterminationist war in Vietnam.[32]

It is no mere coincidence that on January 17, 1989, Patrick Eugene Purdy—clad in combat fatigues and wearing a flak jacket—staged a commando raid on Cleveland Elementary School in Stockton, California, and proceeded to kill five Southeast Asian American children and wounded thirty others with the AK-47 he carried. Born at Fort Lewis, Washington, Purdy was the son of a soldier who reportedly saw combat in Vietnam. In addition to his "hatred of Asians that was tied to the war in Vietnam," it incensed Purdy that the school he once attended had become dominated by Southeast Asian American students.[33] Fully seventy percent of the student body were the children of Southeast Asian American refugees displaced by the U.S.-sponsored wars in Vietnam, Cambodia, and Laos.

Cannibal and Headhunter

The empire of death and its genocidal history are embodied in equal opportunity cannibal killer Jeffrey Dahmer. In an interview with criminal profiler Robert K. Ressler, Dahmer stated that among his seventeen victims the "first one was white, the second one was American Indian, third was Hispanic, the fourth was mulatto."[34] Seven of those murdered were African American, although Dahmer denied that any of the killings were racially motivated. In writing about his infamous son, Lionel Dahmer defended him against accusations that the unassuming Ambrosia Chocolate Factory worker was a "race-killer." "He wanted bodies, muscular, male bodies. . . . The color of their skin hadn't mattered to him in the least," he wrote.[35] Rather, according to the elder Dahmer, the greater availability of black men in need of cash explains their overrepresentation among the murdered.

For one observer, however, it was white "racial power" that allowed Dahmer free rein in oppressing and dominating men of color.[36] Most of his victims had been drugged, tortured, and mutilated; their flesh kept in a freezer for later consumption or to stoke Dahmer's masturbation fantasies. According to those who knew him, Dahmer spoke with unabashed hatred for those who constituted most of his victims: gays and blacks. A street minister in Milwaukee who had spoken to him outside a leather gay bar claimed Dahmer cited Biblical stories to argue that blacks "should be all subservient to the whites."[37]

The lone yellow victim of Dahmer was fourteen-year-old Laotian American Konerak Sinthasomphone. A black teenage girl called policemen to the scene after seeing the "butt naked" teenager stumbling about in a daze after escaping the chamber of horrors while his captor went out for more beer. Dahmer pursued the boy, but neighbors protected him until police officers arrived on the scene. Despite his obvious physical injuries and incoherence from an attempted lobotomy by Dahmer, the white cops left the yellow youth at the apartment. Dahmer had convinced them that the two had been having no more than a lover's quarrel. Once the policemen left, Sinthasomphone was administered one final lethal injection to the brain and later dismembered.

The Sinthasomphone family had come to America in 1980 as refugees from the U.S.-sponsored wars in Vietnam, Cambodia, and Laos. Black residents were outraged by the perceived indifference of city officials and its police department to the fate of the non-white men murdered by the unassuming Dahmer. This attitude was reflected in a recorded radio transmission of the police officers who returned Sinthasomphone to Dahmer shortly before the boy was murdered. One of the policemen reported that the "Intoxicated Asian, naked male, was returned to his boyfriend." The officer continues by saying, "My partner is going to get deloused at the station." Laughter is audible on the recording.[38]

Marriage Material

Career military man Sergeant Jack Wayne Reeves apparently acquired a taste for yellow flesh while on tour of duty in South Korea, leaving his wife and two sons behind in the U.S. During a short visit home in 1978 to settle domestic matters, his wife Sharon Vaughn died of a shotgun blast in an incident that later was ruled a suicide. Because Sharon had been carrying on an affair with an officer stationed at Fort Hood and already had served Reeves with divorce papers, it was strongly suspected that he had a hand in her death.

Reeves returned to duty in South Korea, but soon came back to the U.S. with a woman in her early twenties named Myong Hui Chong. They were married in 1980 in Jacksboro, Texas. Myong died in a drowning accident less than six years later, on July 28, 1986, while on a camping trip with her husband. The very day before Myong's funeral, Reeves drugged and raped her sister Sue. Investigators learned from Sue that Myong was often beaten, drugged, and forced to reenact scenes from the dozens of Asian-themed porn videos (*Deep Inside the Orient; Oriental Explosion*) in the Reeves collection.

After Myong was laid to rest, Reeves pored over the literature provided by a mail-order Asian bride service and selected a young Filipina named Emelita Villa as wife number three. Her parents had hoped that their daughter would marry an American who could lift the family out of the poverty caused by nearly one hundred years of neocolonial rule and military occupation by the U.S. In 1987, Reeves traveled to Cebu City to retrieve Emelita and shortly thereafter returned with her to his Arlington, Texas, home. Predictably, Reeves attempted to keep Emelita as his personal Asian sex-slave against all her efforts at independence from a man she came to detest. Not long after Emelita made preparations to divorce Reeves, she was reported missing on October 11, 1994. One year later, hunters in a remote area found her remains after wild animals unearthed the corpse from its shallow grave.

The role played by yellow women in the sociopathic imaginations of white sex criminals is plain to see in the case of Warren James Bland. He had spent most of his adult life either in prison or in mental institutions for committing numerous violent crimes, but his only known murder victim was an Asian American child. Seven-year-old Phoebe Hue-Ru Ho, the daughter of working-class Taiwanese immigrants who had settled in South Pasadena, California, was abducted by Bland on the way to school on December 11, 1986. Her brutalized body was found one week later in a remote area of Riverside County.

Medical examiners determined that the forty-pound child had been tortured, raped repeatedly, and sodomized while bound hand and foot.

Because of being listed as a "sexual sadist" after thirteen violent felony convictions, Bland came under almost immediate suspicion among registered sex offenders who lived in the vicinity of the Ho residence. When investigators discovered that he had been involved with a Vietnamese American woman who had been trying to rid herself of him, a detective played his hunch that conflict between the couple might have precipitated the attack on Phoebe Ho. Upon being interviewed, divorced mother of three Evie Kingston said that Bland told her of "nightmares he'd been having about going off to war and watching as Soviet soldiers tortured Vietnamese women, using pliers to squeeze their breasts and inserting things into their genital areas."[39]

While on trial for the murder of Phoebe Ho, Bland admitted to the violent fantasies that had been fueled by his extensive reading "about the incident in which American troops had mounted a mutilation-massacre of a Vietnamese village."[40] A fellow inmate claimed that Bland confided to him that "What I did to the kid was no different than what we did in Chu (Vietnam) Lai in 1968 to the women and children when we burned their huts."[41] Having gotten the place-name wrong, no doubt Bland was alluding to the highly publicized civilian massacre at My Lai by the U.S. soldiers attached to Charlie Company of the Americal Division, notorious for torturing suspected communist sympathizers, killing elderly men, and the "gang-raping of young girls."[42] Lieutenant William Calley later was found guilty of murder in the My Lai massacre, but quickly was granted a presidential pardon that allowed him to escape punishment. When asked to comment on the My Lai murders, Calley said that, "It was no big thing."[43]

Although none of his victims were yellow, Arthur J. Shawcross explained away the murder of eleven women between 1972 and 1989 by claiming so-called post-traumatic stress disorder that stemmed from his military service in the Vietnam War. It was in Vietnam that he claimed to have murdered two girls—raping and disemboweling one, while roasting and eating the severed leg of the other—and this set Shawcross free to pursue his pathological predilections once returned to civilian life. The man who came to be known as the "Genessee River Killer" also attested to have killed about twenty-six Vietnamese civilians in cold blood.[44] His designer defense ultimately failed, however, since military records showed that Shawcross was little more than a rear-echelon clerk who had not come close to seeing combat duty.

It is nonetheless noteworthy that Shawcross would fabricate such an outrageous but oddly plausible story in hopes of minimizing punishment for his heinous criminal acts. For within the post-My Lai empire of death, such narratives of atrocity have become somewhat routine. Instead of causing outrage, today the public seems sympathetic to perpetrators of violent crimes against people of color. After former U.S. Senator and ex-Governor of Nebraska J. Robert "Bob" Kerrey was exposed in April, 2001, for having led a Navy SEAL combat mission that led to the "shooting deaths of more than 20 unarmed civilians, mostly women and children" during the Vietnam War, there was little of the shock and revulsion that attends news of the latest civilian mass murder.[45] Indeed, national publications such as *Newsweek* were protective and even forgiving of the man often touted as a prospective presidential candidate, despite the accusation of a fellow squad member who said that "Kerrey ordered the civilians rounded up and shot at point-blank range."[46] Wounded in action in 1969, he was awarded the Congressional Medal of Honor the following year. After leaving office as U.S. Senator, Kerrey entered academia and since January 2001 has served as president of the New School in New York City.

"Highway to Hell"

Born and raised in El Paso, Texas, Ricardo "Richard" Muñoz Ramirez terrorized residents of Southern California for several months during 1985. The fifth and final child of Mexican immigrants, Ramirez is among the few non-Anglos among known serial killers. Like some of his white counterparts, however, the prowling thief dubbed by the press as "The Night Stalker" sought out yellow people as objects of his murderous psychosexual urges. Among the first victims selected by the self-professed Satanist were Asian Americans living in the San Gabriel Valley area of Los Angeles. In one of these killings, thirty-four-year-old Dayle Okazaki was shot to death in March, 1985, while her Latina roommate Maria Hernandez was spared.

In July 1985, Ramirez drove to Sun Valley and entered the home of a Thai American couple who had emigrated to the U.S. only ten years earlier. Chainarong Khovanath, who worked as a parking lot attendant, died instantly after Ramirez fired a .25-caliber bullet into his left ear. Having dispatched this father of two young children, Ramirez took his wife Somkid into the bedroom of the dead man where he raped and sodomized her multiple times. Early the following month, Ramirez committed a similar crime in a Diamond Bar neighborhood. Thirty-one-year-old Pakistani American immigrant Elyas Abowath was shot and killed while he lay in bed, leaving Ramirez free to repeatedly rape and sodomize his twenty-seven-year-old Burmese American wife, Sakina. As a further outrage, he went so far as to drink milk from the breasts of this nursing mother of a newborn infant.

Ramirez moved north to San Francisco in August, 1985, after local law enforcement agencies began to step up their hunt for the man who had been linked to at least fourteen attacks in Los Angeles County. In the early morning hours of August 18, he broke into a house in an upscale neighborhood near Lake Merced. True to his modus operandi, Ramirez shot sixty-six-year-old Taiwanese American immigrant Peter Pan in the head. He sexually assaulted sixty-two-year-old Barbara Pan and then shot her in the head for resisting. One week later, Ramirez was back in Los Angeles. He rented a room in Chinatown, where he could live amidst the yellow people he so loathed. "As he moved about Chinatown," writes Philip Carlo, "he fantasized about committing violence on the people he passed. He imagined them tied up and begging for mercy as he cut them and had sex with them."[47]

The violent fantasies held by Ramirez most likely were shaped by an older cousin, Miguel or "Mike," who had found his calling in the U.S. Special Forces as a Green Beret. A decorated war hero, he took credit for twenty-nine confirmed kills during his two tours of duty in Vietnam. The veteran shared many gruesome war stories with the young Ramirez, including detailed accounts of murder, mutilation, and rape. Miguel often showed his younger cousin Polaroid photos of Vietnamese women forced to perform fellatio on him, a cocked .45 held to their head. Ramirez recognized the decapitated head held by Miguel in one photo as that of a woman seen in other photographs fellating his godlike cousin, who had bragged of the infinite excitement gained by holding the power of life and death over others. The pictures were sexually arousing to Richard Ramirez, who would often masturbate along with the scripted fantasy they conjured. Miguel also taught his cousin the secrets of guerilla warfare. For Miguel and his compatriots who helped feed the fervidly sadistic psychosexual imagination of Richard Ramirez, the slaughter of human beings indeed "could be likened to an orgasmic, charismatic experience."[48]

As the largest Marine base in the world, Marine Corps Air Ground Combat Center (MCAGCC) dominates the life of neighboring Mojave Desert communities populated by large numbers of Samoans, Filipinos, and other Asian Pacific peoples brought under Stateside dominion of the global U.S. military machine. A twenty-year-old Filipina American named Rosalie Ortega had the misfortune of having befriended a Gulf War veteran, a convicted rapist with an extensive history of violence against women prior to his recruitment by the U.S. Marine Corps. Valentine Underwood raped and murdered both Ortega and Amanda Lee Scott on August 2, 1991.

Until age eleven, Ortega lived in Batangas province in the Philippines before being called to join her mother in the U.S. For impoverished Batanguenos living in the shadow of the permanent U.S. military presence, one of the few ways out of their neo-colonial misery was by gaining passage to America via marriage to a serviceman. Ortega's mother, Juanita, had married a black Marine in Manila and had relocated to the U.S. She sent for her children one by one as she earned money to pay for their passage. Beaten regularly by her husband after she was reunited with her children, Juanita divorced him and later took up with a white Marine fifteen years her junior. By 1988, Juanita and her grown children were on their way to resettling in Twentynine Palms, home of MCAGCC. It was there, during the collective euphoria that greeted the return of Gulf War veterans in 1991, that her daughter met her fate at the hand of Underwood. A child of U.S. empire, Rosalie Ortega fell victim to the "longest undeclared war in American history, the military war on female civilians."[49] More specifically, it is yellow female civilians who have been victimized by the "undeclared war" against them by the U.S. military, whose charge it is to enforce Pax Americana throughout the Asian world.

Mass Murder Elite

A recently published indictment against Henry Kissinger offers convincing proof that the former National Security Adviser (later Secretary of State) qualifies as a "war criminal" in accordance with the principles of international human rights law. The indiscriminate bombing of neutral nations during the Vietnam War ordered by Kissinger and President Richard M. Nixon had devastating consequences for the victims of their cynical political ploys. "As a result of the expanded and intensified bombing campaigns," writes Christopher Hitchens, "it has been estimated that as many as 350,000 civilians in Laos, and 600,000 in Cambodia, lost their lives."[50] To this day bombs and land mines maim and kill those unfortunate enough to stumble across the tons of ordnance that remain undetonated thirty-five years after the end of the Vietnam War. In addition, chemical defoliants such as Agent Orange continue to plague the civilian population with serious health problems, including high rates of stillbirths and physical abnormalities among the newborn.

While the list of particulars lodged against former Harvard University professor Kissinger offers irrefutable proof of his central role in inflicting death and destruction upon sovereign states deemed to be crucial U.S. strategic assets, he is but one figure (albeit an especially evil one) within the larger system of imperial conquest and control conceived and managed by the foreign policy and defense elite. Equally culpable are the foreign policy intellectuals (recruited by President John F. Kennedy and later to work for his successor, Lyndon B. Johnson) who decided the fate of colonized Southeast Asian nations struggling to regain national independence within the postwar world order. In his memoirs, former Secretary of Defense Robert S. McNamara credits National Security Adviser McGeorge Bundy with convincing Johnson to accelerate and intensify the bombing campaign in Vietnam.[51] In three years, "Operation Rolling Thunder" was responsible for more bombs being dropped on Vietnam than on all of Europe during World War II. Yet McNamara (at the risk of playfully offending his admitted "friend" Henry Kissinger) describes his former associate Bundy as "by far the ablest national security adviser I have observed over the last forty years."[52]

In ordering the extermination of human life with such utter callousness, elite policy intellectuals and high-level government bureaucrats such as McNamara and Bundy demonstrate that there is little indeed that separates them from the more notorious mass murderers. Only the grand scale and technocratic impersonality of the crimes conceived and directed by the ruling elite acting under cover of state authority distinguish them from garden variety killers.[53]

Imperial Blowback

Beginning with the Cold War, the permanent warfare state aggressively expanded and intensified its material and social investment in militarism as a way of life both domestically and abroad with the aim of maintaining its global empire. Expanding on the concept of "blowback" as explicated in gripping detail by Chalmers Johnson, it has been argued here that one of the unforeseen consequences of U.S. imperial military rule—with all its destructive might—has been the historically unprecedented rise of serial killing and mass murder. On a smaller scale, the string of domestic murders committed in the summer of 2002 by three soldiers who had returned to Ft. Bragg Army base after seeing duty in Afghanistan, exposed the linkage between domestic violence and hyper-militarist American culture.[54]

The notion of blowback is "shorthand for saying that a nation reaps what it sows," writes Johnson, "even if it does not fully know or understand what it has sown." Johnson continues:

> Given its wealth and power, the United States will be a prime recipient in the foreseeable future of all of the more expectable forms of blowback, particularly terrorist attacks against Americans in and out of the armed forces anywhere on earth, including within the United States.[55]

At the formal sentencing of Timothy McVeigh held two months after his June 2, 1997, conviction, the battle-tested soldier invoked the words of Supreme Court Justice Louis D. Brandeis as a summary public statement of his beliefs. "Our government is the potent, the omnipresent teacher," Brandeis wrote in a 1928 dissenting court opinion that reflected his commitment to the preservation of individual rights against the encroachment of state power. "For good or ill, it teaches the whole people by its example." But as pointed out by the authorized biographers of McVeigh, Brandeis goes on to write, "If the government becomes a lawbreaker, it breeds contempt for law; it invites every man to become a law unto himself, it invites anarchy."[56]

In a remarkable correspondence conducted over three years between McVeigh and Gore Vidal, letters from a homegrown terrorist reveal a man waging a clearsighted personal campaign against an "increasingly militaristic and violent" federal government that was becoming "increasingly hostile" toward even its own citizens. McVeigh summed up his motives for the anti-government attack on the Murrah Federal Building by arguing that "what occurred in Oklahoma City was no different than what Americans rain on the heads of others all the time. . . ."[57] The new breed of serial killer and mass murderer, like their counterparts who occupy high office in the service of state-sponsored violence, are but the spawn of what Brandeis perceptively described as our most "potent" and "omnipresent teacher." There is a straight line that connects Ted Bundy with McGeorge Bundy.

Notes

1. Vincent Bugliosi with Curt Gentry, *Helter Skelter: The True Story of The Manson Murders* (New York: W. W. Norton, 1994 [Orig. 1974]), 541. Manson issued this statement after his January 25, 1971, conviction in the Tate-LaBianca murders.
2. Tommy Udo, *Charles Manson: Music Mayhem Murder* (London: Sanctuary, 2002), 35.
3. Colin Wilson, *The Mammoth Book of the History of Murder* (New York: Carroll & Graf, 2000).
4. Ibid., 402.
5. Robert K. Ressler and Tom Shachtman, *Whoever Fights Monsters* (New York: St. Martin's, 1993), 32–33.
6. Robert K. Ressler and Tom Shachtman, *I Have Lived in the Monster: Inside the Minds of the World's Most Notorious Serial Killers* (New York: St. Martin's, 1998), 51.
7. Eric W. Hickey, *Serial Murderers and Their Victims*, 2nd ed. (Belmont, CA: Wadsworth, 1997), 134.
8. Robert D. Keppel with William J. Birnes, *The Riverman: Ted Bundy and I Hunt for the Green River Killer* (New York: Pocket Books, 1995), 454.
9. Ann Rule, *The Stranger Beside Me*, rev. ed. (New York: Signet, 1989), 496.
10. James Alan Fox and Jack Levin, *Overkill: Mass Murder and Serial Killing Exposed* (New York: Dell Books, 1996), 159.
11. Ibid., 190.
12. John Douglas and Mark Olshaker, *The Anatomy of Motive: The FBI's Legendary Mindhunter Explores the Key to Understanding and Catching Violent Criminals* (New York: Pocket Books, 2000), 269.
13. Noam Chomsky, *Rogue States: The Rule of Force in World Affairs* (Boston: South End Press, 2000), 169.
14. Dane Archer and Rosemary Gartner, *Violence and Crime in Cross-National Perspective* (New Haven and London: Yale University Press, 1984).
15. Ibid., 75.
16. The reported relationship between their sexuality, politics, and alleged involvement in the shootings is found in "Gay Secret That Made Snipers Kill," *The National Enquirer* (14 Nov. 02), 34–37.
17. Karen Tumulty and Viveca Novak, "Dodging the Bullet," *Time* (04 Nov. 02), 46.
18. Megan K. Stack and John-Thor Dahlburg, "Pair Had Little Beyond Each Other," *Los Angeles Times*, national edition (27 Oct. 02), 16.
19. Amanda Ripley, "Behind the Killer Smiles," *Time* (04 Nov. 02), 34–41.
20. Stanley Karnow, *In Our Image: America's Empire in the Philippines* (New York: Ballantine Books, 1990), 194.
21. For a brief survey see William Blum, *Rogue State: A Guide to the World's Only Superpower* (Monroe, ME: Common Courage Press, 2000), 125–167.
22. The City of Oklahoma City Document Management Team, *Final Report: Alfred P. Murrah Federal Building Bombing* (Stillwater, OK: Fire Protection Publications, Oklahoma State University, 1996), ix.
23. Robert Jay Lifton, *Destroying the World to Save It: Aum Shinriky, Apocalyptic Violence, and the New Global Terrorism* (New York: Owl Books, 2000), 328.
24. For an excellent investigation into government misconduct against followers of the Branch Davidian sect, see the Academy Award-nominated documentary film *Waco: The Rules of Engagement* (1997), directed by William Gazecki.
25. See Gerry Spence, *From Freedom to Slavery: The Rebirth of Tyranny in America* (New York: St. Martin's Paperbacks, 1995), 17–61. The lead defense attorney for Randy Weaver, Spence warns against abuses of the police state.
26. Bruce Henderson, *Trace Evidence: The Search for the I-5 Strangler* (New York: Onyx, 1999), 288.
27. Michael D. Kelleher and C. L. Kelleher, *Murder Most Rare: The Female Serial Killer* (New York: Dell, 1999), 109.
28. John-Thor Dahlburg, "Serial Killer's Life Still Intrigues on the Eve of Her Death," *Los Angeles Times*, national edition (9 Sept. 02), A6.

29. S. E. Anderson, *The Black Holocaust For Beginners* (New York: Writers and Readers Publishers, 1995), 159.

30. Ward Churchill, *A Little Matter of Genocide: Holocaust and Denial in the Americas, 1491 to the Present* (San Francisco: City Lights Books, 1997), 137.

31. The term "sociopath" has been replaced by the descriptor "antisocial personality disorder."

32. Jim Marrs, *Rule By Secrecy: The Hidden History that Connects the Trilateral Commission, the Freemasons, and the Great Pyramids* (New York: Perennial, 2000), 139.

33. Linedecker, 274.

34. Robert K. Ressler and Tom Shachtman, *I Have Lived in the Monster: Inside the Minds of the World's Most Notorious Serial Killers* (New York: St. Martin's, 1998), 140.

35. Lionel Dahmer, *A Father's Story* (New York: Avon Books, 1995), 155.

36. Richard Tithecott, *Of Men and Monsters: Jeffrey Dahmer and the Construction of the Serial Killer* (Madison: University of Wisconsin Press, 1997), 85.

37. Robert D. Keppel with William J. Birnes, *Signature Killers: Interpreting the Calling Cards of the Serial Murderer* (New York: Pocket Books, 1997), 274.

38. Don Davis, *The Milwaukee Murders: Nightmare in Apartment 213: The True Story*, rev. ed. (New York: St. Martin's, 1995), 12.

39. Kathy Braidhill, *Evil Secrets* (New York: Pinnacle Books, 1996), 147.

40. Ibid., 349.

41. Ibid., 302.

42. Susan Faludi, *Stiffed: The Betrayal of the American Man* (New York: Perennial, 2000), 329.

43. Theo Wilson, *Headline Justice: Inside the Courtroom: The Country's Most Controversial Trials* (New York: Thunder's Mouth Press, 1996), 177.

44. Colin Wilson and Damon Wilson, *The Killers Among Us: Motives Behind Their Madness* (New York: Warner Books, 1996), 334–5.

45. *Yahoo Daily News*, "Ex-Senator Kerrey Admits Role in Vietnam Massacre" (25 Apr. 01), http://dailynews.yahoo.com/h/mm/20010425/ts/politics kerrey dc 1.html

46. Evan Thomas, "Coming to Terms With a Tragedy," *Newsweek* (7 May 01), 37.

47. Philip Carlo, *The Night Stalker: The Life and Crimes of Richard Ramirez* (New York: Pinnacle Books, 1997), 160.

48. Joanna Bourke, *An Intimate History of Killing: Face to Face Killing in 20th Century Warfare* (New York: Basic Books, 1999), 3.

49. Deanne Stillman, *Twentynine Palms: A True Story of Murder, Marines, and the Mojave* (New York: Perennial, 2002), 110.

50. Christopher Hitchens, *The Trial of Henry Kissinger* (New York: Verso, 2001), 35.

51. Genteel criminality runs in the Bundy family. The older brother of McGeorge, William P. Bundy, served as Assistant Secretary of Defense for International Security Affairs under Johnson. Family patriarch Harvey H. Bundy was assistant to Henry L. Stimson. Stimson's career at the service of empire dates to his position as U.S. governor of the Philippines prior to joining the Hoover administration as Secretary of State. Like Kissinger, McGeorge Bundy was a professor at Harvard University before entering government service.

52. Robert S. McNamara with Brian VanDeMark, *In Retrospect: The Tragedy and Lessons of Vietnam* (New York: Vintage Books, 1996), 95.

53. Mass murderers invariably work alone, while government insiders operate under the cover of state authority. Bundy, for example, headed the 303 Committee formed by Kennedy in 1961 after the Bay of Pigs fiasco to manage all U.S. covert operations. Richard H. Shultz, Jr., *The Secret War Against Hanoi: The Untold Story of Spies, Saboteurs, and Covert Warriors in North Vietnam* (New York: Perennial, 2000), 6.

54. Chris Kraul, "Ft. Bragg Murders Prompt Military Efforts to Relieve the Stress of Duty," *Los Angeles Times* (15 Sept. 02), A3.

55. Chalmers Johnson, *Blowback: The Costs and Consequences of American Empire* (New York: Owl Books, 2001), 223.

56. Lou Michel and Dan Herbeck, *American Terrorist: Timothy McVeigh & the Oklahoma City Bombing* (New York: ReganBooks, 2001), 352.

57. Gore Vidal, "The Meaning of Timothy McVeigh," *Vanity Fair* (September 2001), 410.

CHAPTER 13

Militarism and Family Terrorism

RHONDA HAMMER

"Repeat a lie often enough, and people will believe you."
—Joseph Goebbels, Minister of Propaganda, Nazi Party

Recent discussions of terrorism, provoked by the September 11, 2001 attacks on the U.S. and the Bush administration's militarist and unilateralist response to them, generally fail to recognize that terrorism and militarism often find their basis in patriarchal codes which permeate a variety of political, social, economic, and cultural relations of everyday life. Here I want to explore the relationship between militarism and what I call "family terrorism" and to further theorize multiple forms of violence in terms of relations between individualized, familial, public, nationalized, and globalized terrains. I will employ critical feminist theories that offer broad perspectives on terrorism and militarism that include in their rudiments patriarchal violence and domination, in order to address dimensions neglected in many current discussions.[1]

Although some of the most significant debates on war, terrorism, and militarism are being generated by progressive movements, the underlying codes of patriarchy that are so fundamental to any understanding of the concrete and ideological dimensions of terrorism, war, nationalism, and globalization, are often overlooked or underestimated. Moreover, the real human atrocities resulting from these pathological practices are sometimes minimized or reduced to one-dimensional statistics.

The material conditions of militarization and war, especially contemporary warfare, are often forgotten or downplayed within the discourse of much of the discussion of terrorism. As a case in point, the bombing of Afghanistan "has been treated as if human beings are of little consequence."[2] It becomes, instead, a distorted and decontextualized abstraction that is translated as a "war on terrorism," rather than a war on men, women, and children. This is only one manner of ideological mystification of the real, material conditions of human beings that are violated in war and terrorism. Yet, as some feminists reveal, one of the most significant sets of relations, mandatory for any understanding and credible analysis, is recognition of one of the most persuasive lacunae in the interrogations of terrorisms in globalized, nationalized, militarized, and so-called private domains. Gender, or what Cynthia Enloe identifies as "gender blindness," characterizes much work on violence, especially studies of nationalism and the military.[3] What many critical feminists and human rights activists make clear is that "militarization itself, like nationalist identity, is gendered."[4]

This failure to recognize the significance of gender (and sexuality) in war and terrorism is a reflection of a wider disregard for seriously considering gender, and patriarchal codes, in analyzing the escalating violence which defines so much of everyday life. As Catherine Lutz and Jon Elliston put it in their analysis of a recent U.S. epidemic of murders by soldiers of their wives during the summer of 2002 in Fort Bragg, North Carolina:

> In the Pentagon's approach to the problem and virtually all media accounts, *gender has been left hidden in plain sight.* As in the 1990s schoolyard shootings, where a rhetoric of "kids killing kids" disguised the fact that boys were overwhelmingly the killers, here the soldiers are seen simply as an occupational group and the problem, at most, as one of an institutional culture where soldiers have difficulty "asking for help" from family service providers abundantly available at installations like Bragg (*emphasis mine*).[5]

Diana Russell goes on to argue that "the fact that is repeatedly erased by these gender-neutral statements is that it is almost always males, not females, who act out in violent ways" in too many kinds of terrorist situations.[6]

One of the most shocking ideological distortions in describing terrorist activities and/or conditions of war involves the insidious employment of the term "collateral damage." This term has been used extensively in contemporary wars, especially the war against terror in Afghanistan.[7] As Julie Mertis and Jasmina Tesanovic demonstrate, "in contemporary warfare, 95 percent of the casualties are civilians, the majority of them women and children.[8] During the Gulf War, in February, 1991, for example, U.S. planes bombed an air raid shelter in Baghdad, killing 400–500 people—mostly women and children – who were huddled there to escape the incessant bombing."[9] A report published in early December, 2001, estimated that the number of civilian casualties in the first nine weeks of the war against Afghanistan was 3,767.[10] George W. Bush exploited the cause of women in his justification for military attacks on Afghanistan. But in fact:

> This war was not a war for women's liberation; it was a war of revenge. And it was the utmost hypocrisy for George and Laura to shed tears over the oppression of women in Afghanistan when women are treated essentially as badly in Saudi Arabia, and the First Family doesn't say a word about that.[11]

Indeed Bush's claims that he was liberating "women of cover (sic)," would be laughable if the consequences of the attacks were not so dire for the large majority of civilians, most of whom are women, children, and the elderly.[12] Ignoring RAWA's (Revolutionary Association of the Women of Afghanistan) and other Afghan women's opposition to war, Bush and his coalition later dismissed recommendations of women activists from the Human Rights Commission of Pakistan (HRCP) and the European Union as well as RAWA that demanded "the United Nations play a pivotal role in the formation of post-Taliban government in Afghanistan and through elections."[13] Speaking at a news conference in Islamabad on November 3, 2001, representatives of these women's groups "called for the elimination of all fundamentalist groups without any exception or conditions, paving the way for free elections."[14] Sahar Saba of RAWA insisted that Bush and his allies not support replacement of the Taliban with warlords or the Northern Alliance, which she denounced as criminals and enemies of the people. Yet this is exactly what came to pass and the costs to the Afghan people have been enormous.

The American/coalition war forced Afghan civilians into refugee camps in Pakistan, Iran, and elsewhere. Afghan citizens have faced intense poverty, drought, and landmine infestation for decades owing to continuing strife and wars in the country.

> For more than 20 years Afghanistan has also produced the world's largest refugee group ever, at times as high as 6.2 million persons. Currently, numbering 2.6 million, Afghan refugees comprise mostly women, children and the elderly, and are still the largest displaced population in the world. . . . Over one million civilians have been killed as a result of the fighting in Afghanistan, but those that survive face unending hardships. Afghan refugees experience poverty, lack of rights, discrimination, and harassment. Facilities in the refugee villages remain primitive and life is often harsh with a chronic lack of food, medical care and other basic necessities.[15]

> Severe mental illness, distress and post-traumatic syndromes are rampant throughout the civilian population and the many refugee camps they populate. A 1997 UNICEF study found that 54 percent of children had already witnessed seeing someone tortured. Although difficult to document, RAWA found that close to 90 percent of urban women suffered from psychological disorders resulting from terrorist actions provoked by the war.[16]

Sex trafficking, rapes, and other forms of abuse continue under the new regime. "The International Federation of the Red Cross reported that girls in the western part of the country, some as young as 10, were being sold as 'brides' for as little as 100 kilograms of flour."[17] Moreover, it appears that the Taliban's extensive kidnapping and/or purchase of children for sex slavery is not exclusive to their regime. Many of these children and women continue to be missing.[18] Since the rules of law are still "in shambles, the family of a kidnapped girl or woman has no real means of reporting the incident and having the police investigate."[19]

Even First Lady Zeenat Karzai, wife of Afghan President Hamid Karzai, is under tight security and rarely ventures beyond the palace, for fear of abduction.

> Zeenat's family has fears of her being kidnapped by people opposed to the transitional government. If kidnapped, Zeenat could be used to pressure Karzai into possibly giving up his presidency or giving in to warlord interests.[20]

And although women are no longer required to wear the burqa (the rule having been lifted in December 2001), many are too afraid to remove it in public because they are terrified of harassment and/or abduction. Thus most women are frightened to leave their homes at night and feel that even during the day, wearing a headscarf does not provide enough protection.[21]

While the Bush regime would have us believe that life has gotten and will get better for the Afghan people (if you are not Taliban, or a Taliban sympathizer), in reality, the situation for women, and children particularly, has not gotten better, and many argue has gotten worse, since the U.S. intervention. The change in rule from Taliban to Northern Alliance has made little difference regarding imprisonment of women for "offenses such as adultery and dating men not chosen by their families."[22] Violence against women is so extreme that women's rights groups are now calling for expansion of the International Security Assistance Force (ISAF).[23] Yet it has only 5,000 troops and the U.S. has now ruled out the possibility of using U.S. personnel as peacekeepers.[24]

Indeed, Bush and his allies appeared to have reneged on their 4.5 billion-dollar pledge for reconstruction promised at the Tokyo conference in January, 2002. According to Deputy Defense Secretary Paul Wolfowitz, barely 30 percent of what was promised for the year was delivered.[25] Although the U.S. has contributed $300 million for reconstruction and ISAF efforts in Afghanistan, far less than originally pledged, Washington spent "an estimated $1 billion a month on the Afghan war effort—a fact strongly criticized by the UN's special representative for Afghanistan."[26] Meanwhile, conditions in Afghanistan remain horrendous.

> RAWA paints a bleak picture of Afghanistan today, where two decades of war have demolished nearly all infrastructure. They say the country lacks banks, communication systems, and adequate food. "The country's main concern is how to fight for a piece of bread," says [Tamaheena] Faryal. "People have had to sell their own children." The devastation has left Afghani citizens hopeless.[27]

Maternal mortality rates among Afghans are among the highest in the world. One fourth of Afghan children do not survive their fifth birthday. Literacy rates are also extremely low, barely above four percent for women. [And] Afghanistan has the lowest UN gender development ranking in the world.[28] Yet in the George and Laura feminist puppet show, Bush's signing of The Afghan Women and Children Relief Act of 2001, promising educational and medical assistance to Afghan women and children, met a U-turn: "In July, the White House bowed to conservative Christian pressure and cut $34 million from the United Nations Population Fund (UNFPA), which provides reproductive health services for women in 142 countries."[29]

It is within this context of escalating violence against children and women that I refer to the concept "family terrorism" to demonstrate the far-reaching, multidimensional quality, as well as massive quantity, of abuse, terror, and torture, often described as "domestic abuse"—a concept far too benign and limited to signify the complex nature of family violence that, I argue, is better articulated by the expression "family terrorism." This term far better represents the contextual and systemic nature of relations of subordination, domination, and violence through which those in hierarchical positions of power control others. It is these kinds of inequitable power relations, which include the politics of gender, race, class, and ethnicity, that underlie various terrorist ideologies and practices.

To understand the complexities and implications of family terrorism, it is necessary that the multidimensional nature of individual and collective abusive relations be situated in a larger sociopolitical, economic, and cultural context. Myriad interrelated forms of family terrorism must be located within a dialectical understanding of patriarchal codes and ideology, which are hardly exclusive to capitalism. As Enloe reminds us:

> Feminists have shown in their research and in their campaigns for reform that ideas about what constitutes acceptable behavior by men can share patriarchal tendencies and yet vary in surprising ways across cultures. Patriarchy does not come in "one size fits all."[30]

Accordingly, I reexamine the notion of the domestic and private spheres in relation to patriarchal privilege and the abuse and battery of women and children within the wider context of the community, national, global, public, and private spheres.

Patriarchal Violence, Colonization, and Militarism

The employment of colonization theory, applied by many feminists to dissect terror relations at both local and global levels, provides for a deeper understanding of the complexities and multidimensional nature of family terrorism. Translating from classic works on colonization illuminates multifaceted relationships of violence and terror, especially those directed against women, children, and the elderly. Colonization is not just restricted to physical deprivation, legal inequality, and economic exploitation. Sandra Bartky identifies a pathological dimension which is essential to the process of colonization and terrorism that Frantz Fanon, trained as a psychologist before taking up revolutionary writings and practice, described as "psychic alienation."[31]

> To be psychologically oppressed is to be weighed down in your mind; it is to have a harsh dominion exercised over your self-esteem. The psychologically oppressed become their own oppressors; they come to exercise harsh dominion over their own self-esteem. Differently put, psychological oppression can be regarded as the "internalization of intimidations."[32]

The complexities of psychological states of peoples involved in pathologies of colonization and terrorisms are often subordinated or ignored in analytical discussions of these kinds of relations. Yet, understandings of family terrorism necessitate recognition of this most sophisticated dimension of colonization. The pathological characteristics of colonization and its role in family terrorisms reveal the complexities of what is often called the "master/slave dialectic."[33] Distinctions between patriarchal codes and essentialized behaviors of a generalized "class of men" become even more apparent when discussed within the context of colonization as an elaborate process usually involving colonizer, colonized, and collaborator. In relation to women's and children's situations, for example, transformative feminists like Enloe maintain that

> To describe colonization as a process that has been carried on solely by men overlooks the way male colonizers' success depended on some women's complicity. Without the willingness of "respectable" women to see that colonization offered them an opportunity for adventure, or a new chance of financial security or moral commitment, colonization would have been even more problematic.[34]

Colonization cannot be addressed in simplistic Manichean or reductionist terms that essentialize men as oppressors and women as oppressed, or that infer that all women suffer the same degree of subordination. Women can be both colonizer and colonized and can be instruments of family terrorism against children and the elderly as well as instruments of colonization in relation to other women and even men. Thus colonization is a dialectical set of hierarchical relations involving class, race, ethnicity, gender (sexuality), age, nationalism, and other factors that are often interconnected and multiple.

A transformative feminist approach expands upon the notions and realities of battery, terrorization, and abuse of women and children to include relations of the state, cultural and global terrorism of women and children in the forms of feminization of poverty, hunger, exploited labor and slavery, prostitution and the sex trade, arguing that these are expansive forms of the ideology of family terrorism, given that family members, cultural communities, and the state are actively involved in such atrocities. Moreover, as many transformative feminists argue, violence against men—especially during war—is often mediated through the abuse, murder, rape, and torture of familial women and children of the enemy. Gender politics and the relationship between localized and globalized family terrorism, alienation, and colonization, are rarely discussed in terms of violence against women and children in the context of militarism. Yet violence against women, by men, escalates during conditions of war, and many experts argue that modern wars are in themselves acts of terrorism. Thus Zinn argues that: "Terrorism and war have something in common. They both involve the killing of innocent people to achieve what the killers believe is a good end."[35]

Patriarchal family values and violence against women and children must be taken into account in any analysis of "nationalist, communalist and religious fundamentalist social movements which have emerged all over the world," which, as Meredith Tax argues, have moved into "the power vacuum created as local elites have been overwhelmed by the new global financial ruling class."[36] It is within this translation of the patriarchal family to the "localized, national or globalized family" that violence, torture, and rape of women and girls is better understood.

I believe the term family terrorism is even more appropriate given the devastating effects of September 11, especially since certain forces are restricting the term to exclude particular Western actions, as well as patriarchal violence and terror. It is within this contested field of discourse that feminists need to develop critical definitions of terrorisms that go beyond identifying them as purely individual and collective crimes but as an *ideology*. It is within this context that describing specific patriarchal relations of abuse, rape, murder, starvation, poverty, exploitation, torture, and genocide is especially relevant.

"Terrorism": Multiple Realities and Ideological Constructs

A discussion of this polysemous term, "family terrorism," for understanding terrorism, militarism, and a multiplicity of social, political, psychic, and economic relations, is necessary. It is especially relevant given the contentious meaning and use of "terrorism," in Bush's 2001 declaration of a war against terrorism and "evil,"[37] endorsed and supported by a so-called coalition of other nations.[38] Its conflicted meanings have allowed for a plethora of changing delineations that are not only contradictory but are being used to serve hegemonic political interests. Such limited definitions of terrorism are seriously damaging the true impact and contextual meaning of the term, while concealing or ignoring the multidimensionality of terrorism regarding individual and global human rights, including violence directed at disenfranchised peoples, especially women, children, and the elderly.

Regarding what many consider to be a decontextualized reading of "terrorism," Edward Said identifies a serious lack of "analysis and reflection" on the complexities of terrorism within a global context. The absence of this kind of critical thinking has had grave consequences.

> Take the word "terrorism." It has become synonymous now with anti-Americanism, which, in turn, has become synonymous with being critical of the United States, which, in turn, has become synonymous with being unpatriotic. That's an unacceptable series of equations.[39]

Ruth Conniff notes that much of the "media flag waving" in the U.S. since September 11 has been motivated by cynicism and fear, "specifically of being deemed unpatriotic by self-appointed conservative watchdogs . . . who are armed with lists of the unpatriotic compiled by the right-wing Media Research

Center"[40] and Lynne Cheney's Committee to Protect American Civilization.[41] It would seem that not only journalists but educators and intellectuals are especially at risk, given that Ms. Cheney and Senator Joseph Lieberman's American Council of Trustees and Alumni issued a report called "Defending Civilization: How our Universities are Failing America, and What can be Done About It." Their neo-McCarthyist report "cited 100 examples of what it considers unpatriotic acts by specific academics."[42] It appears that the lines have become so blurred and connotations of "patriotism" so obscured within the new American ideology of terrorism, that Democrat Barbara Lee, the sole member of Congress who voted against the September 14 House Bill that "granted President Bush broad authority to use force to counter the terrorist attacks on the World Trade Center and the Pentagon," has had death threats and has been attacked as anti-American and a "traitor."[43]

Anti-terrorism legislation, known as the USA Patriot Act, was signed by Bush on October 26, 2001, after being passed by the House and Senate, with virtually no public hearings, debates, or committee reports. The text has been described as the most unpatriotic measure ever enacted.[44] Employing a vague definition of terrorism, clearly associated with so-called anti-American behavior, the draconian legislation circumvents and negates those very constitutional rights upon which freedom and democracy were established. Ron Paul, a Republican congressman from Texas who voted against the act, characterized the anti-terrorist legislation as "a clear violation of the civil liberties of all Americans."[45] He goes on to describe how this expansive, inaccessible, and often unread bill, "which undermined the principles of individual freedom and liberties in this country," was forced through by Bush and his executive.

> It was called Patriot Act because they didn't want anyone to vote against it, claiming that if you didn't vote for it you weren't a patriotic American citizen.[46]

According to Nadine Strossen, president of the ACLU, these kinds of anti-terrorism mandates have serious implications:

> The term "terrorism" is taking on the same kind of characteristics as the term "communism" did in the 1950s. It stops people in their tracks, and they're willing to give up their freedoms. People are too quickly panicked. They are too willing to give up their rights and to scapegoat people, especially immigrants and people who criticize the war.[47]

Such antiterrorist legislation, combined with U.S. international policies and military actions, is identified by many scholars, activists, and legislators as terrorist in itself. It would seem to fall within the framework of classical American definitions of terrorism in "official U.S. documents: 'the calculated use of violence to attain goals that are political, religious, or ideological in nature. This is done through intimidation, coercion, or instilling fear.' "[48] However, as Chomsky points out, this appropriate meaning of the term has been displaced by an expanding global "propagandistic usage" that is "used to refer to terrorist acts committed by enemies against our allies."[49] Such propagandistic use of "terrorism" not only negates the real essence of the term, but can also reify what are essentially terrorist ideologies and practices within an imaginary antiterror mind-set. For it was this characterization of terrorism that delineated Nazi " 'counter-terrorism' against terrorist partisans."[50] As Zinn observes, new U.S. legislation allows the Secretary of State to designate any organization as terrorist "and his decision is not subject to review."[51] The current U.S. government, in fact, appears to be implementing laws and practices that meet with its country's own established definitions of terrorism, in that:

> The USA Patriot Act defines "a domestic terrorist" as someone who violates the law and is engaged in activities that "appear to be intended to . . . influence the policy of government by intimidation or coercion." This could make many activist organizations subject to designation as terrorist organizations. As for noncitizens—and there are twenty million of them in the United States—they can now be subject to indefinite detention and deportation.[52]

Moreover, the pernicious order that Bush signed on November 13, 2001, which "authorized extra-constitutional military tribunals," allows him to arrogate "the right to apprehend 'any individual who is not a United States citizen' and subject that person to a secret military trial and then impose the death penalty."[53] Here Bush has further ignored traditional notions of terrorism and expanded on his propagandized doublespeak version of the term, mocking any just U.S. usage, further altering its meaning and the powers it affords him and his junta.

The ambiguous nature of the term "terrorism" has serious consequences for human rights at a global level, signalling UN diplomatic work on a counterterror convention is being impeded by lack of agreement on who or what constitutes a terrorist.[54] Moreover, demands "by the Security Council that UN members act against global terrorism are being used to justify repression of domestic dissent, UN officials and independent human rights advocates say."[55] In fact: "The anti-terrorism campaign has been used by authoritarian governments to justify moves to clamp down on moderate opponents, outlaw criticism of rulers and expand the use of capital punishment."[56]

The term "terrorism" has been used for some time as a concept to pursue specific policy objectives. George Shultz, Ronald Reagan's secretary of state, described terrorism as "a threat to Western civilization" and a "menace to Western moral values."[57] Michael Kinsley points out that defining "terrorism" was a major industry in Washington during the 1980s and that there remains no adequate or agreed upon explanation.[58] These lacunae, along with ever-changing, propagandistic definitions of the term, could be viewed as self-serving insofar as they exclude particular U.S. actions.

The U.S. commitment to end terrorism appears especially hypocritical given that in 1997 the government rejected the jurisdiction of the International Court of Justice, which "condemned the U.S. for the 'unlawful use of force,' ordering Washington to cease its *international terrorism*, violation of treaties, and illegal economic warfare, and to pay substantial reparations" (emphasis mine).[59] Yet, as Chomsky notes, this judgment was rarely reported by mainstream mass media.[60] While appalling, it is hardly surprising given escalating corporate concentration within the mass media. It appears that much of the media has collaborated with government and business to carry out propagandistic versions of terrorism and antidemocratic global policies.

The Bush administration manipulation of the discourse of terrorism and media complicity in its war policy makes it all the more urgent to clarify modes of terrorism. One such mode is what I call "family terrorism."

Family Terrorism

I have developed the concept "family terrorism" to provoke a dialectical shift in addressing issues of violence against women, children, and the elderly, which is far more extensive and interrelated with social, political, and economic dimensions than what conventional thinking about violence or abuse of women and children usually signifies. Family terrorism in its first sense reveals and critiques the problematic nature of such ideological references as "domestic violence" or its latest incarnation "intimate partner abuse," which even further neutralizes the complexity of relationships. As Ann Jones explains:

> "Domestic violence"[61] is one of those gray phrases, beloved of bureaucracy, designed to give people a way of talking about a topic without seeing what's really going on. Like "repatriation" or "ethnic cleansing," it's a euphemistic abstraction that keeps us at a dispassionate distance, far removed from the repugnant spectacle of human beings in pain.[62]

According to bell hooks, "domestic violence" has been used to cover up the severity and systematic nature of family terrorism. She argues that it is "a 'soft' term which suggests it emerges in an intimate context that is private and somehow less threatening, less brutal, than the violence that takes place outside the home."[63]

> This is not so, since more women are beaten and murdered in the home than on the outside. Also most people tend to see domestic violence between adults as separate and distinct from violence against children when it is not. Often children suffer abuse as they attempt to protect a mother who is being attacked by a male companion or husband, or they are emotionally damaged by witnessing violence and abuse.[64]

Jones points out that it was during the Carter administration that discourses such as "wife beating" were replaced with neutral "professional vocabularies" such as "spouse abuse," "conjugal violence," "marital aggression," and "domestic violence."[65] "[A] great renaming took place, a renaming that veiled once again the sexism a grass-roots women's movement had worked to uncover."[66] The term "partner abuse" or "intimate partner violence"[67] further neutralizes violent relations in terms of both gender and sexuality. For example, note the ambiguous and potentially misleading statistical findings cited from *National Violence Against Women (NVAW) Survey*, co-sponsored by the National Institute of Justice and the Centers for Disease Control.

> Intimate partner violence is pervasive in U.S. society. Nearly 25 percent of surveyed women and 7.6 percent of surveyed men said they were raped and/or physically assaulted by a current or former spouse, cohabiting partner, or date at some time in their lifetime.[68]

Not only does this finding, in conjunction with the language used, misrepresent the real sexual politics of male violence but also makes it appear as if women's violence against men has become the norm and is even escalating. Moreover, the inclusion of same-sex violence in homosexual relationships is hardly delineated by such research findings and is often only elucidated later. Further, distinctions between lesbian and gay partner violence are not always apparent, although in this study it was documented in later parts, or subsections of such studies, which many people do not read or have access to. Much later in the study it is documented that:

> Intimate partner violence is more prevalent among male same-sex couples than female same-sex couples. . . . These findings [from the NVAW survey] indicate that intimate partner violence is perpetrated primarily by men, whether against same-sex or opposite-sex partners.[69]

Jones points out that "the usefulness of the term [intimate partner violence] lies in its gender neutrality, for it conveniently hides one undeniable fact: that despite the real problem of violence committed by women against women, the assailant in [most] heterosexual *and* homosexual violence is a man."[70] It is here that my use of the term "family terrorism" is also used to address terrorism in a more multidimensional manner, in which the abuse and neglect of children and the elderly is emphasized. Moreover, this term draws on work of feminists like Linda Gordon, who sees family violence as "a political issue."[71] She discusses the abuse and neglect of children within a contextual framework that includes the role of women in terrorizing and/or neglecting their children. Central to Gordon's analysis is the mediating effect of class and money in circumstances of family violence. It is in this sense that bell hooks's use of the term "patriarchal violence" is appropriate. As she explains it:

> The term "patriarchal violence" is useful because unlike the more accepted phrase "domestic violence" it continually reminds the listener that violence in the home is connected to sexism and sexist thinking, to male domination.[72]

The abuse of children and the elderly, as well as escalating global violence against women and children, must be understood as a systemic process. Gordon points out that even a "a mother who might never be violent but who teaches her children, especially her sons, that violence is an acceptable means of exerting social control, is still in collusion with patriarchal violence."[73] She clarifies the relationship of patriarchal violence to parental violence and women's role as collaborator and/or colonizer in this relationship.

As Riane Eisler argues in her discussion of how to analyze the events of September 11 and fundamentalist terrorist extremism, we must begin with examining gender and parent-child relations since these "are the critical, formative relations . . . where we first learn what's normal and moral, where we learn values and behaviors."[74] She emphasizes the context of hate and terror within a transformative and dialectical analysis: "Clearly most women do not use violence to dominate men (even though small numbers of women batter the men in their lives) but lots of women believe that a person in authority has the right to use force to maintain authority."[75]

Many critical feminists have associated patriarchal attitudes and violence with militarism. Moreover, a number of feminist studies demonstrate increases in levels of family violence during wartime.[76]

> The forms of violence inflicted against women in wars vary in form, scale, and intensity from killing, rape, torture, forced impregnation, body searches at checkpoints, imprisonment, settlement in concentration camps and refuges, and forced prostitution to verbal insults and degradation, psychological suffering for losses, and the burden of responsibility that women carry as survivors.[77]

Zillah Eisenstein argues that "war rape is sexualized violence that seeks to terrorize, destroy, and humiliate a people through its women."[78]

> . . . genocidal rape has its own horrors. It takes place in isolated rape camps, with strict orders from above to either force the woman's exile or her death. Rape is repeatedly performed as torture; it is used to forcibly impregnate; it is even used to exterminate. Women in the camps are raped repetitively, some as many as thirty times a day for as long as three consecutive months. They are kept hungry, they are beaten and gang-raped, their breasts are cut off, and stomachs split open.[79]

Even under these conditions, however, women cannot be seen as universal in that, as Enloe reminds us, rape in war is often structured by class, ethnic, and racial "inequalities between women."[80] The commoditization and colonization of different women becomes evident in that the rape of these women, in times of war, upheaval, or political conflict "represents conquered territories."[81]

In other words, women and girls are treated as possessions of husbands, fathers, sons, brothers, and so forth, and their violation, torture, and murder are intended to demoralize and humiliate their enemy. As we have seen, women's mediating role occurs through a process in which the external enemy is imagined by other men, who would defile or denigrate the nation.[82] This was the strategy of the Japanese, during World War II, when they "conscripted" at least 200,000 girls and women from Korea, China, Taiwan, Indonesia, and the Philippines as sex slaves or "comfort women." Countless impoverished Asian girls and women were taken from their homes to serve Japanese soldiers, who beat, raped, and murdered them. Some were recruited by force and deception into sexual slavery during the period 1931–1945.[83] It would be absurd to deny elements of family violence involved in these militaristic outrages, especially given that the Japanese recorded these sex slaves as "ammunition," refusing to even acknowledge that its military ran the program until 1993."[84] Some of these women are finally receiving repatriation from a private fund, although they have been treated as pariahs in their own communities and receive nothing from the Japanese government, which has yet to apologize.

Indeed, respect for the human rights of these Othered women is absent in that such raped, battered, and butchered women are considered the familial property of enemy men. This is just one example of how the hierarchical structure of family terrorism underscores the patriarchal family and is naturally translated and embedded into the relations of the public sphere. In fact:

> A primary reason why forms of violence against women, not just rape but also domestic violence and prostitution, have been kept off the international legal agenda is that so many governments, the principal players in United Nations human rights and war crime tribunal negotiations, are opposed to any outside agency being given authority to intervene in any activity deemed to be related to the "family."[85]

Family terrorism involves a vast set of dominant and often invisible relations and, as Charlotte Bunch points out, much of that violence against women and children "is part of a larger socioeconomic web that entraps women, making them vulnerable to abuses that cannot be delineated as exclusively political or solely caused by states."[86] Hence "family terrorism" seems appropriate for describing the interrelated, hierarchical, and multidimensional forms of violence perpetuated against women and children.

This transformed notion of family transcends the bifurcated mythical distinctions between the public and private and subverts the notion of traditional family values within a patriarchal context. This new idea and metaphoric family resides within the borderlands transcending public, private, local, global divides. The meaning and representation of "family terrorism" has much in common with Eisenstein's reconceptualization and reclamation of the public realm that "presumes the interconnectedness of people and their responsibility for each other."[87]

> The IDEA of "public" allows that individual needs are met socially and collectively, and collective needs are identified individually. . . . My notion of "public"

then is both a process—of thinking through and beyond the self—and a place where this happens.[88]

My use of "family terrorism" is intended as a transformative notion, which signifies more radical and dialectical understandings of both the ideas and realities of family and family terrorism. This epistemology allows for the critique and transcendence of patriarchal familial relations, especially necessary given that

> Just as reworking the rhetoric of family for their own political agendas is a common strategy for conservative movements of all types, the alleged unity and solidarity attributed to family is often invoked to symbolize the aspirations of oppressed groups.[89]

It can also be reappropriated to subvert traditional ideological interpretations, including false distinctions between domestic relations and public life. The importance of such dialectical understanding of family life, according to Hill Collins, draws on the "emerging paradigm of intersectionality."[90]

> As opposed to examining gender, race, class, and nation, as separate systems of oppression, intersectionality explores how these systems mutually construct one another, or, in the words of black British sociologist Stuart Hall, how they "articulate" one another.[91]

It is in this sense that I argue the metaphor "family violence" does not go far enough, that the word "violence" is often overused and so liberally applied that it has lost its real meaning and has become neutral and flat. Amnesty International's Global Campaign Against Torture Report, 2001, makes little distinction between violence and "torture" regarding abuse of women and children nor does it recognize the rights of governments and other bodies to distinguish between private and public violence. The report "urges governments to commit themselves to protecting women and girls from torture. Governments which systematically fail to take action to prevent and protect women from violence in the home and community share responsibility for torture and ill-treatment."[92] The report goes on to contextualize torture within a framework of global violence in that it maintains that: "Torture is fed by a global culture which denies women equal rights with men, and which legitimizes violence against women" and that the "perpetuators are agents of the state and armed groups, but most often they are members of their own family, community or employers. For many women, their home is a place of terror."[93]

Even less progressive organizations define male violence against women as "systemic terrorism." For example:

> The NVAW [National Violence Against Women] Survey provides compelling evidence of the link between violence and emotionally abusive and controlling behavior in intimate relationships. Women whose partners verbally abused them, were jealous or possessive, or denied them access to family, friends, and family income were significantly more likely to report being raped, physically assaulted,

and/or stalked by their partners, even when sociodemographic factors such as race and education were controlled. These findings suggest that many women in violent relationships are victims of *systemic terrorism*; that is, they experience multiple forms of abuse and control at the hands of their partners. Future research should focus on the extent to which violence perpetrated against women by intimate partners consists of systemic terrorism and the consequences of this type of victimization.[94]

Escalating conditions of global slavery and trafficking, often through collaboration of the parents of these women and children, intensifies demand for involvement in global feminisms and human rights movements, at every level. Amnesty International expands upon this as follows:

> Women who have been *bought and sold* for forced labor, sexual exploitation and forced marriage are also vulnerable to torture. Trafficking in human beings is the third largest source of profit for international organized crime after drugs and arms.[95]

Traditional notions of battery are being reevaluated in systemic terms as pathology. "Battering is not usually an isolated incident, but rather it tends to be a cycle that increases in frequency and severity over time."[96] Feminist human rights activists like Charlotte Bunch go on to explain such violent relations in terms of "terrorism" "and torture," arguing that abusing women physically is a reminder of the patriarchal territorial domination or colonization of women's bodies (and minds, perhaps) "and is sometimes accompanied by other forms of human rights abuse such as slavery (forced prostitution), sexual terrorism (rape), imprisonment (confinement to the home) and torture (systematic battery). There are extreme cases such as the women in Thailand who died in a brothel fire because they were chained to their beds. Most situations are more ordinary, like denying women decent education or jobs which leaves them prey to abusive marriages, exploitative work, and prostitution."[97] Amnesty International strongly recommends "the public condemnation of violence against women [and children], criminalizing violence against women [and children], investigating all allegations, and prosecuting and punishing the perpetrators."[98]

Notes

1. For the broader theoretical framework that informs this analysis, see Rhonda Hammer, *Antifeminism and Family Terrorism: A Critical Feminist Perspective*. (Lanham, MD: Rowman and Littlefield, 2002).
2. Howard Zinn, *Terrorism and War* (New York: Seven Stories Press, 2002), 33.
3. Cynthia Enloe, *The Morning After: Sexual Politics and the End of the Cold War*. (Berkeley: University of California Press, 1993), 231.
4. Ibid., *The Morning After*, 245.
5. Catherine Lutz and Jon Elliston, "Domestic Terror," *The Nation*, Oct. 14, 2002, 19.
6. Diana Russell. "Introduction: The Politics of Femicide." In *Femicide in Global Perspective*. Edited by Diana E.H. Russell and Roberta A. Harmes. (New York: Teachers College Press, 2001) 4.

7. Marc Herold, "A Dossier on Civilian Victims of United States Aerial Bombing of Afghanistan: A Comprehensive Accounting." www.cursor.org/stories/civilian-deaths.htm. 2002.

8. As documented by Jennifer Rycenga and Marguerite Waller, in their "Introduction." In *Frontline Feminisms: Women, War, and Resistance.* Edited by Marguerite R. Waller and Jennifer Rycenga. (New York: Routledge), xviii.

9. Zinn, "What War Looks Like," 15.

10. Mathew Rothschild, "Comment: Hold the Applause." *The Progressive*, February, 2002, 9.

11. Ibid.

12. Derrick Z. Jackson, *Boston Globe*, 10/17/2001; http://www.boston.com/dailyglobe 2/290oped

13. *The Dawn*, Nov. 4, 2001; http://www.dawn.com/2001/11/04/top17.htm

14. Ibid.

15. *The Afghan Women's Mission*; http://www.afghanwomensmission.org

16. *Los Angeles Times*, July 7, 2002.

17. Maya Jhani, "Women Fight Terror and War in South Asia and the Middle East." *News and Letters*, March 2002, 1;10.

18. Kevin Sullivan, in the *Washington Post Foreign Service* (December 19, 2001, A01) writes: "Taliban soldiers abducted many women and girls, perhaps hundreds or more, during their five-year rule, according to Afghan families, officials of the incoming government and humanitarian aid groups. Many are still missing, and their stories are only now beginning to emerge in the wake of the Taliban's defeat."

19. Halima Kazem, *Women's Enews*, Sept, 13, 2002; http://www.womensenews.org

20. Ibid.

21. Ibid.

22. Valerie Reitman, *Los Angeles Times*, Nov. 11, 2002.

23. Chris Lombardi, *Women's Enews*, Sept. 8, 2002, http://www.womensenews.org

24. Ahmed Rashid, "Afghanistan Imperiled," *The Nation*, Oct. 14, 2002, 16.

25. Ibid.

26. Ibid.

27. Amanda Scapel, *FEM*, Fall 2001, 10.

28. See The Afghan Women's Mission; http://www. afghanwomensmission.org, 2001.

29. Noy Thrupkaew, Nov. 2002. "Money Where His Mouth Is," *The American Prospect*, Sept. 23, 2002, 17. Moreover, Michele Landsberg argues that Bush "withheld the $45 million that both houses of Congress had agreed to give the United Nations Population Fund" due to pressure from the antichoice right-wing extremists in his party (*The Toronto Star*, Jan. 26, 2002; http://torontostar). It is in this context that any credibility in the Bush government's commitment to women and children is destroyed.

30. Enloe, *The Morning After*, 5.

31. Sandra Bartky, *Femininity and Domination: Studies in the Phenomenology of Oppression.* (New York: Routledge, 1990), 22.

32. Ibid.

33. The master-slave dialectic finds its foundations in the work of 19th-century philosopher G.W.F. Hegel. It has been employed and translated from critical scholarship which attempts to understand the complexities of power relations and relations of domination and subordination. Alexandre Kojeve provides for an indication of Hegel's interpretation, and explains that a seminal aspect of this relationship is characterized by the needs of the dominant member to be recognized by the slave as the master. To do so: "He must overcome him 'dialectically.' That is, he must leave him life and consciousness, and destroy only his autonomy. He must overcome the adversary only insofar as the adversary is opposed to him and acts against him. In other words, he must enslave him." See Alexandre Kojeve, *Introduction To The Reading of Hegel.* (New York: Basic Books, 1969), 15.

34. Cynthia Enloe, *Bananas, Beaches and Bases: Making Feminist Sense of International Politics.* (Berkeley: University of California Press, 1990), 5.

35. Howard Zinn. "A Just Cause, Not A Just War." *The Progressive*, (Dec. 2001), 16.

36. Meredith Tax. "World Culture War." *The Nation*, (May 17, 1999), 24.

37. Attorney General John Ashcroft demonstrates the vagarious and ambiguous nature of this denotation of "evil," which allows for serious abuse of power in this regard. For example, he describes this evil in his prepared remarks to the U.S. mayors' conference: "The men and women of justice and law enforcement are called to combat a terrorist threat that is both immediate and vast; a threat that resides here, at home, but whose reporters, patrons and

sympathizers form a multinational network of evil" ("Prepared Remarks for the US Mayors Conference," October 25, 2001).

38. Bush's decision to evoke "a war on terrorism," many argue, demonstrates widespread misrepresentations of the nature of terrorisms. Indeed there has been extensive U.S. and international opposition to this position, which is far too often silenced or ignored by government and commercial media forms. As the editors of *The Progressive* point out, a wide range of peoples from every walk of life have contested this warfare strategy as the appropriate manner in which to address the terrorist attacks on the United States.

39. Edward Said, cited in David Barsamian, "The Progressive Interview: Edward W. Said." *The Progressive*, (Volume 65, Number 11), 44.

40. Ruth Conniff, "Patriot Games." *The Progressive*, (Jan. 2002, Volume 66, number 1), 15.

41. Kate Clinton, "Dressed for Surveillance." *The Progressive*, (Jan. 2002), 11. Indeed, Clinton provides a daunting description of this committee and its powers. Moreover, she points out that, ironically, Todd Gitlin, who has been castigating members of the left that are in opposition to the war in Afghanistan and elsewhere, is on this list for "the highly inflammatory statement, 'There is lot of skepticism about America's policy of going to war.'"

42. Matthew Rothschild, "The New McCarthyism." *The Progressive*, January, 2002, 23.

43. John Nichols. "The Lone Dissenter." *The Progressive*, November 2001, 28.

44. Chang, Nancy, "The USA PATRIOT Act," Center for Constitutional Rights, November, 2001. www.ccr-ny.org/whatsnew/usa_patriot_act.asp; Ron Paul, 2002. In *The Truth and Lies of 9-11*, Sherman Oaks, CA: Michael C. Rapport, FTW (videotape).

45. Ron Paul, in *The Truth and Lies of 9-11*.

46. Ibid.

47. Cited in Matthew Rothschild, "The New McCarthyism," 19.

48. Noam Chomsky, *9-11*, (New York: Seven Stories Press, 2001), 90.

49. Ibid.

50. Ibid.

51. Howard Zinn, "Operation Enduring War," *The Progressive*, (March 2002), 12.

52. Ibid.

53. Editors Comment, "Assault on the Constitution," *The Progressive* (January 2002) 8.

54. *Los Angeles Times*, Oct. 27, 2001.

55. *Los Angeles Times*, Jan. 2, 2002.

56. Ibid.

57. Eqbal Ahmad, "Terrorism: Theirs and Ours." Presentation at the University of Colorado, Boulder, October 12, 1998.

58. Michael Kinsley, "Defining Terrorism." *Slate*, (Thursday, Oct. 4, 21).

59. Noam Chomsky in *Profit Over People: Neoliberalism and Global Order*. (New York: Seven Stories Press, 1999), 73, goes on to note that "the Democratic-controlled Congress reacted by instantly escalating the crimes while the Court was roundly denounced on all sides as a 'hostile forum' that had discredited itself by rendering a decision against the United States. The Court judgment itself was scarcely reported, including the words just quoted and the explicit ruling that U.S. aid to Contras is 'military' and not 'humanitarian.'"

60. Ibid.

61. "Even feminist advocates for women, who called their cause 'the battered women's movement,' eventually succumbed; they adopted 'domestic violence' in their fund raising proposals, so as not to offend men controlling the purse strings by suggesting that men were in any way to blame for this 'social problem.' So well does the phrase 'domestic violence' obscure the real events behind it that when a Domestic Violence Act (to provide money for battered women's services) was first proposed to Congress in 1978, many thought it was a bill to combat political terrorism within the United States." Ann Jones. *Next Time She'll Be Dead: Battering and How to Stop It*. (Boston: Beacon, 1994), 82.

62. Ibid., 81.

63. bell hooks, *Feminism Is For Everybody*. (Cambridge, MA: South End Press, 2000), 62.

64. Ibid.

65. Ann Jones, *Next Time She'll Be Dead*, 81.

66. Ibid., 82.

67. See, for example, Patricia Tjaden and Nancy Thoennes. "Extent, Nature, and Consequences of Partner Violence: Findings From the National Violence Against Women Survey, NIJCDC." Washington, D.C.: U.S. Department of Justice, Office of Justice Programs, July, 2000.

68. Ibid., iii.
69. Ibid., 56.
70. Ann Jones, *Next Time She'll Be Dead*, 84.
71. Linda Gordon. *Heroes of Their Own Lives: The Politics and History of Family Violence—Boston 1880–1960*. (New York: Viking, 1988), 5.
72. bell hooks, *Feminism Is For Everybody*, 62.
73. Linda Gordon, *Heroes of Their Own Lives*, 64.
74. Riane Eisler, "The School for Violence." *LA Weekly* (Sept. 28–Oct. 4, 2001), 33.
75. bell hooks, *Feminism Is For Everybody*, 64.
76. Vesna Kesic, "From Reverence to Rape," 26.
77. Ibid., 25
78. Eisenstein, *Hatreds*, 59.
79. Ibid., 59.
80. Enloe, *The Morning After*, 239.
81. Eisenstein, *Hatreds*, 41.
82. Enloe, *The Morning After*, 239.
83. K Connie Kang, *Los Angeles Times*, July 22, 2001.
84. Ibid.
85. Enloe, *The Morning After*, 243.
86. Ibid.
87. Zillah Eisenstein, *Global Obscenities: Patriarchy, Capitalism and the Lure of Cyberfantasy* (New York: New York University Press, 1998), 6.
88. Ibid.
89. Patricia Hill Collins, "It's All in the Family: Intersections and Gender, Race, and Nation." *Hypatia* (Summer, 1998), Volume 13, number 3, 63.
90. Ibid.
91. Ibid.
92. "Broken bodies, shattered minds—The torture of women worldwide," *Amnesty International News Release*, March 6, 2001, www.amnesty.org
93. Ibid.
94. Patricia Tjaden and Nancy Thoennes. "Extent, Nature, and Consequences of Partner Violence," 56.
95. Ibid.
96. National Center for Victim Crime Virtual Library, 2000, www.ncvc.org
97. Bunch, "Recognizing Women's Rights as Human Rights," 14.
98. Amnesty International, "Broken Bodies, Shattered Minds."

CHAPTER 14

The Hollywood War Machine

TOM POLLARD

The Hollywood War Machine refers to the production of studio films that depict and glorify wartime heroic exploits while embellishing the military experience itself, from the Revolutionary period to the present. The motion picture industry has from its inception been fascinated with combat as a vital part of the American patriotic legacy. War films have for most of cinematic history rivaled the western genre in terms of popular appeal. A survey of the Hollywood film tradition reveals that a surprisingly large proportion of Hollywood films dramatize U.S. wartime experiences, heroics, and engagements. In exploring the Hollywood War Machine and its enormous cultural impact today, several questions emerge: Why do U.S. filmmakers remain fascinated with the phenomenon of armed conflict? Why do combat films have such different levels of appeal over time? Why do various producers and directors choose to emphasize particular wars over others? Above all, why are war films presently enjoying a renaissance? The answers to such questions will help us comprehend the intricate connection between the war experience and the character of the motion picture industry as well as the broader social attitudes and beliefs upon which the Hollywood war machine is nourished.

Hollywood filmmaking was not always oriented toward glorification of American patriotism and militarism. When the popular mood of the country seemed to favor pacifism or isolationism, as during the years immediately preceding both world wars, films tended either to avoid war altogether or to reflect a certain abhorrence of military conflict itself. On the eve of World War I, films depicting wars either emphasized their horrors or, in a few cases, seemed to advocate an ethic of nonviolence. One such anti-war film was *Civilization, or He Who Remembered* (Thomas Ince, 1914), in which the spirit of Christ returns to earth in the body of a great soldier who eventually restores world peace as he sets out to redeem all of humanity. This film reputedly helped elect Woodrow Wilson president on an anti-war platform when, during the election campaign, Wilson was often compared to the film's Christ-like pacifist hero.[1]

Other films appearing at this time that illuminated the brutality of war included D.W. Griffith's *The Birth of a Nation* (1915), an epic depiction of the Civil War which became an overnight box-office success. While Griffith devoted massive resources to film scenes of epic Civil War battles, his depiction of a devastated Southern life along with the hardships endured by soldiers works against the glorification of war, even as Griffith winds up romanticizing the Ku Klux Klan. Griffith followed this work with *Intolerance* (1917), a film presenting the reality of wars of the distant past as mostly brutal and repugnant. Unfortunately for Griffith, *Intolerance* arrived in theaters just as the U.S. was mobilizing for war, and a previously isolationist public quickly became patriotic to the point of outright jingoism. The point is that during brief periods of pacifism and neutrality, Hollywood films tend to reflect such views. Here as later, when the U.S. enters into armed conflict, any semblance of pacifism evaporates as Hollywood producers gear up to create movies that embellish patriotic and militaristic themes.

Films abundant with anti-war messages have appeared mostly during periods of relative isolationism or widespread opposition to the particular war being fought. Not quite so obvious have been the various twists and permutations anti-war films take. Are all wars cast in a negative light during these periods? Is the entire range of war experience depicted positively during more enthusiastically pro-war periods? The answers to such questions reveal a complex, ever-changing pattern of conflict shown in Hollywood cinema. Only two wars have been especially sanctified by the film industry: the Revolutionary War and World War II. Despite unquestioned blunders and atrocities occurring on both sides of the conflict, it would be difficult to imagine a mainstream American film being made today that characterized the Revolutionary War in a negative light; such a film would immediately be dismissed as heretical, unpatriotic. Similarly, it would be difficult to imagine a contemporary World War II film presented from a German or Japanese viewpoint. Insofar as these two wars have become part of contemporary American mythology, they have become sacrosanct in the realm of popular culture. Other conflicts, most notably World War I, the Vietnam War, the Cold War, and the Gulf War, at the outset inspired films embracing the righteous aims of the conflict, but over time they often produced more critical, jaundiced representations. In the case of Indochina, America's first military defeat, films continued to appear for more than a decade questioning the viability and morality of the war.

The decades between World War I and World War II constitute a rare pacifistic period in American history in which the majority of Americans viewed war as horrific and brutal. Griffith, the leading American filmmaker at that period, released *Hearts of the World* in 1918, just as the "Great War" was ending. Griffith's film focuses on the horrors of the war as brutal German troops invade and occupy a peaceful French village. Some locals resist, and those that the Germans capture are tortured and then murdered. Lillian Gish plays the heroine, the daughter of an American expatriate painter who meets the son of another expatriate painter. After they fall in love and become engaged the young man, played by Robert Harron, patriotically enlists in the French army to defend his adopted homeland. On her wedding night, Gish survives horrific bombardment by German troops, though her fiancé is not so lucky. Driven to madness by his death and the shock of bombardment, she decides to spend the night with his corpse. In another scene, three small boys bury their mother in order save her body from brutish German desecration. These powerful scenes convey the message that, in General Sherman's words, "War is hell." In a similar vein, Rex Ingram's *The Four Horsemen of the Apocalypse* (1921) also depicts World War I as horrific, yet not without its unexpected benefits. In Ingram's film two well-to-do cousins end up being raised in two cultures: French and German. When war breaks out both enlist in the army. One of the young men, Julio (Rudolph Valentino), the film's handsome star, had previously lived a carefree, degenerate, superficial life as a wastrel and rake whose greatest accomplishment was dancing the tango. Eventually, however, war's grim realities force him into a belated maturity. Ultimately, the two cousins confront each other on the battlefield on opposing sides, both swept up by war's upheaval.

William Wellman's *Wings* (1927) portrays a fairly realistic portrait of World War I fighter pilots as perhaps only a veteran combat aircraft commander like Wellman himself could have done. The film's co-stars include Charles "Buddy" Rogers as Jack and Richard Arlen as David, two young American pilots who begin as rivals and end as bosom friends. Clara Bow plays Mary, who is in love with Jack and who also enlists after Jack and David ship out for the French front. The two men successfully shoot down several German planes and become flying aces, decorated by the French for courage. Ultimately, the two end up tragically after David, who had been shot down by a German pilot, makes his way behind enemy lines to a German air base and steals one of their aircraft. Jack encounters his friend and unwittingly shoots him down, assuming he is an enemy. This plot structure later reappears in *Pearl Harbor* (2000). After the war Jack and Mary unite and seem destined for matrimonial happiness. *Wings* was followed three years later by Howard Hawks's *The Dawn Patrol* (1930), starring Richard Barthelmess and Douglas Fairbanks, Jr. as British bomber pilots fighting in France. In one sequence Barthelmess and Fairbanks attack a German airfield in a heroic response to German taunts about their aviation skills. As in *Wings, The Dawn Patrol* showcases air battles and pilot courage as the two men destroy an entire German air squadron. These two films adopt the typical Hollywood treatment of war as heroic, sanctified armed conflict waged for just causes, despite inevitable tragic losses.

The thirties brought film audiences seeking escape from the harsh economic realities of the Depression to musicals, screwball comedies, gangster films, westerns, and historical melodramas. Victor Fleming's *Gone With the Wind* (1939) appeared on the eve of World War II and painted a bitter portrait of the Civil War and its aftermath in the South. Fleming's film, appearing at the precise moment when war loomed, reflects the mood of isolation then gripping the country. Scarlett O'Hara's (Vivian Leigh) very first lines, which she directs at two of her suitors, perfectly reflect this ambivalence: "Fiddle-dee-dee.

War, war, war. This war talk's spoiling all the fun at every party this spring!" Public opinion took a dramatic swing toward war, however, as World War II engulfed the U.S. in late 1941; with Hollywood cinema quickly adopting a strongly pro-war stance. Patriotic films of that period include *Casablanca*, *Destination Tokyo*, *Thirty Seconds Over Tokyo*, and *They Were Expendable*. They feature serious, determined heroes waging war against menacing, brutal enemy forces.

Heroes and villains who populate the classic combat films resemble in many ways those of the classic westerns, except that most combat films celebrate the exploits of tight-knit combat units whereas westerns traditionally emphasize the lone "outlaw hero" who usually disappears into the sunset having achieved his goal. Unlike the squalid, nightmarish scenarios often depicted during peacetime, however, wartime films more likely portray the combat experience through a backdrop of striking scenery where heroic deeds frequently take on epic proportions. Popular sentiment during wartime typically glorifies and magnifies war encounters, minimizing its boredom and fatigue as well as its undeniably gritty, dangerous, and unromantic aspects. As feelings of patriotism intensify during popular wars, the battlefield actors wind up deified by the media. During such wars, public demand for war films intensifies, with the result that numerous combat films appear.

The Good War

What can be referred to as "good wars" can be understood as essentially noble causes, including the American struggle for independence and the campaign against the Nazis in order to "save democracy" during World War II. By the time World War II came along, the mass media created patriotic slogans and heroic images, which were fully internalized by millions of average filmgoers who flocked to the theaters soon after the conflict began. In contrast with many of the war films of earlier decades, in which shocking images of battlefield carnage were common, films shot during and after World War II romanticized it as a war in which heroic men and women triumphed over brutal, sinister, semi-human villains steadfastly opposed to freedom and democracy. Memorable works included David Miller's *Flying Tigers* (1941), John Farrow's *Wake Island* (1942), Howard Hawks's *Air Force* (1943), Delmer Daves's *Destination Tokyo* (1943), Mervyn LeRoy's *Thirty Seconds Over Tokyo* (1944), and John Ford's *They Were Expendable* (1945). These were followed, after the war, by Nicholas Ray's *Flying Leathernecks* (1951) and Fred Zinneman's *From Here to Eternity* (1953), each of which contains rather similar plot elements that refer to a necessary, urgent struggle against demonic enemies. In *Thirty Seconds Over Tokyo*, for example, Lieutenant Colonel James Doolittle (Spencer Tracy) inspires his volunteer airmen, ready to embark on a secret mission to bomb Tokyo, by promising, "You're going to do things with a B-25 you thought were impossible!" In *From Here to Eternity*, Private Robert E. Lee

Prewitt (Montgomery Clift) expresses similar jingoistic feelings as he promises that the Japanese will come to deeply regret their attack on Pearl Harbor. "Who do they think they're fighting? They're pickin' trouble with the best army in the world!" says Prewitt. Missing from such films, of course, is any depiction of American flaws, blunders, or atrocities, including the massive "relocation" of Japanese-Americans, Allied fire bombings of Hamburg, Dresden, and Tokyo, and the nuclear annihilation of Hiroshima and Nagasaki. These and similar episodes were largely absent from any Hollywood combat films owing to their "controversial" subject matter and, above all, to the fear they might transform a good war into something more politically and morally troublesome.

In some cases directors created war films that, far from featuring glorious battles fought by heroes, acquainted viewers with the horrific, unglamorous side of military engagements. In this vein Alfred Hitchcock's *Lifeboat* (1944), departing from classic war films by depicting survivors of a torpedoed American passenger ship, was met with a wave of critical and popular hostility. One critic wrote that, "Unless we had seen it with our own eyes, we would have never believed that a film could have been made which sold out democratic ideals and elevated the Nazi supermen."[2] Hitchcock's unpardonable sin was that his German submarine captain, far from being simply a demonic Nazi madman, possessed almost superhuman strengths and skills. The director explained that "at that time, 1940–41, the French had been defeated, and the Allies were not doing too well. Moreover, the German . . . was actually a submarine commander; therefore, there was every reason for his being better qualified than the others to take over the command of the lifeboat. But the critics apparently felt that a nasty Nazi couldn't be a good sailor." One reviewer was so incensed at Hitchcock's film that she gave it "ten days to get out of town."[3]

John Huston attempted in 1945 to release a short documentary titled *Let There Be Light*, part of the War Department's "Why We Fight" series ostensibly made for indoctrinating raw recruits, which in fact attempted to show war in all its gory details. Alarmed, the War Department decided against showing Huston's film to recruits, shelving it behind a curtain of secrecy even while most critics strongly advocated its release.[4] James Agee actually included Huston's film on his list of "Best Films of 1946."[5] All efforts were to no avail, however, as the film enraged the military as well as members of the general public. Huston's film was finally released decades later and has become something of a cult classic because of its anti-war sentiments.

As Hitchcock and Huston learned, critical depictions of popular wars encounter massive cultural and financial problems. The vast majority of World War II films made during the forties and fifties presented war in a strongly positive light, replete with similar, predictable narrative structures. Thus we have a hugely successful prewar action film in which airplane pilots risk death in order to deliver mail to South America—*Only Angels Have Wings* (Howard

Hawks, 1939). Hawks's movie stars Cary Grant as Jeff, a hardened pilot administering a rag-tag airline, and Jean Arthur as a professional dancer who falls in love with Jeff's ruggedly macho character. It also stars Richard Barthelmess of *Dawn Patrol* fame as one of the courageous pilots. The flyers constitute an all-male group who gamble with death during each mission, reprising a formula of heroic men embarking stoically on dangerous missions that remains popular in contemporary war films like *Three Kings, Pearl Harbor, Saving Private Ryan, U-571,* and *The Thin Red Line.* The formula is constructed, allowing for some variation, as follows:

- An isolated male group involved in a life-and-death mission functions as a "group hero."
- The group is composed of distinctly varied personality types, its success depending on both teamwork and individual heroic acts.
- The stoicism, professionalism, and coolness of the heroes in the face of dangers, obstacles, and death comprise the major thematic elements of the film. Although not all members may initially exhibit courage, survivors will predictably do so by the end of the film.
- Any outsiders who enter the group will threaten what has become a highly unified, even hermetic world.
- Outsiders are forced to earn admission to the group by accepting its ethos and stoicism when confronted with danger and death. Acceptance does not come easily, a tension providing an important dimension to the plots.[7]

In its most basic form, as a series of plot motifs, this pattern continues to appeal to audiences even today, although it has been modified and refined to suit new audiences. It is a testimony to its adaptability that this basic structure is readily apparent in such contemporary films as *Pearl Harbor, U-571,* and *Black Hawk Down.* Each of these films chronicles the exploits of males engaged in dangerous combat missions. In each of these, and in most other war films, both past and present, protagonists overcome fear and anxiety by evincing stoical, devil-may-care attitudes toward danger. Having diverse characters also provides countless opportunities for dramatic dialogues and interesting character interactions, both essential in maintaining audience interest. Including outsiders among the other characters also provides many splendid dramatic opportunities for character development as they confront the group and, usually, gain admission to it, but only on its terms. The combat formula worked well not only in depicting armed warfare; it also contained within it vital narrative elements that helped create dramatic tension. It is no wonder, then, that this early combat pattern has remained popular with audiences as well as filmmakers.

Samuel Fuller's *The Steel Helmet* (1951) serves as a classic example of the war film genre, even though its setting is the Korean War, not World War II. Fuller presents survivors of a North Korean offensive operation that has nearly wiped out major elements of the American forces. These survivors unite around a tough, cigar-smoking sergeant played by Gene Evans. The other diverse characters include an African American medic, a Japanese American soldier, a former conscientious objector, and a young Korean boy. They cooperate to kill enemy snipers that had them pinned down, then advance to a Korean temple and set up an observation post. Eventually, they capture a North Korean major who had been hiding in the temple. Fuller's film fully incorporates the established combat pattern of males bonding under fire, of a close-knit group practicing stoicism and courageous behavior, and of outsiders having to conform to the group ethos. This pattern was repeated over and over again during this period, and even into our own.

During the late fifties and sixties numerous films appeared which corresponded to the earlier combat patterns. These films glorified the U.S. role in World War II and paid homage to the valiant men and women who participated in it. Henry Koster's *D-Day, the Sixth of June* (1956) celebrated the historic landing of the Allies on France's Normandy beaches. Ken Anaken followed with his own version of D-Day in *The Longest Day* (1962), starring John Wayne, Robert Mitchum, Henry Fonda, Robert Ryan, Richard Todd, and Richard Burton among forty-three stars in all. The battle scenes in this film were superb enough to receive two Academy Awards for Best Black and White Cinematography and Best Special Effects. Here too World War II was celebrated as an undeniably good war that of course had to be fought and won in order to defeat the Nazis and the Axis. The battles of Brittany and Normandy help to define the good war concept in which losing became totally unthinkable. Other films depicting the victorious battles of Guadalcanal and Midway eventually became part of American wartime mythology.

Franklin Shaffner's well-received *Patton* (1970), an epic tribute to the European Theater tank commander, casts George C. Scott as the brilliant and colorful general. Patton established war on a practical level by exhorting his troops to kill for their country rather than die for it. "I want you to remember," he instructs his assembled troops, "that no bastard ever won a war by dying for his country. He won it by making the other poor dumb bastard die for his country." Schaffner's film follows the well established genre convention dramatizing the exploits of heroic combat groups but departs from the standard formula insofar as it focuses on a single leader in the person of General Patton. By showing the implausible deeds of such a gritty tank commander, *Patton* gained wide popularity along with critical acclaim upon release, appealing especially to audiences longing to bask in military glory. This film was reportedly President Richard Nixon's personal favorite; he kept a White House copy to show friends and visiting dignitaries. Filmed during the far less popular Vietnam War, *Patton* hearkened back to the glories and Manichean categories of World War II, when combat was unambiguous, noble, heroic, and decisive.

Vietnam: The Not-So-Good War

The concept of a righteous war became more difficult for the American public to comprehend during and after both the Cold War and Vietnam, which stirred unprecedented dissent over what had been achieved that could possibly justify such huge losses of human life. During earlier combat experiences the Hollywood studios, with few exceptions, cooperated fully with the U.S. military to give the fullest possible representation of its interests and views. This Hollywood propagandistic war machine, however, broke down during and just after the Vietnam War; films conforming to the formulaic combat genres in which distinctly American (usually white male) heroes are portrayed as courageous, decent, and victorious now become scarce, most of them poorly made and attracting few viewers. *The Green Berets* (1968), co-directed by John Wayne (with Ray Kellogg), constitutes the best known of this genre. It still airs on television, notably in the TBS action film series, and remains on the shelves of major video rental stores. This film stars Wayne as Colonel Michael Kirby, a patriotic commander defending the merits of war against all doubters, a leader willing to suspend human rights and liberties on the battlefield since, "Out here," he explains to a skeptical reporter who questions an execution, "due process is a bullet!" The film contains most of the stereotyped military characters and battlefield heroics, courageous soldiers who sacrifice themselves to save their comrades and the indigenous villagers located near their Special Forces outpost deep in Vietcong territory. At one point a sergeant explains to a crowd of onlookers Stateside that "what's involved here is Communism's domination of the world!" Virtually everything Colonel Kirby says and does is also designed to persuade, culminating in his ringing pro-war speech in which he satirically challenges his troops, in a variation of the old "tell it to the Marines" battle cry, to "tell it to Captain Colman [a martyred hero], and shout it loud, 'cause Arlington Cemetery is a long way from here!" This film was a straightforward attempt to sway public opinion in favor of the war, which had already proved unpopular by 1968. Despite its sensational appeal to patriotism, however, and perhaps due in part to the film's overt propagandistic aspects, Wayne's movie failed to attract either large audiences or favorable reviews, and for a time Hollywood avoided films depicting the Vietnam War altogether.

The Green Berets failed to inspire like-minded sequels, even though the film consciously attempts to emulate the most popular melodrama genre of all: westerns. Kirby's base camp, a lonely jungle enclave deep in Vietcong territory, bears a more than passing resemblance to Western frontier outposts like Fort Apache. In case anyone in the audience missed the similarities, Wayne included a prominent sign at the base gate welcoming visitors to "Dodge City." It does not take much imagination to substitute Apache or Lakota Indians for the shadowy Vietcong military units, and rugged jungle-filled canyons represent natural obstacles similar in ferocity to the most parched American deserts. This film, like many in the combat genre, is, in fact, a thinly disguised western. By evoking the quintessential American genre, the "war machine" combat film industry strives to appeal to the widest possible audience. In the case of Wayne's film, however, the effort was largely unsuccessful: the film appealed primarily to those already committed to the undeclared war in Vietnam.

Robert Altman's *M*A*S*H* (1970) ostensibly depicted events that occurred during the Korean War, but the film appeared long after that conflict subsided. Released during the turbulent sixties, it presents an ironic, jaundiced view of military conflict and its human sagas behind the front lines. Altman examines the exploits of a cast of characters assigned to a medical unit, in which military personnel (played by Donald Sutherland, Elliott Gould, Tom Skerrit, Sally Kellerman, and Robert Duvall) engage in amorous adventures and other mock-heroic exploits that detract from contemplating the war's serious and heroic aspects. Although *Patton* depicts its besieged protagonist as rife with human foibles, the general is still regarded as a serious military commander, quite in contrast to the physicians, nurses and hospital administrators of *M*A*S*H*. The contrast between the two films becomes even more heightened by Altman's frank, comedic coverage of the adventures and misadventures of characters like Major Hot Lips Houlihan (Sally Kellerman) and Trapper John McIntyre (Elliott Gould). The film's last lines, uttered by a loudspeaker, effectively summarize this irreverent portrait of the war's lighter side: "Attention: Tonight's movie has been *M*A*S*H*. Follow the zany antics of our combat surgeons as they cut and stitch their way along the front lines, appearing as bombs—I mean bombs and bullets—burst around them, snatching laughs and loves amid amputations and penicillin."

Mike Nichols's *Catch-22* (1970), also appearing at the height of the Vietnam War, portrays World War II through a darkly comedic lens. This film satirizes the heroic ideal of the good war while strongly suggesting that the conflict was neither so serious nor so heroic as had been conveyed in earlier propagandistic films. In fact, Nichols portrays war as both dangerous and absurd, as the film's title refers to a mind-boggling clause in the military code that allows combat soldiers to apply for a medical discharge on the grounds of insanity, but simultaneously assuring that all such appeals are doomed to failure. As psychologist Doc Daneeka (Jack Gilford) explains to Yossarian (Alan Arkin), "Anyone who wants to get out of combat isn't really crazy so I can't ground him." As in *M*A*S*H*, earlier military encounters served as a backdrop for critiquing the war of the moment. Hence these two movies have far more to do with the Vietnam experience—generally seen as a moral and military quagmire—than about World War II or Korea, although they do include historical details pertaining to earlier conflicts. These films depict military adventures and horrors such as sniper fire, armed attacks, aerial bombardment, long-distance shelling, and exploding land mines along with various group-bonding activities (tests of strength and will, struggles for dominance, competing beliefs and ideologies that eventually find common ground) that depart little from their World War II predecessors. Those include the heroes of *M*A*S*H* and *Catch-22*, who offer alternative perspectives on the merits of military conflict. Here the viewer can see that war itself must be regarded as barbaric, something that can no longer be sanctioned or celebrated or defined as "just."

In contrast to previous wars, Vietnam gave rise to abundant popular confusion and hostility that found its way into films of the period. There was the pathetic effort of Wayne, in *The Green Berets*, to apply the "good war" label to Vietnam, but critics and audiences alike refused to go along, partly because of the stereotyped characters, partly owing to the hackneyed dialogue and thin plot, and partly as a result of war's very absurdity. As the anti-war movement grew and fewer Americans came to support the war, film audiences avoided the few works attempting to cast Vietnam in the same heroic, sanctified terms as World War II. By the seventies and eighties, responding to ever-growing revulsion towards the war, producers and directors were making films that consistently rejected the appellation of "good war" to the Vietnam debacle.

As the Vietnam War drew to a conclusion in 1975, filmmakers began to produce scathingly ironic critiques of U.S. intervention, focusing above all on the terrible human casualties the war inevitably produced. Michael Cimino's *The Deer Hunter* (1978) gave audiences a realistic portrait of the Vietnam War starkly different from the romanticized one embellished by Wayne. In Cimino's narrative, lifelong friends from a small Pennsylvania town are reunited during a battle in Vietnam but are captured by the Vietcong and forced to play a form of Russian roulette by their captors. Escaping from their captors, two of the Americans are unable to find peace with themselves owing to their awful experiences that included seeing a Vietnamese soldier kill a civilian family with a hand grenade. Mike (Robert De Niro), having witnessed the atrocity, executes the offending soldier on the spot by incinerating him with a flame-thrower. Mike and close friend Nick (Christopher Walken) later participate in Russian roulette in a Saigon bar, this time for money. Mike begs Nick not to go through with it, asking: "Is this what you want? I love you, man." But Mike's display of love for Nick is not enough to stop Nick from going through with the game. With characters forced to endure mental and physical anguish and torture, being driven to the point of suicide, it would be difficult for audiences to perceive Vietnam as anything akin to a "good war" although, as Robin Wood observes, Cimino refused to make any direct political statement.[8]

One year after *The Deer Hunter*, Francis Ford Coppola's *Apocalypse Now* (1979) appeared, based on Joseph Conrad's story *Heart of Darkness*, probing the darkest sides of the human condition. Coppola constructs his narrative deep inside Cambodia at the time of the Vietnam War, where Captain Benjamin Willard (Martin Sheen), a special forces officer, embarks on a dangerous mission deep into forbidden territory to discover the whereabouts of (and "terminate with extreme prejudice") renegade Colonel Kurtz (Marlon Brando). Willard's mission takes him deeper and deeper into chaos, suffering, and death, leading him ultimately to the very embodiment of evil, namely Kurtz's residence. Kurtz surrounded his house with a display of the decapitated heads of his enemies. A gun battle terminates with the death of everyone but Captain Willard. Amidst such a total apocalypse, Kurtz utters the film's final line, his chilling final words summarizing Coppola's simple message about war: "The horror! The horror!" Coppola portrayed war as essentially evil in itself, the quintessential outpost of hell on earth. Once war had its grip on Colonel Kurtz, there was no letting go until he and everything around him were completely destroyed.

No work on the Hollywood war machine would be complete without a discussion of at least the first Rambo film, *First Blood* (1982). Ted Kotcheff chose Sylvester Stallone to play John Rambo, a Green Beret Vietnam vet who arrives at the town of Hope seeking information about a buddy who, it turns out, had died after being exposed to the deadly Agent Orange. Douglas Kellner observes that Kotcheff deliberately positioned Rambo and his war buddy as social victims, unable to succeed in civilian life and betrayed by the U.S. government.[9] It follows that society in general and the federal government in particular are to blame for Rambo's difficult plight. There can be no doubt that, for Kotcheff, Vietnam was not quite the "good war" because of problems like Agent Orange. In his struggles Rambo discovers that he must fight a new kind of war against police arrogance and brutality. After failing to receive a ride hitchhiking, Rambo walks into Hope and is immediately arrested for vagrancy by the local sheriff, who tells him he needs a haircut. In jail he suffers abuse by sadistic deputies, then escapes and attempts to hide out in the woods. He defeats the sheriff by killing all of his deputies and then even prevails over the National Guard, a unit of which was activated at the sheriff's request. Finally, the unruffled Rambo is talked into surrendering by his former commanding officer, Colonel Troutman (Richard Crenna). Troutman thereupon announces that Rambo's job in Vietnam "was to dispose of the enemy personnel. To kill, period. Win by attrition. Well, Rambo was the best." Rambo's tragedy is that he was abandoned by the social order in which he believed, for which he fought, and for which he risked death. Although Rambo represents the tough, macho, superpatriotic military superhero, he also co-opts the counterculture lifestyle of the sixties and seventies with his long hair, natural-foods diet, and rebellious lifestyle.

First Blood was soon followed by *Uncommon Valor* (1983), Kotcheff's commercially successful movie featuring Gene Hackman as a former special forces colonel returning to Southeast Asia at the behest of a wealthy businessman, played by Robert Stack, whose son remained a prisoner in Laos, nearly a decade after the war's end. Hackman's son is also missing, so the two agree that Hackman will head up a clandestine rescue mission. The prisoners are being held, it turns out, not in Vietnam but in Laos, and their jailers are elements of the Laotian military. This film outwardly blames the U.S. government, not Laos, for the ineffectiveness of lengthy negotiations over the fate of the MIAs (missing in action). This "dangerous mission" modality follows the typical combat-film pattern as it brings together a disciplined group of men able to display battlefield heroics. Joseph Zito's *Missing in Action* (1984) recreates this scenario, with Chuck Norris replacing Gene Hackman in a commando-type assault to rescue MIAs being held prisoner in Vietnam. Such films attempt to rehabilitate the Vietnam morass by depicting military superheroes who now seem capable of prevailing through even the most dangerous missions.

Rambo embodies not merely the forgotten warrior, but also the self-disciplined macho character with awesome mental and physical powers—with the capacity to kill any number of human beings where he deems it necessary. During the Reagan-Bush years, Rambo emerged as a symbol of patriotic, betrayed manhood. Indeed Reagan's own public relations handlers made expert use of this rugged national symbol by associating it with Reagan's aggressive anti-Communist foreign policy. Susan Jeffords argues that Stallone's portrayal of a Vietnam-veteran superhero in the Rambo series, coupled with Arnold Schwarzeneger's extreme macho roles in *The Terminator* (1984) and similar films, became an integral part of Ronald Reagan's "imagery." She writes that "these hard bodies came to stand not only for a type of national character— heroic, aggressive, and determined—but for the nation itself."[10]

Such early post-Vietnam war films strove valiantly to resuscitate the image of that disastrous conflict. In fact, they proved more successful than John Wayne's earlier artless tribute to those commandos who fought in actual combat, working-class heroes who, like earlier counterculture heroes in such movies as *Easy Rider* and *Butch Cassidy and the Sundance Kid*, opposed the establishment, distrusted and hated government, and took on rebellious lifestyles. Kellner suggests that "the films can be read diagnostically as symptoms of the victimization of the working class."[11] They can also be interpreted as attempts to redefine Vietnam as a "good war."

Platoon (1986) represents Oliver Stone's desire to involve audiences in the day-to-day nightmare he himself experienced as a soldier in Vietnam. Stone's film centers on two diametrically opposed platoon leaders—the well-intentioned, kindly, even Christ-like Sergeant Elias (Willem Dafoe) and the cynical, sadistic Sergeant Barnes (Tom Berenger), who tells platoon members stationed near the Cambodian border, "I am reality. That's the way it ought to be, and that's the way it is." Sergeant Elias, on the other hand, dresses down another sergeant for expressing an overtly macho, dictatorial attitude. "O'Neill, take a break. You don't have to be a prick every day of your life, you know." Ultimately, two such disparate soldiers cannot survive in the same platoon, and Barnes decides to murder Elias.

The narrator, a green recruit named Chris Taylor (Charlie Sheen), explains that both men influenced the entire platoon: "There are times since when I've felt like a child born of these two fathers. But be that as it may, those of us who did make it have an obligation to build again, to teach others what we know, and to try with what's left of our lives to find a goodness and meaning to this life." The two sides of war, noble and savage, are thus reconciled in Stone's powerful and devastatingly critical film. The episodes in *Platoon* hardly add up to a "good war," but rather illustrate the terrible unpredictability of war along with its endless pain and suffering. Taylor tells the audience that, "Somebody once wrote, 'Hell is the impossibility of reason.' That's what this place feels like, Hell. I hate it already, and it's only been a week."

One ingredient missing from Stone's film is a visual sense of the enemy. The soldiers in *Platoon* face shadowy Vietcong opponents who are never seen and, for that reason, seem to represent more abstract forces of destruction lurking in the jungle than real social groupings. By creating a faceless enemy, Stone effectively distances his film from the typical "good war" film in which enemies are depicted as subhuman stereotypes. In contrast, combat films such as *Pearl Harbor* and *Saving Private Ryan* show enemy faces as typically contorted by hatred for Americans. The defacing of the enemy has the effect of making the audience question the righteousness and effectiveness of the war.

Stanley Kubrick's *Full Metal Jacket* (1987) contains yet another ironic statement about Vietnam. He casts Gunnery Sergeant Hartman (Lee Emery), a tough-as-nails drill instructor, along with Private Joker (Matthew Modine), a jaded observer who challenges Hartman by mimicking John Wayne's voice in response to Hartman's tough repartee and asking, under his breath, "Is that you, John Wayne? Is this me?" A third character, Private Pyle (Vincent D'Onofrio), goes crazy and shoots Sergeant Hartman just after Hartman asks, with his usual tough irony, "Didn't Mommy and Daddy show you enough attention when you were a child?" Private Joker utters the film's last line while walking through a hellishly-burned village, "I'm so happy that I am alive, in one piece, and short. I'm in a world of shit, yes. But I am alive. And I am not afraid." This bleak portrait of the Vietnam conflict, one year after *Platoon*, demonstrates the force of disillusion with what had come to be recognized as America's first military defeat.

John Irvin's *Hamburger Hill* (1987) appeared in the same year as *Full Metal Jacket*. It, too, paints a depressing picture of the conflict. The film follows the life of an army platoon from their initial R and R in Saigon to their deployment in a futile and tragic assault on a small plot of raised ground. While resting one night between one of their eleven assaults on Hamburger Hill, some of the men listen to a radio program beamed from North Vietnam warning them that, "like your shadow, death is following you everywhere." Shortly thereafter, some of the same men are mowed down by friendly fire from an army chopper. From that point onward, their situation deteriorates, and they are picked off one by one by enemy forces. Soldiers lose limbs and even their faces in the relentless conflict, while the battlefield increasingly resembles the mythological realm of dead souls. As the men slog through mud and blood on their tragic and futile quest, this film's starkly realistic depiction of the war's brutal events place it not only in the anti-Vietnam War category but in the anti-every-war category as well. Although this film, and others of the Vietnam era, express anti-war sentiments, they still conform to the established combat film pattern.

Stone's *Born on the Fourth of July* (1989) carried a harshly critical view of war even further in telling the life story of an attractive, likable, initially gung-ho Marine, Ron Kovic (Tom Cruise). Kovic enlists directly out of high school, forgoing college, his girlfriend, and a promising athletic career. Once in Vietnam, things go well for Kovic until his second tour of duty, where the situation quickly starts to unravel. As a platoon leader, Kovic orders his men to fire upon a village from which sniper fire emanates. Upon closer inspection, however, the snipers have disappeared, leaving only severely wounded civilians, including children. Kovic and his men then engage in a fire fight with units of the North Vietnamese Army, when in the confusion Kovic kills one of his own men, a private from Georgia. After being shot in the foot he continues fighting, only to receive a bullet that severs his spine, crippling him for life. He returns home after enduring not only the horrors of the war but also the trials of a Veterans Administration Hospital, where he discovers his troubles have only begun, encountering an America bitterly divided over the war. He embarks upon an odyssey of self-discovery that leads for a time to life as an expatriate in Mexico. Kovic eventually regains a sense of meaning by dedicating himself to the anti-war movement. He addresses the 1972 Democratic Convention, where his words of profound disillusionment with the war and the life of a disabled veteran reach millions, and one member of the audience responds warmly with "Welcome home, Ronnie!" Kovic's struggles are now over: he fully accepts his identity as both disabled vet and anti-war activist.

The Vietnam era films of Stone, Kubrick, and Irvin, reaching large audiences long after the war ended, articulated a generation's anti-war yearnings and sentiments that ultimately found their way into the cinematic world. By dwelling upon more critical images of the Indochina debacle, they helped educate audiences concerning wartime atrocities and the gross failures of American military and foreign policy spanning the JFK, Johnson, and Nixon years. The Vietnam films constitute a dramatic record of one of the most tragic and tumultuous periods in American history. By depicting the war in all of its innate brutality, futility, and grim reality, these films ultimately questioned the morality of all wars. As vivid anti-war statements, they present an exception to the normal combat-film pattern of heroic deeds committed on hot, bitterly fought battlegrounds.

Cold War and Popular Culture

During the early phases of the Cold War, in the late 1940s and early 1950s, Hollywood cinema reflected the deep fear and paranoia gripping American society at the time. Many early films presented the ideological antagonism between the U.S. and the USSR as essentially a noble historical crusade in defense of Western Civilization. Don Siegel's *Invasion of the Body Snatchers* (1956) dramatized the role of concerted action in defeating a group of aliens (stand-ins for Communists) working clandestinely and ruthlessly to destroy the U.S. government and enslave its citizens. Siegel's film appeared at the same time as a popular television series about Herb Philbrick, double agent for both the U.S. and the USSR: *I Led Three Lives* achieved high ratings for several years. These media representations carried forward many elements of the World War II combat film, including the plight of a dedicated group of citizens battling to protect cherished values and lifestyles threatened by hordes of cold, aggressive, life-negating aliens. The late fifties and early sixties witnessed a number of more jaundiced Cold War films, beginning with Stanley Kramer's *On the Beach* (1959), based on Nevil Shute's best-selling novel about a submarine crew that manages to avoid nuclear Armageddon by being submerged at the time of detonation. With all continents except Australia already laid waste by nuclear radiation, the submarine's commander (Gregory Peck) and his crew head for Australia to enjoy their last days before they all perish from radiation poisoning.

Sidney Lumet's *Fail Safe* (1964) explored one of the Cold War's recurrent nightmares—a nuclear war set off accidentally between the U.S. and the USSR. Kubrick covered much the same ground in his British black comedy of 1964, *Dr. Strangelove; or How I Learned to Stop Worrying and Love the Bomb*, which remains today one of the most powerful anti-war movies ever made. Hitchcock later contributed to this genre with some highly imaginative thrillers, including *Torn Curtain* (1966) and *Topaz* (1969). *Torn Curtain* stars Paul Newman as a fake defector to East Germany whose real mission is to obtain Communist defense secrets, while *Topaz*, based on the best-selling novel by Leon Uris, stars Frederick Stafford as a French intelligence agent who uncovers a vast conspiracy of spies in high places—yet another Cold War fear amounting at times to paranoid hysteria. Such films revealed the nasty, brutal side of the Cold War, with its intrigue, duplicity, and unending surveillance of civilians, blackmail, imprisonment, torture, and of course assassination. Heroes in these pictures fight nameless, shadowy villains, at times even more shadowy than the Vietcong in *Platoon*. Hitchcock's thrillers capitalized on Cold War rivalries that could have taken place during virtually any war, always replete with vast networks of spies and counterspies. Hitchcock never seemed to question whether or not the Cold War was a "good war," as directors like Lumet and Kubrick did, but seemed to accept it as something akin to a conflict of civilizations, as a necessary element of global politics.

Kubrick usually relied upon black comedy to make fun of the sanctity of Cold War hostilities which, of course, were never too far from precipitating a hot war. His *Dr. Strangelove* was perhaps the first film to embellish a sense of ironic distance from the East/West conflict that engrossed so many American politicians and filmmakers. The film revolves around the (at times very real) possibility of a nuclear confrontation between Russia and the U.S. Dr. Strangelove (Peter Sellers) calmly envisions a post-nuclear war universe in which only a few, including himself and others in the underground War Room, would survive. The survivors would ultimately be forced to repopulate the planet, since no one else would be able to survive the nuclear exchange. Strangelove addresses the American president in the War Room, saying: "I hasten to add that each man will be required to do prodigious service along these lines, and the women will have to be selected for their sexual characteristics, which will have to be of a highly stimulating nature." Strangelove's words give the impression that he welcomes the coming holocaust. Though humorous in its narrative structure, the total annihilation of humanity depicted by Kubrick can only be viewed as the most extreme "bad war" ever concocted by human beings.

Norman Jewison's *The Russians Are Coming! The Russians Are Coming!* (1966) offered a strikingly different comedic perspective on the Cold War. Jewison's narrative centers on a Russian submarine crew that is stranded after running aground off a small New England seaport. The crew comes ashore looking for supplies to make repairs, but their humorously inept efforts at impersonating Americans only succeed in frightening nearly everyone in town. The British James Bond series lends dramatic action to the espionage tales of the Cold War, beginning with *From Russia With Love* (1963), which depicts the dapper Bond (Sean Connery) attempting to steal a top-secret Russian decoding machine from the Soviet embassy in Istanbul. Never a reluctant hero like other combat film protagonists, Bond takes on his assignments with cool professionalism, even indifference, in the face of death. When he is threatened at gunpoint by villain Red Grant (Robert Shaw) who intones "the first one won't kill you. Nor the second. Not even the third. Not till you crawl over here and kiss my foot," Bond calmly replies, "How 'bout a cigarette?" This coolly detached attitude toward death is common in the more familiar combat genre, yet Bond's exploits turn out to be strictly his own, not those of some dedicated battle group.

Toward the end of the Cold War and into the present, Hollywood cinema persisted in its tried-and-tested formulas perfected by World War II combat films which glorified daring escapades of heroic individuals assisted by their professional military brethren. Tony Scott's *Top Gun* (1986) is one of the best examples of this approach, featuring Lieutenant Pete Mitchell (Tom Cruise), a skillful navy fighter pilot who manages to fly close enough to a Russian MIG fighter to photograph it. Mitchell is assigned to the prestigious Top Gun flying school, but once there he establishes the reputation of an out-of-control maverick. He is obsessed with himself and his own laurels. "I feel the need—the need for speed!" Mitchell proclaims tellingly. He learns to temper his youthful exuberance enough to be asked to return to the academy as instructor, obviously quite an honor for a young pilot. Mitchell's legacy would never have been realized, however, if it were not for the underlying (though unstated) message that the Cold War was essentially a good war. Indeed Scott's film depicts the anti-Communist crusade as not only good but as winnable. Kellner notes that Mitchell here can be compared with Rambo and other militaristic heroes of the eighties as a prime "Reaganite wet dream" glorifying militarism while also celebrating a host of conservative values.[12] This is a far cry from earlier films such as *On the Beach, Fail Safe*, and *Dr. Strangelove* that affirmed that the Cold War was insane and out of control, with the potential to annihilate human civilization.

Disguised Combat Films

Just as the western narrative structure appeared in other genres, such as war films (*Casablanca*) and police films (*Dirty Harry*), the combat film pattern underlies what might be called "disguised combat films." Indeed the narratives of many non-combat films conform to a surprising degree to the established combat movie formula. That structure, in which heroes cooperate to achieve noble, patriotic objectives in the face of terrible obstacles, can readily be adapted to any genre. Westerns, police films, gangster films, and comedies have borrowed liberally from combat-style narrative strategies and motifs. Even before the combat formula crystallized during World War II, a few non-combat films had anticipated the genre. Thus *Only Angels Have Wings*, though not strictly a combat film, served as the prototype for later World War II combat movies. Hawks's film depicts a group of closely bonded male pilots who could just as well be flying combat missions. Instead of an enemy air force, however, the characters in Hawks's film face jagged mountains with needle-like peaks surrounded by steep-sided gorges, along with some of the nastiest flying weather ever depicted. The conflict focuses on the humans versus nature motif, with nature usually emerging victorious. Glue-thick fog banks and horrendous downpours are punctuated by rare periods of clear weather. The pilots, under Jim's (Cary Grant) direction, form deep personal bonds while exuding a seemingly cold disregard for human life.

Hollywood moguls came to realize that the combat motif which had proven so successful in attracting audiences could work just as well in westerns, crime dramas, science fiction, horror films, and even comedy. Beginning in the late fifties, as the American public seemed to tire of combat films, the formulaic combat pattern began to appear in these other genres. Westerns merely substituted Western landscapes and had Indians stand in for the Nazis or Huns or Japs of traditional combat films. Both the western and combat genres, of course, are male-dominated, both stress extremely violent action, and both feature organized groups of heroes taking on a militarized enemy. Westerns that closely resembled war films, allowing for differences in costume and locale, included *Rio Bravo* (1959), *The Good, the Bad, and the Ugly* (1966), *The Magnificent Seven* (1967), *Bandolero* (1968), *Butch Cassidy and the Sundance Kid* (1969), *The Wild Bunch* (1969), and *Silverado* (1985). Sam Peckinpah's *The Wild Bunch* (1969) is a classic example of the disguised combat film, featuring a small band of outlaws headed by the aging Pike Bishop (William Holden). Bishop and his men hijack a munitions train in order to sell arms to Pancho Villa's revolutionary army, but they meet their match when attacked by large forces of the Mexican army. The men display the kind of courage and coolness under fire that makes heroes of combat films the object of envy, and their personal bonds are just as strong as those forged by regular combat soldiers in wartime.

George Roy Hill proved that the combat motif can be effective with only two heroes: *Butch Cassidy and the Sundance Kid* (1969) features two famous Western outlaws, played by Paul Newman and Robert Redford, who embark upon commando-like adventures such as robbing banks and trains. After one spectacular train robbery, the two are pursued by an implacable, ever advancing posse they cannot elude. Like military commandos, the two face recurrent dangers as they travel incognito through rugged Southwestern terrain, much like the pair of commandos in Guy Hamilton's *Force 10 from Navarone* (British, 1970), played by Robert Shaw and Harrison Ford, who go behind enemy lines to commit terrorist acts against the German occupation forces in Yugoslavia. The posse that pursues Butch and Sundance, in fact, comprises an even more professional and formidable fighting team than the German occupation forces in Hamilton's film, and both exhibit survival skills and combat acumen that would do credit to any combat film. Narrative structures in westerns like *The Wild Bunch* and *Butch Cassidy and the Sundance Kid*, along with more recent films like *Dances with Wolves* (1990), *The Last of the Mohicans* (1992), and *Unforgiven* (1992), evoke a certain "special forces" aura in the character of military engagements presented. Western filmmakers have simply substituted posses and units of the Mexican army for combat film villains such as Nazis and Japanese.

Gangster movies also have been known to adopt combat motifs as they depict an entirely different kind of combat: urban street fighting and gang warfare. The *Godfather* series, for example, constitutes a prime focus of the disguised combat genre. Thus when the Corleone family "goes to the mattresses" in its war against rival Mafia families it conducts itself as essentially a military "unit." Here it matters very little structurally whether combat takes place on a battlefield deep behind enemy lines or in urban city centers. Male bonding, carefree attitudes toward death, outsiders who menace the groups—all of these motifs appear writ large in *The Godfather*, as in other gangster films like *Prizzi's Honor* (1985), *Bugsy* (1991), and *Casino* (1995).

The *Star Wars* episodes, starting with George Lucas's original in 1977, can also be viewed as thinly disguised combat films, depicting courageous rebel forces locked in a life-and-death struggle with ruthless, evil empires. In the case of *Star Wars* it was simply called The Empire, whereas in *Star Trek* it was the militaristic Klingon Empire. It was these fictional empires, reminiscent of Nazi Germany, which President Ronald Reagan had in mind when making his famous reference to the Soviet Union as an "evil empire." These filmic empires have served, of course, as stand-ins for the USSR, whereas the heroic freedom fighters represented by Luke Skywalker, Princess Leia Organa, and Obi-Wan Kenobi are doubles for U.S. trained and controlled "freedom fighters" of the various Cold War fronts, including Afghanistan's *mujahideen* and Nicaragua's Contras, as well as U.S. soldiers in Vietnam. The *Star Wars* and *Star Trek* films are not only disguised war films, they are, in fact, thinly disguised Cold War films in which storm troopers, aliens, and even friendly androids stand in for alien military forces.

The combat structure has also proved adaptable for comedic purposes. Thus in *First Wives Club* (1996), Hugh Wilson adapted the combat pattern to fit an urban farce about disgruntled ex-spouses of rogue males pooling their resources in order to obtain the upper hand over their former husbands. The males, played by Dan Hedaya, Victor Garber, and Steven Collins, have spurned their wives in favor of younger women. The wives, played by Goldie Hawn, Bette Midler, and Diane Keaton, are former college roommates who recognize each other decades later at the funeral of one of their roommates who committed suicide after her husband departed for a much younger woman. The club members bond by singing "You Don't Own Me" and organize what amounts to an urban "strike force" designed to wrest control of their property from their wretched ex-husbands. After establishing their organization and strategy, which includes freezing their ex-husbands' assets and exposing (in one case) their fraudulent business practices, one of them exclaims gleefully, "This is just like *Mission Impossible!*"

Like combat films, *First Wives Club* includes an outsider who longs to become part of the group. Keaton's alienated daughter, who is a college student, confesses that she is a lesbian. In order to succeed in freezing her husband's assets, Keaton brings her daughter into the group, forcing her to pass some tests. Unlike ordinary combat films, however, the only danger facing these heroines is that of irrelevance. At the beginning they are castaways, aging women past their prime with nothing to look forward to—an existence that, in some ways, resembles the actual deaths of men suffered in combat.

The Coen brothers' *O Brother Where Art Thou?* (2000) likewise employs the combat motif for comedic purposes. Here a group of felons, led by Ulysses

Everett McGill (George Clooney), escapes from a Southern chain gang and successfully eludes law enforcement agents while eventually winning fame and release when they become "The Foggy Bottom Boys," a country singing group. The male group in this movie functions much like groups of commandos in combat films like *The Guns of Navarone* (1961) and *A Bridge Too Far* (1977); rural Mississippi seemingly becomes as dangerous for McGill as Nazi Germany was for Allied commandos.

Such instances of adapting basic combat plot structures to different genres illustrate the powerful dramatic elements that inhere in combat situations. It is true that all films depict conflict at some level, but few dramatic situations can compete with organized warfare for sheer conflict. Audiences often find catharsis in viewing warfare heroes confronting ruthless, powerful enemies. Conflicts that predominate in war films seem to toughen and harden the protagonists, reducing the human drama to its most primordial elements. Heroes in combat movies carry out acts of aggression regarded as taboo in non-combat situations: blowing up bridges, shooting people, throwing grenades, hijacking military equipment, and so forth. Disguised combat films permit audiences to explore conflicted, violent scenarios, but in generally more subdued and refracted form.

Cinematic Terrorism: Old and New

The combat pattern also underlies the majority of films that have incorporated terrorist motifs over the past two decades. Terence Young's *Thunderball* (1965) signaled the first whisperings that terrorists might obtain a nuclear device for purposes of blackmail. Sean Connery's James Bond managed to thwart the terrorists on that occasion, but Young's film now appears disturbingly prescient in the post-September 11 world. In the aftermath of the terrorist attacks on the World Trade Center and the Pentagon, millions of people fear that terrorists will use chemical, biological, or even nuclear weapons against the U.S. or other Western nations. *The Sum of All Fears* (2002) portrays a worst-case scenario in which terrorists explode a nuclear warhead in Baltimore. Not since the early decades of the Cold War, when schoolchildren across the U.S. were drilled to follow defensive measures in case of a Soviet nuclear attack, have Americans been so fearful of being attacked by weapons of mass destruction.

Not surprisingly, the plots of films depicting terrorists tend to emulate the modalities of real-world international terrorists. Alfred Hitchcock's *Saboteur* (1942), for example, projects a Nazi plot to sabotage American war industries at a time when public fears of espionage and industrial terrorism were at a peak. Similarly, John Frankenheimer's *The Manchurian Candidate* (1962), depicting an attempted assassination of a presidential candidate, appeared during a period of political killings—it was actually still in theatrical release when JFK was assassinated in 1963. Here of course the similarities between film and reality proved much too close for comfort. Frank Sinatra, who owned a controlling interest in the production, pulled it from theatrical distribution in the wake of the Kennedy assassination; it would not be released for another two decades. In yet another case of film merging with political reality, George Seaton's *Airport* (1970) depicts a psychopathic suicide bomber who attempts to hijack an American airliner, reflecting public anxiety regarding airplane hijackings during a period when real hijackings began to take place.

Phillip Robinson's *The Sum of All Fears* combines familiar combat elements with overtones of terrorism. In this film, begun prior to 9/11, the world faces imminent threat of nuclear war—not by a "rogue state" or even Islamic terrorists but rather from Nazis. In actuality, they are neo-Nazis, since the film strives to be contemporary, but the fact that they are mostly older men sets them apart from gangs of skinheads and other neo-Nazi youth. The confusion arises because Robinson decides to turn a flashback in the Tom Clancy novel into part of the ongoing narrative. The Nazis do bring to mind some European ultra-rightist politicians, but they mostly hark back to World War II. The threat of total nuclear annihilation is ultimately thwarted by the hero, Dr. Jack Ryan (Ben Affleck), an ex-Marine turned historian, but not before the U.S. experiences its first nuclear strike, destroying much of Baltimore. Though the attack was carried out with just one small atom bomb, it nonetheless dwarfs the September 11 attacks. Viewing it post-September 11 cannot fail to provoke emotions of fear and anxiety. Gradually, Ryan uncovers a Nazi plot to goad the U.S. and Russia into waging nuclear war, providing the Nazis a golden opportunity to move in and reverse their 1945 defeat. "You get Russia and America to fight each other and destroy each other," the Nazi leader exhorts his terrorist colleagues on the eve of their horrific project. The bomb destroys the Baltimore sports arena and kills thousands of football fans who have come for the Super Bowl. *The Sum of All Fears* evokes the "good war" by having Nazis as its villains, while Russia too emerges as a dangerous enemy, thus recycling the familiar Cold War myths and demons.

One problem with such films is the inevitable question of how one defines terrorism itself. The U.S. has organized a worldwide coalition against "terrorism," but there is no consensus as to what it constitutes—or how it might apply to forms of *state* violence. Thus when the U.S. brazenly and unilaterally invaded Panama ostensibly to depose its dictator, killing several thousand civilians in the process, did that amount to an act of terrorism? Were the American colonists acting as terrorists when they destroyed private property at the Boston Tea Party or when they fought against British forces in the Revolutionary War? The term is innately murky and nebulous, suggesting a multitude of (largely ideological) definitions. Hollywood films depicting terrorism tend to reflect ideological biases prevalent in the dominant culture.

Hollywood and the New Militarism

The 1990s witnessed a dramatic resurgence of military films celebrating rebirth of noble warmaking, tied in great measure to the cultural and political dictates of U.S. empire, solidified in the decade since the breakup of the Soviet system. At the same time, two maverick films appeared that challenged this paradigm and sought to portray war in realistic terms. The first film of the decade to endow war with such realism was Edward Zwick's *Courage Under Fire* (1996), the first to be set in the Gulf War. It immediately generated controversy as the Army refused to lend equipment unless the script was altered to depict the Army in a better light. Zwick refused to water down his script and was forced to do without the usual assistance the military provides to filmmakers. The film presents some spectacular and chilling scenes involving U.S. forces' conduct under fire, scenes that bear an uncomfortably close resemblance to actual events in the Persian Gulf. In the first instance, Lieutenant Colonel Nathaniel Serling (Denzel Washington) leads a tank battalion in pursuit of retreating Iraqi forces when his tank formation is suddenly penetrated by Iraqi tanks. In the confusion, Serling orders his tank to fire at one of the suspected enemy vehicles, only to discover later it was one of his own. As in real cases of friendly fire during the war, he had inadvertently killed some of his own men. Later, Serling investigates a situation in which Captain Karen Walden (Meg Ryan), a Medevac helicopter pilot, was killed in action while covering for retreating American forces. Serling's investigation leads to conflicting, *Rashomon*-like reports from several eyewitnesses. Beyond acts of heroism, he discovers callousness, cowardice, and incompetence on the part of other combatants. These two episodes give rise to an anti-war atmosphere as the misadventures of U.S. forces in the Gulf War appear in symbolic form. This film, however, was soon out of step with a series of new war films that appeared over the next several years.

To recover a sense of the "good war" that might correspond to expanded U.S. military ventures within the New World Order, much filmmaking of the late nineties turned to the great patriotic triumphs of World War II. Terrence Malick's *The Thin Red Line* (1998) depicts the Battle of Guadalcanal, one of the most intense engagements of the Pacific Theater. This long-awaited film was somewhat disappointing to critics, who remembered the director's skillful production of *Badlands* in 1973. In his new film Malick manages to achieve a thoughtful, philosophical air through effective use of narration. At one point a battle-weary character wonders aloud about the origins of war, "this great evil. Where'd it come from? How'd it come into the world? What seed, what root did it come from?" Malick's version also presents war as a fundamental source of conflict within nature itself. "Why does nature vie with itself, the land contend with the sea?" asks the narrator. "Is there an angry power in nature?"

Andrew Martin's 1964 film, also called *The Thin Red Line*, covered much the same ground as Malick's, though without Malick's philosophizing. Both films are based on the same James Jones novel, but they treat the war experience quite differently. In Martin's early version, World War II is presented as a good war, despite many gory battle scenes. Both films also dwell on the conflict between idealistic Captain Staros and his superior officer who takes a more pragmatic approach to the horrors of combat. The Captain Staros character in both films refuses to risk the lives of his men needlessly and is ultimately relieved of his command and sent home, clearly signaling that humane values are irrelevant to the business of war. Both films reflect the notion, attributed to General Sherman and echoed by many others, that "War is hell!"

Steven Spielberg's *Saving Private Ryan* (1998) returns to the safe terrain of the quintessential good war, namely the Allied invasion of Normandy in 1944. This was Spielberg's first World War II drama since *Schindler's List* (1993). Its cast includes Captain John Miller (Tom Hanks) and the members of his squad, including Sergeant Horvath (Tom Sizemore), Privates Reiben (Edward Burns), Jackson (Barry Pepper), Mellish (Adam Goldberg), Caparzo (Vin Diesel), and Medic Wade (Giovanni Ribisi). The squad embarks upon the difficult and treacherous mission of locating Private James Ryan (Matt Damon), who was among the landing forces now spread out along the French coast. All of Ryan's three brothers have been killed in action, and War Department policy dictated that the "sole surviving son" should be removed from combat as soon as possible. Once located, Ryan becomes the typical outsider, forced to accept the group's norms before being allowed full membership. The film dramatizes the travails of a private who urges his would-be rescuers to do something heroic for the war effort. Since it is intended to assist the U.S. military effort, the rescuers readily agree to help Ryan destroy a German convoy in France. They enlist all their battlefield skills, including the arts of subterfuge, to defeat the Nazis in a crucial battle. German soldiers are shown as demonic enemies fighting for a doomed cause. Only the Allies, exemplified by Captain Miller and his courageous squad, are fighting for a just cause that requires no explication in the film. What could be more sanctified than sending a young boy home to console his distraught mother? From this standpoint, *Saving Private Ryan* depicts World War II in the heroic pattern of the forties and fifties combat genre.

By choosing to set his film on the Normandy battlefields, Spielberg made certain that audiences would identify with the mission of saving Private Ryan and, by extension, with the larger U.S. war effort. Had he chosen to set the action during one of the less popular wars, as in Vietnam or the Gulf War, the film would have evoked different visceral responses. Whether a war is deemed "good" or "bad" determines a film's plot as well as its emotional tone.

Jonathan Mostow's submarine-warfare thriller *U-571* (2000) gets so absorbed in celebrating World War II as a euphorically good war that it even rewrites history in a manner that seems almost Orwellian. Mostow renders the heroic exploits of British submariners in obtaining the Enigma German secret code in a way that suggests the mission had been carried out by an *American* submarine crew. He subverts historical authenticity with the apparent intent of reassigning the U.S. to its accustomed hegemonic role in world affairs;

British military exploits are recast to appear as U.S. combat triumphs. Mostow himself stated, "If it's possible to call a war a 'good war,' that label would have to apply to World War II. Never before in our history was there such a clear-cut case of good versus evil." He further explains, "There is no ambiguity about our involvement in that war," unlike more recent conflicts from Korea to the Gulf, "and we rose up as a nation to defeat Hitler."[13] *U-571* pays tribute to past U.S. military glory by deliberately falsifying actual events.

Michael Bay's *Pearl Harbor* (2001) outdoes Mostow's and Spielberg's films in its dramatic romanticization of World War II. Bay's deeply flawed epic begins in rural Tennessee where two young boys grow up fascinated by aircraft. They mature into young Air Force pilots, Rafe McCawley (Ben Affleck) and Danny Walker (Josh Hartnett), years before the Japanese attack Pearl Harbor. After completing his training, Rafe volunteers to fly with the Eagle Squadron, a fighter group then engaged in the bitterly fought Battle of Britain. Before he leaves, Rafe falls in love with young nurse Lieutenant Evelyn Johnson (Kate Beckinsale), and she vows to wait for his return. Rafe became an "ace" by downing five German planes before being shot down over enemy territory and reported dead. The announcement of Rafe's death brings Kate and Danny together, although reluctantly at first. The couple fall in love and plan marriage. At that point Rafe, who was missing in action but not deceased, and had fought his way back to British lines, suddenly joins them at Pearl Harbor. Rafe explains that only his love for Evelyn saved him from death in the Battle of Britain, but he decides to give up his claims on her when he learns she is pregnant with Danny's child. At this point Bay interrupts the romantic triangle by staging the December 7, 1941, Japanese attack on Pearl Harbor, deftly recreating the horror and bloodshed of the massive aerial bombardment of the U.S. fleet. Trapped sailors drown in the hulls of their battleships while Japanese planes continue strafing other sailors desperately swimming for their lives. Using the element of surprise, the Japanese destroy most American planes, but Rafe and Danny, with precious little time to change from Hawaiian shirts to military uniforms, somehow manage to commandeer two fighters and take off to launch a counterattack. During the contrived fierce air battle, Rafe and Danny emerge as heroes, shooting down several Japanese zeroes as they return to their aircraft carriers.

The action shifts to a secret Air Force base, whereupon the two volunteer for a top secret mission commanded by Lieutenant Colonel James Doolittle (Alec Baldwin). Their task is the now-famous Doolittle Raid over Tokyo, a highly politicized operation achieving more symbolic than military success. Rafe and Danny crash land on the coast of China, heavily infested with Japanese military units. Danny fails to survive the landing, after saving both Rafe and his crew by turning the plummeting plane's guns on an advancing squad of Japanese soldiers. In the denouement we see Rafe and Evelyn as a happy family, playing with a small boy. This family group, including the son of a slain hero, his fiancée, and his best friend, shows the profound loss of innocence among all the surviving characters. Much like *Titanic, Pearl Harbor* presents a conventional love story as the centerpiece of the film narrative, with epic historical events relegated to backdrop. The film also sacrifices historical accuracy for the sake of questionable dramatic objectives. The actual raids on Pearl Harbor took place in the very early morning and thus could not have been observed by many people, yet in Bay's version they occur later in the morning with many bystanders watching obliviously as Japanese planes suddenly appear over Oahu. Moreover, U.S. flyers were unable to mount any serious defense against the attack, which makes the heroic aerial scenes in *Pearl Harbor* quite implausible. Like Mostow in *U-571*, Bay seems willing to recast history for the purpose of recreating an impressive patriotic spectacle. The result is an almost comic book characterization of the events preceding and surrounding the attack. Bay does seem to admire Admiral Yamamoto (Mako), presenting the Japanese Navy mastermind as a brilliant strategist who is able to destroy much of the U.S. Pacific Fleet in response to the harsh American oil embargo imposed on Japan. Bay glosses over the failure of U.S. political and military actors in the weeks leading up to the attack, ignoring any mention of the oft-repeated rumor that FDR (Jon Voight) and his senior military advisors had advance warning of Japanese plans but allowed the flotilla to proceed in order to galvanize the American public behind the impending war effort. Forsaking any nuanced approach, *Pearl Harbor* embellishes World War II at its inception (for the U.S.) as a good war that, however, resulted in the loss of American innocence.

David O. Russell's *Three Kings* (1999), like Zwick's *Courage Under Fire*, offers a rare filmic portrayal of the Gulf War, which departs from the good war formula. The viewer winds up distanced from the official moral and political rationale for U.S. military intervention, which included freeing Kuwait from Iraqi occupation and removing Saddam Hussein from the presidency of Iraq. Russell sets the tone in the first scene, where an American soldier shoots and kills an Iraqi soldier who refuses to lay down his weapon. "Congratulations, my man, you got yourself a rag head!" exclaims one of his buddies. The heroes, a small group of soldiers led by Special Forces Major Archie Gates (George Clooney), embark on a *Kelly's Heroes*-type adventure to steal Kuwaiti gold taken by the Iraqis during their brief occupation of Kuwait. *Three Kings* exposes the shallowness and duplicity of American foreign policy toward Iraq, notably toward the Iraqi people. It follows the familiar combat genre, including a cool, detached, professional manner of dealing with danger. When a soldier expresses fear to Major Gates over the upcoming battle against the Republican Guards, Gates explains, "the way this thing works is you do this thing you're scared shitless of, and then you get the courage after you do it."

Although *Three Kings* follows many established plot lines, it differs from World War II combat films in one vital respect: it resolutely denies the "good war" label for the Gulf War, which came instantaneously to Americans in the form of a glorified TV spectacle. Instead of a rejuvenating war experience, Russell finds a callous American military totally unsympathetic to the fate of the Iraqi people. At one point Chief Elgin (Ice Cube) orders a soldier to stop using racist expressions in reference to Iraqis, but when the soldier expresses confusion he is told to use "Towel Head" and "Camel Jockey" in lieu of "Dune Coon" and "Sand Nigger." The U.S. armed forces treat the Iraqis as condescendingly as these epithets imply, even though Iraqi rebels encountered in the field turn out to be courageous and disciplined. The Americans finally succeed in escorting a large group of refugees into Iran, saving their lives; they end up trading these lives, however, for millions of dollars in gold bars they had recovered from the Iraqis and hidden in the desert.

Three Kings encourages the viewer to identify vicariously with a military action that appears to save Iraqi lives. Of course the action is nothing more than a fantasy: U.S. troops did nothing to assist Iraqi rebels or refugees, preferring to turn the matter of rebels over to Iraqi forces as an "internal matter" for Iraq. In reality President Bush had called on the Iraqi people to rise up and overthrow Saddam Hussein, only to turn neutral once some Iraqis actually tried to carry this out, leaving them open to imprisonment and execution. The answer to Iraqis' queries as to when the U.S. Army can be expected to provide needed military assistance is basically "never."

William Friedkin's *Rules of Engagement* (2000) brought war films into the realm of terrorism, in this case Islamic fundamentalism. Friedkin, best known for his earlier work (*The French Connection*, 1971, and *The Exorcist*, 1973) eerily anticipates the later U.S. "war against terrorism," though still rather naïvely as the events of September 11 were to prove; the film dwells on powerful terrorist threats to U.S. targets around the world. *Rules* opens with a flashback of a Vietnam combat scene in which Marine Corps Colonel Terry Childers (Samuel L. Jackson) rescues another officer, Colonel Hays Hodges (Tommy Lee Jones), from withering artillery attack by Vietcong soldiers. The scene shifts to Yemen as the U.S. ambassador, facing a hostile crowd of demonstrators, makes a panicky phone call asking for military evacuation. Childers accepts the assignment and flies to the U.S. Embassy aboard a military helicopter along with a platoon of special forces. He rescues the ambassador (Ben Kingsley) and his family, even snatching the embassy flag despite a hail of gunfire coming from the crowd. At last, wounded and pinned down by enemy gunfire, Childers orders his men to fire into the crowd, a response usually justified only by dire circumstances. The Marines fire into the crowd, allowing Childers, the ambassador, and his family, and the remaining Marines to evacuate by helicopter.

At this point Childers's troubles are far from over, as he becomes the target of an intensive military investigation into his decision to use deadly force against what appeared to be foreign civilians. In desperation, he turns to his friend, Colonel Hays Hodges, a former infantry commander turned lawyer.

Hodges initially refuses to take the case, arguing that he is not a good enough attorney to get his friend exonerated, but at last agrees and immediately flies to the Yemeni capital, Sana, where he discovers that a terrorist organization with radical Islamic ideology planned the embassy attack. Back in the U.S., Hodges uses every courtroom tactic available to defend Childers from what seems a blatant attempt by the U.S. National Security Advisor (Bruce Greenwood) to wrongly prosecute the officer for using deadly force against innocent civilians. The NSA had earlier destroyed a videotape obtained from a surveillance camera that showed the "peaceful crowd" firing guns and trying to kill the ambassador and other Americans. After Hodge's discrediting of both the advisor and the ambassador (pressured into lying about the incident in order to convict Colonel Childers), coupled with his depiction of Childers as a heroic, dedicated commander, the court finds him not guilty. Thus Friedkin's picture vindicates the colonel while indicting U.S. leaders for not moving against terrorism.

Three Kings being a notable exception, the Hollywood film industry has been obsessed with the "good war" theme over the past decade—a theme looming large in *Saving Private Ryan, U-571,* and *Pearl Harbor.* World War II is resurrected as a heavily mythologized, sanctified historical moment through which the national will was dramatically tested and then just as dramatically triumphed. No recent war attained such status, of course, either in Hollywood or in the general culture. World War II has joined the Revolutionary War and the Civil War as venerated, romanticized, indeed *necessary* historical combat dramas.

Filmmakers Spielberg and Stone offer competing filmic views on both the morality and efficacy of the American war experience. Spielberg, who spent no time in Vietnam, has looked to World War II as a watershed conflict that deeply influenced him as he was growing up in the 1950s. His father served in the war as a radio operator on B-52s. Spielberg started making 8-millimeter films about the war and his father's involvement in combat when he was just 12 years old. World War II later served as the setting for no less than eight of his most popular films, including *1941* (1979), the three *Indiana Jones* films (1981–1990), *Empire of the Sun* (1987), *Schindler's List* (1993), and *Saving Private Ryan* (1998). He completed yet another wartime film for the HBO television network—a spinoff from *Saving Private Ryan*—titled *Band of Brothers* (2001).

Like Spielberg, Stone was born shortly after World War II but his view of combat was gained firsthand during Vietnam. He volunteered for the 25th Infantry Division, U.S. Army, in 1967 and was sent to Vietnam, where he served with distinction, being awarded the Bronze Star for Valor and a Purple Heart with Oak Leaf Cluster. Disillusioned with U.S. militarism in Indochina, Stone nonetheless forged his views during combat, while Spielberg's came mostly from his father's personal memories of combat in World War II. Stone's movies are famous for depicting Vietnam as a horrific and immoral military adventure. In 1986 Stone made *Platoon*, a realistic depiction of Vietnam, as well as *Salvador*, a film presenting U.S. intervention in the Salvadoran civil war as both stupid and immoral. *Born on the Fourth of July* (1993), however, is undoubtedly Stone's bitterest depiction of the horrors of war and the terrible consequences for its victims. While Stone's films seem to attack the very legitimacy of contemporary warfare, at least in the context of American militarism, Spielberg's glorify it largely through the military legacy of World War II.

Conclusions

The events of September 11, 2001, are sure to lead to some dramatic changes in the production of combat films and the opening of a new phase in the evolution of the Hollywood War Machine. An initial reaction to the terrorist attacks was to informally censor films straying too close to real-life terrorist narratives that might force viewers to relive the nightmare. Executives at Warner Brothers and Disney temporarily shelved three films (*Collateral Damage, Big Trouble*, and *Bad Company*) that depicted terrorists attacking U.S. targets. Other films containing graphic images of terrorism were placed on hold, though matters could change once the studios decide the public has recovered from the September trauma. The wait is sure to be a briefer one than that for *The Manchurian Candidate*, which depicted an assassination attempt on a presidential candidate and was withdrawn from theaters after the JFK assassination. The film was not released again theatrically until 1987, fully 25 years after it was originally produced.

Combat films serve as dramatic historical artifacts that reflect changing views of the combat experience, offering barometers of patriotic sentiment. Of twentieth century armed conflicts, only World War II has been consistently portrayed as a good war, rekindling strong memories of patriotism, glory, and victory. Although the U.S. had no full-blown military entanglements just before the events of September 11, the film industry was still busy making pictures within the good-war propaganda style. If Hollywood was correct in its reading of the public mood, the proliferation of pro-war movies suggested the presence of a mass audience ready to embrace future wars so long as they were not too costly or protracted. From this standpoint, the unofficial ban on terrorist pictures will surely be superseded as the war on terrorism continues to call forth films dramatizing noble wars against evil adversaries.

In the aftermath of September 11, the Bush administration, behind the leadership of presidential advisor Karl Rove, set out to enlist the participation of the Hollywood community in the war on terrorism—the first such efforts since World War II. Many politicians hoped to see a convergence of foreign policy agendas and film content, Bush himself arguing for a "seamless web of unity" around the war effort. Of course the Pentagon has for many years insisted upon the right to monitor film scripts before allowing its facilities or resources to be used in moviemaking, and more recently such agencies as the CIA and NSA have followed this pattern. During a trip to Hollywood, however, Rove encountered resistance from film industry people such as Robert Redford and Oliver Stone, who wanted little to do with U.S. war propaganda efforts. While such resistance to Pentagon influences captures the general mood of the industry, the general thrust of combat pictures, judging by the role of directors like Spielberg, Bay, and Mostow, can be expected to follow the path of the Hollywood War Machine.

In October 2001, two extremely brutal films depicting terrorism, *Training Day* and *Don't Say a Word*, were released and met with unexpectedly strong box-office returns. At the same time, production was resumed on two other terrorist-related films, *Behind Enemy Lines* and *Black Hawk Down*, both having been nearly completed by September 11. *Behind Enemy Lines* depicts the frightful adventures of American pilot Captain Burnett (Owen Wilson), shot down on Christmas day over Bosnia during UN actions in Yugoslavia. A senior U.S. officer, Admiral Leslie Reigart (Gene Hackman), bucks NATO and orders a mission to rescue Burnett, but is soon overruled by his NATO commander. Burnett is forced to flee to another rendezvous point deep in hostile territory and is then pursued by Serb forces intent upon shooting him down and destroying his photos after he accidentally flies over a "killing field" and catches Serb soldiers in the act of murdering and burying innocent civilians. Admiral Reigart defies NATO authorities at severe risk to his career as a Naval officer and orders a secret mission to rescue Burnett. The message of this film is clear: U.S. forces may defy the international community in order to rescue one of their own, especially if they are in the clutches of "barbarians" like the Serbs. The film is anti-NATO peacekeeping operations, which are depicted as ineffectual and contrary to U.S. interests.

Black Hawk Down, directed by Ridley Scott, reached the widest audience of any post-September 11 war film. This darkly atmospheric film portrays a botched 1993 military mission to capture top officials of Somali warlord General Mohammed Farah Aidid as part of yet another UN "peacekeeping" effort. The mission goes awry when militia loyal to Aidid mount a fierce firefight against U.S. forces. The battles heat up after an Army Black Hawk helicopter is downed by hostile fire. Although U.S. forces fight heroically against overwhelming odds they are eventually driven back to the confines of their military base. By the end, U.S. forces are able to secure their retreat, after many special forces soldiers and pilots have been killed. More than one thousand Somalis also died in some of the fiercest fighting since the Vietnam War.

Scott's film shows the U.S. military to be courageous, tenacious, and skillful in battle. The Somali forces also appear courageous as they absorb the loss of hundreds of fighters, although they are seen as being arrogant and cruel toward the only American soldier captured during the fighting. Somalis, labeled "skinnies" by Americans, are never shown as individuals with common bonds of humanity. The audience never learns the sources of their fierce hostility to-wards Americans, as if anti-American sentiment were some kind of national bias or chauvinism. There can be no question that Somalis voiced many legiti-mate objections to UN forces, deeming them unwarranted intrusions into a local civil war. Moreover, U.S. troops hardly behaved as honorably or as coura-geously as the film indicates, if we are to believe eyewitness accounts of Soma-lis present during the battle. One of them, Mrs. Weheliya, described how she and her family were taken hostage by U.S. troops attempting to rescue their comrades in a downed helicopter; the Americans warned they would kill everyone in the family unless the militia troops retreated. "We were clinging to each other," she recalled. "We were terrified."[14] If U.S. forces held Somali civil-ians hostage at gunpoint during the battle this was never acknowledged, and no such incident or anything remotely like it can be seen in Scott's film. If the actual events occurred just as *Black Hawk Down* depicts, then no U.S. soldier even threatened Somali civilians. Every personal and combat activity shown in the film merely polishes the reputation of U.S. Army Rangers and helicopter pilots. And therein lies the rub: if American troops behaved like paragons of bravery and heroism, why the persistent reports of civilian hostages taken at gunpoint? Which version of history is to be believed, eyewitness participants or filmmakers ensconced within the Hollywood War Machine striving for pa-triotic appeal at the box office? The film's creators, of course, maintain that it reflects no political or nationalistic ideology. Eric Roth, the screenwriter, ex-plained: "For me, the film is less about patriotism and flag waving. It's a study in heroism under fire, by a couple of soldiers who are outmanned and in over their heads. I found it stirring and, frankly, slightly apolitical."[15] In fact, every film, even avowedly apolitical ones, cannot help but reflect the values and be-liefs held by filmmakers working within contours of the culture industry. No doubt it has become politically incorrect in Hollywood today to convey nega-tive images of the U.S. military.

Although *The Sum of All Fears* seems laughable in the post-9/11 period, with its nostalgic evocation of World War II and the Cold War, it may actually represent a possible line of future cinematic development. In its combination of genres and strongly nostalgic invocation of military triumph, Robinson's film may well capture the essence of the future combat genre. The War on Ter-rorism will be a protracted, costly struggle, with terrorist attacks no doubt continuing at perhaps an even more intensive, destructive pace. The Holly-wood War Machine could well continue to weave a complex tapestry of film noir stylings and combat-film action, frantically invoking past military glories and victories in order to legitimate the present one.

Notes

1. Lewis Jacobs, "Movies in the World War," in Gerald Mast (ed.), *The Movies in Our Midst* (Chicago: University of Chicago Press, 1982), 164–165.

2. Donald Spoto, *The Dark Side of Genius: The Life of Alfred Hitchcock* (New York: Ballantine Books, 1983), 283.

3. François Truffaut, *Truffaut/Hitchcock* (New York: Simon and Schuster, 1983).

4. See James Agee, *Agee on Film* (New York: Grosset and Dunlap, 1958), 236.

5. Leonard Quart and Albert Auster, *American Film and Society Since 1945*, second edition. (Westport, CT: Praeger, 1991), 1.

6. Robert Ray, *A Certain Tendency of the Hollywood Cinema, 1930–1950* (Princeton, NJ: Princeton University Press, 1985), 113–118.

7. Ibid.

8. Robin Wood, *Hollywood From Vietnam to Reagan* (New York: Columbia University Press, 1986), 271–2.

9. Douglas Kellner, *Media Culture.* (New York: Routledge, 1995), 64.

10. In Robert Sklar, *Movie-Made America: A Cultural History of American Movies* (New York: Random House, 1994), 346.

11. Kellner, *Media Culture*, 65.

12. Ibid., 75.

13. *Los Angeles Times*, April 25, 2000.

14. Donald G. McNeil, Jr., "For the Somalis, a Manhunt Movie to Muse Over," *New York Times*, Jan. 22, 2002.

15. Dana Calvo and Rachel Abramowitz, "Uncle Sam Wants Hollywood but Hollywood Has Qualms," *Los Angeles Times*, Nov. 19, 2001.

Conclusion
The Real Axis of Evil

GEORGE KATSIAFICAS

Long before North Korea announced, in October 2002, that it possessed nuclear weapons, Bush's infamous "axis of evil" speech was a clear sign that his administration had made North Korea a target.[1] In early 2002, the U.S. not only labeled North Korea part of an "axis of evil," it also threatened to use nuclear weapons against it.[2] In the first year and a half of the Bush presidency, there were no serious talks between the U.S. and North Korea. Moreover, under pressure from right-wing congressmen, the Bush administration reevaluated the 1994 U.S. agreement with North Korea, known as "The Agreed Framework."[3] Although most Americans remain completely unaware of it, in 1994 the U.S. came very close to bombing North Korea unilaterally. "The Agreed Framework" narrowly averted a new Korean War that, in the estimation of the U.S. military commander in Korea, would have killed more than the three million people who lost their lives from 1950–1953.[4]

Alongside its looming war against Iraq and hostile actions against North Korea, Bush and Co. are today waging wars in Afghanistan, the Philippines, and Colombia; they arm Israel and permit it to overrun and destroy Palestinian towns and cities; they are encouraging the revival of German and Japanese militarism; they are attempting to overthrow the Chavez government in Venezuela; they have withdrawn from the International Criminal Court, scrapped the Anti-Ballistic Missile Treaty and the Kyoto protocols, refused to sign a new international protocol to the 1972 biological warfare treaty, and have dramatically increased military spending. Most ominously, Bush adopted a new "first-strike" strategic doctrine, replacing decades of U.S. policies based on "deterrence" and "containment."

When I say Bush and Co., I do not refer only to one man and his administration; it is the *system* that is the problem. No matter who sits in the White House, whether George Bush or Bill Clinton or someone else, militarism has long been and will surely remain at the center of U.S. foreign policy and economic development. The U.S. Congress has been little better than Bush: among other things, it rejected the nuclear test ban treaty signed by 164 nations and has fully endorsed Bush's foreign policy on every issue. With Congressional funding, the U.S. now has over 250,000 troops in 141 countries— and it is seeking new bases and attempting to install more troops in places like

Uzbekistan and Tajikistan. In Northeast Asia, 100,000 U.S. troops are stationed indefinitely.

In a phrase, military madness defines the mentality of leading U.S. decision-makers. It would therefore be irresponsible to regard recent military threats emanating from the White House as empty gestures. The world desperately needs a viable peace movement capable of mobilizing millions of people across the globe in order to stop U.S. military madness before it gives rise to perpetual new wars. In the following remarks, I hope to clarify the historical character of this disease and recommend a possible cure.

The Historical Pattern of Violence

Before they became organized as nation-states, white European settlers in America committed genocide to steal the land of indigenous peoples. Beginning in the sixteenth century, peripheral areas were rapidly assimilated into a capitalist world system based in Europe. Whether in what is now Mexico, Peru, or the U.S., the pattern was generally the same: besides massacring tens of millions of Native Americans, European colonialists enslaved tens of millions of Africans to build up their new empires. Estimates of the number of Africans *killed* in the slave trade range from 15 to 50 million human beings, with tens of millions more enslaved and harshly exploited. From its earliest days, the U.S. practiced biological warfare. Lord Jeffrey Amherst, after whom towns in Massachusetts, New York, and New Hampshire were named, was celebrated because he devised a scheme to rid the land of indigenous people without risking white lives. He gave Native Americans blankets carrying the smallpox virus, thereby wiping out entire villages under the guise of providing assistance. In the century after the American Revolution, nearly all native peoples were systematically butchered and the few survivors compelled to live on reservations. Have people in the U.S. apologized for and renounced such violence? Unfortunately, the answer is no. Indeed, towns are still named for Amherst, and one of the fanciest restaurants near prestigious Amherst College is today called the "Lord Jeff."

In 1848, the U.S. annexed almost half of Mexico with the aim of expanding "Anglo-Saxon democracy" and "Manifest Destiny." Even though dozens of U.S. soldiers were executed under orders of General Zachary Taylor for refusing to fight against Mexico, U.S. expansionism accelerated. At the end of the nineteenth century, as manufacturers looked for international markets, the U.S. (led by men experienced in the Indian wars) conquered the Philippines. Six hundred thousand Filipinos perished from the war and disease on the island of Luzon alone. William McKinley explained that "I heartily approve of the employment of the sternest measures necessary." The director of all Presbyterian missions hailed the slaughter of Filipinos as "a great step in the civilization of the world."[5] For Theodore Roosevelt, the murders in the Philippines were "for civilization over the black chaos of savagery and barbarism." In 1900, Senator Albert Beveridge of Indiana summarized the colonialist mentality: "We are the ruling race of the world. . . . We will not renounce our part in the mission of our race, trustee, under God, of the civilization of the world." One cannot help but wonder precisely what idea of "civilization" he had in mind.

Although Mark Twain and the Anti-Imperialist League stood in opposition to U.S. policy, imperial ambitions were far too strong. Between 1898 and 1934, U.S. Marines invaded Honduras seven times, Cuba four times, Nicaragua five, the Dominican Republic four, Haiti and Panama twice each, Guatemala once, Mexico three times, and Colombia four times. In 1915, over 50,000 Haitians were killed when U.S. troops mercilessly put down a peasant rebellion.[6] Marines were sent to China, Russia, and North Africa—in short, wherever the masters of U.S. imperialism needed them.

With the Great Depression of 1929, militarism became more than an instrument of colonial conquest: it emerged as the primary solution to stagnation in the world economy. Since 1948, the U.S. has spent more than $15 trillion on the military—more than the cumulative monetary value of all human-made wealth in the U.S.—more than the value of all airports, factories, highways, bridges, buildings, machinery, water and sewage systems, power plants, schools, hospitals, shopping centers, hotels, houses, and automobiles. If we add the current Pentagon budget (over $346 billion in fiscal 2002) to foreign military aid, veterans' pensions, the military portion of NASA, the nuclear weapons budget of the Energy Department, and the interest payments on debt from past military spending, the U.S. spends $670 billion every year on the military—more than a million dollars a minute.[7] The U.S. military budget is larger than those of the world's next 15 biggest spenders combined, accounting for 36 percent of global military expenditures.

Although the main problem is obviously the U.S., nearly two-thirds of global military spending today occurs outside the U.S. Japanese and German militarism are being revived, while in South Korea the military budget has increased by 12.7 percent for 2003 to more than $14 billion.

American Militarism and Asia

Bush's "axis of evil" is entirely in Asia. This is no accident. Lest we forget history, it is in Asia where in the last half century the U.S. slaughtered over five million people in regional wars so distant from the U.S. (and Russian) mainlands that historians refer to this period as the "Cold" War. In just three years, somewhere between three and five million people were killed in Korea, the vast majority of them innocent civilians. Although thousands of civilian refugees were massacred and the U.S. employed biological weapons,[8] it still will not admit to nor apologize for these actions. Instead it moved the killing fields to Indochina, where it used more firepower than had been used in all previous wars in history combined, killing at least two million people and leaving millions more wounded or made refugees. Chemical warfare, euphemistically called Agent Orange, was systematic and deadly: over 20 million gallons of Agent Orange were sprayed on Vietnam. For every man, woman, and child in South Vietnam, the U.S. dropped more than 1000 pounds of bombs (the equivalent of 700 Hiroshima bombs), sprayed a gallon of Agent Orange, and used 40 pounds of napalm and half a ton of CS gas on people whose only wrongdoing was to struggle for national independence.[9] The kill ratio in these two Asian wars was about 1000 times that of wars in Central America and perhaps just as high for the more than 200 other U.S. military interventions during the "Cold War."

East Asia's importance as a market for military goods has been increasing dramatically. After the end of the Cold War, when demand for such products leveled off in North America, Western Europe, and the former Soviet Union, arms suppliers looked to other markets. U.S. arms exports rose from $8 billion in 1989 to $40 billion in 1991, while British arms exports rose nearly 1000 percent from 1975 to 1995 (when they reached $4.7 billion). In 2001, global military spending (conservatively estimated) rose two percent to $839 billion, 2.6 percent of world GNP or about $137 for every man, woman, and child on the planet. According to the International Institute for Strategic Studies: "Between 1990 and 1997, East Asia's share of global defence imports by value almost tripled, from 11.4 percent to 31.7 percent. In 1988, only 10 percent of U.S. arms exports went to the region. By 1997, this had increased to 25 percent."[10] Within East Asia, South Korea's share of military spending in 1997 ($14.8 billion) was nearly as large as the combined total spending of Indonesia, Malaysia, Singapore, and Thailand.[11] In the wake of the Asian financial crisis, military buildups were delayed, but Malaysia's recent purchase of three French submarines for $972 million, South Korea's decision to acquire 40 F-15s for $4.23 billion and its rapidly increasing military budget are indications of military spending taking off in the region. According to Kim Kook Hun, a major general and director of the South Korean Defense Ministry's arms control bureau, 7 of 17 countries in the world with nuclear weapons or weapons programs were in the Asia/Pacific region, as were 16 of 28 with missile programs, 10 of 16 with chemical weapons, and 8 of 13 with biological weapons.[12]

Even more alarming is the revival of Japanese militarism. Japan's annual military spending is now second only to that of the U.S., amounting to some five trillion yen (about $40 billion), and the international deployment movement of its military (banned since 1945) has resumed. In April 2002, Ichiro Ozawa, leader of Japan's second largest opposition party, stated that Japan could easily make nuclear weapons and eventually become stronger than China. Shinzo Abe, deputy chief cabinet secretary, publicly explained that Japan could legally possess "small" nuclear weapons, while Yasuo Fakuda, chief secretary of the Japanese cabinet, said that Tokyo could review its ban on nuclear weapons. Rather than reaping a peace dividend with the end of the Cold

War, East Asia is poised for what could become a regional nuclear arms race and massive buildup of conventional military forces.

The need for global peace movements is strongly indicated by the above dynamics. Without massive and militant peace movements, political elites cannot be kept from using military spending in order to prevent global stagnation, aggrandize national power, and enrich large defense contractors. One countertrend can be found in the Filipino example of expelling the U.S. from its huge base at Subic Bay, an important trendsetter for anti-militarism movements. But as we watch U.S. troops conducting military operations in the Philippines today, we must reflect upon the urgent need to cure the disease of military madness beyond temporarily addressing the symptoms. To be strategically effective, popular movements will have to inject a longterm vision into moments of crisis. Seemingly necessary for the dynamism of the existing world system, militarism is a scourge that squanders humanity's vast resources and threatens to destroy hard-won popular gains and victories. The impetus for militarism resides in the capitalist world economic system, and it is there that peace movements must focus if a cure for the disease is to be found.

The Imperial Crusade

The key recognition here is that the real axis of evil is composed of the World Trade Organization, the World Bank, and the International Monetary Fund. Like their predecessors in the colonial world, these global institutions masquerade as bringing people more freedom and rights. "Free" trade, IMF "bailouts" and World Bank "assistance," however, too often mean more poverty for people at the fringes of the world system—not more freedom. Historically there is an inverse relationship between the expansion of prosperity and democracy in the core of the world system and the growth of poverty and dictatorship in the Third World, a dialectic of enslavement meaning that greater "progress" in Europe and the U.S. spells increasing misery in the periphery.

Conventional wisdom holds that increasing core democracy should mean more enlightened policies towards the Third World and improvement in the conditions of life for all human beings. One exponent of such conventional wisdom is Francis Fukuyama, who argues that we have reached the "end of history"—that contemporary European/American political institutions are the desired endpoint of human development. Fukuyama believes that the battle of Jena in 1806 (when Napoleon defeated the Prussian monarchy) marks the consolidation of the liberal-democratic state, and that "the principles and privileges of citizenship in a democratic state only have to be extended." For Fukuyama, "There is nothing left to be invented" in terms of humanity's social progress.[13]

For Fukuyama, the spatial extension of the principles of the French Revolution means that the rest of the world will likewise experience human progress.

Evidence abounds, however, that the extension of those principles has resulted in just the opposite—increasing dependency and poverty for the Third World. The American and French revolutions helped propel the nascent world system centered in Europe into a framework of international domination, concentrating military power in nation-states and accumulating the world's wealth in the hands of giant corporations and banks. The worldwide penetration of the economic and political system produced by the American and French revolutions has, to be sure, resulted in rapid economic development and some of the most important forms of political liberty that our species has enjoyed. For a majority of its people, the U.S. is arguably the freest society in the world. The dialectical irony of history means that it is simultaneously a white European settler colony founded on genocide and slavery as well as on freedom and democracy. But one must ask: what are the costs of living in such a society? Slavery in the Third World? Ecological devastation? Military madness?

The dynamic of increasing political democracy in the North coinciding with intensified exploitation in the South has a long history. French colonialists in Vietnam provided a particularly graphic example when they placed a copy of the same statue of liberty that France gave to the U.S. atop the pagoda of Le Loi in Hanoi. Le Loi was the national leader who in 1418 had helped defeat the Mongols when they invaded Vietnam. Today he is still regarded as a national hero, a man whose mythology includes Hoan Kiem (Returned Sword) Lake, where the golden turtle that gave him the magical sword he used to drive the Mongols out subsequently reappeared to reclaim the sword—a story not unlike that of King Arthur in British folklore. The placing of a statue of liberty on Le Loi's pagoda certainly was an affront to the Vietnamese, one symbolizing how the spatial extension of the principles of the French Revolution can be brutally offensive to the Third World.

French colonialism was indeed brutal and deadly: Indochinese recall that dead human beings fertilize each tree in the country's vast rubber plantations. During the great war against fascism, French exploitation of Vietnam was intensified. In a famine from 1944 to 1945, at least a million and a half and possibly two million Vietnamese starved to death in the north (where the population was less than 14 million), at the very time rice exports to France were fueling its liquor industry—in blatant disregard for human life in the midst of the war against "fascism." In American popular culture, President John Kennedy is often associated with the word "Camelot" and remembered for his beautiful wife. Tragically, it was he—one of the most "liberal" U.S. presidents in history—who ordered massive use of Agent Orange in Vietnam. Similarly, the strongest French imperial expansionists were staunch anti-clerical "progressives" who regarded themselves as ideological heirs of the French Revolution. They were "enlightened" liberals, much the way John Kennedy and members of his administration were "enlightened" liberals who believed they were carrying on the tradition of the U.S. revolutionary heritage and Manifest Destiny.

As minister of education, Jules Ferry defied the Catholic Church in France by making education universal, secular, and obligatory, but he was later the first French prime minister to make intensification of colonialism his overriding platform. Ferry believed that it was France's duty to civilize inferior people, and on May 15, 1883, a full-scale expedition was launched to impose a protectorate on Vietnam.[14] Conservatives in France objected to this colonial expansion. As Vietnam disappeared, subsumed under the names of Tonkin, Annam, and Cochin China, even the identity of the Vietnamese people was attacked, as the French referred to them as Annamites. Here we can see the spatial expansion of the liberal values of the Enlightenment and the French Revolution—values that became the basis for France's "civilizing mission" ("*mission civilisatrice*") just as the American Revolution was later turned into "Manifest Destiny." It was the same French troops, bringing with them "civilization," who in 1885 burned the imperial library at Hue, which contained ancient scrolls and manuscripts and was a repository for thousands of years of wisdom.

In 1831 Alexis de Tocqueville, a disciple of the French Revolution and author of *Democracy in America*, watched in Memphis, Tennessee, the "triumphant march of civilization across the desert," as he put it. As he observed 3,000 or 4,000 soldiers drive before them "the wandering races of the aborigines," that is, those Native Americans who were lucky enough to survive "Jacksonian democracy" (named after a man who ordered his men to exterminate "bloodthirsty barbarians and cannibals"), Tocqueville was duly impressed that Americans could deprive Indians of their liberty and exterminate them, as he put it, "with singular felicity, tranquility, legally, philanthropically, without shedding blood," and most importantly "without violating a single great principle of morality in the eyes of the world"—the European world, one should say. "It was impossible," Tocqueville said, "to kill people with more respect for the laws of humanity."[15] Fukuyama's spatial extension of the liberal principles of the French and American revolutions could not be more eloquently enunciated.

In the name of civilization and liberal democracy, the British destroyed the communal ownership of village land in India, structures that had sustained local culture for centuries, a communal tradition surviving invasions by Persians, Greeks, Scythians, Afghans, Tartars, and Mongols but which could not, as Fukuyama would insist, resist the perfection of the liberal principles of the British state. Under British enlightenment, large estates developed and peasants were turned into sharecroppers. In 1867 the first fruits of British liberalism appeared: in the Orissa district of India alone, more than one million people died in a famine. Such famines were hardly indigenous to India, with its "backward" traditions (according to European values), but were brought by the "enlightened" liberalism of European democracy, through the spatial extension of the principles of "democratic" capitalism.

Under the direct influence of its great revolution, France proclaimed a crusade against Algerian slavery and anarchy and, in the name of instituting orderly and civilized conditions, was able to break up Arab communal fields of villages, including lands untouched by the "barbarous" and "unenlightened" Ottoman rulers. As long as Islamic culture had prevailed, hereditary clan and family lands were inalienable, making it impossible for the land to be sold. But after fifty years of enlightened French rule, the large estates had again appeared and famine made its ugly appearance in Algeria.

Civilization or Barbarism?

I have indicated how European capitalist "civilization"—particularly its most "enlightened" forms—systematically slaughtered native peoples and created a centralized world system that demands militarism as a key organizing principle. If this were simply history, we could all breathe a sigh of relief. But these tendencies are today stronger than ever. According to the United Nations, in the 1990s more than 100 million children under the age of five died of unnecessary causes: diarrhea, whooping cough, tetanus, pneumonia, and measles—diseases easily preventable through cheap vaccines or simply clean water. UNICEF estimates that up to 30,000 children under the age of five die of easily preventable diseases *every day* in the Third World.[16] Kofi Annan declared in 2001 that as many as 24,000 people starve to death every day.[17] Altogether one billion people are chronically malnourished while austerity measures imposed by the IMF have resulted in a drop in real wages in the Third World and declining gross national products in many countries. While 70 percent of the world's wealth is in the hands of 20 percent of its population, one in ten human beings suffers starvation and malnutrition.

Despite—or more accurately, because of—the spatial extension of liberal values in the period after World War II, there were four times as many deaths from wars in the forty years *after* World War II than in the forty years before it. While the world spends something like a trillion dollars a year on its militaries, one adult in three cannot read and write, one person in four is hungry, the AIDS epidemic accelerates, and we are destroying the planet's ecological capacity to sustain life. The absurdity and tragedy of such a world is made even more absurd and tragic by the profound ignorance and insensitivity of the wealthiest planetary citizens regarding the terrible plight of human beings in the periphery.

In such a world, of course, there can be no lasting peace. As long as the wretched of the earth, those at the margins of the world system, are dehumanized, branded as terrorists, and kept out of decision-making, they have no alternative but to carry out insurrection and wage war in order to find justice. In order to remedy this irrational system, a crucial task is to redefine what civilization means. We know what it is not for the billion or more "wretched of the earth" for whom increasing planetary centralization and dependence upon transnational corporations, militarized nation-states, and the international axis of evil mean living hell. With the passing of time it becomes more obvious that this same "civilization" squanders humanity's wealth, destroys traditional cultures wholesale, and plunders the planet's natural resources.

The structural violence of an economic system based upon short-term profitability is a crisis that all peace and justice movements will have to address. Even if some of the above irrationalities of the present system are reduced, the structural contradictions of the system will inevitably be displaced to other arenas. As long as vast social wealth remains dominated by the "enlightened" and "rational" principles of efficiency and profitability, there will be militarism, brutal degradation of human lives along with unbridled destruction of the natural ecosystem; there will be mammoth socially wasteful projects, for example tunnels in the Alps and Pyrenees, bridges connecting Denmark and Sweden or Prince Edward Island and the Canadian mainland, redundant World Cup stadiums—rather than constructive use of humanity's enormous social wealth. A few hundred multinational corporations today control this social wealth through the most undemocratic of means and for ends benefiting only a small minority. According to the logic of "enlightened" neoliberal economics, these corporations must either grow or die. Only a fundamental restructuring of the world system can lead us toward an ecologically viable life-world, one in which we decentralize and bring under self-management the vast social wealth of humanity.

If we allow ourselves to indulge in a brief moment of utopian speculation— today more difficult than ever in the aftermath of the carnage of September 11—few people would disagree with the idea of totally abolishing weapons of mass destruction—not just nuclear, chemical, and biological weapons but also so-called conventional ones like fighter jets, bombers, landmines, artillery, and economic sanctions. Acting strategically, global peace movements will have to be directed toward the abolition (not just the reform) of military power around the globe. In a world where even peaceful means of transportation are turned into weapons of mass destruction, nearly everyone would consider such a proposition foolish, but with major weapons systems in the hands of governments, how else can the powerless fight back? Only through universalization of the non-military forms of conflict resolution will humanity's future fate improve beyond the abysmal reality it currently faces. Of course the destruction of world military power would undoubtedly send the global economic system into a calamitous depression—which is all the more reason for people to discuss this issue as part of the need to develop a completely different world system.

Popular strength resides in forging a new international civil society that can delegitimize militarized nation-states and socialize predatory transnational corporations. The transformation of Eurocentric capitalist civilization requires nothing less than an international movement, with lessons from past liberation movements central to this project. A few years ago, Vo Nguyen Giap, military commander of Vietnamese forces against the French and Americans, summarized the reasons why the Vietnamese were able to defeat the U.S. Among those, the anti-war movement that developed inside the U.S. was prominent. For years Vietnamese leaders cultivated this movement until it grew into a force with which they were able to coordinate their battlefield tactics.[18]

Building an International Peace Movement

While the need for constraining U.S. military power has never been more urgent, many peace and anti-war movements around the world support the war against "terrorism." The German Greens, founded upon the principle of pacifism, served a key role in legitimating the NATO war against Yugoslavia and the U.S. war in Afghanistan, to say nothing of endorsing the first foreign deployment of German combat troops since Hitler. Historical parallels can be found in the German Social Democrats' support of the Kaiser in World War I and in the French Communist Party's support for the war in Algeria. In the U.S. many progressives naïvely accept the Bush administration's comparison of bin Laden with Hitler, a distorted view that makes virtually any military offensive seem reasonable. Incredibly, the main U.S. opposition to Bush's plans for war against Iraq comes from the Joint Chiefs of Staff—the top military elites in the Pentagon who have waged "a determined behind-the-scenes campaign" to question "Iraq hysteria" among senior Bush administration officials.[19]

The Bush administration now possesses a unique window of opportunity to have its way with the world. Not a single government besides Iraq registered any opposition to the war in Afghanistan. While many nations do oppose escalation of the war to Iraq, it is likely they will fall in line once the U.S. carries out its unilateral military actions. For eleven years the U.S. and Britain have steadily bombed Iraq, and if their new levels of military aggression bring a quick and easy victory, it follows that Bush and Co. would become so filled with triumphal euphoria that taking on such countries as North Korea might be a thinkable next step. Russia and China might acquiesce to U.S. militarism, particularly since they would probably be left untouched while Japan and South Korea (China's main regional competitors) would be military targets. Throughout the past century war has been the primary solution to stagnation in the world economy. With the high-tech sector appearing to have run its course, Japan and Germany in the economic doldrums, the stock market suffering its biggest losses in decades, and industries everywhere contracting, what mechanism besides war is there for renewed growth?

The U.S. could have responded to September 11 in a manner quite different than it has. Why not withdraw troops from Saudi Arabia and compel justice for Palestinians? Neither of these measures would create any great hardship for the U.S. Could it be that the U.S. economy, dependent more than ever on war for its health, demands military action? I am reminded of the Sean Connery movie, *The Rock:* Taking over Alcatraz Island, a group of army officers aims weapons of mass destruction at San Francisco, demanding $100 million for destitute families of servicemen who sacrificed their lives in various secret wars. Although millions of people might be killed, the authorities never even discuss paying the $100 million (a relatively paltry sum). At the present historical juncture, it similarly appears that the U.S. government has never condescended to take into account the grievances of others—despite the horrific dangers a new war poses for people around the world.

It is no accident that peace movements in 2002 are strongest in Korea and other regions of Asia. From their recent experiences, the Korean people understand the urgent need for peace and the strategic importance of fighting militarism. A non-Islamic country with a citizenry deeply sensitive to issues of war and peace, Korea has a voice that speaks to governments and activists everywhere.

Instead of relying on "liberal" governments to constrain U.S. militarism, people can use extraparliamentary tactics to isolate the U.S.—just as earlier international groups and movements turned the apartheid regime in South Africa into an international pariah. Wherever in the world Bush or senior U.S. officials travel, protests should be as militant and massive as possible. Grassroots rebellions in Argentina, Mexico, and Nigeria reflect the high level of consciousness people in many countries have developed and are ready to act upon.[20] In this context, far-reaching protests can help unleash a global peace offensive that will compel governments to stop war by raising their costs and disrupting domestic tranquility.

In the U.S., where regime change is most desperately needed to prevent use of weapons of mass destruction and fight militarism, an extraparliamentary opposition was galvanized by the Seattle anti-WTO protests. Although reactionary forces now command overwhelming majority allegiance, vital countertrends have appeared, as seen in the 200,000 or more people who marched in Washington at the end of October along with the great popularity enjoyed by such critics as Michael Moore and Noam Chomsky. Gradually breaking with the ideological and organizational power of reaction will necessarily proceed from small steps to giant leaps.

Since 1968 the international character of popular movements has been recognized as a primary factor in their emergence and impact. Two more examples of the spread of movements across borders, involving a process of mutual amplification and synergy, can be found in the disarmament movement of the early 1980s in the U.S. and Europe and in the wave of democracy movements in Asia in the mid and late 1980s.[21]

From a handful of nuclear disarmament protesters in the 1970s, an enormous peace movement changed world history in the 1980s, helping end the Cold War and alter the global balance of power. Movements grew from years of grassroots initiatives in a variety of arenas,[22] spreading rapidly and bringing hundreds of thousands of people into the streets of New York, Paris, London, Rome, Brussels, and Bonn. The situation in northeast Asia today is very similar to that of Europe in the early 1980s, when the U.S. and the USSR stationed intermediate range Pershing and SS-20 nuclear missiles in the region. Such new missile deployment meant that the U.S. and USSR could have fought a "limited" nuclear war in Europe without either country being directly engaged in military hostilities. The emergence of the Green Party in Germany and the presence of huge protest movements helped Gorbachev convince Russian generals that Western Europe would not attack them, allowing the USSR to change peacefully, release its East European buffer states, and take the initiative to end the arms race.

Today in northeast Asia, a regional war could be waged without directly involving the U.S. In a worst-case scenario, U.S. policymakers could opt to initiate a "limited" war in which Koreans would fight other Koreans. Minimal U.S. casualties would make such a war more palatable to the American public.[23] So long as the U.S. exercises operational command over the South Korean armed forces, the outbreak of war is more likely, especially given Bush's "first-strike" policy. (There are very few other nations that permit their military to be governed by a foreign power.) Demanding Korean control of its own military forces could unite nearly all Koreans and would encourage North Korean leaders to reengage the South in dialogue while sending a message to the U.S. that war in Korea is totally unacceptable.

Whatever short-term demands peace activists make, popular movements in Korea will inevitably have a significant international role to play. Koreans have long inspired other countries in Asia. In building the Korean movement for democracy in the 1980s, leaders sought to find ways to unite people in the struggle—and the answer was to call for direct presidential elections. In June 1987, after hundreds of thousands of people took to the streets for 19 consecutive days, that demand was realized. Movements for democracy soon blossomed in many Asian countries: Burma in 1988, China in 1989, Tibet, Taiwan, and Nepal in 1990, and Thailand in 1992. These struggles were related to each other and today are all treated as manifestations of "people power," a term coined during the Filipino revolution of 1986, itself inspired by the Kwangju Uprising in Korea in 1980. If there is something people everywhere can learn from prior waves of social movements, it is that actions mutually amplify each other in different parts of the world.

Forging strategic goals means to insist upon outlawing weapons of mass destruction, above all nuclear weapons, and to secure a pledge of no first-strike by the U.S. As movements grow and mature, the role of conscious elements within them must be to keep *longterm* goals at the forefront: a nuclear-free world; a world free of weapons of mass destruction; a world where peace and justice can freely exist; demilitarization of the U.S. and other economies; the use of vast social wealth for human needs rather than for profits of giant transnational corporations; development of autonomous regions where people can freely choose how to use their resources. Together the people of the world can accomplish these goals, but only on a foundation of international solidarity and cooperation.

Notes

1. On November 25, 2001, the Sunday *New York Times* featured a story entitled "After the Taliban, Who? Don't Forget North Korea."
2. In March 2002, a Pentagon review of U.S. nuclear policy recommended that the U.S. threaten to use nuclear weapons against seven countries—including North Korea.
3. North Korea agreed to shut down and eventually dismantle its nuclear weapons program. In return, the U.S., Japan, and South Korea agreed to provide the North with two light-water nuclear reactors for generating electricity. These reactors were never built.
4. See "Engaging North Korea," by Jimmy Carter, *New York Times*, October 27, 2002, wk13.
5. Noam Chomsky, "The United States and Indochina: Far From an Aberration," in Douglas Allen and Ngo Vinh Long (editors), *Coming to Terms: Indochina, the United States and the War* (Boulder, CO: Westview Press, 1991), 165.
6. See the illustrated book by Joel Andreas, *Addicted to War: Why the U.S. Can't Kick Militarism* (Oakland, CA: AK Press, 2002).
7. Ibid., 39.
8. International Scientific Commission on Biological Warfare in Korea and China, *Report*, 1952. Available from Koreatruthcommission@yahoo.com
9. *Vietnam Documents*, edited by George Katsiaficas (New York: ME Sharpe, 1992), 146.
10. Tim Huxley and Susan Willett, *Arming East Asia* (International Institute for Strategic Studies/Oxford University Press, 1999), 23.
11. Ibid., 15.
12. Michael Richardson, "Fears spread that other Asia nations will seek nuclear arms," *International Herald-Tribune*, June 6, 2002, 5.
13. See his article "The End of History," *Foreign Affairs* 1988, 5.
14. See *Greater France, A History of French Overseas Expansion*, Robert Aldrich (New York: St. Martin's, 1996), 98.
15. See Chomsky, op. cit.
16. "UN Says Millions of Children Die Needlessly," by Elizabeth Olson, *New York Times*, March 14, 2002, 13.
17. " 'Time to Act' on Hunger, Annan says," *International Herald-Tribune*, June 11, 2002.
18. We all owe Vietnam a debt for helping preserve the principles of liberty and democracy. It was their sacrifice and resistance that preserved the idea of national independence, and it was the resistance to the war inside the U.S. that both helped preserve principles of individual liberty and prevent direct U.S. military intervention in Central America in the 1980s. If the truth about U.S. massacres during the Korean War had been known, how many Vietnamese lives would have been saved?
19. Thomas E. Ricks, "Military trying to head off Iraq strike," *International Herald-Tribune*, May 25–26, 2002, 1.
20. See Amory Starr and Jason Adams, "Anti-globalization: The Global Fight for Local Autonomy," *New Political Science* 25:1 (March 2003).
21. These are examples of what I call the "eros effect." See www.eroseffect.com
22. For a full analysis, see my book *The Subversion of Politics: European Autonomous Social Movements and the Decolonization of Everyday Life*, published in 1997.
23. Here is one pragmatic reason why keeping U.S. troops in Korea may actually serve as a deterrent to war. The U.S. would be less likely to use weapons of mass destruction in Korea if it were to mean many American soldiers would also die in the ensuing conflict. Paik Nak-chung first brought this insight to my attention.

Contributors

Carl Boggs is Professor of Social Sciences at National University in Los Angeles. He is the author of many books, including *The Two Revolutions: Antonio Gramsci and the Dilemmas of Western Marxism* (1984), *Social Movements and Political Power* (1986), and *The Socialist Tradition: from Crisis to Decline* (1996). His most recent book is *The End of Politics: Corporate Power and the Decline of the Public Sphere* (2000).

Noam Chomsky is a longtime political activist, writer, and Institute Professor of Linguistics at MIT. He writes extensively and lectures around the world on international affairs, U.S. foreign and military policy, and human rights. His long list of influential books includes *American Power and the New Mandarins, The Fateful Triangle, Manufacturing Consent* (with Edward Herman), *Turning the Tide, Propaganda and the Public Mind, Rogue States, The New Military Humanism,* and *9–11.*

Irene Gendzier is a professor at Boston University and works in the area of U.S. foreign policy in the Middle East. Her books include *Frantz Fanon: A Critical Biography, Development Against Democracy,* and *Notes from the Minefield: United States Intervention in Lebanon and the Middle East 1945–1958.* She is on the editorial board of *New Political Science.*

Darrell Y. Hamamoto is Professor of Asian American Studies at the University of California, Davis. He has explored both the mundane and outer reaches of American culture and human behavior in a number of books including *Nervous Laughter* (1989), *Monitored Peril* (1994), *New American Destinies* (1999), and *Countervisions* (2000). His current research interests include Asian American criminality, Yellow sexuality, and independent Asian American media.

Rhonda Hammer is a research scholar at the UCLA Center for the Study of Women and coauthor of *Rethinking Media Literacy: A Critical Pedagogy of Representation.* She is the recent author of *Antifeminism and Family Terrorism* (2001).

Chalmers Johnson is author of *Blowback: The Costs and Consequences of American Empire* (Metropolitan Books, 2000) and many other works. He is president of the Japan Policy Research Institute located near San Diego,

California. He taught for thirty years (1962–1992) at the Berkeley and San Diego campuses of the University of California and held endowed chairs in Asian politics at both of them. At Berkeley he served as chairman of the Center for Chinese Studies and as chairman of the Department of Political Science. His B.A., M.A., and Ph.D. degrees in economics and politics are all from the University of California, Berkeley.

George Katsiaficas is Professor at Wentworth Institute of Technology and former editor of *New Political Science*. His book *The Imagination of the New Left* was recently translated into Korean. He is author of *The Subversion of Politics: European Autonomous Social Movements and the Decolonization of Everyday Life*, which was co-winner of the 1999 Michael Harrington Award. Long active in movements for social justice, he is working on several projects related to contemporary Korean social movements.

Douglas Kellner is George F. Kneller Philosophy of Education professor in the Graduate School of Education and Information Studies at the University of California, Los Angeles. Previously he taught in the philosophy department at the University of Texas in Austin. He is the author of many books, including *The Persian Gulf TV War* (1992), *Media Culture* (1995), *The Postmodern Turn*, with Steven Best (1997), *The Postmodern Adventure*, with Steven Best (2001), and *Grand Theft 2000* (2001).

Peter McLaren is known internationally for his educational activism and scholarly writings on critical pedagogy, critical literacy, the sociology of education, cultural studies, and Marxist theory. He is currently Professor at the Graduate School of Education and Information Studies at UCLA. His recent books include *Revolutionary Multiculturalism, Pedagogy of Dissent for the New Millennium, Critical Pedagogy and Predatory Culture, Life in Schools*, and *Che Guevara, Paulo Freire, and the Pedagogy of Revolution*.

Morris Morley is Associate Professor of Politics at Macquarie University, Sydney, Australia, and a senior research fellow at the Council on Hemispheric Affairs, Washington, D.C. He is the author of *Washington, Somoza, and the Sandinistas* (1994), coauthor of *Latin America in the Time of Cholera* (1992), and *Unfinished Business: America and Cuba Since the End of the Cold War* (2002).

Michael Parenti has taught at a number of colleges and universities, and lectures widely around North America and abroad. He is the author of over 250 articles and fifteen books, including the recently published *Against Empire, Blackshirts and Reds, Dirty Truths, America Besieged, History as Mystery, To Kill a Nation: The Attack on Yugoslavia*, and most recently *The Terrorism Trap* along with the seventh edition of *Democracy for the Few.* Dr. Parenti's writings have appeared in a wide range of scholarly and political journals. He lives in Berkeley, California. For more information, consult his web site at www.michaelparenti.org.

James Petras is Emeritus Professor of Sociology at the State University of New York at Binghamton and Adjunct Professor in International Development Studies at Saint Mary's University, Halifax, Nova Scotia. He is coauthor of *Latin America in the Time of Cholera* (1992), *Democracy and Poverty in Chile* (1994), *The Dynamics of Social Change in Latin America* (2000), and *Globalization Unmasked: Imperialism in the 21st Century* (2001).

Tom Pollard is Professor of Social Sciences at National University in San Jose. He received his Ph.D. in American Studies at the University of Kansas. He is coauthor (with Carl Boggs) of *A World in Chaos: Social Crisis and the Rise of Postmodern Cinema,* and he has written several articles in the areas of film studies and American popular culture. He is a screenwriter and researcher for documentary films. His productions include *Paradise Bent* and *Maya Pompeii,* among others. He has been involved with several television documentaries during the past several years.

Ted Rall is a nationally-syndicated cartoonist and columnist. He has twice won the Robert F. Kennedy Journalism Award and been a Pulitzer Prize finalist for his cartoons. A former radio talk show host, he is the author of ten books. His most recent works include the award-winning graphic travelogue "To Afghanistan and Back" about his coverage of the U.S. invasion of fall 2001 and "Gas War: The Truth Behind the American Occupation of Afghanistan," an investigation of the Trans-Afghanistan oil and pipeline project. He is currently working on a new book about the Democratic Party. He lives in New York City.

R. Claire Snyder is Assistant Professor of Government and Politics in the Department of Public and International Affairs at George Mason University. She is the author of *Citizen-Soldiers and Manly Warriors: Military Service and Gender in the Civic Republican Tradition* (1999), as well as numerous articles and essays on topics related to democratic theory and citizenship. Her current research focuses on the radical republican tradition, progressive theories of civil-military relations, and conservative attempts to reconsolidate patriarchy.

Norman Solomon is the founder of the Institute for Public Accuracy and author of many books, including *The Habits of Highly Deceptive Media* and *Adventures in Medialand* (with Jeff Cohen). His most recent book is *Target Iraq: What the News Media Didn't Tell You* (with Reese Erlich). He organized two trips to Baghdad in late 2002, the first with Representative Nick Rahall and other delegates, the second with actor/director Sean Penn.

Loring Wirbel is editorial director for communications properties at CMP Media, LLC, a publishing company based in London and New York. He has worked on military and civil liberties issues with national and regional activist groups for more than twenty years, and he is currently member of the board of directors of Global Network Against Weapons and Nuclear Power in Space. He has won such awards as Project Censored and Scripps-Howard writer of merit, and he has a forthcoming book on militarization of space with Pluto Press. He lives in Colorado Springs, Colorado, with his wife and daughter.

Index